SPATIAL DATA CONFIGURATION IN STATISTICAL ANALYSIS OF REGIONAL ECONOMIC AND RELATED PROBLEMS

ADVANCED STUDIES IN THEORETICAL AND APPLIED ECONOMETRICS
VOLUME 14

For a complete list of volumes in this series see final page of this volume.

Spatial Data Configuration in Statistical Analysis of Regional Economic and Related Problems

by

Giuseppe Arbia

Istituto di Statistica Economica, Faculty of Statistics,
University of Rome "La Sapienza", Italy
and Fitzwilliam College, Cambridge, U.K.

KLUWER ACADEMIC PUBLISHERS
DORDRECHT / BOSTON / LONDON

Library of Congress Cataloging in Publication Data

Arbia, Giuseppe.
Spatial data configuration in statistical analysis of regional economic and related problems / Giuseppe Arbia.
p. cm. -- (Advanced studies in theoretical and applied econometrics ; v. 14)
Includes index.
ISBN 0-7923-0284-2
1. Space in economics--Statistical methods. 2. Regional economics--Statistical methods. I. Title. II. Series.
HB137.A72 1989
330'.01'5195--dc20 89-8210

ISBN 0-7923-0284-2

Published by Kluwer Academic Publishers,
P.O. Box 17, 3300 AA Dordrecht, The Netherlands.

Kluwer Academic Publishers incorporates
the publishing programmes of
D. Reidel, Martinus Nijhoff, Dr W. Junk and MTP Press.

Sold and distributed in the U.S.A. and Canada
by Kluwer Academic Publishers,
101 Philip Drive, Norwell, MA 02061, U.S.A.

In all other countries, sold and distributed
by Kluwer Academic Publishers Group,
P.O. Box 322, 3300 AH Dordrecht, The Netherlands.

Printed in The Netherlands

To Paola and Elisa

TABLE OF CONTENTS

FOREWORD BY ROBERT J BENNETT

Spatial Statistics and econometrics has long been a *Cinderella* aspect among the statistical sciences. For various reasons it seems that either its problems were too complex, or research priorities lay elsewhere. However, with the emergence of the demands of economic planning, pattern recognition, remote sensing and artificial intelligence the requirements for a sound basis of econometric theory for handling spatial data has become essential. Much of this framework has now been established following key studies by Moran, Geary, Kendall, Whittle, Granger, Ord, Besag and Ripley in Statistics, and by such researchers as Curry, Tobler, Paelinck, Haggett, Cliff, Haining and Openshaw in the applied fields of econometrics and geography. This is the lineage to which this book contributes. Yet some of the problems in spatial statistics have stubbornly remained. Particularly important amongst these has been that of the modifiable areal unit problem and the influence of spatial data configuration in general on spatial autocorrelation and associated analytical and estimation techniques.

This book represents a major contribution to the solution of these issues. The so-called *modifiable areal unit* problem arises as the result of the influence on subsequent statistical procedures of variable scales of spatial zonal data, and variable aggregation of cases within different zones. The book presents for the first time an integrated theoretical presentation of the consequences of the interaction of the effects of scale and aggregation in spatial data and their influence on the statistical properties of estimation and significance testing. The book presents the theory, evaluates its properties using simulation techniques and then works through simple hypothetical as well as empirical examples. It represents the most fundamental contribution to the modifiable areal unit problem since the work of Gehlke and Biehl in 1934 and Kendall and Yule in 1950. Hence the book makes a contribution of fundamental importance to spatial statistics and it is particularly appropriate that it should appear in this series of Advanced Studies in Theoretical and Applied Econometrics. That the scholar who has produced this work is still a young researcher with much still to offer bodes well for the development of this field.

I was pleased to have been able to support the author as his advisor on his PhD at Cambridge University, from which the book derives. It was a pleasure to assist him. Giuseppe Arbia is to be congratulated on this, his first book; and it is a pleasure to commend the work to its readers.

Professor Robert J Bennett
London School of Economics

ACKNOWLEDGEMENTS

This book derives from my PhD thesis written during my stay in Cambridge in various period of times from 1985 to 1987. I am pleased to fulfil the pleasant duty of thanking the many people who have contributed in one way or another to the preparation of this volume.

Special thanks are due to Professor R.J.Bennett of London School of Economics without whose guidance and encouragement this book would not have been completed. His constructive criticism on various drafts of the manuscript enabled me to improve it substantially. During the period in which he assisted me as a PhD advisor he has been a constant example to follow and his influence is evident throughout the book.

The environment plays a crucial role in a scholar's work. For this reason I wish to thank the staff of the Department of Geography in Cambridge for providing me with a stimulating atmosphere. A special mention is due to Dr. A.D. Cliff.

Thanks are also due to Dr. R.P. Haining of Sheffield University and to Dr. G.A. Young of the Statistical Laboratory in Cambridge for various comments made in many lively discussion and on various drafts of the book, to Dr.C.Kenyon of the Department of Mathematics in Cambridge for assisting me in writing some of the Fortran programs, and to the anonymous referee for enriching the work by giving numerous helpful suggestions.

Of my colleagues at the University of Rome I express my deepest gratitude to Professor A.Erba for much encouragement during many years.

A human being is a unity and the scholar is not separate from the man. During my stay at Cambridge University I was lucky enough to meet a number of very good friends that made the life in Cambridge be worthwhile. I wish to thank especially Dr. J.E. Zucchi of McGill University of Montreal and Dr. A.L. Sawaya of Sañ Paulo University for constantly reminding me that life is much more than writing a book. The proofreading and the revision of the text has been demanding. I would like to thank Mrs. Tricia Goodwin-Williams for her assistance with this. While pursuing the research reported here I was generously supported by the British Council, by the N.A.T.O. and by the Italian National Research Council (C.N.R.) through scholarships and through the project "Economia". Their financial assistance is acknowledged here. The text processing of the book took place in Fitzwilliam College in Cambridge and in the Centro Interpartimentale di Calcolo Scientifico of Rome University. Thanks are due respectively to Dr. Pearl and to Prof. Schaerf for the access to the computer facilities.

I gratefully acknowledge the permission of the publisher Pion Limited for the reproduction of Figures 2.2.4 and 5.2.1 from Cliff A.D. and Ord J.K. (1981) and Figures 2.2.5 and 6.3.3 from Openshaw S. and Taylor P.J. (1979).

Finally I acknowledge the constant help and encouragement of my beloved wife Paola and of my daughter Elisa to both of whom this book is dedicated.

All Saints, 1988

Giuseppe Arbia
University of Rome

NOTATION SHEET

The following abbreviations and symbols are used

PDF	Probability distribution function
DF	Probability density function
JPDF	Joint probability distribution function
JDF	Joint probability density function
CJPDF	Conditional joint probability distribution function
CJDF	Conditional joint probability density function
JBPDF	Joint bivariate probability distribution function
JBDF	Joint bivariate probability density function
~N	Normally Distributed
~MVN	Multivariate Normally Distributed
$\int$	Unless differently specified implies $_{-\infty}\int^{\infty}$
Π	Unless differently specified implies $\Pi_{i=1}^{n}$
Σ	Unless differently specified implies $\sum_{i=1}^{n}$
$\Sigma_{(2)}$; $\Sigma_{(3)}$; $\Sigma_{(4)}$	$\Sigma_j \Sigma_k \; {}_{j \neq k}$; $\Sigma_j \Sigma_k \Sigma_l \; {}_{j \neq k \neq l}$; $\Sigma_j \Sigma_k \Sigma_l \Sigma_p \; {}_{j \neq k \neq l \neq p}$
$O(n^{-1})$	Terms of order n^{-1}
G(i)	A group of sites indexed by i
G	Is a grouping matrix
g_{ij}	Is the typical element of **G** such that $g_{ij}=1$ if $j \in G(i)$ and zero otherwise
r_i	Is the cardinality of G(i)
N(j)	The set of neighbors of site j
W	Is the connectivity matrix of a spatial system
w_{jk}	Is the typical element of **W** such that $w_{jk}=1$ if $k \in N(j)$ and zero otherwise
v_j	Are the number of neighbors of site j (or nodality) $v_j = \Sigma_k w_{jk}$

A	Is the total number of joints ("connectivity") of a spatial system $A = \Sigma_{(2)} w_{ij} = \Sigma v_j$
v^*	Is the average connectivity $v^* = A\, n^{-1}$
A_i	Is the connectivity within group i $A_i = \Sigma_{k \, \varepsilon \, G(i)} \Sigma_{j \, \varepsilon G(i)} w_{jk}$
t_{il}	Is the connectivity between group i and group l
i,j,k,l,p	Integer used as summation indices
n	Integer indicating the number of sites at an *individual-process* level
m	Integer indicating the number of sites at a *group-process* level.
X,**Y**	Are vectors or matrices written boldface
X	Is a random variable at an *individual-process* level
X^*	Is a random variable at a *group-process* level

As to general mathematical statistical concepts, the terminology is chosen in accordance with Kendall and Stuart (1976). In particular:

-Upper case (e.g. X,Y) indicate stochastic processes, while lower case (e.g. x,y) indicate the realizations of the same processes.

-Greek letters indicate the stochastic process moments (e.g. $\mu, \sigma, \gamma, \rho$), while Latin letters are used to indicate the corresponding sample moments (m,s,c,r)

For the moments of any order the general form is as follows:

$_{XY}M_{ij}{}^{e}$

where M is a bivariate moment, X (and Y) are the variate(s) to which the moment refers, i(and j) are the observation(s) to which it refers (j is omitted in the case of univariate moments; when the process is stationary both i and j are omitted) and e is the exponent.

Everybody knows that geography is about maps

(Unwin, 1981; p.1)

The fundamental notion in statistical theory is that of group or aggregate

(Kendall & Stuart, 1976; p.1)

1. Introduction: spatial effects and the role of configuration of data

1.1. OBJECTIVES AND APPROACHES

Spatial data in regional economic analysis have two distinctive features. First of all they cannot be thought as randomly generated from the classical urn models; rather they are dependent in that "the value of, say, prosperity in one region gives statistical information about the likely value of adjacent areas "(Unwin and Hepple, 1974). This is usually referred to as the *spatial autocorrelation* problem (Cliff and Ord , 1981). Secondly they are constituted by aggregation of the characteristics of individuals within portions of space. The population in a country is the sum of the individuals living in that country, the total income of a region is the sum of the income of the population in that region: the per-capita consumption of an area is the mean of the individual consumption of that area, and so on. However the borders of the zones in which a study area is divided are not just *divinely given*; rather there is a very large number of different ways in which the individuals can be aggregated to form areal data. Analysis is often made more complex by the common situation faced in geographical investigation that the variable of interest is recorded on a system of irregular collecting areas. Thus the study area is divided into territorial units which are, in general, different in size and shape and which connect to one another in an arbitrary and irregular way. The problem of the arbitrariness and irregularity of spatial units will be referred to as the *modifiable areal unit problem* following Openshaw and Taylor (1979).

The interaction between these two intrinsic features of spatial data, between spatial autocorrelation and modifiable areal units, creates a number of problems if we seek to use the observed data to estimate statistical relationships. These problems have been recognised extensively in the literature and there is now a large number of empirical investigations of the effects of different spatial data configurations. Some of these will be reviewed in Chapter 2. However no theoretical explanation has yet been provided which allows prediction and control for the effects of spatial data configuration during geographical investigations.

The main aim of this book is to propose a statistical framework within which the spatial autocorrelation problem is taken into account, to explain, and therefore to control for, the effects of the modifiable areal unit problem. In addition a number of related problems will also be investigated. Furthermore the whole work is based on the conviction that a statistical approach to spatial series in regional economics has to be, at the same time, truly geographical incorporating *in some way* the information contained in the map on which the data are laid. This is what we call the *configuration of spatial data*. We use this term to describe the variety of relevant information which fully specify the geography of a particular situation: the links of neighbourhood between regions, their shape, their size, and their relative and absolute location in the study area.
The emphasis throughout the book is on theory which allows us to explain and suggests the ways to controlling for some spatial data effects. However, where possible, we will also propose solutions to reduce or to eliminate these effects.

1.2. AN OVERVIEW OF THEORETICAL PROBLEMS

A first manifestation of the modifiable areal unit problem is the **scale problem** or the problem of the level of resolution. Consider, for example, Figure 1.1.a which shows the map of the British counties and Figure 1.1.b which displays the map of British regions . If we are examining a single variable and we want to study, say, the spatial inequality of its distribution through its variance, our conclusions will depend on the scale we choose. For example the distribution of income can be close to a situation of equity at a regional level, but very unequal at a county level. Furthermore if we consider associations between two or more variables it is well known (Yule and Kendall, 1950) that the correlation coefficient changes with different scales of areal units. This applies either to direct correlation analysis, or to indirect uses with multivariate techniques based on correlation, such as factor analysis. As a matter of fact it is not unusual in the literature to find data aggregated to a level so that high correlation is demonstrated.
A second, closely related aspect of the modifiable areal unit problem is the **aggregation problem**. Consider, for example, Figures 1.2.a and 1.2.b. In both cases we are dealing with the map of Italy divided into 32 territorial units. However the borders between the units are different in the two cases. Again the value of statistical measures, like the variance and the correlation, changes greatly with changing zone boundaries.
A third analytical problem arises when aggregated data are the only source available while the object of the study are individual characteristics and relationships. This is often the case when dealing with Census data tracts or with electoral results. In Figures 1.3.a and 1.3.b are shown the percentage of votes of the Communist Party in the 1987 Italian political elections and, respectively, the percentage of population over 75 years in the 32 polling districts. Looking at Figures 1.3.a and 1.3.b one may conclude that the probability of voting Communist Party is higher for elderly people. However this conclusion is fallacious. In fact it has been shown in several studies (Robinson, 1950) that the correlation measured using areal data is never a substitute for individual correlation. This is usually referred to in the literature as the **ecological fallacy** problem.

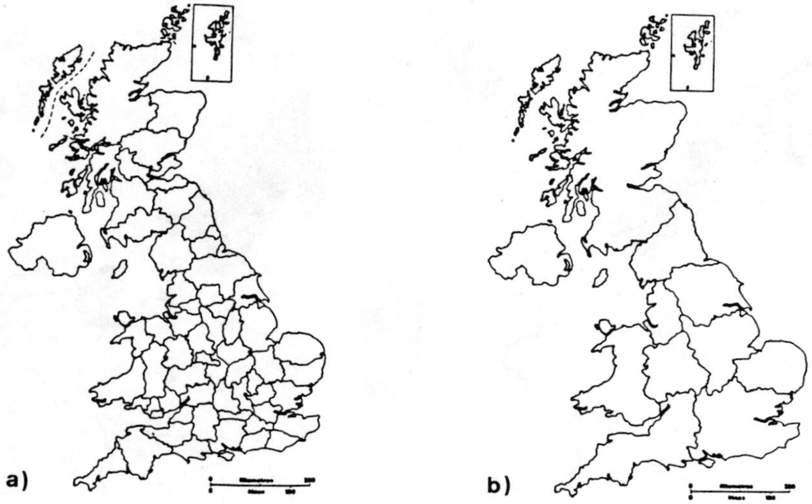

Figure 1.1: Map of Great Britain at two different scale levels:(a) Counties, (b)Regions.

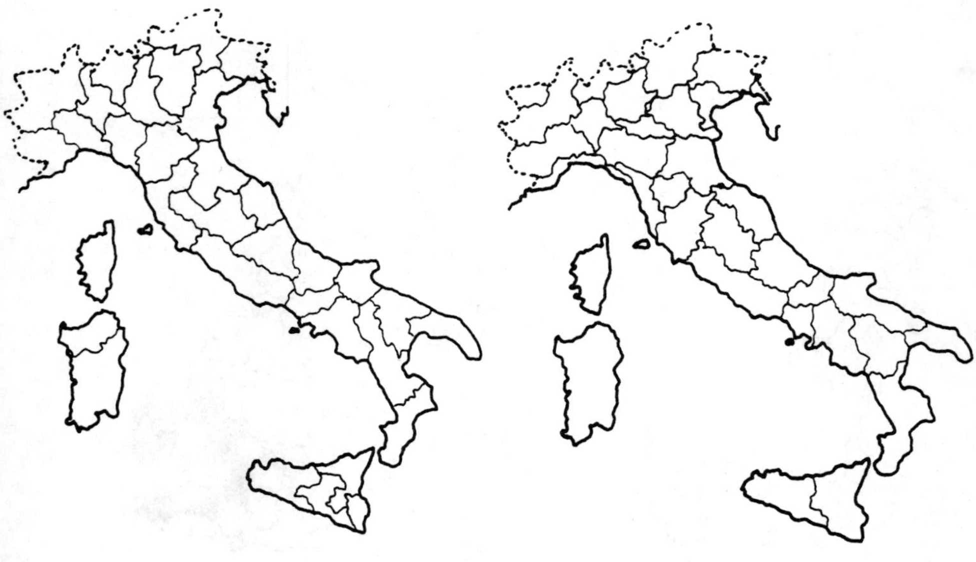

Figure 1.2: Two alternative aggregations of the Italian provincie in 32 larger areas

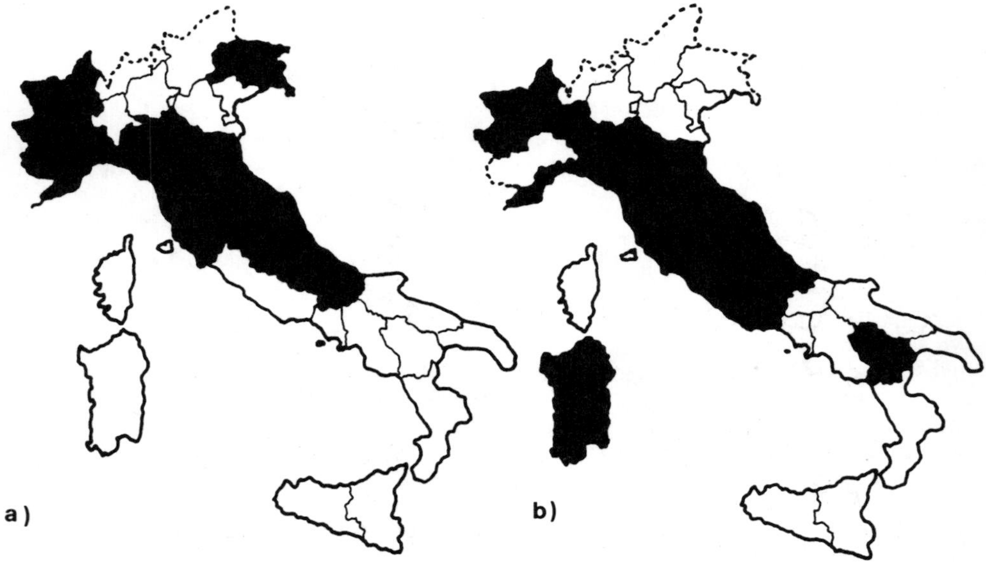

Figure 1.3 Percentage of votes of the Communist Party in the 1987 Italian political elections (a) and percentage of population over 75 years (b) in 1981 Italian Census in 32 polling districts. The polling districts with values above the average are shaded.

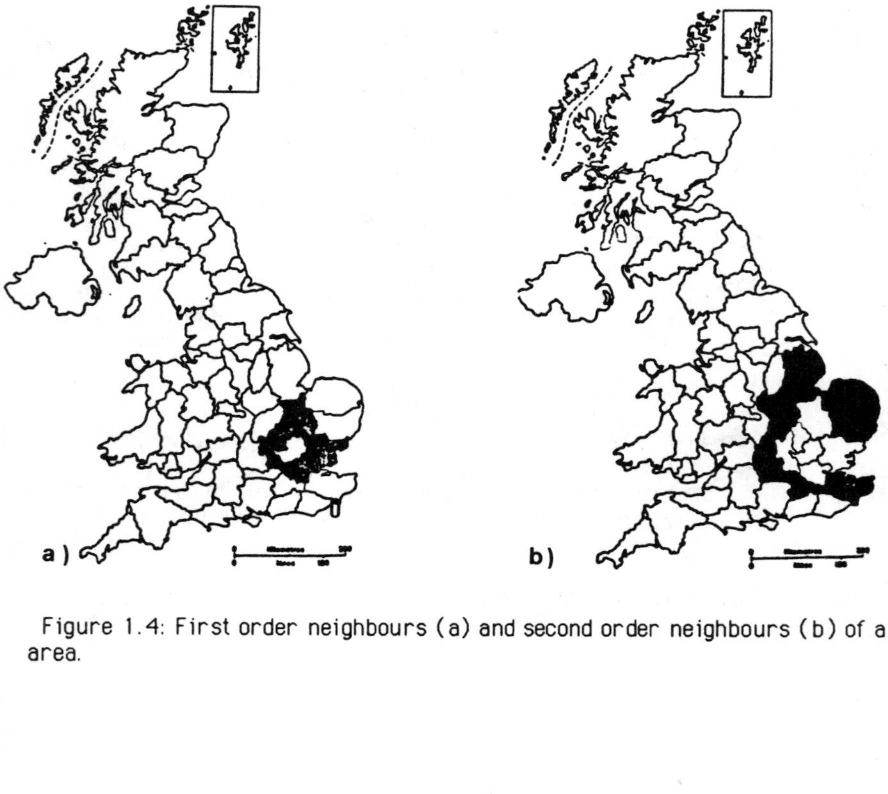

Figure 1.4: First order neighbours (a) and second order neighbours (b) of a reference area.

While there are several other problems relating to the analysis of areal data, the problem of estimating a **spatial correlogram** merits special attention. The concept of the correlogram has been borrowed in the spatial literature from the time series analysis. Figure 1.4.a shows the first-order neighbours of a reference area, while Figure 1.4.b displays the second-order neighbours of the same area. Higher-order neighbours can be defined in a similar fashion. While it is clear that the dependence is strongest between immediate neighbouring areas a certain degree of dependence may be present among higher-order neighbours. This has been shown to be an alternative way of looking at the scale problem (Cliff and Ord, 1981, p.123).
However, unlike the case of a time series where each observation depends only on past observations, here dependence extends in all directions. This fact poses new problems for the estimation of the correlogram.
We will show in the next chapters that the problem of estimating a spatial correlogram of a spatial series shares the same characteristic as the other problems mentioned in this section; therefore it can be treated within the same methodological framework.
In all the problems which we have briefly introduced here, a paramount role is played by the configuration of the spatial data i.e. by the fact that each unit on which a variable is recorded possesses its own unique size and shape and connects to other units in an irregular way. The investigation of the effects of data configuration within the context of spatial autocorrelation and modifiable areal units leads us to the need for an appropriate methodology. We introduce this below.

1.3. A SKETCH OF THE METHODOLOGY

Throughout the book we will assume that a good representation of reality can be obtained by assuming that a spatial series is a finite realization of a stochastic process in two dimensions. To make any progress with such an approach we are forced to accept as a starting point the hypothesis of normality and stationarity of the process itself. (Some theoretical results, however, can be applied to other kind of processes). There are a number of practical situations in which it is not unreasonable to assume that the process has a stationary multivariate normal distribution. When this is not the case we will assume that it is always possible to subdivide the areal units into sufficiently small units (ultimately the individual economic agents) where the assumption of stationarity becomes more plausible. The advantage of this approach is that we are able to study the effects on the moments of the generating process of any statistical manipulation of the original data.
For example, dealing with the scale problem, provided we know the distribution of the generating process at a county level and provided we know the way in which data are aggregated up to the regional level, we can specify the distribution of the generating process at a regional level. In doing so we are also able to exploit all the relevant information about the configuration of the spatial data.
In each chapter attention is given to explaining classical results found in the literature and to confirming these theoretical results by analysis of sets of real economic data. Furthermore, in some cases, artificial computer-generated data are also examined. For example the theoretical results obtained in Chapter 7 on the *ecological fallacy* problem, are tested by exploiting a microsimulation approach where the individual behaviour is simulated and the results aggregated up to a geographical level. In all the simulation studies new computer programs had to be written. The listing of these programs, written in FORTRAN-77 on the IBM-3081 system of Cambridge University Computer Centre, are contained in the appendices to the relevant chapters.

1.4. AN OUTLINE OF THE BOOK

The plan of the book is as follows. Before entering into the theoretical discussion, we first introduce in more detail the set of problems of concern. In Chapter 2 we review the results found in the literature on the effects of the spatial configuration of data on statistical analysis. In Chapter 3 we seek to clarify the concept of *spatial configuration of data* in order to introduce the essential concepts and notation used in the rest of the book.

Chapter 4 introduces the methodological basis for the theoretical contribution of the book. Here we introduce some basic notions of spatial stochastic processes and we derive the fundamental theoretical results used in later chapters.

Chapter 5 is concerned with the analysis of the problems arising in statistical analysis of **univariate** spatial series. In particular in sections 5.2 and 5.3 we analyse the scale problem in situations involving a single variable, while in section 5.4 the aggregation problem is attacked. The effects of the configuration of spatial data in **bivariate** statistical analysis of spatial series are discussed in Chapters 6 and 7. In Chapter 6 we consider again the scale and aggregation problems in correlation analysis of two spatial series, whereas in Chapter 7 we consider the *ecological fallacy* problem. Chapter 8 is devoted to discussing the problems of estimating the spatial correlogram in irregular lattices. Finally the appendices to the book contain some of the data used for our empirical studies (Appendices A.1 to A.4) and a review of the methods available for simulating two-dimensional random surfaces (Appendix A.5).

1.5. OMITTED TOPICS

It is clear that the aim of this book is not to give an exhaustive account of all the problems that occur when a statistical analysis is performed with data which are distributed over space. Consequently a number of topics are omitted from the discussion.

First of all, while the most common situation in regional economics is that of variables recorded in *irregular collecting areas*, there are situations in which the actual location of geographical entities is of interest. This is the case of microanalytical studies in the spatial economy such as the detection of housing patterns or the study of the location of industrial plants or of public facilities (Wilson and Bennett, 1985). The study of *point patterns* of this kind are not considered here, although some indication is given of the way in which the methodological framework developed in this book could be extended to deal with these situations.

Secondly, data are always considered for a single cross-section in time; consequently no attention is given to problems related to *spatial-time series* (Bennett, 1979).

Thirdly, the effects of spatial configuration of data in the analysis of more than one series is restricted to bivariate regression analysis while no consideration is given to *multivariate techniques* like factor analysis or principal component analysis (Streitberg, 1978).

Finally, other interesting topics like the *missing data* problem (Haining, Griffith and Bennett, 1984) or *spatial sampling* (Cochran, 1963; Ripley, 1981) are also omitted because of lack of space.

2. Theoretical problems motivation

2.1. INTRODUCTION

In this chapter we wish to discuss to a deeper extent the theoretical problems reviewed in Chapter 1. In particular in Section 2.2 the modifiable areal unit problem will be analysed in its two manifestations of *scale* and *aggregation*. Section 2.3 contains a review of the literature on the *ecological fallacy*. Finally the problem of estimating a *spatial correlogram* will be discussed in Section 2.4.

2.2. THE MODIFIABLE AREAL UNIT PROBLEM

2.2.1. The nature of the modifiable areal unit problem: modifiable versus unmodifiable units

Yule and Kendall (1950) lucidly introduce a fundamental distinction between two different kinds of data to which a statistical analysis may be applied.
It sometimes happens that we have to deal with statistical units which cannot be further decomposed into smaller units. Consider, for example, the case in which we measure the income or the level of consumption of a single economic agent. The ultimate unit of analysis is the individual whose income and consumption is a "unique non-modifiable numerical measurement" (Yule and Kendall, 1950). It is not conceivable to divide the individual economic agent into smaller units. The same thing is true if we consider, for example, the age of an individual, or the level of production of a single firm or the price of a commodity. This kind of data are related to units which are intrinsically *non-modifiable* .
The same is not true when dealing with spatial units which are, in contrast, *modifiable*. "Since it is impossible, or at any rate impracticable, to grow wheat and potatoes on the same piece of ground simultaneously we must, to give our investigation a meaning, consider an area containing both wheat and potatoes; and this area is modifiable at choice"(op.cit.; p.312). Similar examples may be found in economics where, for example, a regional unemployment rate, the percentage of commuters, the total male population, the votes cast for a political candidate, can only be referred to a modifiable geographical unit. The relevance of this distinction is that the value of any statistical measure "will, in general, depend on the unit chosen if that unit is modifiable" (Yule and Kendall, 1950).
Openshaw and Taylor (1979) distinguished two aspects of the modifiable areal unit problem in a geographical context. The first aspect relates to the different results one may get in statistical analysis with the same set of data grouped at different scale levels (e.g. counties or regions) and it is therefore referred to as the *scale problem*; the second considers the variability of results not due to variations in the size of the areas,

but rather to the shape of them. This is therefore referred to as the *aggregation problem*. We will deal with the two aspects separately in the next two sections.

2.2.2. The scale problem

The scale problem in geographical studies arise for different reasons. First of all, human society is organized in territorial units usually arranged into nested hierarchies like town, counties, regions and states; it is therefore common to have to cope with data aggregated in terms of such spatial units. In these cases the problem arises of choosing the level of resolution that describes best the phenomenon under study (Moellering and Tobler, 1972). A second situation arises from the procedure in geographical studies of superimposing on a map a regular grid of contiguous quadrats in order to investigate the pattern of a particular phenomenon (Greig-Smith, 1952). This procedure is most commonly used in plant ecology, but there are examples also in human geography (see for example, Cliff and Ord,1981; p.133).
In both the regular and the irregular case the scale problem can be summarized by saying that "generalizations made at one level do not necessarily hold at another level, and that conclusions we derived at one scale may be invalid at another" (Haggett, 1965).

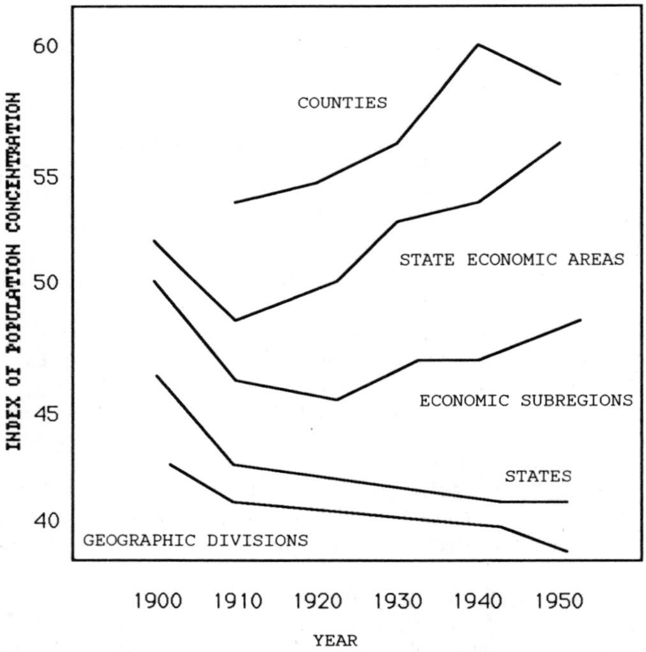

Figure 2.2.1: Index of population concentration in U.S. from 1900 to 1950. Source Duncan et al. (1961).

To give an idea of how serious the problem of scale is, let us start with an example. Figure 2.2.1 shows the index of population concentration, for different areal subdivisions of the United States through time. The figure (taken from Duncan et al. 1961, p.86) shows that the population concentration has increased over the 50 years considered, if we measure it at a *county* level or at a *state economic area* level. In contrast the index remains approximately constant at the level of *economic subregion* . Finally the population concentration decreases if we measure it at a *state* level or at the level of *geographic divisions*. This example shows that because of the modifiable areal unit problem we are not even able to give an answer in a conclusive way to the simple question: "what happened to the population concentration in the U.S. in the period considered?"

The problem has been recognised for a long time and researchers have concentrated on its effects on statistical measures, particularly on the correlation coefficient and on the variance. In a short paper Gehlke and Biehl (1934) studied the effects on the correlation coefficient between male juvenile delinquency and median monthly income in 252 census tracts in Cleveland. The correlation coefficient was first computed for the 252 census tracts and then for the same data grouped successively into fewer and larger units with the contiguity constraint. The results are shown in Table 2.1 for the raw data and for ratios. It is useful to remark, however, that due to the loss of degrees of freedom, the estimates of the correlation coefficient become less reliable as sample size decreases.

The main conclusion is that, in both cases, the correlation coefficient increases monotonically in absolute value. When census tracts are grouped at random rather than by contiguity, the two authors obtained the results displayed in Table 2.2 .

In this case no systematic scale effect occurs. The result is interesting and suggests that the dependance between areas can be at the origin of the problem: dependence plays a role when we group contiguous areas; in contrast, it is eliminated when we group areas at random.

number of units	Correlation coefficient	
	Raw data	Ratios
252	-0.502	-0.516
200	-0.569	-0.504
175	-0.580	-0.480
150	-0.606	-0.475
125	-0.662	-0.563
100	-0.667	-0.524
50	-0.685	-0.579
25	-0.763	-0.621

Table 2.1 : Correlation coefficients at different scale levels where data are grouped with the contiguity constraint, for juvenile delinquency and monthly income in Cleveland , USA. Source Gehlke and Biehl (1934).

In a second experiment, whose results are displayed in Table 2.3, Gehlke and Biehl confirmed the previous conclusions studying the correlation between farm products and the number of farmers for 1,000 rural counties.
In the same issue of the Journal of the American Statistical Association, J. Neprash (1936) warned that " the correlation of spatially distributed variables must be accepted with very severe limitations of interpretation". He further remarked that these limitations originated from the fact that data violate the condition of the independence of the units of which the traits are measured.
Yule and Kendall (1950) reinforced Gehlke and Biehl argument observing that, in practical situations, the correlation coefficient tends to increase with scale. Figure 2.2.2 shows the map of 48 agricultural counties of England in 1936. For each county Table 2.4 shows the yields per acre of wheat and potatoes. Yule and Kendall found a correlation between the two yields of + 0.2189. They then combined successively the counties in pairs (note that the areas grouped are not always contiguous). The values of the correlation coefficient at different scales are shown in Table 2.5.
Although the results at the higher scales are not significant due to the diminished degrees of freedom, the tendency to increase found by Gehlke and Biehl is confirmed in the Yule and Kendall study.

Number of units	Correlation coefficient
252	-0.502
175	-0.434
25	-0.544

Table 2.2 : Correlation coefficients at different scale levels where data are grouped at random, for juvenile delinquency and monthly income in Cleveland, USA. Source Gehlke and Biehl (1934).

Number of units	Correlation coefficient	
1000	-0.649	*
63	-0.859	*
40	-0.725	**
31	-0.756	*
8	-0.826	**

Table 2.3 : Correlation coefficients between farm products and number of farmers at different scale levels where data are grouped at random (*) and with the contiguity constraint(**). Source Gehlke and Biehl (1934).

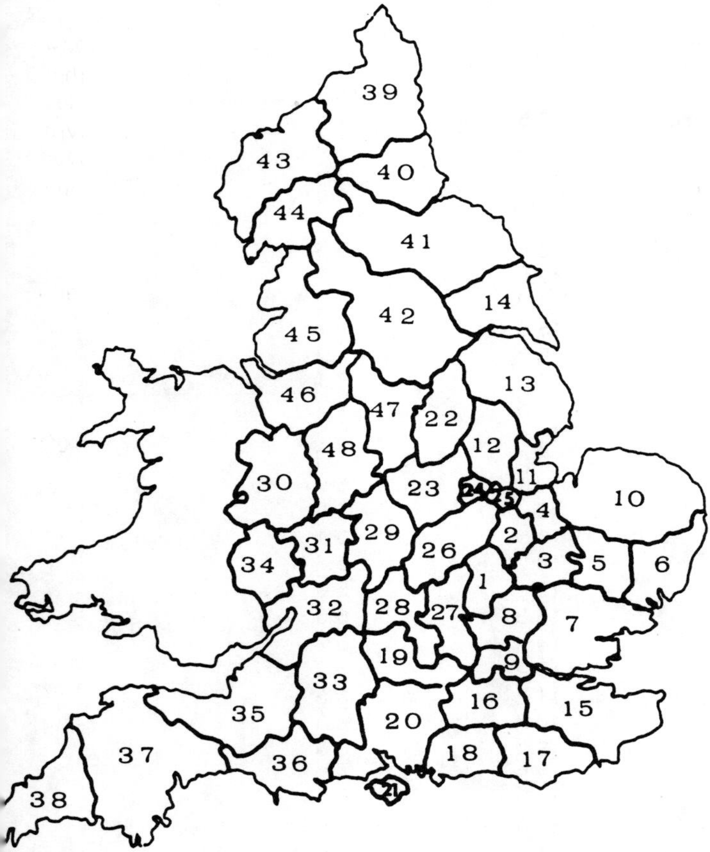

Figure 2.2.2 : Map of 48 agricultural counties in England in 1936.

Code	County	Wheat	Potatoes
1	Bedford	16.0	5.3
2	Huntington	16.0	6.6
3	Cambridge	16.4	6.1
4	Ely	20.5	5.5
5	Suffolk, West	18.2	6.9
6	Suffolk, East	16.3	6.1
7	Essex	17.7	6.4
8	Hertford	15.3	6.3
9	Middlesex	16.5	7.8
10	Norfolk	16.9	8.3
11	Lincoln (Holland)	21.8	5.7
12	Lincoln(Kesteven)	15.5	6.2
13	Lincoln (Lindsey)	15.8	6.0
14	Yorkshire (E.Riding)	18.5	6.6
15	Kent	18.5	6.6
16	Surrey	12.7	4.8
17	Sussex E.	15.7	4.9
18	Sussex W.	14.3	5.1
19	Berkshire	13.8	5.5
20	Hampshire	12.8	6.7
21	Isle of Wight	12.0	6.5
22	Nottingham	15.6	5.2
23	Leicester	15.8	5.2
24	Rutland	16.6	7.1
25	Northampton	14.3	4.9
26	Peterborough	14.4	5.6
27	Buckingham	15.2	6.4
28	Oxford	14.1	6.9
29	Warwick	15.4	5.6
30	Shropshire	16.5	6.1
31	Worcester	14.2	5.7
32	Gloucester	13.2	5.0
33	Wiltshire	13.8	6.5
34	Hereford	14.4	6.2
35	Somrset	13.4	5.2
36	Dorset	11.2	6.6
37	Devon	14.4	5.8
38	Cornwall	15.4	6.3
39	Northumberland	18.5	6.3
40	Durham	16.4	5.8
41	Yorkshire N.R.	17.0	5.9
42	Yorkshire W.R.	16.9	6.5
43	Cumberland	17.5	5.8
44	Westmorland	15.8	5.7
45	Lancashire	19.2	7.2
46	Cheshire	17.7	6.5
47	Derby	15.2	5.4
48	Stafford	17.1	6.3

Table 2.4 : Yields of wheat and potatoes in 48 agricultural counties in England in 1936.

Number of units	Correlation coefficient
48	0.2189
24	0.2963
12	0.5757
6	0.7649
3	0.9902

Table 2.5 : Correlation coefficient between wheat and potatoes in Yule and Kendall (1950) study.

The two authors realized that it is virtually possible " to produce any value of the correlation from 0 to 1 by choosing an appropriate size of the unit of area for which we measure the yields . Is there any real correlation between wheat and potatoes yields or are our results illusory?" They went on by saying that "our correlation will accordingly measure the relationship between the variates for the specified unit chosen for the work. They have no absolute validity independent of these units , but are relative to them.
They measure, as it were, not only the variations of the quantities under consideration, but also the properties of the unit-mesh which we have imposed on the system in order to measure it". This is the first time that the scale problem is connected with the configuration of maps.
Yule and Kendall proposed a possible theoretical explanation to the problem. This can be summarized as follows. First of all suppose that we are dealing with two variables X and Y, say, and assume that they can be regarded as the sum of two uncorrelated elements: a systematic component and a random component

$$X = Z + E$$
$$Y = W + F$$

Their variance can be similarly decomposed as

$$\mathrm{Var}(X) = \mathrm{Var}(Z) + \mathrm{Var}(E)$$

and

$$\mathrm{Var}(Y) = \mathrm{Var}(W) + \mathrm{Var}(F)$$

The argument of Yule and Kendall is that in aggregating the units the element of choice cancels out so that Var (E) and hence Var(X) diminishes (and similarly Var(F) and Var(Y)). It follows that the denominator of the correlation coefficient (given by $[\mathrm{Var}(X)\ \mathrm{Var}(Y)]^{-1/2}$) will also be reduced by an increase of the size of the area. Consequently the correlation coefficient will increase as we aggregate the data.
A.H.Robinson (1956) introduced the problem to geographers. In his paper he presented a simple example to indicate that it is possible to get virtually any value we like for the correlation coefficient simply by changing the zone boundaries. His example is shown in Figure 2.2.3 .
Three alternative zoning schemes were laid out for two densities X and Y. In the first there are six zones, in the second, one of the areas was doubled in size and the density recalculated; finally in a third scheme, the process is repeated and a larger area obtained. The result of the aggregation process is that the correlation coefficient assumes the values displayed in Table 2.6.

The example is, perhaps, too simple and the small number of values does not allow any conclusive proof. However it has the merit of having made geographers aware of the problem. Robinson concluded by proposing as a solution the weighting of density values by the area to which they refer, a procedure which is now widely accepted (Bachi, 1957; Thomas and Anderson, 1965; Williamson, 1971).
We will show that this procedure does not remove the problem of scale (see Chapter 5). However it indicates a way to bring into consideration the physical characteristics of geographical data.
A further contribution to the problem is given by Blalock (1964). The author computed the correlation coefficient between a first variable X (the percentage of non-white population), and a second variable Y which involves a measure of the differential between white and non-white incomes using data collected for 150 Southern American Counties (op.cit.; p.103). Similarly to previous studies, data are grouped in pairs, fives, tens and fifteens by employing four different criteria:
a) Random grouping of the counties
b) Grouping so as to maximize the variance of X
c) Grouping so as to maximize the variance of Y
d) Grouping by proximity
The results are displayed in Table 2.7. The feature, of increasing correlation in geographical grouping and of constancy in random grouping , previously noted (Gehlke and Biehl, 1934) is again present. Furthermore Blalock also recognises that a role is played by the variance of the two variables involved: when the groups are made in order to maximize the variance, the correlation increases more sharply than in the case of grouping by proximity.

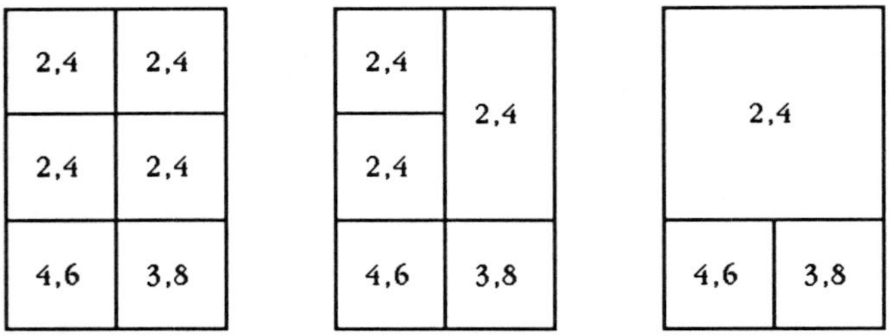

Figure 2.2.3 : Layouts of Robinson's (1956) experiment.

Number of units	Correlation coefficient
6	0.715
5	0.875
3	0.500

Table 2.6 : Correlation coefficient between the two densities in the example of Robinson (1956).

In recent years there has been a reappraisal of the problem through the work of P.Taylor and S.Openshaw. According to Taylor (1977) the rising correlation with increasing scale can be regarded as the result of spatial autocorrelation "whereby grouping by proximity maintains more of the variable's variance" (p.222). This fact explains heuristically why no scale effect occurs with random observations.
This conjecture has been tested by Openshaw and Taylor (1979) who had the merit of having introduced for the first time the problem of the spatial autocorrelation explicitly into consideration. The two authors considered the 99 counties in the state of IOWA (U.S.A.) and selected two variables: the percentage of votes for Republican candidates in the congressional election of 1968 and the percentage of population over 60 years. The value of the correlation coefficient at the 99 county level was found equal to 0.34. The two authors described a procedure to simulate, for the 99 counties, observations drawn from a bivariate normal distribution with a correlation equal to that observed in the real data. Three levels of the spatial autocorrelation coefficient (Cliff and Ord, 1981) were chosen: (a) A maximum negative level in both variables, (b) No spatial autocorrelation in both variables, and (c) A maximum positive level in both variables. Finally they performed 10,000 permutations of the 99 counties at different scale levels and computed, at each scale, the correlation coefficient. The results are summarized in Table 2.8.
Commenting on the results of the simulation Openshaw concluded that " the artificial data with negative spatial autocorrelation has the least biased results...whereas increasing positive spatial autocorrelation produces results which are increasingly biased....The zero autocorrelation state confers no particular benefits" (Openshaw, 1981, p.18).
Openshaw and Taylor in a number of successive studies, sought after a general theory of the modifiable areal unit problem, but concluded, rather sceptically, that no systematic relationship emerged. "We have been able to find a very wide range of correlations. We simply do not know why we have found them. Hence we can make no general statements about variations in correlation coefficient so that each areal unit problem must be treated individually for any specific piece of research" (Openshaw and Taylor, 1979; 142-143).

Method	Correlation coefficients				
	Ungrouped	n=75	n=30	n=15	n=10
Random	0.54	0.67	0.61	0.62	0.26
Max variation of X	0.54	0.67	0.84	0.88	0.95
Max variation of Y	0.54	0.67	0.87	0.91	0.95
By proximity	0.54	0.63	0.70	0.84	0.81

Table 2.7 : Comparison of correlation coefficients for various methods of grouping at different scales. Source Blalock (1964).

number of zones	average group size	correlation $_x\rho=-0.57$ $_y\rho=-0.71$		$_x\rho=$ $_y\rho=0.0$		$_x\rho=0.82$ $_y\rho=0.92$	
		Mean	Standard deviation	Mean	Standard deviation	Mean	Standard deviation
6	16.5	.31	.443	.61	.294	.60	.247
12	8.2	.30	.370	.47	.263	.52	.176
18	5.5	.29	.350	.42	.227	.48	.142
24	4.1	.31	.309	.40	.192	.44	.121
30	3.3	.32	.277	.39	.166	.42	.108
36	2.7	.32	.242	.38	.146	.40	.098
42	2.4	.33	.209	.37	.128	.39	.087
48	2.0	.33	.183	.36	.112	.38	.080
54	1.8	.33	.160	.36	.100	.34	.072

Table 2.8 : Values of the correlation for three different levels of spatial autocorrelation in the two variables. Source : Openshaw (1981) .

A final work which is of interest in this section is that of Cliff and Ord (1981; p.132). They studied some data taken from the Atlas of London (Jones and Sinclair, 1968; sheets 43-45) about the area of floorspace in office, commercial and industrial use in 1962. The data are laid on a 24-by-24 square lattice grid and are displayed in Figure 2.2.4. Two regressions were performed between commerce and offices and between industry and offices. Data were analysed at different levels of spatial resolution with successive aggregation obtained by combining 4,4,4,3 and 3 cells of the previous level at each step. The results are displayed in Table 2.9.

Scale level	Var(X)	Var(Y)	Corr(X,Y)
(a) X= Commerce Y=Offices			
1	116712	886554	0.19
2	71547	700432	0.36
3	46203	414767	0.67
4	17557	197011	0.71
5	9211	78547	0.97
(b)X=Industry Y= Offices			
1	88954	886554	0.09
2	49935	700432	0.16
3	32080	414767	0.33
4	162289	197011	0.34
5	7923	78547	0.32

Table 2.9 : Variance and correlation at different scales of London land-use data. Source Cliff and Ord, 1981; p.133.

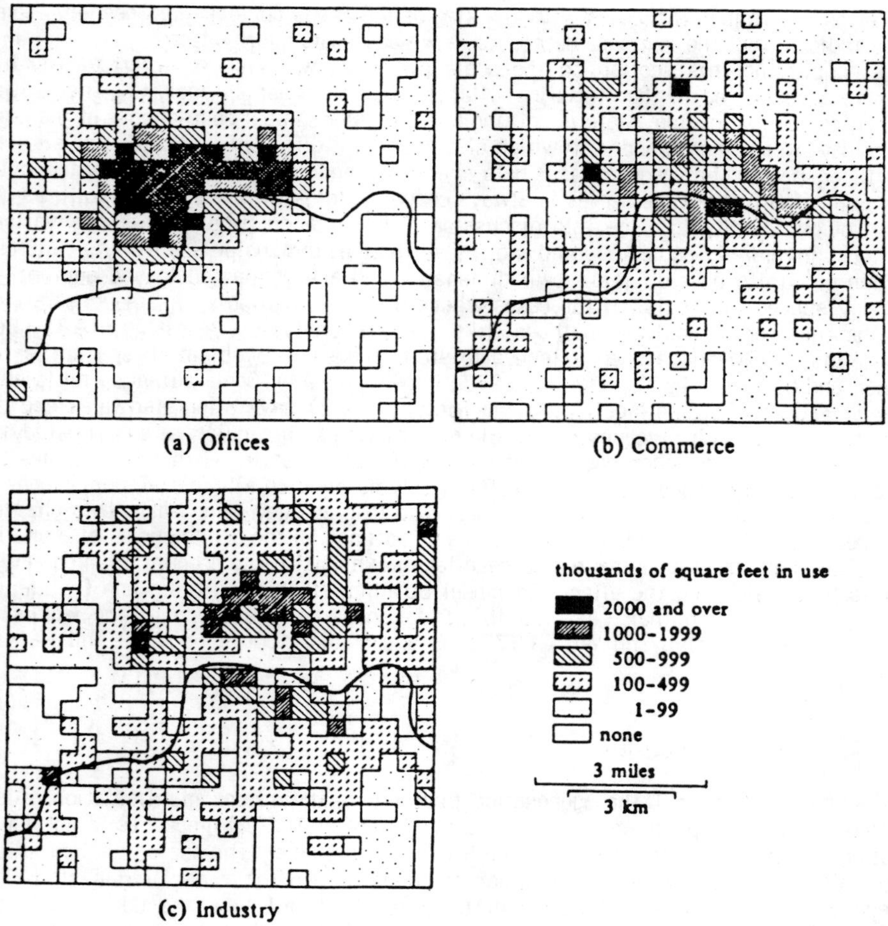

Figure 2.2.4 : Floorspace occupied by (a) Office, (b) Commerce and (c) Industry in part of London County Council in 1962. Source Cliff and Ord, 1981; p.132.

The conclusions were that the correlation increases and the variance decreases with increasing scale. Elsewhere Cliff and Ord (1981,p.130) come to the conclusion that " the degree of correlation between the variables is a function of the size of area considered". They go on to say that " if a suitable functional form describing the change in correlation with size could be found, it might be calibrated from the estimated values" (op.cit.; p.130).

At the end of this review it appears clear that the scale problem has at least two consequences for statistical analysis of areal data. First, there is evidence that the

correlation coefficient increases with the size of the areas considered. Secondly, some studies indicate that the variance decreases as we aggregate observations.
Before concluding this section on the scale problem, we wish to refer to similar problems encountered in the statistical literature of time series analysis. The spatial hierarchies county, region, state is nothing but the geographical counterpart of the time units of day, week, month and year which also represent different scales of analysis. The main difference is that geographical data are finite and irregularly distributed over space. Even if finite, a time series is always conceivable as infinite, and this allows the concept of periodicity to come into discussion. Furthermore time series observations are almost invariably equally spaced and, by definition, dimensionless. On the contrary geographical units possess their own dimension and are connected to one another in unequally spaced intervals. In the cases where data are available on a square lattice grid, the time series analysis methods, like spectral analysis (Priestley, 1981; Box and Jenkins, 1970) have been extended to study the scale problem in spatial series (Rayner and Golledge, 1972; Rayner, 1971; Rogers, 1974). Some authors (noticeably Curry, 1970, 1972; and Moellering and Tobler, 1972) have attempted to extend the idea of decomposition by frequency or scale of variation to irregular data units studying how variance and regression coefficient vary with scale. Dealing with a time series the analysis of the correlogram and the spectral analysis provide alternative approaches to the problem of scale. We will come back again to this analogy later on in this chapter when dealing with the problems which arise in estimating the correlogram of a spatial series. The problem of scale have also been taken explicitly into account in time series analysis by considering the effects on model building of shifting from one frequency wave (e.g. days) to another (e.g. month). References can be found in the works of Telser(1967), Amemiya and Wu (1972); Granger and Morris (1976) and Harvey (1981).

2.2.3. The aggregation problem

As we stated in Chapter 1 the aggregation problem is the second manifestation of the modifiable areal unit problem. Here the variability of statistical measures is not due to variations in the size of the areas, but rather to their shape: "The scale problem arises because of uncertainty about the number of zones needed for a particular study.The aggregation problem arises because of uncertainty about how the data are to be aggregated to form a given number of zones. It should be noted that for any reasonably sized data set there is considerably more spatial freedom in the choice of aggregation than there is in the choice of the number of zones" (Openshaw, 1981, p.8).
This subproblem of the modifiable areal unit is more subtle. Dealing with scale there occurs an obvious loss in information when shifting from a finer to a coarse scale. In contrast, when dealing with the aggregation problem, no loss of information occurs if we shift from one boundary system to another; rather there is an alteration of information. Geographical studies have been traditionally concentrated on the scale problem (Clark and Avery, 1976) so that considerably less work has been done on the aggregation problem. The aggregation problem is, however, a feature long known by politicians because it forms the basis of the gerrymander (Taylor and Johnston, 1979), that is "drawing electoral boundaries to suit one's own political affiliation" (Unwin, 1981). As a matter of fact the problem has been fully recognised in geography only after a series of papers by Openshaw and Taylor in the late seventies (Taylor, 1973; Openshaw, 1977a, 1977b, 1977c, 1978a, 1978b; and Openshaw and Taylor, 1979) on whose work we shall need to draw heavily in this section.

The importance of Openshaw and Taylor's work is that they performed the first large-scale simulation on the problem in order to demonstrate its magnitude and severity. The two authors were seeking an answer to the question "what are the worst cases or real limits of the aggregation effects?" (Openshaw, 1981; p.21). In a now famous study Openshaw and Taylor (1979) simulated 10,000 different aggregations of the 99 IOWA counties (see Section 2.2.2) at different scales and computed the correlation coefficient for each aggregation. Table 2.10 summarizes the main results.

It can be seen that a very wide range of values of the correlation coefficient can be produced by juggling with zone boundaries. Openshaw (1981) commented that "for 99 IOWA zones, a small data set by current standards, a very wide range of results can be obtained. The amount of aggregation variability, or spatial freedom, will be even greater with larger data sets". In another paper Openshaw and Taylor (1981) commented that "For a small data set of 99 IOWA counties, 12 zones aggregation could be engineered that produce correlation between -0.97 and +0.99; a regression slope of between - 12.7 and + 12.2 and a level of fit which could be nearly perfect or incredibly poor, and a robust regression coefficient that varied from -14.6 to +16.2". Their conclusion was that " the magnitude of the zoning effect that has been observed is too large to be ignored".

Openshaw and Taylor, perhaps, underestimated the influence of the spatial autocorrelation when they say that "different amounts of the spatial autocorrelation have no noticeable effects" (Openshaw and Taylor, 1979; p.22). As a matter of fact looking at Table 2.10 it appears that the range of variability of the correlation coefficient is, instead, sensitive to the level of spatial autocorrelation. In fact the wider ranges are associated with negative spatial autocorrelations and the smaller ranges to positive spatial autocorrelation. In the case of no spatial autocorrelation the range assumes intermediate values.

In a second simulation experiment Openshaw and Taylor (1979) went further by studying not only the minimum and the maximum of the correlation coefficient in alternative aggregations of the same data set, but its complete distribution when the zoning criterion changes. Some results of this second experiment have already been displayed in Table 2.8. Some interesting features emerge also from Figure 2.2.5.

As in the first experiment three levels of spatial autocorrelation in the two variables were employed: autocorrelation coefficients in the two variables both negative, both positive and both null.

The following conclusions can be drawn :

1) The distribution of the correlation coefficient when the zoning criterion changes has an approximately Gaussian shape.

2) The variance of the distribution of the correlation coefficient increases with the scale.

3) When a positive spatial autocorrelation is present the distribution exhibits less spread and less bias if compared with the distribution under the hypothesis of no spatial autocorrelation.

Openshaw and Taylor concluded their series of studies on the subject with a sceptical position: "Aggregation variability is not susceptible to a statistical approach since no systematic empirical regularities could be found" (Openshaw and Taylor, 1981; p.13). We will see in a later chapter however, that this sceptical conclusion was reached because the two authors did not take into account in their simulation all the relevant elements.

number of zones	average group size	spatial autocorrelation $_x\rho=-0.57$ $_y\rho=-0.71$		$_x\rho=$ $_y\rho=0.0$		$_x\rho=0.82$ $_y\rho=0.92$	
		Min	Max	Min	Max	Min	Max
6	16.5	-.99	.99	-.99	.99	-.99	.99
12	8.2	-.97	.99	-.99	.99	-.99	.99
18	5.5	-.97	.99	-.97	.99	-.92	.99
24	4.1	-.98	.99	-.90	.99	-.89	.98
30	3.3	-.93	.98	-.86	.98	-.78	.95
36	2.7	-.93	.98	-.80	.98	-.61	.93
42	2.4	-.92	.97	-.79	.96	-.52	.93
48	2.0	-.87	.96	-.66	.95	-.39	.89
54	1.8	-.85	.95	-.52	.91	-.32	.88

Table 2.10 : Some approximate limits of the correlation coefficient in different aggregations. Source: Openshaw (1981, p.22).

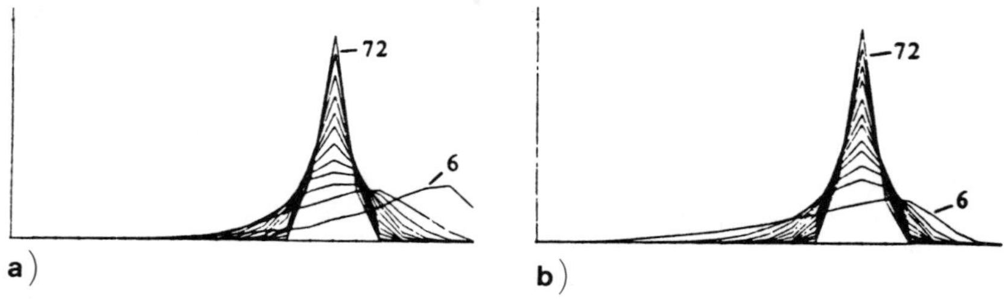

Figure 2.2.5 : Distribution of the correlation coefficient when the zoning criterion changes in the simulation study of Openshaw and Taylor(1979,p.138). (a) random observations. (b) positive spatial autocorrelation.

2.2.4. Conclusion

In this section we have reviewed the results found in the literature on the modifiable areal unit problem in its two manifestations of *scale* and *aggregation* subproblem. In spite of a large amount of empirical work on the subject that shows its severity, no full theoretical explanation has been found, at present, to the problem. Even if some hypothesis on the nature of the modifiable areal unit problem have been expressed by some authors (noticeably Yule and Kendall, 1950; Taylor, 1977; and Blalock, 1964) no conclusive proof has been reached nor results that can be used for prediction or correction purposes. Hence from this review of the literature we can conclude with the words of Openshaw: that "the modifiable areal unit problem is today one of the most important unresolved problems in spatial analysis" (Openshaw, 1981; p.6).

2.3. THE ECOLOGICAL FALLACY PROBLEM

2.3.1 Individual versus group behaviour

The problem of ecological fallacy concerns the different results obtained in statistical analysis when dealing with individuals as the unit of analysis instead of aggregations to Census tracts or other geographical units. The problem has been known for a long time in the literature. It was pointed out first by W.S.Robinson (1950) who in a famous paper distinguished between two kinds of correlations. The *individual correlation* "is the correlation in which the statistical object or thing described is indivisible" (W.S.Robinson, 1950; p.351). In terms of the analysis of Section 2.2 this is a correlation between non-modifiable units. A second kind of correlation is what the author termed the *ecological correlation* in which " the statistical object is a group of persons" (W.S.Robinson, 1950; p.351).

The individual correlation inferred from areal data such as Census tracts, may be seriously biased as to the magnitude. In fact it can be even erroneous as to the sign.

In many statistical studies "ecological correlations are used with the obvious purpose to discover something about the behaviour of individuals. Ecological correlation are used simply because correlation between the property of individuals are not available" (W.S.Robinson, 1950; p.352).

The typical example is that of studies of voting behaviour in which the researcher is not allowed to know the individual observations, but can obtain percentages of the votes in polling districts. The best one can do in this situation is to match voting proportions against aggregate characteristics of the voters in the smallest areas for which votes are available.

We can note here incidentally, that this is by no means a problem typical of human geography. In fact it is nothing but the geographical counterpart of analogous statistical problems encountered in other fields such as, for instance, the possible inconsistency between micro-economic theories and macro relationships (Klein, 1946) and the general problem of creating class-intervals for statistical observations. A classification of various typologies of ecological fallacies in social sciences is contained in Alker (1974).

2.3.2 Individual correlation versus group correlation

In the paper already quoted W.S.Robinson (1950) reports the results of an experiment based on the correlations between colour, illiteracy and nativity for the population with more than 10 years in the U.S. in 1930. Table 2.3.1 shows the results of Robinson's study.

The results are analogous to those which we have reviewed when dealing with the scale problem: they show an increase in the absolute value of the correlation coefficient when the number of observations decreases. Furthermore, the example shows that a change in the sign of the correlation coefficient can also occur when shifting from individuals to areal units.

Another important contribution to understanding the problem was given by Openshaw (1983). The author analysed a set of 40 variables for 122,342 households records collected by the regional Government of Tuscany (Italy) from the Census organised by ISTAT (the Italian Central Bureau of Statistics). The method Openshaw used to investigate the ecological fallacy problem was to cross-tabulate the individual and the zonal correlation coefficient as shown in Table 2.3.2. The distribution of the off-diagonal elements indicates the magnitude of the problem. In most cases less than 40 percent of the values remain in the diagonal and, therefore, are not affected by grouping.

Some authors have attempted to find a theoretical explanation for this phenomenon. According to Blalock "in shifting from one unit of analysis to another we are likely to affect the manner in which outside and possibly disturbing influences are operating on the dependent and the independent variables under consideration" (Blalock, 1964; p.98). He goes on suggesting that "in shifting units we may be affecting the way in which other unknowns or unmeasured variables are influencing the picture" (Blalock, 1964; p.99).

A more formal explanation is suggested by Duncan et al.(1961) following an argument originally due to Robinson (1950). The demonstration which is outlined in the next pages represents an extension of the standard statistical discussion for nested ANOVA models (Sheffe', 1959) to the case of correlation with the areal units acting as the discriminating effects (See also Cliff and Ord, 1981; p.129).

Define x_{ij} and y_{ij} as the observations of the i-th individual ($i=1,.....,n_j$) in the j-th areal unit ($j=1,....,k$) and $\sum_j n_j = N$. Suppose further that $x_j = n^{-1} \sum_i x_{ij}$, $\bar{x} = N^{-1} \sum\sum x_{ij}$ and similarly for y. Define now the total sum of squares of x as

Level of aggregation	Number of units	Correlation Regression 1	Correlation Regression 2
Individuals	98,000,000	0.203	0.118
State	48	0.773	-0.526
Census divisions	9	0.946	-0.619

Table 2.3.1 : Robinson's aggregation experiment. Regression 1 : Negro and illiteracy. Regression 2 : Nativity and illiteracy. Source: Robinson, 1950.

Zonal correlations Individual correlations categories	1	2	3	4	5	6	7	8	9	Total
1: -1.0 to -0.8	**100**									1
2: -0.8 to -0.6		**0**								0
3: -0.6 to -0.4			**100**							2
4: -0.4 to -0.2	2	19	31	**24**	17	6				83
5: -0.2 to 0.0		1	7	21	**32**	23	14	2		603
6: 0.0 to 0.2			1	6	10	**28**	28	22	3	78
7: 0.2 to 0.4							**18**	27	55	11
8: 0.4 to 0.6								**100**		1
9: 0.6 to 0.8									**100**	1
Totals	3	21	72	154	214	167	106	33	10	

Table 2.3.2 : Crosstabulation of individual and ecological correlation coefficients (percentage of rows totals. Source Openshaw (1983).

$$ {}_xS_t = \sum\sum (x_{ij} - \overline{x})^2 \qquad (2.3.1)$$

the *within area* sum of squares as

$$ {}_xS_w = \sum\sum (x_{ij} - x_j)^2 \qquad (2.3.2)$$

the *between area* sum of squares as

$$ {}_xS_b = \sum n_j (x_j - \overline{x})^2 \qquad (2.3.3)$$

and similarly for y. The *total correlation* is defined as

$$ r_t = \sum\sum (x_{ij} - \overline{x})(y_{ij} - \overline{y}) ({}_xS_t\, {}_yS_t)^{-1/2} \qquad (2.3.4)$$

Finally define the *ecological correlation* as

$$ r_e = \sum n_j (x_j - \overline{x})(y_j - \overline{y}) ({}_xS_b\, {}_yS_b)^{-1/2} \qquad (2.3.5)$$

and the *average within area* correlation as

$$ r_w = \sum\sum (x_{ij} - x_j)(y_{ij} - y_j) ({}_xS_w\, {}_yS_w)^{-1/2} \qquad (2.3.6)$$

The following decomposition holds

$$ r_t = r_w(1\ {}_xS_b\, {}_xS_t^{-1})^{1/2} (1 - {}_yS_b\, {}_yS_t^{-1})^{1/2} + r_e({}_xS_b\, {}_xS_t^{-1})({}_yS_b\, {}_yS_t^{-1}) \qquad (2.3.7)$$

hence

$$r_e = r_t k_1 - r_w k_2 \tag{2.3.8}$$

where

$$k_1 = ({}_xS_b{}^{-1}\,{}_xS_t)({}_yS_b{}^{-1}\,{}_yS_t) \tag{2.3.9}$$

and

$$k_2 = k_1 (1 - {}_xS_b\,{}_xS_t{}^{-1})^{1/2} (1 - {}_yS_b\,{}_yS_t{}^{-1})^{1/2} \tag{2.3.10}$$

Therefore the ecological correlation r_e is the weighted difference between the total individual correlation and the average within-areas individual correlation. From (2.3.8) we have that the ecological correlation is greater than the individual correlation whenever

$$r_w \leq k_3 r_t \tag{2.3.11}$$

where

$$k_3 = k_2{}^{-1} (k_1 - 1) \tag{2.3.12}$$

Since the minimum of k_3 is unity this implies that "the ecological correlation will be numerically greater than the individual correlation whenever the within-area individual correlation is not greater than the total individual correlation, and this is the usual circumstance" (W.S.Robinson, 1950; p.356).
The author does not explain in full detail the substantive meaning of the weights k_1, k_2 and k_3, nor does he attempt to relate them to the characteristics of the map imposed on the individuals in order to study them.

2.3.3. Micro versus macro economic relationships

We stated at the beginning of this section that a problem closely related to the ecological fallacy problem is that of the possible inconsistency between micro and macro relationships in economics (Pesaran et al., 1987). A relationship estimated at an individual level is what the economists call *behavioural* relationship. Typical examples are the single firm production function or the single consumer consumption function. For the single enterprise the production function embodies a particular interpretation of the causal mechanism that links input and output. The same relationship at an aggregate level does not depend on profit maximization, or whatever, but purely on technological factors (Klein, 1946). The individual relationships at an aggregate level are regarded in economics as *technical* relationships. If we estimate with aggregate data the linear consumption function, the derivative of consumption with respect to income has nothing in common with individual marginal propensity to consume (As Modigliani and Brunberg, 1954, have proved. See also Stocker, 1982).

The relatively cavalier fashion with which most empirical studies shift from one unit level to another or use existing data, has been only seldom criticized in the literature (Green, 1964; Hannan, 1971; Haitowsky, 1971). Traditionally economists and econometricians have been faced with this problem in the analysis of family budgets. Prais and Aitchinson (1954) examined the effect of carrying out a regression analysis on grouped data when individual observations are not available or they are too numerous to allow computation (prior to modern computers). They concentrated on the effects on the regression coefficient and found that (i) whatever the method of aggregation, the estimates were always unbiased; (ii) the variance of the estimates based on the ungrouped data is always smaller, and (iii) if the grouping is carried out in accordance with the value of the independent variable the loss in the efficiency is not very large. Cramer (1964) completed the analysis by considering the effect of grouping on the squared correlation coefficient R^2. He considered the transformation $c= R^2(1 - R^2)^{-1}$ and found that this quantity increases substantially with aggregation, the increase being proportional to the ratio

$$(m-2)\, S(x^2)\, [(n-2)\, S(x'^2)]^{-1} \qquad (2.3.13)$$

where $S(x^2)$ is the sum of squares of the independent variable in the individual data, $S(x'^2)$ is the sum of squares in the grouped data, n is the number of individuals and m the number of groups considered. Cramer also remarks that a random grouping, while producing a minimum increase in R^2 reduces the efficiency of the regression coefficient, whereas a grouping role defined as *efficient*, i.e. minimizing the variation of the independent variable in each group, produces only a small reduction of efficiency in the regression coefficient, but a greater increase in the value of R^2. Note here incidentally that, in a geographical context, the minimization of the within-group variance corresponds to the presence of a positive spatial autocorrelation in that area. In fact, in this case, similar values tend to cluster. Finally Orcutt, Watts and Edwards (1968; p.783), after a microsimulation study, pointed out that "detailed study of the individual regression indicates a tendency to reject the null hypothesis more frequently the usual sampling theory would suggest". They concluded that "perhaps this is why economic theories are almost never rejected on the basis of empirical evidence" (op.cit.; p.786).

2.3.4. Conclusion

In this section we have reviewed some of the existing literature on the ecological fallacy problem and on related problems in economics. The empirical works examined allows us to conclude that:

1) The ecological correlation is usually greater in absolute value then the individual correlation and can differ from it even as to the sign.

2) The regression coefficient estimate although unbiased is less efficient if based on grouped data.

Similarly to the modifiable areal unit problem, in spite of a lot of empirical examples describing the disturbing effects of the ecological fallacy problem, no theoretical explanation exists and very little is yet known about the magnitude of the bias or of the loss in efficiency. Therefore, even if some techniques may be derived that can help in certain particular situations in sociology (Duncan and Davies, 1953; Goodman, 1959; Johnston, 1976) and in econometrics (Johnston, 1972), no general solution yet exists.

2.4. PROBLEMS IN THE ESTIMATION OF THE SPATIAL CORRELOGRAM

2.4.1. Introduction

As we said in Chapter 1 a further set of problems we want to examine in this book are those arising in the estimation of the spatial correlogram. To introduce the topic it is necessary to define formally the concept of *spatial lag* by analogy with the time series analysis and this accomplished in Section 2.4.2. In Section 2.4.3 we refer to some empirical examples, while Section 2.4.4 contains some conclusions.

2.4.2. Spatial lag and spatial correlogram

A correlogram is a graph which shows how the spatial autocorrelation changes with distance. The correlogram has traditionally had an application dealing with time series (Box and Jenkins, 1970) so that distance is usually employed to mean time distance. Geographers have tried to adapt the idea to spatial series using, in contrast, spatial distance (Cliff and Ord 1973, 1981; Lebart, 1966). Sokal and Oden (1978) describe imaginatively the concept in this way: "Imagine throwing a stick of specific length over and over again at a certain study area, while noting the values of a variate at the points at which ends of the stick lands. Affirming that spatial autocorrelation is tantamount to saying that the values at the ends of the stick are usually like each other, or they are usually different". If we now imagine throwing sticks of different lengths at the same study area the outcoming plot of autocorrelations against the stick length is the correlogram.
A correlogram in time series analysis is given by the mean correlation between the original series and the so-called *lagged* series: that is the series shifted, say, τ steps ahead. (See Figure 2.4.1).
In symbols we have that the lagged series can be expressed as

$$L^{t^*}(x_i) = x_{i-t^*}$$

where L(.) is the lag operator.
If we imagine a theoretical spatial series laid on a infinite regular square lattice grid, it makes sense to define the spatial lag operator along the two axes, say, s and r (Whittle, 1954; Hooper and Hewings, 1981; Ripley, 1981)

$$L^s L^r (x_{ij}) = x_{i+s,j+r}$$

where x_{ij} is the observation corresponding to the i-th row and the j-th column of the lattice. The relaxing of infiniteness introduces the need for edge corrections analogous to those for time series (Priestley, 1981; Guyon, 1982; Griffith and Amrhein, 1983) but does not affect the essence of the problem which is basically of a multiple time series (Whittle, 1962). However the regular lattice grid case is only a theoretical situation very rarely found in human geography. The traditional way (Cliff and Ord, 1981) of dealing with irregular spatial schemes is through the definition of a set of neighbours for each site i, say N(i). We also define a weights matrix $\mathbf{W} = w_{ij}$ with zero elements in its diagonal and the remaining non-negative elements scaled to sum to unity in each row, and being non-zero only if $j \in N(i)$. (See Chapter 3 for details). Given these definitions the term

$$L(x_i) = \Sigma_{j \in N(i)} w_{ij} x_j \tag{2.4.1}$$

plays the role of the *spatially lagged* series. An extension of Formula (2.4.1) to higher-order lags is also possible by defining a hierarchical spatial ordering of neighbours (see Figure 1.4) of each site in a sequence of sets ${}_gN(i)$ and, accordingly, a sets of g-th order weights matrices $\mathbf{W(g)} = w(g)_{ij}$.
Various definitions of neighbourhood are available (Cliff and Ord, 1981). Two areas i and j are said to be g-th order neighbours if either
(i) the shortest path from i to j passes through $g - 1$ intervening areas, or
(ii) the distance between i and j falls within the g-th distance class.
Starting from this spatial lag definition, a number of estimators are available for the spatial correlogram (Lebart, 1969; Cliff and Ord, 1981; Bennett, 1979). These will be examined in fuller detail in Chapter 8.

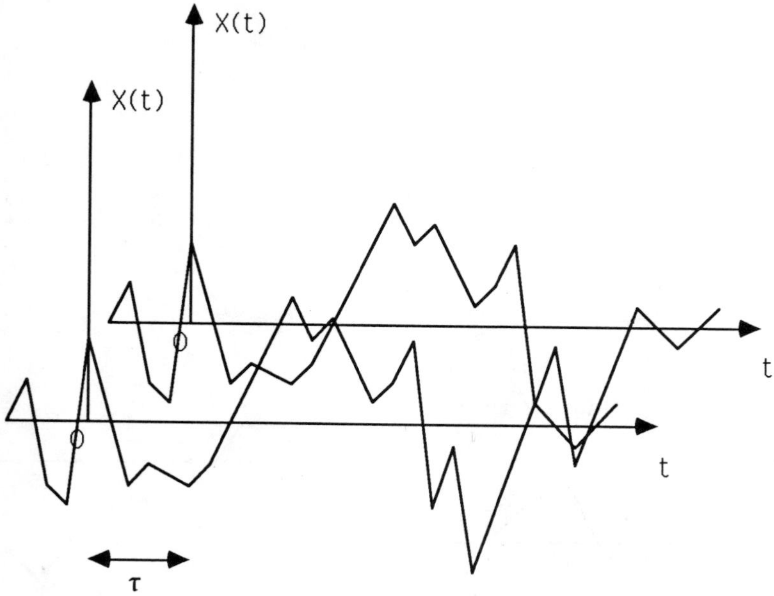

Figure 2.4.1 : A time series and the corresponding lagged series at lag τ.

2.4.3. Some empirical spatial correlograms

In this section we wish to report some results concerning the estimation of empirical correlogram found in the literature. The typical behaviour of spatial correlograms is to diminish rapidly towards zero with successive lags. As a consequence in most empirical studies significant correlation after the first lag is only very rarely observed. As a first example consider the burnt savanna data collected by Hopkins (1967). The Middle Belt of Nigeria consists largely of savanna which is regularly burnt every year. Hopkins collected the data relative to the herbs remaining after burning, using a 40-by-40 grid of contiguous quadrats with a side of 0.5 metre. The data are displayed in Table 2.4.1. Upton and Fingleton (1985) analysed the correlogram of the burnt savanna data which is displayed in Figure 2.4.2. The decreasing shape of the spatial correlogram is confirmed. Peaks seem to emerge at lag 4, 8 and 10 in Figure 2.4.2.a. However the authors did not give any substantive interpretation of these peaks. Figure 2.4.2.b shows the same correlogram based on distance classes instead of contiguity. The overall decrease is confirmed. Furthermore "there is the additional feature of a steep upward rise to high positive autocorrelation at about d=25" (Upton and Fingleton, 1985, p.195).

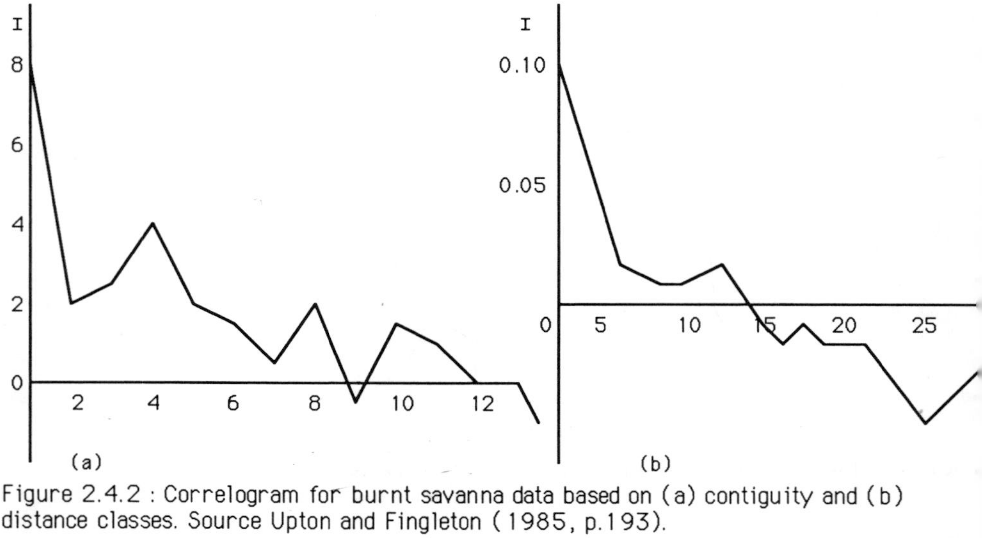

Figure 2.4.2 : Correlogram for burnt savanna data based on (a) contiguity and (b) distance classes. Source Upton and Fingleton (1985, p.193).

0 0 0 0 1 1 2 0 0 0 0 1 0 0 2 1 0 2 1 1 1 1 0 0 0 1 3 0 2 0 0 0 0 0 0 0 0 0 0 0
0 2 1 1 0 1 0 0 0 0 3 1 0 0 0 0 3 2 1 0 0 0 2 5 0 0 0 0 0 2 5 0 0 2 1 1 2 0 0 0
0 1 1 3 0 0 1 0 1 0 2 0 1 1 2 1 1 2 0 1 1 0 2 3 1 0 0 0 0 0 2 0 0 0 0 0 0 0 1 1
0 0 2 1 0 0 0 0 0 1 2 0 0 0 0 0 1 2 2 5 2 2 2 1 1 0 0 2 1 0 0 0 0 2 1 0 2 0 1 2
0 0 1 0 0 0 2 1 0 2 1 1 0 0 0 0 0 0 1 2 0 1 0 1 3 0 0 0 1 0 0 1 0 2 1 4 0 1 0 1
0 0 1 0 0 0 0 3 1 1 1 0 1 1 1 4 0 1 0 0 0 0 0 2 0 0 1 1 0 1 2 3 1 1 1 0 0 0 0 0
0 0 1 0 0 0 1 0 0 1 1 1 1 6 0 0 0 2 1 0 0 0 0 1 3 2 1 1 1 0 0 1 2 1 2 0 2 1 0 1
0 0 0 1 0 0 0 2 0 0 0 0 0 1 0 1 0 0 0 0 2 3 1 0 1 2 2 1 1 1 1 2 4 1 0 2 1 1 1 0
0 0 1 0 0 0 0 0 0 0 0 2 0 1 1 0 0 0 0 0 0 0 0 0 0 0 0 0 0 4 0 0 1 0 0 3 1 0 1 0
1 0 1 0 0 0 0 0 0 0 2 0 2 2 0 0 0 1 0 0 0 0 0 1 0 0 3 5 0 1 4 2 2 1 0 0 0 1 1 1
0 1 2 0 0 0 0 1 0 0 0 1 0 0 0 2 2 0 0 1 0 0 0 2 2 0 2 1 0 0 7 2 2 6 120 0 6 2 0
0 0 2 0 0 0 0 0 0 0 0 0 1 0 1 0 0 0 2 0 0 1 2 0 1 0 2 1 1 1 1 0 0 2 144 2 0 0 1
0 0 0 0 0 0 0 0 0 0 1 0 0 0 0 0 0 1 1 0 1 0 0 3 0 0 1 3 0 2 0 0 1 0 0 3 4 3 0 1
0 0 1 0 1 0 0 0 1 0 0 1 0 1 0 2 0 0 0 0 0 0 0 0 0 1 0 0 0 0 1 1 1 2 1 0 0 1 1 0
1 0 0 0 0 0 0 0 0 0 0 1 0 2 0 0 0 0 0 0 0 1 0 4 1 0 0 0 0 0 0 0 0 2 0 2 0 0 0 1
0 0 0 0 0 0 0 2 0 0 1 0 0 0 0 1 0 0 0 0 0 0 1 2 1 0 0 1 0 0 2 1 0 0 3 0 1 0 0 2
0 0 0 0 0 0 0 0 0 0 0 0 1 0 2 0 0 2 1 0 0 0 0 0 0 0 2 0 0 0 0 0 0 3 2 3 0 1 0 0
0 1 0 0 0 3 1 0 0 2 0 0 1 1 1 0 0 1 2 0 1 0 0 0 0 3 1 0 1 0 0 2 1 1 0 0 0 2 1 0
1 0 0 0 0 0 1 0 0 2 0 0 0 0 0 0 0 0 0 0 0 1 0 0 0 0 1 1 0 0 2 1 2 0 0 0 0 1 1 1
1 2 2 3 0 0 1 0 0 0 0 1 1 0 0 3 0 1 0 0 0 0 1 2 0 2 1 0 2 0 0 2 0 0 0 0 1 0 1 0
1 0 2 0 0 0 0 1 1 1 0 0 0 0 0 1 3 1 0 0 1 1 0 0 0 1 0 0 0 0 3 1 2 1 1 2 1 0 0 0
0 2 1 0 0 0 3 0 0 0 0 0 0 1 2 5 3 0 0 0 0 0 0 0 0 0 3 1 1 0 0 1 0 0 0 1 1 1 0 1
1 1 1 1 0 4 2 0 1 0 0 1 1 0 0 0 2 2 0 0 0 0 0 2 1 1 1 1 0 1 0 0 0 0 1 2 1 0 1 0
1 2 1 1 0 2 2 0 0 1 1 0 0 1 1 0 0 0 0 0 0 0 0 1 0 0 0 0 0 0 0 2 1 0 1 0 1 0 1 3
0 1 0 2 0 3 1 1 0 1 0 0 1 0 2 0 1 1 2 1 0 0 1 0 0 0 0 0 4 0 1 1 0 4 1 0 0 0 2 1
2 1 3 1 0 4 1 1 1 0 0 0 0 0 0 3 0 1 1 0 0 1 1 2 1 0 0 1 9 0 0 0 0 0 0 0 2 2 3 1
1 1 1 0 0 2 2 0 1 0 0 0 0 1 0 0 0 0 0 0 0 0 0 1 0 3 0 0 0 0 0 2 0 2 0 0 0 1 0 0
1 1 1 1 2 1 3 1 0 0 1 0 1 0 0 0 0 0 0 0 0 1 0 0 0 0 0 0 3 0 0 0 0 0 1 1 0 0 1 1
0 0 0 2 1 1 1 0 0 0 0 0 2 0 0 0 0 2 0 0 0 0 0 0 0 4 0 0 1 0 0 1 1 1 2 0 0 4 0 0
1 0 0 1 2 2 2 1 0 1 0 0 0 0 2 1 0 0 0 0 0 0 2 0 0 0 0 0 1 0 2 0 0 0 0 0 2 1 0 0
1 0 2 0 3 0 0 6 0 1 0 1 0 0 0 0 0 2 0 0 0 0 1 0 2 1 0 0 0 0 0 1 0 0 0 2 0 4 0 1
0 0 0 0 1 2 1 0 0 1 4 1 0 1 0 2 2 1 1 0 0 0 0 0 0 0 0 0 0 0 0 0 0 0 0 1 0 0 0 0
0 0 1 1 0 0 1 0 0 0 0 1 1 0 0 0 0 1 0 1 0 0 0 0 0 0 0 0 0 0 0 0 0 0 1 0 0 0 0 0
0 2 1 0 0 2 3 0 1 2 0 2 0 0 1 0 0 1 0 0 2 1 0 0 0 0 0 0 0 0 0 0 0 0 0 0 1 0 0 1
0 0 3 0 0 0 1 0 0 1 0 4 1 1 0 0 0 0 1 0 0 0 0 0 0 0 0 0 0 0 0 0 0 0 1 0 0 0 0 0
3 1 4 2 0 2 0 2 0 0 3 3 2 1 4 2 0 1 0 1 0 0 1 0 0 0 0 0 0 0 0 0 0 0 0 0 1 8 1 0
1 1 1 1 0 0 0 3 0 0 5 1 1 3 0 0 1 1 0 1 0 0 0 0 0 0 0 0 0 0 0 0 0 0 0 1 0 1 0 1
1 0 2 2 0 0 0 0 0 0 0 0 0 1 4 2 4 0 1 2 1 0 0 0 0 0 2 1 4 3 0 0 0 1 0 0 0 0 0 0
0 0 0 0 1 0 0 0 3 0 0 0 0 0 0 1 4 2 0 0 1 2 1 0 1 0 0 0 1 0 0 0 0 0 0 3 0 0 0 0
1 0 2 2 0 0 0 2 1 1 2 0 0 0 1 1 4 2 1 0 1 2 0 1 0 1 0 0 0 1 0 0 0 2 1 0 0 0 1 0

Table 2.4.1 : Density diagram of the distribution of herb remains after burning savanna. Source: Hopkins (1965).

As a second example let us consider a study reported in Cliff et al.(1975). The authors considered a set of data on the notifications of measles outbreaks supplied weekly by the Medical Officer of Health for each local authority in England. The study area considered included the counties of Cornwall, Devon, Dorset, Gloucester, Somerset and Wiltshire. Data were considered at a level of disaggregation of the 178 General Register Offices (GRO's). The authors estimated the spatial correlogram considering the definition of neighbours based on contiguity. Cliff et al.(1975) noticed that the average distance between the 178 areas was of seven spatial lags while the maximum distance was of 22 spatial lags. Figure 2.4.3 shows the estimates of the spatial correlogram in the first 15 lags. The distinctive feature of decrease of the correlogram after the first lag is confirmed. Furthermore there appear to be an increase in the absolute value of the correlogram in the last lags. Finally the turning point of the correlogram is at lag seven that is it corresponds to the average distance between sites.

While there are several other examples (See e.g. Bennett, 1975; Hooper and Hewings, 1981; Martin and Oeppen, 1975; Pfeiffer and Deutsch, 1980), those reviewed here serve for the purpose of illustration. They all confirm the distinctive feature of the spatial correlogram to decrease sharply after the first lag.

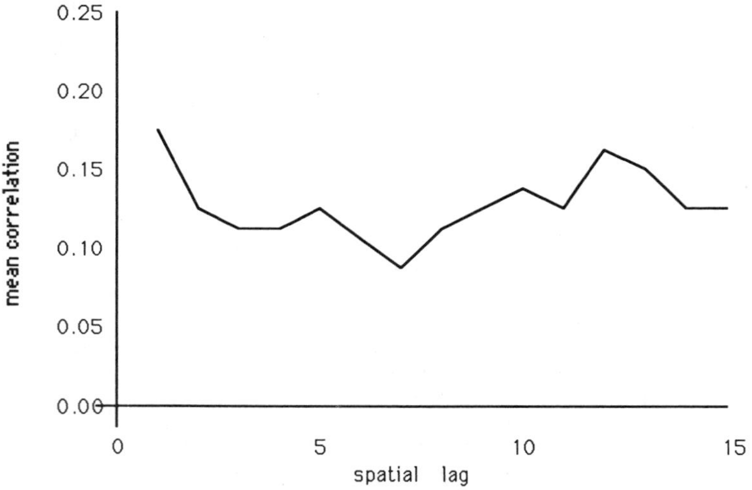

Figure 2.4.3: Spatial correlogram for the measles data in 178 GRO's in South-West of England. Source: Cliff et al. (1975).

2.4.4. Conclusion

In this section we have introduced the spatial correlogram as a statistical tool that helps in study of how the spatial autocorrelation changes with distance. A number of empirical examples have also been reported. The common feature of these examples is that there is a general decrease in the absolute value of the correlogram as soon as a lag is introduced. An increase in absolute value of the highest lags is also sometimes observed. Finally where peaks in the correlogram are suspected it is very difficult to attach to them substantive interpretations. This behaviour of the correlogram can be used as the empirical substantiation of a distance decay of spatial interaction. However we will show that perhaps the behaviour of most empirical correlograms could be due to statistical effects produced by spatial data configuration and not only to a genuine distance decay of interaction. This hypothesis is considered in detail in Chapter 8.

2.5 SUMMARY AND CONCLUSION

In this chapter we have reviewed some of the problems arising in human geography from the use of statistical methods based on areal data. For the scale problem (Section 2.2) it emerges from the literature that by increasing the scale of analysis we obtain, in most empirical cases, a monotonic increase in the absolute value of the correlation coefficient towards unity. Similar results are found in Section 2.4 for the ecological fallacy problem. For the aggregation problem (Section 2.3) no systematic result is found in the literature and the general belief is that aggregation variability cannot be controlled for through a statistical approach. Finally, in Section 2.5 we examined the spatial correlogram as an alternative means of studying the scale of a spatial process. In the literature a tendency emerges for the correlogram to decrease sharply soon after the first lag. This can be due to a genuine distance decay of geographical phenomena, but it can also depend on the inadequacy of the existing estimators. This fact requires more investigation.

We claim a feature to be common to all the above mentioned problems: that they reflect in various guises the way in which data are collected, i.e. the physical characteristics of the map imposed on the phenomenon in order to study it . This is what we call the *configuration of spatial data* and which is the central subject of this book. We give a precise definition and formalization of configuration in the next chapter.

3. The configuration of spatial data in regional economics

3.1. INTRODUCTION

In the previous Chapters we defined the area of interest of the book by discussing some of the problems arising in statistical analysis of areal data. All the problems examined arise as a consequence of the particular way in which data are collected, a characteristic that we summarized by the term *spatial configuration of data*. These problems will be discussed in the next chapters within a unified methodological framework. Before proceeding to present formally this framework it is necessary, however, to better define what we mean by spatial configuration of data and to introduce some notation. This chapter gives this introduction. In Section 3.2 we discuss the nature of spatial data and in Section 3.3 we introduce some useful notation.

3.2. THE NATURE OF SPATIAL SERIES IN REGIONAL ECONOMIC ANALYSIS

Spatial data can be observed in various forms. A first distinction can be drawn between *continuous* areal data and *discontinuous* data. A similar distinction is usually made when dealing with time series data. For example, the time series of the stock market prices is essentially a continuous one which can be recorded at any point in time. In contrast, the total level of production in one country can be defined only over intervals of time, as the sum of units produced in that interval.
Continuous areal data are fairly common in meteorology (Dixon and Spackman, 1970) and in ecology (Kershaw, 1964). For example annual rainfall totals can be, in principle, observed at all points over the entire study area. In the case when data are intrinsically continuous we can consider the observations at some points in space as a sample from a continuous random process. It is, however extremely difficult to find examples of such data when we deal with regional economic analysis where phenomena occur which often have sharp discontinuities between areas. The most common situation in economics is to deal with discrete data. While in time series analysis we have only one way in which data can be discrete, in spatial analysis we can distinguish between four different kinds of discontinuities, namely *points, lines, areas* and *surfaces*. A *point* refers to a single place and is usually considered as having no dimension or having a dimension which is negligible if compared with the study area. There is a large number of examples of point data in human geography such as, for instance, the location of industrial plants or of houses. Furthermore it may happen sometimes that areal data are reduced to point form as, for instance, when studying central-place theories of settlement structure (Wilson and Bennett, 1985) or in order to interpolate a trend surface (Haggett, 1976). *Line* data or *networks* arise in regional economics to specify features like travel-to-work flows or transportation network. *Areal* data have a paramount relevance in the study of regional economics. In fact most of the empirical studies in human geography are based upon Census information collected over discrete

areal units such as counties or regions. Finally we can have *surfaces* as in a contour map of altitude. However, while this kind of data are very common in physical geography, no example can be found in human geography.
When we deal with areal data a second distinction can be made between data laid on a *regular Cartesian lattice* and data located on an *irregular grid*. Examples of the first kind of data in human geography are very rare. Some Census information for the U.K. are grid-referenced (e.g. in the 1971 Census). Similarly other countries like Sweden and U.S.A. (Hågerstrand, 1955; Passoneau and Wurman, 1966) record some population data on regular grid. Finally some example exist dealing with geography at a micro scale. (See, for example, Jones and Sinclair, 1968).
The far more common typology of spatial data in human geography, however, is when we have our information recorded on territorial units, often administrative units, which, in general, are of variable size and shape. It is usual to refer to this kind of data as to *irregular collecting areas* (Haggett, 1967).
A final distinction can be made with reference to the kind of variable recorded. This can be either continuous or discrete. The distribution of most socio-economic variables is likely to be discrete as, for instance, population or income. However the number of individuals or things considered is usually so large that their distribution can be conveniently approximated by a continuous one.

3.3. DESCRIBING THE CONFIGURATION OF IRREGULAR COLLECTING AREAS

3.3.1. Introduction

This section is devoted to introducing some of the methods used by human geographers and regional scientists to describe their maps. (For a larger review see Haggett, Cliff and Frey, 1977; p.291; Unwin, 1981; p.85).
When spatial data are observed in a continuous form, as frequently happens in physical geography or in meteorology, the best way to describe them through maps is to fix an arbitrary point as the origin and superimpose a simple system of coordinates such as a Cartesian, polar scheme or global latitude and longitude. In this way each observation can be described in terms of its coordinates and the internal relationships between observations in terms of their distance. A similar approach can also be employed when the spatial observations are observed on regular square grid lattice.
The far more common situation faced in analysis of regional economic analysis, however, is to have the variables of interest recorded on a system of *irregular collecting areas* (Haggett, Cliff and Frey, 1977; p.348); that is a study area divided into territorial units, often administrative regions, which are, in general, different in their size and shape. In this case the spatial system is described more conveniently in terms of the *contiguity relations* among the areas.
Some of the methods available for the description of such systems are now reviewed. The central idea of this book is that the spatial configuration of data (i.e. the physical characteristics of the maps) is an element that has to be taken into account in the statistical analysis of economic variables if we wish to avoid serious bias. The concepts and notation introduced in this section, give a formalization of what we mean by the *spatial configuration of data* and as such it is a key starting point for the formal theoretical development of the whole book.

3.3.2. Systems of irregular collecting areas

Let us start by considering a study area completely divided into n non-overlapping sub-areas, as for example the 48 English counties that existed in 1936 in the Yule and Kendall (1950) study (See Chapter 2). For each site j of the study area ($j = 1,......,n$) we can specify the *neighbourhood*, as the set of those sites which are *in some sense* in the proximity of site j. Let us call this set N(j) and any site $k \in N(j)$, the *neighbours* of site j.

A system of sites each with specified neighbours may be thought of as a *graph*; consequently the description of the spatial system can draw upon the methods commonly employed in graph theory (See Tinkler, 1977). The *nodality* of site j, say v_j, is the number of sites in proximity with site j or, in other words, the cardinality of the set N(j). The total nodality or *connectedness* of the system is given by

$$A = \sum v_j \qquad (3.3.1)$$

and the *average connectedness* by

$$v^* = An^{-1} \qquad (3.3.2)$$

A *totally connected* spatial system is a systems in which each site is connected with all the others (See Cliff and Ord, 1981,p.174). In this extreme case we have that

$$v_j = n - 1 \quad \text{each } j \qquad (3.3.3)$$

and

$$A = n(n-1) \qquad (3.3.4)$$

This provides an upper bound to the values of v_j and A.

At the other extreme we can have *time-like* connected spatial systems in which each site is connected with only one other site. In this case we have

$$v_j = 1 \quad \text{each } j \qquad (3.3.5)$$

and

$$A = n \qquad (3.3.6)$$

Another special case, more common in geographical studies, is the *line transect* case (Bartlett, 1966; p.217) in which the sites are laid on a line and each site is connected with only the previous and the next site. In this case

$$v_1 = v_n = 1 \qquad (3.3.7)$$

and

$$v_j = 2 \quad \text{,each } j \neq 1,\ j \neq n \qquad (3.3.8)$$

Consequently

$$A = 2(n - 1) \tag{3.3.9}$$

and

$$An^{-1} = 2(n - 1)n^{-1} \tag{3.3.10}$$

As a consequence in a spatial scheme when the *line transect* and the *totally connected* case are considered the limits, the theoretical range of A is

$$2(n - 1) \leq A \leq n(n - 1) \tag{3.3.11}$$

and the range of v^*

$$2(n - 1)n^{-1} \leq v^* \leq (n - 1) \tag{3.3.12}$$

However, it is necessary to notice here that the theoretical range of the connectedness is based on two extreme cases, which are only rarely found in practice. In particular the upper bound almost never is $n(n - 1)$, due to the planar constraint. As a consequence in most empirical cases the range of the connectedness will be sensibly smaller than in Formula (3.3.12). (See Section 5.4 for details).

A tool which is often useful, especially when dealing with a large number of sites, is that commonly referred to as the *connectivity* (or adjacency) matrix (Unwin, 1981; Cliff and Ord, 1981).

The connectivity matrix of a spatial system of sites is an n-by-n matrix **W** of typical element w_{jk} such that

$$w_{jk} = \begin{cases} 1 & \text{if } j \in N(k) \\ 0 & \text{otherwise} \end{cases} \tag{3.3.13}$$

$(k = 1,\ldots,n\ ;\ j = 1,\ldots,n)$.

The various concepts of nodality previously introduced can now be expressed in terms of the **W** matrix. The nodality of site j can now be defined as

$$v_j = \Sigma_k\, w_{jk} \tag{3.3.14}$$

The total connectedness by

$$A = \Sigma\, v_j = \Sigma_{(2)}\, w_{jk} \tag{3.3.15}$$

and the average connectedness by

$$v^* = n^{-1}\ \Sigma_{(2)}\, w_{jk} \tag{3.3.16}$$

When n is very large the specification of a connectivity matrix can be considerably simplified using the algorithm described in Appendix 3.1.
An alternative way of describing the configuration of a system of irregular collecting areas is through the principal eigenvalue of the connectivity matrix as shown by Boots (1982, 1984, 1985) and Griffith (1982, 1984). However this kind of approach is not considered here in detail because it does not contribute to the main concern of the book.

3.3.3. Systems of grouped irregular collecting areas

Let us now assume that the economic variable of interest is recorded at two different levels of spatial resolution (e.g. counties and regions). Let us further assume the two levels constitute a fully nested hierarchy in that each site at the more disaggregated level is contained in one and only one site at the more aggregated level.
In terms of the previously introduced notation the n sites constituting the spatial system at the lower scale are grouped into m fewer and larger areas to form a new configuration of the spatial system at the higher scale. The set of sites at the lower scale, contained in the i-th group is called G(i), i = 1, ...,m. In addition r_i represents the cardinality of the set G(i), that is the number of lower scale sites entering group i.
It is useful also to define an m-by-n grouping matrix **G** (Prais and Aitchinson, 1954) with typical element g_{ij} such that

$$g_{ij} = \begin{cases} 1 & \text{if } j \in G(i) \\ 0 & \text{otherwise} \end{cases} \qquad (3.3.17)$$

(i = 1,...,m ; j = 1,....,n).
Similarly to the connectivity matrix, the specification of a grouping matrix can be made simpler by using the algorithm described in Appendix 3.2.
The previously defined concepts of connectedness can now be easily extended to this two-level representation of a spatial system.

The connectedness internal to group i, or *within group* connectedness, is defined by

$$A_i = \Sigma_{j \in G(i)} \Sigma_{k \in G(i)} w_{jk} \qquad (3.3.18)$$

The within group average connectedness is defined by

$$v^*_i = A_i r_i^{-1} \qquad (3.3.19)$$

and the total within group connectedness by

$$A_W = \Sigma A_i \qquad (3.3.20)$$

The total connectedness of the spatial system at the lower scale, therefore, can be split into two components

a) a *within group connectedness*, that indicates the links between sites belonging to the same group and

b) a *between group connectedness*, that indicates the links between sites belonging to different groups. In symbols we have

$$A = \sum A_i + \sum_{(2)} t_{il} \qquad (3.3.21)$$

where t_{il} represents the number of neighbouring sites at the lower spatial scale, taken one in group i and one in group l. The values t_{il} can be ordered in an m-by-m matrix **T** called the *matrix of the between group links* of the spatial system.

The minimum of the *between groups connectedness* is reached when there is only one point of contact between each pair of groups, in which case $t_{il}=2$. In contrast, the maximum of t_{il} occurs when all the sites in group i are in contact with all the sites in group l in which case $t_{il} = r_i r_l$. It follows than that the range of the *between groups connectedness* is

$$2 \le t_{il} \le r_i r_l \qquad (3.3.22)$$

Finally a system of neighbours and a connectivity matrix can also be defined at the group level. Let us call **W*** the m-by-m connectivity matrix with typical element w^*_{il} such that

$$w^*_{il} = \begin{cases} 1 & \text{if } i \in N(l) \\ 0 & \text{otherwise} \end{cases} \qquad (3.3.23)$$

3.3.4. Systems of hierarchical spatial order of neighbours

We have so far assumed that for each site j of a study area we can specify its neighbourhood , that is the set of sites with which site j is in proximity. This description of a system of irregular collecting areas will be assumed throughout most of the book. However in Chapter 8, when dealing with the spatial correlogram, we will relax this hypothesis by allowing for the possibility of having, instead of a single set of neighbours for each site, several sets which refer to sites that are one, two, or more steps apart by analogy with time series analysis. In this case we define a hierarchical spatial ordering of neighbours of each site in a sequence of sets ${}_gN(j)$, called g-th order neighbours of site j, such that

$$\sum_{g=1}^{D} {}_gN(i) + 1 = n \text{ each } i \qquad (3.3.24)$$

where D is the diameter of the graph associated to the spatial scheme. Formula (3.3.24) indicates that the hierarchical spatial ordering is exhaustive in that each site is classified as a neighbour, of a given order, of site j.

We define accordingly a set of g-th order connectivity matrices **W(g)**, with elements $w(g)_{jk}$, such that

$$w(g)_{jk} = \begin{cases} 1 & \text{if } k \in N(j) \\ 0 & \text{otherwise} \end{cases} \qquad (3.3.25)$$

As a consequence we have that

$$\sum_{g=1}^{D} \mathbf{W(g)} + \mathbf{I} = \mathbf{U} \qquad (3.3.26)$$

where **I** is the diagonal identity matrix, and **U** is a matrix with all elements equal to unity.

3.4. CONCLUSION

The aim of this short chapter is to provide a bridge between the introductory discussion of the problems associated with spatial data configuration outlined in Chapter 2 and the formal theoretical development of the next chapters. In Section 3.2 we discussed the nature of spatial data in human geography while Section 3.3 was devoted to introducing some methods and notation used by geographers to describe their maps. Now that the subject matter has been defined and that the basic notation introduced, we can move on to attack the core of our problem.

APPENDIX 3.1

```
C        Program to generate  a connectivity matrix with a considerably
C        smaller matrix as an  input .  N is the number of sites of the
C        system. V is the maximum number of neighbour of a site.
         REAL A(N,V),W(N,N)
         READ (5,*) N,V
         DO 6 I = 1,N
         READ (5,*)(A(I,J),J=1,V)
6        CONTINUE
         DO 10  I = 1,N
         DO 11 L = 1, N
         W(I,L) = 0.0
11       CONTINUE
10       CONTINUE
         DO 3 L = 1, N
         DO 1 I = 1, N
         DO 2 J = 1, V
         IF (A(I,J) .NE. 0   .AND.   A(I,J) .EQ. L) THEN
                      W(I,L) = W(I,J) + 1.0
         ENDIF
2        CONTINUE
1        CONTINUE
3        CONTINUE
C        Eliminates values not equal one arising from multiple definitions
C        of some elements of the matrix W
         DO 20  I = 1, N
         DO 21  L = 1,N
         IF ( W(I,L)  .NE. 0) THEN
                      W(I,L) = 1.0
         ENDIF
21       CONTINUE
20       CONTINUE
         DO 4 L = 1,N
         WRITE (6,5) (W(I,L), I= 1,N)
5        FORMAT (N(1X,F2.0))
4        CONTINUE
         STOP
         END
```

EXAMPLE

INPUT DATA

```
2 0 0 0 0 0
1 3 7 8 0 0
2 5 6 7 0 0
5 0 0 0 0 0
3 4 6 7 0 0
3 5 0 0 0 0
2 3 5 0 0 0
2 7 9 0 0 0
7 8 10 11 12 0
9 11 12 0 0 0
7 9 10 12 13 0
9 10 11 13 14 15
11 12 14 0 0 0
12 13 15 16 0 0
12 14 16 17 0 0
14 15 17 0 0 0
15 16 18 0 0 0
17 0 0 0 0 0
0 0 0 0 0 0
0 0 0 0 0 0
```

FOR THE ITALIAN REGION SPATIAL SYSTEM (See APPENDIX A.1)

APPENDIX 3.2

```
C          Program to generate a grouping matrix with a considerably
C          smaller matrix as an input . N is the number of sites of the
C          system. R is the maximum number of sites contained in a group
C          M is the number of groups.
C
           REAL A(M,R),G(M,N)
           READ (5,*) M,N,R
           DO 6 I = 1,M
           READ (5,*)(A(I,J),J=1,R)
6          CONTINUE
           DO 10 I = 1,M
           DO 11 L = 1, N
           G(I,L) = 0.0
11         CONTINUE
10         CONTINUE
           DO 3 L = 1, N
           DO 1 I = 1, M
           DO 2 J = 1, R
           IF (A(I,J) .NE. 0  .AND.  A(I,J) .EQ. L) THEN
                         G(I,L) = G(I,J) + 1.0
           ENDIF
2          CONTINUE
1          CONTINUE
3          CONTINUE
            DO 4 L = 1,N
           WRITE (6,5) (W(I,L), I= 1,M)
5          FORMAT (M(1X,F2.0))
4          CONTINUE
           STOP
           END
```

EXAMPLE

INPUT DATA

```
1 2 3 4 0
5 6 0 0 0
7 8 9 10 0
11 12 13 14 15
16 17 0 0 0
18 0 0 0 0
19 20 0 0 0
```

OUTPUT

```
1 0 0 0 0 0 0
1 0 0 0 0 0 0
1 0 0 0 0 0 0
1 0 0 0 0 0 0
0 1 0 0 0 0 0
0 1 0 0 0 0 0
0 0 1 0 0 0 0
0 0 1 0 0 0 0
0 0 1 0 0 0 0
0 0 1 0 0 0 0
0 0 0 1 0 0 0
0 0 0 1 0 0 0
0 0 0 1 0 0 0
0 0 0 1 0 0 0
0 0 0 1 0 0 0
0 0 0 0 1 0 0
0 0 0 0 1 0 0
0 0 0 0 0 1 0
0 0 0 0 0 0 1
0 0 0 0 0 0 1
```

FOR THE FOLLOWING GROUPING

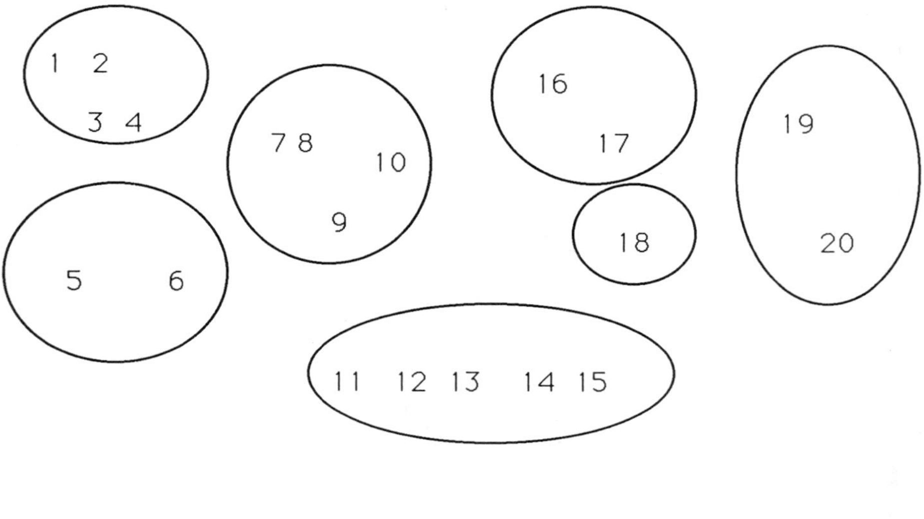

4. Stochastic spatial processes

4.1. STATIONARY STOCHASTIC PROCESSES IN TWO DIMENSIONS

4.1.1. Introduction

In this section some basic concepts and theorems in the theory of stochastic processes in two dimensions are reviewed (For details see Bartlett, 1966; Whittle 1954; Ripley, 1981). In particular we are interested to give a formal description of processes that may be thought as underlying a geographical distribution of an economic variable. This is the main concern of the whole book. The most general situation in regional economics is to have to cope with data recorded in irregular collecting areas such as counties, regions or states. (Haggett, Cliff and Frey 1964, p.349). For this reason, when we speak of *sites*, we often have in mind portions of space rather than points, and when we say *set of sites* we normally think of irregular rather then regular lattices. Furthermore most of the economic variables are likely to be continuous and therefore the focus will be, throughout the chapter, on continuous processes recorded on a discrete space.

4.1.2. Univariate processes in two dimensions

In rather formal terms we want to describe the situation in which we are given *n* sites with a given spatial sequence indexed by the integer i, and a vector $\mathbf{x}=(x_1,x_2,\dots,x_n)$ of observations on the variable X which is considered to be a finite realization of a process $\{X_i\}$ of dependent variables $X_1, X_2 ......X_n$.
For each i, we can imagine that X_i will have some probability distribution in that some values of the admissible range are more likely than others. We can therefore define, for each X_i, the *probability distribution function* (PDF) of X_i, $F(x_i)$ by

$$F(x_i)=P[X_i \leq x_i] \qquad (4.1.1)$$

In the situation we are more interested in, i.e. when X_i is a continuous random variable, $F(x_i)$ is absolutely continuous and we can condense all its properties into its *probability density function* (DF) $f_i(x)$ defined as

$$f_i= dF(x_i) \;/\; d\,x_i \qquad (4.1.2)$$

which exists almost everywhere, or inversely

$$F(x_i) = \int_{-\infty}^{x} f_i(u)\, du \qquad (4.1.3)$$

From the above definitions the moments of the process can be derived. In particular the mean and the variance of X_i will be given by

$$\text{Mean}\ \{X_i\} = E(X_i) = \int x\, f_i\,(x)\, dx = \mu_i \qquad (4.1.4)$$

say, and

$$\text{Var}\ \{X_i\} = E[(X_i-\mu_i)^2] = \int (x-\mu_i)^2\, f_i(x)\, dx = \sigma_i^2 \qquad (4.1.5)$$

So far no specific assumption has been made on the nature of the random process. To introduce the form of the random process we have to allow for the possibility that the DF of X_i can change from one site to another, i.e. that $f_i(x)$ is a function both of x and i. As our aim is to study the joint variation of a set of random variables at different points in space, we must at this stage introduce the *joint probability distribution function* (JPDF). First we consider the case of two random variables X_i and X_j recorded at sites i and j. The JPDF $F(X_i,X_j)$ is defined by

$$F(x_i x_j) = P\ [X_i \le x_i;\ X_j \le x_j\ ] \qquad (4.1.6)$$

Again if F(.) is absolutely continuous we can also define, almost everywhere, the *joint probability density function* (JDF)

$$f_{i,j} = \partial^2 F(x_i x_j)\ /\ \partial x_i\, \partial x_j \qquad (4.1.7)$$

or inversely

$$F(x_i x_j) = \int_{-\infty}^{x_i} \int_{-\infty}^{x_j} f_{ij}(u_i u_j)\, du_i du_j \qquad (4.1.8)$$

Following from these definitions the bivariate moments about the mean of the joint distribution are given by

$$E[(X_i-\mu_i)^r (X_j-\mu_j)^s] = \int\int (x_i-\mu_i)^r (x_j-\mu_j)^s\, f_{ij}(x_i x_j)\, dx_i dx_j \qquad (4.1.9)$$

In particular their covariance is given by

$$\begin{aligned} &\text{Cov}\{X_i X_j\} = E[(X_i-\mu_i)\,(X_j-\mu_j)] \\ &= \int\int\ (x_i-\mu_i)\,(x_j-\mu_j)\, f_{ij}(x_i x_j)\, dx_i dx_j\ =\ \gamma_{ij} \end{aligned} \qquad (4.1.9.a)$$

All the previous concepts can be extended to the whole set of random variables $X_1,X_2,...,X_n$ to give the complete JPDF $F(x_1,x_2,...,x_n)$

$$F(x_1,x_2,...,x_n) = P\ [X_1 \le x_1; X_2 \le x_2; .... ; X_n \le x_n] \qquad (4.1.10)$$

say, and the complete JDF $f_{1,2,\dots n}(x_1,x_2,\dots,x_n)$

$$f_{1,2,\dots n}(x_1,x_2,\dots,x_n) = \partial^n F(x_1,\dots x_n)/\partial x_1\dots\partial x_n \tag{4.1.11}$$

Inversely

$$F(x_1,x_2,\dots x_n) = \int_{-\infty}^{x_1}\dots\int_{-\infty}^{x_n} f_{1,\dots n}(u_1,\dots,u_n)\, du_1,\dots,du_n \tag{4.1.12}$$

with joint moments

$$\begin{aligned}&E[(X_1-\mu_1)^{h_1}..(X_n-\mu_n)^{h_n}]\\&=\int\dots\int(x_1-\mu_1)^{h_1}\dots(x_n-\mu_n)^{h_n}f_{1,\dots,n}(x_1,\dots x_n)dx_1,\dots dx_n\\&=\mu_{h_1\dots h_1}\end{aligned} \tag{4.1.13}$$

The individual DF's $f_1(x_1)\dots f_n(x_n)$ represent the marginal distributions of $X_1,X_2,\dots,X_n$, respectively, and can, of course, be calculated from $f_{1\dots n}(x_1,\dots,x_n)$ through the integral

$$f_i(x_i) = \int\dots\int f_{1,\dots,n}(u_1,\dots u_n)du_1,\dots du_{i-1},du_{i+1},\dots du_n \tag{4.1.14}$$

Given $F(x_1,\dots x_n)$ as a JPDF of $X_1,X_2,\dots,X_n$, we may wish to find the marginal JPDF of a subset of $X_1,X_2,\dots,X_n$, say $X_1,X_2,\dots,X_r$ $(r<n)$ defined by

$$\begin{aligned}&P[X_1 \le x_1,\dots X_r \le x_r]=P[X_1 \le x_1,\dots X_r \le x_r,X_{r+1} \le\infty,\dots X_n \le \infty]\\&= F(x_1,\dots x_r,\infty,\dots,\infty)\end{aligned} \tag{4.1.15}$$

The marginal JDF of $X_1,X_2,\dots,X_r$ is

$$f_{1\dots r}(x_1\dots x_r) = \int\dots\int f_{1\dots n}(u_1\dots u_n)du_{r+1}\dots du_n \tag{4.1.16}$$

Furthermore the joint moments of the same subset of variables can be computed from the joint distribution. For example

$$\begin{aligned}&E[(X_1-\mu_1)^{h_1}\dots(X_r-\mu_r)^{h_r}]\\&=E[(X_1-\mu_1)^{h_1}\dots(X_n-\mu_n)^{h_n},,X_{r+1}{}^0\dots X_n{}^0]\\&= \int\dots\int (x_1-\mu_1)^{h_1}\dots(x_r-\mu_r)^{h_r} f_{1..n}(x_1\dots x_n)\, dx_1\dots dx_n\\&=\int..\int(x_1-\mu_1)^{h_1}..(x_r-\mu_r)^{h_r}[\int\dots\int f_{1..n}(x_1\dots x_n)dx_{r+1}\dots dx_n]dx_1\dots dx_r\end{aligned} \tag{4.1.17}$$

We may also desire to derive the *conditional distribution* (CD) of a set of random variables, say $X_1,X_2,\dots,X_r$, given that the other variables $X_{r+1},X_{r+2},\dots,X_n$ assume certain values. The *conditional joint probability distribution function* (CJPDF) of $X_1\dots X_r$ given $X_{r+1}<x_{r+1}\dots X_n<x_n$ is defined by

$$P[X_1 \le x_1 \ldots X_r \le x_r | X_{r+1} \le x_{r+1} \ldots X_n \le x_n]$$
$$= P[X_1 \le x_1 \ldots X_n \le x_n] / P[X_{r+1} \le x_{r+1} \ldots X_n \le x_n] \quad (4.1.19)$$

The *conditional joint probability density function* (CJDF) of $X_1, X_2, \ldots, X_n$ given $X_{r+1}=x_{r+1} \ldots\ldots X_n=x_n$ is

$$f_{1..r}(x_1 \ldots x_r | x_{r+1} \ldots x_n)$$
$$= f_{1\ldots n}(x_1 \ldots x_n) / \int \ldots \int f_{1\ldots n}(u_1 \ldots u_r x_{r+1} \ldots x_n) du_1 \ldots du_r \quad (4.1.20)$$

(A general discussion of conditional probability is given by Kolmogorov, 1950).

INDEPENDENCE

The interesting feature of studying the geographical distribution of an economic variable as a random process is that interdependence between sites can be formally expressed and, eventually, modelled. The interdependence of the various random variables is , therefore,a basic assumption for the study to be worthwhile. It is therefore important to define statistical independence formally.
Two random variables X_i, X_j are said to be statistically independent if

$$F(x_i x_j) = F(x_i) G(x_j) \quad (4.1.21)$$

where $F(x_i)$ is the marginal PDF of X_i and $G(x_j)$ is the marginal PDF of X_j. In terms of probability density we have, similarly that

$$f_{ij}(x_i x_j) = \partial^2 F(x_i x_j) / [\partial x_i \partial x_j]$$
$$= \partial^2 F(x_i) G(x_j) / [\partial x_i \partial x_j] = f_i(x_i) f_j(x_j) \quad (4.1.22)$$

with obvious notation. Conversely

$$F(x_i x_j) = \int_{-\infty}^{x_i} \int_{-\infty}^{x_j} f_{ij}(u_i u_j)\, du_i du_j = \int_{-\infty}^{x_i} \int_{-\infty}^{x_j} f_i(u_i) f_j(u_j)\, du_i du_j$$
$$= \int_{-\infty}^{x_i} f_i(u_i) du_i \int_{-\infty}^{x_j} f_j(u_j) du_j = F(x_i x_j)$$
$$(4.1.23)$$

The whole process $\{X_i\}$ is said to be constituted by *mutually independent* random variables if

$$F(x_1 \ldots\ldots x_n) = F_1(x_1) \ldots\ldots F_n(x_n) \quad (4.1.24)$$

Also, a subset $X_1, X_2, \ldots, X_r$ is said to be independent of the set $X_{r+1}, \ldots, X_n$ if

$$F(x_1 \ldots x_n) = F(x_1 \ldots x_r, \infty \ldots \infty)\, F(\infty, \ldots, \infty, x_{r+1} \ldots x_n) \quad (4.1.25)$$

One result of independence is that joint moments will factor. For example if $X_1, X_2, \ldots, X_n$ are mutually independent, then

$$E[(X_1-\mu_1)^{h_1} \ldots\ldots (X_n-\mu_n)^{h_n}]$$
$$= \int \ldots \int (x_1-\mu_1)^{h_1} \ldots (x_n-\mu_n)^{h_n} f_1(x_1) \ldots f_n(x_n)\, dx_1 \ldots dx_n$$
$$= \prod \int x_i^{h_i}\, f_i(x_i)\, dx_i = \prod E(X_i^{h_i}) \qquad (4.1.26)$$

As already stated, because of its importance for spatial processes, we are interested in the departure from the assumption of statistical independence. The "first law in geography" (Tobler 1970) states as: "Everything is related with everything else, but near thing are more related than distant things". This is at the basis of the *local dependence* hypothesis and assumes a "distance decay" or "neighbourhood" effect. We may introduce local dependence in terms of a conditional or in terms of joint density function.

In the former case of local dependence as a conditional model, the conditional distribution of X at site i depends only upon the values at those sites which are, somehow, in the proximity of site i. This is the essence of local (or Markov) statistical dependence in the spatial context (Besag, 1974; Haining, 1977).

Formally, define N(i) as the set of neighbours of site i, then we have the condition that a process is locally dependent if

$$f_i(x_i \mid X_j = x_j,\ i \neq j) = \begin{cases} f_{1 \ldots n}(x_1 \ldots x_n) \,/\, [\,\int f(u_i, x_j)\, du_i\,] & \text{if } j \in N(i) \\ f_i(x_i) & \text{otherwise} \end{cases} \qquad (4.1.27)$$

In the second case, of the joint model, we have the condition that a process is locally dependent if

$$f_{1..n}(x_1 \ldots x_i \ldots x_n)$$
$$= f_{1 \ldots r}(x_1 \ldots x_i \ldots x_r)\ f_{r+1 \ldots n}(x_{r+1} \ldots\ldots x_n) \qquad (4.1.28)$$

where the set $\{1,2,\ldots r\} \in N(i)$ and the equation holds for each i and for the appropriate N(i). Further developments of these models are given by Whittle (1954,1963), Heine (1955), Besag(1972, 1974), and Haining (1977, 1978a, 1982).

STATIONARITY IN TWO DIMENSIONS

The class of random processes we have been looking at so far is too large and general to enable methods of analysis to be designed or to allow statistical estimation of all the unknown parameters of the density function. Consequently some restrictions have to be introduced. We can introduce the concept of *stationarity* in a spatial context. Stationarity of a spatial process implies that its statistical properties do not change

over space. In a *strict sense* this means that a process is stationary if the JPDF of any subset of random variables remains unchanged when we *shift* the subset under consideration across the space.
Because we are dealing with a process in two-dimensions, a subset of random variables from a spatial process can be shifted in two ways. We can operate either a translation or a rotation. Stationarity under translations is termed *homogeneity* (as opposed to *heterogeneity*) and implies that the pattern of the process does not vary in a systematic way from place to place. Stationarity under rotation is termed *isotropy* and implies that the process does not exhibit any preferred direction, or *anisotropy*. Homogeneous and isotropic processes are said to be stationary under rigid motion (or in a strict sense).
A consequence of *strict* stationarity is that the univariate and the joint moments of any order in a subset remain unchanged if the subset is *shifted* A weaker condition is to require that the process is stationary only up to a certain order of moments. For an important class of processes, the Gaussian processes (as we will see in a later paragraph), however, stationarity up to second order also implies stationarity in a strict sense (See Kolmogorov, 1941; Yaglom, 1962; Bennett, 1979). It is therefore important to look specifically at this kind of stationarity. Stationarity up to second order in a spatial context can be expressed by saying that the mean and the variance do not change between sites:

$$\mu_i = \mu \qquad \text{each } i \tag{4.1.29}$$

$$\sigma^2_i = \sigma^2 \qquad \text{each } i \tag{4.1.30}$$

and the covariance between two values of X (i and j) depends only on the relative location of the two sites and not on their actual position i.e. (Granger, 1969; p.15)

$$E[(X_i - \mu_i)(X_j - \mu_j)] = \gamma_{ij} = \gamma(r, \theta) \tag{4.1.31}$$

where r is the distance between site i and site j, and θ is the angle in polar coordinates formed by the direction of the segment joining site i and site j. If the process is also isotropic then no directional bias occurs. Hence γ depends only on r, that is to say

$$E[(X_i - \mu_i)(X_j - \mu_j)] = \gamma(r) \tag{4.1.32}$$

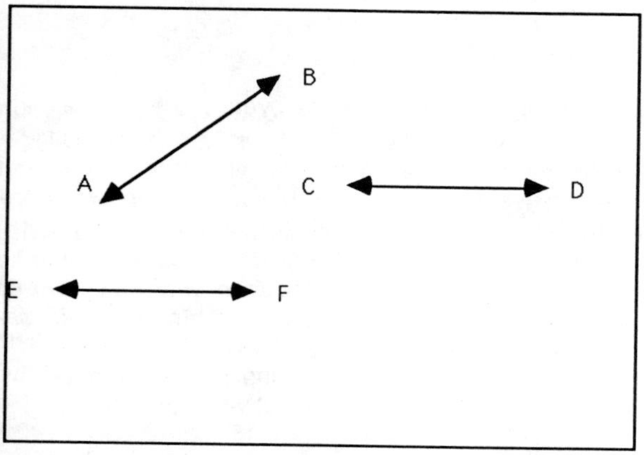

Figure 4.1 : Homogeneity and isotropy: If the process is homogeneus then Cov (C,D)=Cov(E,F)≠ Cov(A,B) . If the process is also isotropic then Cov(C,D)=Cov(E,F)=Cov(A,B).

Returning to the previous definition of local dependence we can now also define the concept of *local stationarity* with reference to the covariance of a process. In this case the previous Formula (4.1.32) holds only if r is less than a certain threshold, while the covariance vanishes when the threshold is overtaken. We can express this in a general form

$$E\,[(X_i - \mu_i)(X_j - \mu_j)] = \begin{cases} \gamma = \rho\sigma_i\sigma_j = \rho\sigma^2 & \text{if } j \in N(i) \\ 0 & \text{otherwise} \end{cases} \qquad (4.1.33)$$

where ρ is the stationary correlation coefficient between pairs of random variables within the threshold. The previous expression is general in that it contains as a subcase the instance of a circular neighbourhood, with centre on i and with radius r. It also allows for patterns of local stationarity for discrete parameter processes like the ones we are more interested in.

Starting from a general description of random processes the introduction of the constraint of stationarity of the second order, although sometimes too strong, enables us to describe the whole process only by its mean and variance-covariance matrix. Furthermore, the local dependence constraint reduces the covariance matrix to a much simpler form (This simpler case will be analysed in detail in paragraph 4.2.3).

We must however, remark here that stationarity is a useful, but often unrealistic, property of a process underlying the kind of data examined by human geographers. If a process was stationary we would have to accept that the degree of dependence, or at least of correlation, between a variable recorded, for example, at London and Oxford, is the same as between any other pair of villages 55 or so miles apart (as noted by Granger 1969) which is in conflict with any common sense notion of the behaviour of social and economical variables.

4.1.3 Multivariate processes in two dimensions

We have so far considered the behaviour of a single process over space. Let us now extend the previous definitions to the case of multivariate processes. Multivariate processes arise when, instead of considering a single process $\{X_i\}$ at various sites i, we observe simultaneously several processes $\{X_i\}$, $\{Y_i\}$, $\{Z_i\}$, say. Just as we have discussed in dealing with univariate processes, we can examine the relationships between random variables only after knowing their joint probability distribution, so, in dealing with multivariate processes we have a very similar framework to describe not only the properties of the individual univariate processes , but also their *cross-links* (Priestley, 1981).
To introduce this let us start considering a bivariate process. Suppose we are given two stochastic processes $\{X_i\}$ and $\{Y_i\}$, i=1,....n. Their joint bivariate probability distribution function (JBPDF) is

$$F(x_i y_j) = F(x_1 ... x_n y_1 ... y_n)$$
$$= P [X_1 \le x_1 .. X_n \le x_n, Y_1 \le y_1 ... Y_n \le y_n] \qquad (4.1.34)$$

and, for absolutely continuous F(.), their joint bivariate probability density function (JBDF) is

$$f_{(1..n)(1..n)}(x_1 ... x_n y_1 ... y_n)$$
$$= \partial^{2n} F(x_1 ... x_n y_1 .. y_n) / [\partial x_1 .. \partial x_n \partial y_1 ... \partial y_n] \qquad (4.1.35)$$

Inversely

$$F(x_1 ... x_n y_1 .. y_n)$$
$$= \int_{-\infty}^{y_1} \cdots \int_{-\infty}^{y_n} \int_{-\infty}^{x_1} \cdots \int_{-\infty}^{x_n} f_{(1,..,n)(1,..,n)} \; (u_1, \ldots, u_{2n}) \; du_1, \ldots, du_{2n} \qquad (4.1.36)$$

From the joint bivariate DF we can, of course, go back to the univariate DF

$$f_{1...n}(x_1 .. x_n) = \int ... \int f_{(1..n)(1...n)}(u_1 ..... u_{2n}) \, du_{n+1} ... du_{2n} \qquad (4.1.37)$$

and, hence to the univariate moments e.g.

$$E(X_i)$$
$$= \int x_i [\int ... \int f_{(1.n)(1..n)}(x_1 .. x_n y_1 .. y_n) dx_1 .. dx_{i-1} x_{i+1} .. dx_n dy_1 .. dy_n] \, dx_i$$
$$= {}_x\mu_i \qquad (4.1.38)$$

say, and

$$Var(X_i) = E [(X_i - {}_x\mu_i)^2]$$
$$= \int (x_i - {}_x\mu_i)^2 [\int .. \int f_{(1..n)(1..n)}(x_1 .. x_n y_1 .. y_n) dx_1 .. dx_{i-1} x_{i+1} .. dx_n dy_1 .. dy_n] \, dx_i$$
$$= {}_x\sigma_i \qquad (4.1.39)$$

All the joint moments can also be derived by the integral:

$$E[(X_1-{}_x\mu_1)^{h_1}\dots(X_n-{}_x\mu_i)^{h_n}(Y_1-{}_y\mu_1)^{h_{n+1}}\dots(Y_n-{}_y\mu_n)^{h_{2n}}]$$
$$=\int..\int\int..\int x_1^{h_1}..x_n^{h_n}y_1^{h_1}..y_n^{h_n}f_{(1..n)(1..n)}(x_1..x_ny_1..y_n)dx_1..dx_ndy_1..dy_n \quad (4.1.40)$$

A particular meaning assume the joint moments of first order

$$E[(X_i-{}_x\mu_i)(Y_j-{}_y\mu_j)] \quad (4.1.41)$$

When i=j we have

$$E[(X_i-{}_x\mu_i)(Y_i-{}_y\mu_i)] = {}_{xy}\gamma_{ii} = {}_{xy}\rho_{ii}\,{}_x\sigma_i\,{}_y\sigma_i \quad (4.1.41.a)$$

which are usually referred to in the literature as the *cross-covariance* (Anderson, 1958; Priestley, 1981) between the process $\{X_i\}$ and the process $\{Y_i\}$, and ${}_{xy}\rho$ as the corresponding cross-correlation.
In contrast when $i \neq j$

$$E[(X_i-{}_x\mu_i)(Y_j-{}_y\mu_j)] = {}_{xy}\gamma'_{ij} = {}_{xy}\rho'_{ij}\,{}_x\sigma_i\,{}_y\sigma_j \quad (4.1.41.b)$$

which we will refer to as the *lagged cross-covariance* between the process $\{X_i\}$ and the process $\{Y_i\}$. This term is sometimes referred to in the spatial literature as the "spill-over effect" (Paelinck and Nijkamp, 1975; p.450) and describes the effect that a variable at site i produces on a second variable in the neighbourhood of i.

We can also derive the conditional distribution of one process given the other. In particular we can have the conditional joint probability distribution function of $\{X\}$, given some values of $\{Y_i\}$, expressed by

$$P[X_1\le x_1..X_n\le x_n \mid Y_1\le y_1..Y_n\le y_n]$$
$$= P[X_1\le x_1..X_n\le x_n\,,\,Y_1\le y_1..Y_n\le y_n] \,/\, [P[Y_1\le y_1..Y_n\le y_n] \quad (4.1.42)$$

and the conditional joint probability density function is given by :

$$f_{1...n}(X_1..X_n|Y_1...Y_n)$$
$$=f_{(1..n)(1..n)}(x_1.x_ny_1..y_n)/[\int.\int f_{(1..n)(1..n)}(u_1..u_ny_1..y_n)du_1..du_n \quad (4.1.43)$$

Furthermore the concept of independence can be easily extended to multivariate processes. Two processes $\{X_i\}$ and $\{Y_i\}$ are said to be statistically independent if

$$F(x_1..x_ny_1..y_n) = F(x_1..x_n\,\infty......\infty)\;F(\infty.....\infty\,y_1..y_n) \quad (4.1.44)$$

Similarly, in terms of density functions, independence implies that

$$f_{(1..n)(1..n)}(x_1..x_n y_1..y_n) = f_{1..n}(x_1..x_n)\, f_{1..n}(y_1..y_n) \qquad (4.1.45)$$

with obvious notation.
The concept of stationarity can be also extended to the consideration of bivariate processes. We say that $\{X_i,Y_i\}$ is a stationary bivariate process, or that $\{X_i\}$ and $\{Y_i\}$ are jointly stationary, if
a) each of them is stationary, and
b) their cross-properties are also stationary.
Focusing on stationarity up to second order, this can be formally expressed by the univariate conditions

$$_x\mu_i = {_x\mu} \qquad _y\mu_i = {_y\mu} \qquad (4.1.46)$$

$$_x\sigma_i^{\,2} = {_x\sigma^2} \qquad _y\sigma_i^{\,2} = {_y\sigma^2} \qquad (4.1.47)$$

$$_x\gamma_i = {_x\gamma}(r,\theta) \qquad _y\gamma_i = {_y\gamma}(r,\theta) \qquad (4.1.48)$$

and by the cross-covariance stationarity conditions

$$_{xy}\gamma_i = {_{xy}\gamma}(r,\theta) \qquad (4.1.49)$$

$$_{xy}\gamma_{ij} = {_{xy}\gamma'}(r,\theta) \qquad (4.1.49.a)$$

where γ' is now the stationary lagged cross-covariance.
As in the previous section, r and θ are respectively the distance between site i and site j and the angle of the segment joining them. In the case of local stationarity this becomes

$$_x\gamma_{ij} = {_x\gamma} \qquad _y\gamma_{ij} = {_y\gamma} \qquad _{xy}\gamma_{ij} = {_{xy}\gamma'} \quad \text{and} \quad _{xy}\gamma_{ii} = {_{xy}\gamma}$$

$$\text{if } j \in N(i) \qquad (4.1.50)$$

The covariances are zero if $j \in N(i)$.
All the concepts of this paragraph can also be extended to multivariate rather then bivariate spatial processes. The extension is straightforward, but leads to a complicated notation. For this reason the more general case is not expressed formally here.

4.2 LINEAR TRANSFORMATIONS OF RANDOM PROCESSES

4.2.1 "Individual-processes" and "group-processes"

Spatial data in human geography are constituted, as a rule, by *aggregation* (or *accumulation* as Granger says, 1974) of individual characteristics in portions of space, either in the form of sums or in the form of averages. For example, population in a county is the sum of the individuals living in that county, the total income of a region is the sum of the individual income of the population in that region, the per-head

consumption in an area is the mean of the individual consumption in that area and so on (Granger, 1969; p.14). Furthermore, for various reasons it sometimes occurs that aggregate spatial units are further aggregated into larger portions of space e.g. by shifting the scale of analysis from a town to a county level, or from one zoning system to another. We have already seen the kind of problems which are caused by this intrinsic feature of spatial data in terms of statistical bias. They can be summarized basically in the *modifiable areal unit problem* (zoning and scale problems) and the *ecological fallacy problem* (See Chapter 2). In each of these cases we start by considering a certain generating process and we end up, after aggregation, with a different process. We will from now on refer to the original generating process as to the *individual-process*, whether it is constituted by actual individuals or by small areas, and we will refer to the process after aggregation as to the *group-process*.
The aim of this section, and the rest of this chapter, is to derive the group-process probability distribution in terms of the individual-process probability distribution. We will follow two different approaches. The first consists in developing a general scheme to derive the joint probability density function of a group-process given a distribution of any kind underlying the individual-process. This is only possible if the form of the individual-process is completely specified. The second, less ambitious approach consists in deriving only some significant moments of the group-process in terms of the individual-process. For the special case where we deal with Gaussian processes, in effect, the study of only the first and the second moments exhausts the problem because these are enough to determine the whole distribution of the process. Furthermore, we have the convenient property analogous to the central limit theorem, that for a large family of well-behaved stationary processes, linear combinations of observations tend to normality even when they are constituted by mutually dependent components (Marsaglia, 1954; Parzen, 1957; Klopotowsky, 1977).
For this reason a major section of this chapter will be devoted to Gaussian processes.

4.2.2. Density function of linear transformations of random processes

Let the JPDF of $\{X_i\}$ $i=1,...n$ be $f_{1,...n}(x_1,....x_n)$. Consider n real-valued functions

$$x_i^* = x_i^*(x_1,...x_n) \qquad i = 1,...,n \qquad (4.2.1)$$

The inverse transformation is

$$x_i = x_i(x_1^*,....,x_n^*) \qquad (4.2.2)$$

Let the random variables $X^*_1.....X^*_n$ be defined by

$$X_i^* = x_i^*(X_1....X_n) \qquad i = 1,....,n \qquad (4.2.3)$$

Then the JDF of $\{X^*_i\}$ is (Anderson, 1958; p.11)

$$g_{1,\dots,n}(x_1^*,\dots x_n^*) = f[x_1(x_1^*\dots x_n^*);\dots;x_n(x_1^*\dots x_n^*)]\ J(x_1^*\dots x_n^*) \tag{4.2.4}$$

where $J(x_1^*,\dots,x_n^*)$ is the Jacobian

$$J(x_1^*,\dots,x_n^*) = \text{mod} \begin{vmatrix} \partial x_1/\partial x_1^* & \partial x_1/\partial x_2^* \dots \partial x_1/\partial x_n^* \\ \partial x_2/\partial x_1^* & \partial x_2/\partial x_2^* \dots \partial x_2/\partial x_n^* \\ \dots & \\ \dots & \\ \partial x_n/\partial x_1^* & \partial x_n/\partial x_2^* \dots \partial x_n/\partial x_n^* \end{vmatrix} \tag{4.2.5}$$

assuming that the derivatives exist.
In the case of linear transformations we have that

$$x_i^* = \Sigma_j\ g_{ij}\ x_j \qquad i=1,\dots,n \tag{4.2.6}$$

or, in matrix notation

$$\mathbf{x}^* = \mathbf{G}\ \mathbf{x} \tag{4.2.7}$$

The inverse transformation is

$$\mathbf{x} = \mathbf{G}^{-1}\mathbf{x}^* \tag{4.2.8}$$

with $\{h_{ji}\} \varepsilon\, \mathbf{G}^{-1}$. Now, letting the random variables $X^*_1,\dots,X^*_n$ be defined by

$$X_i^* = \Sigma_j\ g_{ij}\ X_j \qquad i = 1,\dots,n \tag{4.2.9}$$

or in matrix notation

$$\mathbf{X}^* = \mathbf{G}\ \mathbf{X} \tag{4.2.10}$$

the density of $X^*_1,\dots,X^*_n$ is the same as (4.2.4), but with Jacobian now explicitly given by

$$J(x_1^*,\dots x_n^*) = \text{mod} \begin{vmatrix} h_{11} & h_{12} \dots h_{1n} \\ h_{21} \dots & \\ \dots & \\ \dots & \\ h_{n1} & h_{n2} \dots h_{n2} \end{vmatrix} \tag{4.2.11}$$

As an example we will derive the marginal density function of the sum X^* of two random variables X_1 and X_2 with JDF $f_{1,2}(x_1,x_2)$. Consider the transform

$$X_1^* = X_1 + X_2 \qquad (4.2.12)$$
$$X_2 = X_2$$

and its inverse

$$X_1 = X_1^* - X_2 \qquad (4.2.13)$$
$$X_2 = X_2$$

The JDF of x_1^* and x_2 is

$$g(x_1^* x_2) = f_{12}\,[x_1(x_1^*, x_2),\ x_2(x_1^* x_2)]\ J(x_1^* x_2) \qquad (4.2.14)$$

with Jacobian

$$J = \begin{vmatrix} \partial x_1/\partial x_1^* & \partial x_1/\partial x_2 \\ \partial x_2/\partial x_1^* & \partial x_2/\partial x_2 \end{vmatrix} = \begin{vmatrix} 1 & -1 \\ 0 & 1 \end{vmatrix} = 1 \qquad (4.2.15)$$

Integrating out x_2 yields the probability density function of $X^*_1 = X_1 + X_2$, namely,

$$g(x_1^*) = \int f_{12}\,[\,(x_1^* - x_2),(x_2)\,]\,dx_2 \qquad (4.2.16)$$

In this way we can obtain the distribution of any one individual component of the group-process in terms of all its other individual components. In other words, if the distribution for all the individuals within a study-area is known, we can derive from the previous formulae the distribution for the whole area.
We have assumed so far that the transformations from the x-space to the x^*-space is one-to-one. The typical situation we are interested in is, in contrast, the case in which, through linear transformations, we operate a reduction from the original space of n random variables to a subspace of m $(m<n)$ larger spatial units. In this case the matrix of derivatives becomes singular and the Jacobian cannot be computed.
To illustrate through an example how this problem can be overcome, we consider transformations of the process $\{X_i\}$ $i=1,..,5$

$$X_1^* = X_1 + X_2$$
$$X_2^* = X_3 + X_4 \qquad (4.2.17)$$
$$X_3^* = X_5$$

and then we add two extra identical transformations, say

$$X_2 = X_2 \qquad (4.2.18)$$
$$X_4 = X_4$$

The inclusion of these two identical transformations is just a mathematical devise to have a non-zero value for the Jacobian. For this reason the choice of the variables is completely arbitrary and the solution of the problem do not depend on them. The inverse transformation is now

$$\begin{aligned} X_1 &= X_1^* - X_2 \\ X_2 &= X_2 \\ X_3 &= X_2^* - X_4 \\ X_4 &= X_4 \\ X_5 &= X_3^* \end{aligned} \tag{4.2.19}$$

The JDF $f_{1,\ldots,5}(x_1,\ldots,x_5)$ is now transformed into

$$\begin{aligned} & g_{1..5}(x_1^*,x_2^*,x_3^*,x_2,x_4) \\ &= f_{1.5}[x_1(x_1^*,x_2^*,x_3^*,x_2,x_4)..x_5(x_1^*,..,x_4)]J(x_1^*,x_2^*,x_3^*,x_2,x_4) \\ &= f_{1..5}[(x_1^*-x_2),x_2,(x_2^*-x_4),x_4,x_3^*]\ J(x_1^*,x_2^*,x_3^*,x_2,x_4) \end{aligned} \tag{4.2.20}$$

with the Jacobian

$$J = \begin{vmatrix} 1 & 0 & 0 & -1 & 0 \\ 0 & 0 & 0 & 1 & 0 \\ 0 & 1 & 0 & 0 & -1 \\ 0 & 0 & 0 & 0 & 1 \\ 0 & 0 & 1 & 0 & 0 \end{vmatrix} = |-1| = 1 \tag{4.2.21}$$

Integrating out the redundant variables X_2 and X_4 we obtain the JDF of the group-process $\{X^*_i\}$, $i=1,2,3$

$$\begin{aligned} & g_{1,2,3}(x_1^*,x_2^*,x_3^*) \\ &= \int\int f_{1,..,5}[(x_1^*-x_1),x_2,(x_2^*-x_4),x_4,x_3^*]\ dx_2 dx_4 \end{aligned} \tag{4.2.22}$$

Generalizing the previous notation, suppose we are given an individual-process $\{X_j\}$ $j=1,\ldots,n$ with JDF $f_{1,\ldots,n}(x_1,\ldots x_n)$. Then consider m real-valued functions $(m<n)$

$$x_i^* = x_i^*(x_1 \ldots x_n) \qquad i = 1,\ldots,m \tag{4.2.23}$$

and $(n-m)$ real-valued functions

$$x_{.1} = x_{.1} \qquad 1=1,\ldots,(n-m) \tag{4.2.24}$$

In the linear case this can be summarized in the matrix notation

$$\mathbf{X^*} = \mathbf{G}\ \mathbf{X} \tag{4.2.25}$$

with $\mathbf{X^*}=(X^*_1\ldots\ldots X^*_m \mid X_{.1}\ldots\ldots X_{.(n-m)})$, $\mathbf{X} = (X_1\ldots X_n)$, and

$$\mathbf{G} = \left| \begin{array}{l} g_{11}\, g_{12} \cdots g_{1n} \\ \cdots\cdots\cdots\cdots \\ g_{m1}\, g_{m2} \cdots g_{mn} \\ ----------- \\ 0\ 0 \ldots 1 \ldots 0 \\ \cdots\cdots\cdots\cdots \\ 0\ 0 \ldots 0 \quad 1 \end{array} \right| \tag{4.2.26}$$

The inverse of the transform is

$$x_j = x_j\,(x_1{}^* \ldots x_m{}^* x_{.1} \ldots x_{.(n-m)}) \quad j = 1,..,n \tag{4.2.27}$$

and the JDF of the group-process is given by

$$\begin{aligned} &\int \ldots \int f_{1..n}[x_1(x_1{}^* \ldots x_m{}^* x_{.1} \ldots x_{.(n-m)}) \ldots\ldots x_n(x_1{}^* \ldots x_m{}^* x_{.1} \ldots x_{.(n-m)}) \\ &J\,(x_1{}^* \ldots x_m{}^* x_{.1} \ldots x_{.(n-m)})\,]\; dx_{.1} \ldots dx_{.(n-m)} \\ &= g(x_1{}^* \ldots x_m{}^*) \end{aligned} \tag{4.2.28}$$

Let us now consider a bivariate individual-process $\{X_jY_j\}$, j=1,...,n, with JDF $f_{(1....n)(1....n)}(x_1 \ldots\ldots x_n, y_1 \ldots\ldots y_n)$. The extension of the previous results is straightforward. Define 2m real-valued functions

$$\begin{aligned} x_i{}^* &= x_i{}^*(x_1 \ldots x_n y_1 \ldots y_n) \quad i = 1,..,m \\ y_i{}^* &= y_i{}^*(x_1 \ldots x_n y_1 \ldots y_n) \quad i = 1,...,m \end{aligned} \tag{4.2.29}$$

Define 2(n−m) additional identities

$$\begin{aligned} x_{.l} &= x_{.l} \qquad l = 1,...,(n-m) \\ y_{.l} &= y_{.l} \qquad l = 1,...,(n-m) \end{aligned} \tag{4.2.30}$$

and define the inverse transformations

$$\begin{aligned} &x_i = x_i\,(x_1{}^* \ldots x_m{}^* x_{.1} \ldots x_{.(n-m)} y_1{}^* \ldots y_m{}^* y_{.1} \ldots y_{.(n-m)}) = x_i(\,.\,) \\ &y_i = y_i\,(x_1{}^* \ldots x_m{}^* x_{.1} \ldots x_{.(n-m)} y_1{}^* \ldots y_m{}^* y_{.1} \ldots y_{.(n-m)}) = y_i(\,.\,) \\ &i = 1,...,m \end{aligned} \tag{4.2.31}$$

The JDF of the bivariate group-process $\{X_i{}^*Y_i{}^*\}$, i=1,...,m is now defined by

$$\begin{aligned} X_i{}^* &= x_i{}^*\,(X_1 \ldots X_n Y_1 \ldots Y_n) \\ Y_i{}^* &= y_i{}^*\,(X_1 \ldots X_n Y_1 \ldots Y_n) \end{aligned} \tag{4.2.32}$$

After the transformation we now have :

$$f_{(1..n)(1..n)}(x_1^* .. x_m^* y_1^* .. y_m^*)$$
$$= \int ... \int f_{(1..n)(1..n)} [x_1(.) ... x_n(.) y_1(.) ... y_n(.)]$$
$$J(.) dx_{.1} ... dx_{.(n-m)} dy_{.1} .. dy_{.(n-m)} \qquad (4.2.33)$$

Furthermore the CJDF of $\{X^*_i\}$ given $\{Y^*_i\}$ can be derived substituting by (4.2.33) into (4.1.20)

$$f_{1..m}(x_1^* ... x_m^* \mid y_1^* ... y_m^*)$$
$$= \{\int .. \int f_{(1..n)(1..n)}[x_1(.) .. x_n(.) y_1(.) .. y_n(.)] J(.) dx_{.1} .. dx_{.(n-m)} dy_{.1} .. dy_{.(n-m)}\}$$
$$\{\int .. \int [\int .. \int f_{(1..n)(1..n)}[u_1(.) .. u_n(.) y_1(.) .. y_n(.)] J(.) du_1 .. du_n] dx_{.1} .. dx_{.(n-m)}$$
$$dy_{.1} .. dy_{.(n-m)}\}^{-1}$$
$$(4.2.34)$$

We thus have the general conditions for describing the probability density functions of a group-process from its individual components for the general case in which there is not a one-to-one transformation between the two processes.

4.2.3. Linear transformations of Gaussian processes

The formulae developed in the previous section lead to the group-process distribution only if we are able to specify exactly the individual-process distribution. In many cases, however, the distribution of the individual-process may not be completely known or, more frequently, the previous formulae can lead to distributions that cannot be solved analytically so that the results may be of limited or no practical relevance. However relatively simple results can be reached by considering the case of *Gaussian processes*. Consequently this section is devoted to the introduction of the class of univariate and multivariate Gaussian process. For this class of processes the distribution of group-process is derived in terms of individual-processes.

THE NORMAL DENSITY FUNCTION

The JDF of a Gaussian process $\{X_i\}$ is

$$(2\pi)^{-n/2} |_X\mathbf{V}|^{-1/2} \exp\{-(1/2)(\mathbf{X} - {}_X\boldsymbol{\mu})' \, {}_X\mathbf{V}^{-1} (\mathbf{X} - {}_X\boldsymbol{\mu})\} \qquad (4.2.35)$$

where ${}_X\boldsymbol{\mu} = \{\mu_1, ..., \mu_n)$ is the vector of the means, ${}_X\mathbf{V}^{-1}$ is a n by n symmetric matrix such that ${}_X\mathbf{V}$ is the matrix of variances and covariance of the variables (or the dispersion matrix of the process). We denote the density (4.2.35) as MVN $({}_X\boldsymbol{\mu}; {}_X\mathbf{V})$. The correlation coefficient between the random variables X_i and X_j is defined as

$${}_X\rho_{ij} = {}_X\gamma_{ij} / [{}_X\sigma_i \, {}_Y\sigma_j] \quad \text{and} \quad {}_X\rho_{ij} = {}_X\rho_{ji} \qquad (4.2.36)$$

If, in addition, the Gaussian process is also locally stationary, we have that ${}_X\mu_i = {}_X\mu$ for each i, ${}_X\sigma^2_i = {}_X\sigma^2$ for each i and

$$ {}_X\gamma_{ij} = \begin{cases} {}_X\gamma & \text{if } j \in N(i) \\ 0 & \text{otherwise} \end{cases} \qquad (4.2.37) $$

and, hence,

$$ {}_X\rho = {}_X\gamma \,/\, {}_X\sigma^2 \qquad (4.2.38) $$

If we consider, for instance a simple process $\{X_i\}$, i=1,2, the mean vector is

$$ E\,(X_1, X_2) = ({}_X\mu_1, {}_X\mu_2) = {}_X\boldsymbol{\mu} \qquad (4.2.39) $$

The covariance matrix can be written

$$ \mathbf{V} = E \begin{pmatrix} (X_1 - {}_X\mu_1)^2 & (X_1 - {}_X\mu_1)(X_2 - {}_X\mu_2) \\ (X_2 - {}_X\mu_2)(X_1 - {}_X\mu_1) & (X_2 - {}_X\mu_2)^2 \end{pmatrix} $$

$$ = \begin{pmatrix} {}_X\sigma_1{}^2 & {}_X\rho\, {}_X\sigma_1\, {}_X\sigma_2 \\ {}_X\rho\, {}_X\sigma_2\, {}_X\sigma_1 & {}_X\sigma_2{}^2 \end{pmatrix} \qquad (4.2.40) $$

It is easily verified that the inverse of ${}_X\mathbf{V}$ is

$$ \mathbf{V}^{-1} = (1 - \rho^2)^{-1} \begin{pmatrix} 1/{}_X\sigma_1{}^2 & -{}_X\rho/({}_X\sigma_1\, {}_X\sigma_2) \\ -{}_X\rho/({}_X\sigma_2\, {}_X\sigma_1) & 1/{}_X\sigma_2{}^2 \end{pmatrix} \qquad (4.2.41) $$

so that the JDF of X_1 and X_2 is

$$ [2\pi\, {}_X\sigma_1\, {}_X\sigma_2 \sqrt{(1 - {}_X\rho^2)}]^{-1} $$
$$ \exp\{-[2(1-{}_X\rho^2)^{-1}][(x_1-{}_X\mu_1)^2({}_X\sigma_1)^{-2} - 2\rho(x_1-{}_X\mu_1) $$
$$ (x_2-{}_X\mu_2)({}_X\sigma_1 {}_X\sigma_2)^{-1} + (x_2 - {}_X\mu_2)^2({}_X\sigma_2)^{-2}]\} \qquad (4.2.42) $$

If, in addition, the process is also stationary we have

$$ [2\pi\, {}_X\sigma^2 \sqrt{(1 - {}_X\rho^2)}]^{-1} $$
$$ \exp\{-[(x_1-{}_X\mu)^2 - 2\rho(x_1 - {}_X\mu)(x_2 - {}_X\mu) + (x_2 - {}_X\mu)^2]/ $$
$$ /\,[2{}_X\sigma^2(1 - {}_X\rho^2)]\} \qquad (4.2.43) $$

Generalizing the previous notation we have that the JDF of a bivariate Gaussian process $\{X_i Y_i\}$, i=1,...,n, is given by

$$(2\pi)^{-n} |\mathbf{V}|^{-1/2} \exp\{-(1/2)\ (\boldsymbol{\xi}-\boldsymbol{\mu})' \mathbf{V}^{-1}(\boldsymbol{\xi}-\boldsymbol{\mu})\} \tag{4.2.44}$$

where $\boldsymbol{\xi}$ is a bivariate random vector partitioned into components $\mathbf{X}$ and the $\mathbf{Y}$

$$\boldsymbol{\xi} = (\mathbf{X}\ \mathbf{Y}) = (X_1 ... X_n\ \ Y_1 ... Y_n) \tag{4.2.45}$$

$\boldsymbol{\mu}$ is a vector of means

$$\boldsymbol{\mu} = ({}_x\boldsymbol{\mu}, {}_y\boldsymbol{\mu}) = ({}_x\mu_1, ..., {}_x\mu_n, {}_y\mu_1, ..., {}_y\mu_n) \tag{4.2.46}$$

$\mathbf{V}$ is the matrix of variance, covariance and cross-covariances

$$\mathbf{V} = \begin{pmatrix} {}_x\mathbf{V} & {}_{xy}\mathbf{V} \\ {}_{yx}\mathbf{V} & {}_y\mathbf{V} \end{pmatrix} \tag{4.2.47}$$

${}_x\mathbf{V}$ and ${}_y\mathbf{V}$ are the matrices of variance and covariances of, respectively, the process $\{X_i\}$ and $\{Y_i\}$. ${}_{xy}\mathbf{V} = {}_{yx}\mathbf{V}$ are the matrices of cross-covariances of the two processes. An interesting feature of a Gaussian process is that its distribution is uniquely determined by the vector of means ${}_x\boldsymbol{\mu}$ and by the dispersion matrix ${}_x\mathbf{V}$ (Anderson, 1958). This result also holds for a bivariate process which is uniquely determined by the vector of means $\boldsymbol{\xi}$, the variance-covariance matrices ${}_x\mathbf{V}$ and ${}_y\mathbf{V}$ and the cross-covariance matrices ${}_{xy}\mathbf{V} = {}_{yx}\mathbf{V}$. Furthermore, if $\{X_i\}$ has a joint normal distribution, a necessary and sufficient condition that one subset of random variables, and the subset consisting of the remaining variables, be independent is that each covariance of a variable from one set and a variable from the other set be zero (Anderson, 1958; p.22). Hence for a Gaussian process zero correlation implies independence.

"UNIFORMLY COVARIANT" AND "LOCALLY COVARIANT" PROCESSES

Due to the central role played in multinormal processes by the variance-covariance matrix it is necessary to introduce at this stage some hypotheses about its form which embodies a plausible pattern of dependence for the case we are considering. We will now distinguish two different patterns of dependence which will be used in all the subsequent discussion:

a) **Uniform covariance.** When we are dealing with individual-processes which refer to actual individuals interacting in the study-area we can postulate that all the random variables are equally pair-wise correlated. This hypothesis implies, in turn, that interaction among individuals is not restricted within *cliques* (Besag, 1974) in the study-area. Although sometimes unrealistic, this is the only way out of the impasse of defining a matrix of dispersion which is, in most applications, very large. Furthermore, in the case in which the number of individuals is large compared with the size of the area (i.e. the area is very dense) the hypothesis is not very far from reality.

We will refer to this kind of dependence as *uniform covariance* which, in a stationary bivariate Gaussian process, is expressed formally by

$$
\begin{aligned}
{}_x\gamma_{jk} \in {}_x\mathbf{V};\quad {}_x\gamma_{jk} &= E[(X_j - {}_x\mu_j)(X_k - {}_x\mu_k)] = {}_x\rho\, {}_x\sigma^2 && \text{each } j=k \\
{}_{xy}\gamma_{jk} \in {}_{xy}\mathbf{V};\quad {}_{xy}\gamma_{jk} &= E[(X_j - {}_x\mu_j)(Y_k - {}_y\mu_k)] = {}_{xy}\rho\, {}_x\sigma\, {}_y\sigma && \text{each } j=k \\
&= {}_{xy}\rho'\, {}_x\sigma\, {}_y\sigma && \text{each } j\neq k
\end{aligned}
\qquad (4.2.48)
$$

b) **Local covariance.** When we are dealing with individual-processes which are constituted by small areas which are then grouped into larger zones, the previously mentioned hypothesis of local dependence is the most plausible (Smith, 1980). In a Gaussian process this is formally expressed by

$$
\begin{aligned}
{}_x\gamma_{jk} \in {}_x\mathbf{V};\quad {}_x\gamma_{jk} = E[(X_j - {}_x\mu_j)(X_k - {}_x\mu_k)] &= {}_x\rho\, {}_x\sigma^2 && \text{when } j \in N(k) \\
&= 0 && \text{otherwise}
\end{aligned}
\qquad (4.2.49)
$$

and in a bivariate Gaussian process by

$$
\begin{aligned}
{}_{xy}\gamma_{jk} \in {}_{xy}\mathbf{V};\ {}_{xy}\gamma_{jk} = E[(X_j - {}_x\mu_j)(Y_k - {}_y\mu_k)] &= {}_{xy}\rho'\, {}_x\sigma\, {}_y\sigma && \text{when } j \in N(k) \\
&= {}_{xy}\rho\, {}_x\sigma\, {}_y\sigma && \text{each } j=k \\
&= 0 && \text{otherwise}
\end{aligned}
\qquad (4.2.50)
$$

We will refer to this second kind of dependence as the *local covariance* hypothesis.

SOME PROPERTIES AND THEOREMS

Apart from the already mentioned properties, the reason that the study of Gaussian processes is worthwhile is that the marginal distributions and the conditional distributions derived from a multivariate normal process are also multivariate normally distributed. Moreover, linear combinations of normal variates are again normally distributed.

For this reason the study of the distribution of a group-process is far simpler if the individual-process is multinormally distributed. Although it has been shown elsewhere (Springer, 1980) how to derive the group-process distribution using the previously depicted approach, in this section different lines will be followed. In particular a central role is played by the following theorem (Anderson, 1958; p.25):

THEOREM 4.2.1: If $\{X_j\}=X_1,\ldots,X_n$ is distributed according to the law $N({}_x\boldsymbol{\mu}, {}_x\mathbf{V})$ then $\{X^*_i\}=X^*_1,\ldots,X^*_m$, $(m<n)$ such that $\mathbf{X^*}=\mathbf{GX}$ is distributed according to the law $N(\mathbf{G}_x\boldsymbol{\mu}, \mathbf{G}_x\mathbf{VG'})$, where $\mathbf{G}$ is an m-by-n grouping matrix of rank $m<n$.

COROLLARY : If $\{X_jY_j\}$, $j=1,\ldots,n$, is a bivariate process distributed according to the law

$$
\mathbf{N} \sim \begin{pmatrix} {}_x\boldsymbol{\mu} \\ {}_y\boldsymbol{\mu} \end{pmatrix} ; \begin{pmatrix} {}_x\mathbf{V} & {}_{xy}\mathbf{V} \\ {}_{yx}\mathbf{V} & {}_y\mathbf{V} \end{pmatrix}
$$

then the bivariate process $\{X^*_i Y^*_i\}$, $i=1,\ldots,m$, $(m<n)$ such that $\mathbf{X}^*=\mathbf{GX}$ and $\mathbf{Y}^*=\mathbf{GY}$, is distributed according to the law

$$\mathbf{N} \sim \begin{pmatrix} \mathbf{G}\,{}_x\boldsymbol{\mu} \\ \mathbf{G}\,{}_y\boldsymbol{\mu} \end{pmatrix} ; \begin{pmatrix} \mathbf{G}\,{}_x\mathbf{V}\,\mathbf{G}' & \mathbf{G}\,{}_{xy}\mathbf{V}\,\mathbf{G}' \\ \mathbf{G}\,{}_{yx}\mathbf{V}\,\mathbf{G}' & \mathbf{G}\,{}_y\mathbf{V}\,\mathbf{G}' \end{pmatrix}$$

From this theorem all the results we need for this book will follow. We will develop them separately for each of the two sets of cases of aggregation from a simple sum and of aggregation through averaging.

AGGREGATION THROUGH SUMS

We are given an individual random process $\{X_j\}$, $j=1,\ldots,n$, $N({}_x\boldsymbol{\mu},{}_x\mathbf{V})$ with ${}_x\boldsymbol{\mu}$ and ${}_x\mathbf{V}$ defined as in (4.2.35), and a group-process $\{X^*_i\}$, $i=1,\ldots,m$, such that $\mathbf{X}^*=\mathbf{GX}$. In this case $\mathbf{G}$ is an m-by-n grouping matrix with elements g_{ij} which assume the values

$$g_{ij}=\begin{cases} 1 & \text{if } j \in G(i) \qquad r_i \text{ times in the i-th row} \\ 0 & \text{if not} \qquad n-r_i \text{ times in the i-th row} \end{cases} \tag{4.2.51}$$

where $G(i)$ is the set of random components of the individual-process included in the i-th random component of the group-process, and r_i is the cardinality of $G(i)$.
From Theorem 4.2.1 we have for the mean vector

$$E(\mathbf{X}^*) = E(\mathbf{GX}) = \mathbf{G}\,{}_x\boldsymbol{\mu} \tag{4.2.52}$$

and in particular for the i-th component

$$E(X_i^*) = \Sigma_{j\in G(i)}\, {}_x\mu_j \tag{4.2.53}$$

If the individual-process is stationary in mean with ${}_x\boldsymbol{\mu}_j = {}_x\boldsymbol{\mu}$ for each j, then this reduces to

$$E(X_i^*) = r_i\, {}_x\mu \tag{4.2.54}$$

Now setting ${}_x\boldsymbol{\mu}=0$, without loss of generality, we have for the diagonal variance matrix of the group-process

$$E\{\text{diag}\,(\mathbf{X}^*\mathbf{X}^{*\prime})\} = \text{diag}\,(\mathbf{G}\,{}_x\mathbf{V}\,\mathbf{G}') \tag{4.2.55}$$

and, in particular for the i-th component

$$E(X_i^{*2}) = {}_{x*}\sigma^2_i = \Sigma_{j\,\in\,G(i)}\ {}_x\sigma^2_j + \Sigma_{(2)\,j,k\,\in\,G(i)}\, {}_x\gamma_{jk} \tag{4.2.56}$$

As a result we have, in case that the individual-process is stationary with stationary variance equal to ${}_X\sigma^2$, Equation (4.2.56) reduces to

$$E(X_i^{*2}) = {}_{X*}\sigma^2{}_i = r_i\ {}_X\sigma^2 + \Sigma_{(2)\ j,k\ \varepsilon\ G(i)}\ {}_X\gamma_{jk} \qquad (4.2.57)$$

If we assume, in addition, that the process is "uniformly covariant" (See §.4.2.3) i.e.

$${}_X\gamma_{jk} = {}_X\rho_X\sigma^2 \qquad \text{each } j,k$$

we have

$${}_{X*}\sigma^2{}_i = r_i\ {}_X\sigma^2\ [\ 1 + (r_i - 1)\ {}_X\rho\ ] \qquad (4.2.58)$$

When, in contrast, we are in the local covariance hypothesis we have

$${}_{X*}\sigma^2{}_i = r_i\ {}_X\sigma^2 + \Sigma_{(2)\ j,k\ \varepsilon\ G(i), j\ \varepsilon\ N(k)}\ {}_X\gamma_{jk} \qquad (4.2.58.a)$$

where N(k) is the already mentioned set of neighbours of site i (see Formula 4.1.27). Let us now call A_i the level of internal connectedness of group i given by the total number of non-zero covariances within the group i (see § 3.3.3). In the hypothesis of local stationarity Formula (4.2.58.a) reduces to

$${}_{X*}\sigma^2{}_i = r_i\ {}_X\sigma^2 + A_i\ \ {}_X\gamma_{jk}$$

$$= r_i\ {}_X\sigma^2\ [\ 1 + A_i\ r_i^{-1}\ {}_X\rho_{jk}] \qquad (4.2.58.b)$$

Finally for the covariance of the group-process we have

$$E(\mathbf{X^*X^{*'}}) = \mathbf{G}\ {}_X\mathbf{V}\ \mathbf{G'} \qquad (4.2.59)$$

and for the i-th and l-th component

$$E(X_i^*X_l^*) = \Sigma_{j\ \varepsilon\ G(i)}\Sigma_{k\varepsilon\ G(l)}\ {}_X\gamma_{jk} \qquad (4.2.60)$$

The result is that the spatial autocovariance between two sites of the group-process equals the sum of the covariance at the individual-process level of one random variable from one group and a variable from the other; this is the covariance between individuals that cross the group boundaries to interact.

Now, if all pairs of random variables are equally correlated (that is if we are in the *uniformly covariant* hypothesis) we have that

$$E(X_i^*X_l^*) = {}_{X*}\gamma = r_i r_l\ {}_X\rho_X\sigma^2 \qquad (4.2.61)$$

for all $j\ \varepsilon\ G(i)$ and $k\ \varepsilon\ G(l)$, $k \neq l$. If alternatively we have stationarity but only a locally covariant process, then

$$E(X_i^* X_l^*) = t_{il}\ {}_x\rho_x \sigma^2 \tag{4.2.62}$$

where $j \in G(i)$, $k \in G(l)$ and where t_{il} is the number of non-zero covariances at the individual-process level between i and l. (See § 2.3).
Consider now the bivariate individual-process $\{X_j Y_j\}$, $j=1,\ldots,n$ which is distributed

$$\mathbf{MVN} \sim \begin{pmatrix} {}_x\boldsymbol{\mu} \\ {}_y\boldsymbol{\mu} \end{pmatrix} ; \begin{pmatrix} {}_x\mathbf{V} & {}_{xy}\mathbf{V} \\ {}_{yx}\mathbf{V} & {}_y\mathbf{V} \end{pmatrix}$$

with ${}_x\boldsymbol{\mu}$, ${}_y\boldsymbol{\mu}$, ${}_x\mathbf{V}$, ${}_y\mathbf{V}$, ${}_{xy}\mathbf{V} = {}_{yx}\mathbf{V}$ are defined as in (4.2.47).
Consider in addition the bivariate group-process $\{X^*_i Y^*_i\}$, $i=1,\ldots,m$, such that

$$\mathbf{X^*} = \mathbf{GX} \qquad \text{and} \qquad \mathbf{Y^*} = \mathbf{GY} \tag{4.2.63}$$

where $\mathbf{G}$ is an m-by-n matrix defined as in (4.2.51).
Consequently the cross-covariance of the bivariate group-process is

$$E(\mathbf{X^* Y^*}) = \mathbf{G}\ {}_{xy}\mathbf{V}\ \mathbf{G'} = \mathbf{G}\ {}_{yx}\mathbf{V}\ \mathbf{G'} \tag{4.2.64}$$

In particular for the two groups i and l

$$E(X^*_i Y^*_l) = {}_{x^*y^*}\gamma_{il} = \Sigma_{(2)\ j,k \in G(i)}\ {}_{xy}\gamma_{jk} \tag{4.2.65}$$

For the cross covariance in the same group

$$E(X^*_i Y^*_i) = {}_{x^*y^*}\gamma_{ii} = \Sigma_{j \in G(i)}\ {}_{xy}\gamma_{jj} + \Sigma_{(2)\ j,k \in G(i)}\ {}_{xy}\gamma_{jk} \tag{4.2.66}$$

This shows that the group correlation (or ecological correlation) splits into two terms, where the first term represents the individual correlation (Duncan, Cuzzort and Duncan, 1961), and the second term is an interaction term representing the effect of other individuals (or the *environment*) on the individual behaviour.
Furthermore if the bivariate individual-process is jointly stationary with

$$_{xy}\gamma_{jj} = {}_{xy}\gamma = {}_{xy}\rho\ {}_x\sigma_y\sigma \qquad \text{each } j \tag{4.2.67}$$

and

$$_{xy}\gamma'_{jk} = {}_{xy}\gamma' = {}_{xy}\rho'\ {}_x\sigma_y\sigma \qquad \text{each } j,k (j \neq k) \tag{4.2.68}$$

where ${}_{xy}\rho' = {}_{xy}\gamma\ ({}_x\sigma_y\sigma)^{-1}$ is the joint lagged cross-correlation, and we have the uniform covariance hypothesis then we have

$$_{x^*y^*}\gamma_i = r_i\ {}_{xy}\gamma + r_i(r_i - 1)\ {}_{xy}\gamma' \tag{4.2.69}$$

If, in addition, ${}_x\sigma={}_y\sigma=\sigma$, then

$$ {}_{x^*y^*}\gamma_i = \sigma^2 r_i [{}_{xy}\rho + (r_i - 1)_{xy}\rho'] \tag{4.2.70}$$

Alternatively, if the process is stationary and locally covariant with

$$ {}_{x^*y^*}\gamma_{jk} = \begin{cases} {}_{xy}\rho'\,{}_x\sigma\,{}_y\sigma & \text{if } j \in N(k) \quad ; j \neq k \\ {}_{xy}\rho\,{}_x\sigma\,{}_y\sigma & \text{if } j = k \\ 0 & \text{otherwise} \end{cases} \tag{4.2.71}$$

then

$$ {}_{x^*y^*}\gamma_i = r_i\ {}_{xy}\rho\,{}_x\sigma\,{}_y\sigma + A_i\ {}_{xy}\rho'\,{}_x\sigma\,{}_y\sigma \tag{4.2.72}$$

where A_i is the number of non-zero covariances between X_j ,$j \in G(i)$, and Y_j ,$j \in G(i)$. This is equal to the connectedness within group i. (See § 3.3.3 and Figure 4.2).

AGGREGATION THROUGH AVERAGING

The development of the case of grouping by averaging closely follows the same lines as the case of aggregation through sums. In this case we are given a process $\{X_j\}$, $j=1,\ldots,n$

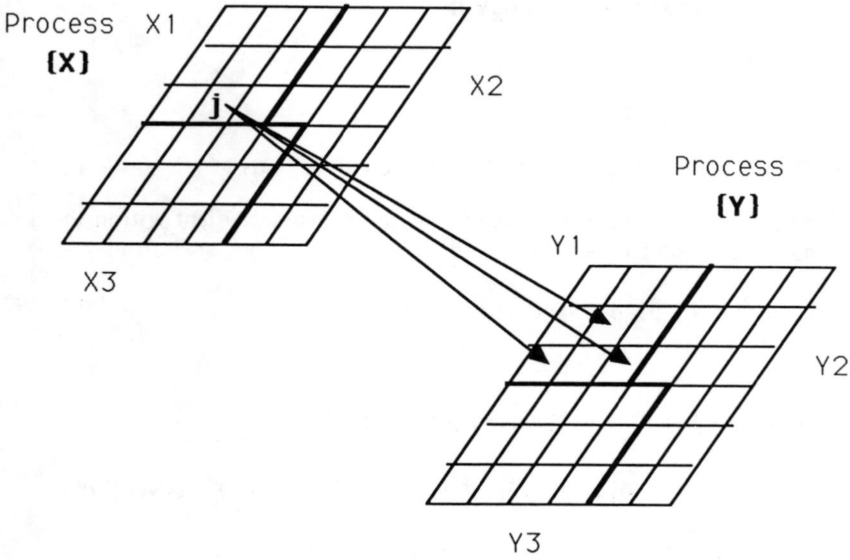

Figure 4.2 : Non-zero cross-covariaces between group X1 and group Y1 for site j.

$N({}_X\boldsymbol{\mu}, {}_X\mathbf{V})$ and we are seeking the distribution of $\{X^*{}_i\}$, $i=1,\ldots,m$ $(m<n)$ where $\mathbf{X}^* = \mathbf{G}\mathbf{X}$ and $g_{ij} \in \mathbf{G}$ such that

$$g_{ij} = \begin{cases} r_i^{-1} & \text{if } j \in G(i) \quad r_i \text{ times in row } i \\ 0 & \text{otherwise} \quad (n - r_i) \text{ times in row } i \end{cases} \qquad (4.2.73)$$

The result for the mean in the group-process is

$$E(\mathbf{X}^*) = E(\mathbf{G}\,\mathbf{X}) = \mathbf{G}\,{}_X\boldsymbol{\mu} \qquad (4.2.74)$$

and for the i-th component

$$E(X_i^*) = r_i^{-1} \textstyle\sum_{j \in G(i)} {}_X\mu_j \qquad (4.2.75)$$

which, in the stationary case, reduces to

$$E(X_i^*) = {}_X\mu \qquad (4.2.76)$$

Again, setting ${}_X\boldsymbol{\mu}=\mathbf{0}$ we have, for the variance of the group-process:

$$E\{\,\mathrm{diag}\,(\mathbf{X}^*\mathbf{X}^{*\prime})\,\} = \mathrm{diag}\,\mathbf{G}\,{}_X\mathbf{V}\,\mathbf{G}' \qquad (4.2.77)$$

and for the i-th component

$$E(X_i^{*2}) = {}_{X^*}\sigma_i^2$$
$$= r_i^{-2} \textstyle\sum_{j \in G(i)} {}_X\sigma_j^2 + r_i^{-2} \sum_{(2)\, j,k \in G(i)} {}_X\gamma_{jk} \qquad (4.2.78)$$

If we assume again that the individual-process is uniformly covariant within the group with ${}_X\gamma_{kj} = {}_X\rho\,{}_X\sigma^2$ for each j,k, we have

$${}_{X^*}\sigma_i^2 = r_i^{-1}\,{}_X\sigma^2 + r_i^{-1}(r_i - 1)\,{}_X\rho\,{}_X\sigma^2 \qquad (4.2.79)$$

If the local covariance hypothesis holds, we have instead

$${}_{X^*}\sigma_i^2 = r_i^{-2} \textstyle\sum_{j \in G(i)} {}_X\sigma_j^2 + r_i^{-2} \sum_{(2)\, j,k \in G(i);\, j \in N(k)} {}_X\gamma_{jk}$$
$$= r_i^{-1}\,{}_X\sigma^2 + r_i^{-2} A_i\,{}_X\gamma = r_i^{-1}\,{}_X\sigma^2\,[1 + A_i\, r_i^{-1}\,{}_X\rho] \qquad (4.2.79.a)$$

The covariance element in the group-process is

$$E(\mathbf{X}^*\mathbf{X}^{*\prime}) = \mathbf{G}\ {}_x\mathbf{V}\ \mathbf{G}' \tag{4.2.80}$$

and for the i-th and l-th component

$$E(X_i^*X_l^*) = (r_ir_l)^{-1}\Sigma_{k\,\varepsilon\,G(i)}\Sigma_{l\,\varepsilon\,G(k)}\ {}_x\gamma_{jk} = {}_{x^*}\gamma_{il} \tag{4.2.81}$$

Again we may face two situations. If the individual-process is stationary and uniformly covariant with covariance equal to ${}_x\rho_x\sigma^2$ we have simply

$$E(X_i^*X_l^*) = {}_x\rho_x\sigma^2 \tag{4.2.82}$$

If alternatively the individual-process is only locally covariant, where ${}_x\gamma_{jk} = {}_x\rho_x\sigma^2$ if $j\varepsilon N(k)$ and zero otherwise, then

$$E(X_i^*X_l^*) = t_{il}\ (r_ir_l)^{-1}\ {}_x\rho_x\sigma^2 \tag{4.2.83}$$

where again t_{il} is the number of non-zero covariance at the individual-process level between i and l. Finally for the cross-covariance of the group-process we have

$$E(\mathbf{X}^*\ \mathbf{Y}^*) = \mathbf{G}\ {}_{xy}\mathbf{V}\ \mathbf{G}' = \mathbf{G}\ {}_{yx}\mathbf{V}\ \mathbf{G}' \tag{4.2.84}$$

and

$$E(X_i^*Y_l^*) = {}_{x^*y^*}\gamma_{il}$$
$$= \Sigma_{j\,\varepsilon\,G(i)}\ \Sigma_{k\,\varepsilon\,G(l)}\ (r_ir_l)^{-1}\ {}_{xy}\gamma_{jk} \tag{4.2.85}$$

For the cross-covariance in the same group

$$E(X_i^*Y_i^*) = {}_{x^*y^*}\gamma_{ii}$$
$$= (r_i)^{-2}\Sigma_{j\varepsilon\,G(i)}\ {}_{xy}\gamma_{jj} + (r_i)^{-2}\ \Sigma_{j\,\varepsilon\,G(i)}\ \Sigma_{k\,\varepsilon\,G(i)}\ {}_{xy}\gamma_{jk} \tag{4.2.86}$$

In the case where the bivariate individual-process is jointly stationary with

$${}_{xy}\gamma_{jj} = {}_{xy}\rho\ {}_x\sigma\ {}_y\sigma$$
$${}_{xy}\gamma_{jk} = {}_{xy}\rho'\ {}_x\sigma\ {}_y\sigma \tag{4.2.87}$$

and all pairs are equally correlated, we have

$${}_{x^*y^*}\gamma_i = r_i^{-1}\ {}_{xy}\rho\ {}_x\sigma\ {}_y\sigma + (r_i-1)r_i^{-1}\ {}_{xy}\rho'\ {}_x\sigma\ {}_y\sigma \tag{4.2.88}$$

If, in addition ${}_x\sigma = {}_y\sigma = \sigma$ (4.2.88) simplifies further to give:

$${}_{x^*y^*}\gamma_{il} = {}_x\sigma^2[\ r_i^{-1}\ {}_{xy}\rho + (r_i-1)r_i^{-1}\ {}_{xy}\rho'\ ] \tag{4.2.89}$$

Alternatively if the process is stationary and locally covariant with

$$ {}_{xy}\gamma_{jk} = \begin{cases} {}_{xy}\rho' \, {}_{x}\sigma \, {}_{y}\sigma & \text{if } j \in N(i) \; ; j \neq k \\ {}_{xy}\rho \, {}_{x}\sigma \, {}_{y}\sigma & \text{if } j = k \\ 0 & \text{otherwise} \end{cases} \qquad (4.2.90) $$

the cross-covariance in the group-process is

$$ {}_{x^*y^*}\gamma_i = r_i^{-1} \, {}_{xy}\gamma + A_i \, (r_i)^{-2} \, {}_{xy}\gamma' \qquad (4.2.91) $$

where A_i is as already defined in (4.2.72) (See also § 3.3.3). For the case ${}_x\sigma={}_y\sigma=\sigma$

$$ {}_{x^*y^*}\gamma_i = {}_x\sigma^2 \, r_i^{-1} [{}_{xy}\rho + A_i r_i^{-1} \, {}_{xy}\rho'] \qquad (4.2.92) $$

CONDITIONS OF STATIONARITY OF THE GROUP-PROCESS

Let us now summarize the results for Gaussian processes and draw some conclusions. We will consider the effect of grouping in the simplest case in which the bivariate individual-process $\{X_i Y_i\}$ is jointly stationary, ${}_x\mu, {}_y\mu$ are the stationary means, ${}_x\sigma^2$, ${}_y\sigma^2$ the stationary variances ${}_x\gamma={}_x\rho_x\sigma^2$, ${}_y\gamma={}_y\rho_y\sigma^2$ the stationary covariances, and ${}_{xy}\gamma = {}_{xy}\rho_x\sigma_y\sigma$ the stationary cross-covariances. The conditions under which the group-process is also stationary are summarized here.

Case of sums

Given the hypothesis that $\{X_i\}$ is Gaussian and stationary we have that $\{X_i^*\}$ is Gaussian and

a) stationary in mean if $r_i=r$ for each i with mean

$$ {}_{x^*}\mu = r \, {}_x\mu \qquad (4.2.93) $$

If in addition the individual-process is locally covariant

b) stationary in variance if $r_i = r$ and $A_i = A$ (a constant) for each i, with variance

$$ {}_{x^*}\sigma^2 = r \, {}_x\sigma^2 \, [\, 1 + A \, r^{-1} \, {}_x\rho] \qquad (4.2.93.a) $$

c) stationary in covariance if $t_{il}=t$ (a constant such that $t \leq r_i r_l$) for each i and l, with covariance

$$ {}_{x^*}\gamma = t \, {}_x\rho_x\sigma^2 \qquad (4.2.94) $$

If alternatively the individual-process is uniformly covariant

b') stationary in variance if $r_i=r$ for each i, with variance

$$ {}_{x^*}\sigma^2 = r \, {}_x\sigma^2 \, [\, 1 + (r-1) \, {}_x\rho] \qquad (4.2.95) $$

c') stationary in covariance if $r_i r_l = r^*$ (a constant), and in particular if $r_i r_l = r^2$, for each i and l, with covariance

$$_{X^*}\gamma = r^2 \ _X\rho_X\sigma^2 \tag{4.2.96}$$

If the bivariate process $\{X_iY_i\}$ is locally covariant, then the group-process is
d) stationary in cross-covariance if A_i=A (a constant) and r_i=r for each i, with cross-covariance

$$_{X^*Y^*}\gamma = r_X\sigma_Y\sigma\,[_{XY}\rho + A\,r^{-1}\ _{XY}\rho'] \tag{4.2.97}$$

If alternatively the individual bivariate process is uniformly covariant, then the process is
d') stationary in cross-covariance if r_i=r for each i, with cross- covariance

$$_{X^*Y^*}\gamma = r\ _X\sigma_Y\sigma\,[_{XY}\rho + (r-1)\ _{XY}\rho'] \tag{4.2.98}$$

Case of mean
$\{X_i^*\}$ is Gaussian and
a) stationary in mean <u>always</u> with

$$_{X^*}\mu = {_X\mu} \tag{4.2.99}$$

If in addition the individual-process is locally covariant
b) stationary in variance if r_i =r and A_i = A (a constant) each i, with variance

$$_{X^*}\sigma^2 = r^{-1}\,_X\sigma^2\,[\,1 + A_i r_i^{-1}\ _X\rho] \tag{4.2.99.a}$$

c) stationary in covariance if $t_{il}/(r_i r_l)=t^*$ (a constant) for each i and l, with stationary covariance

$$_{X^*}\gamma = t^*\ _X\rho_X\sigma^2 \tag{4.2.100}$$

If alternatively the individual-process is uniformly covariant
b') stationary in variance when r_i=r with variance

$$_{X^*}\sigma^2 = r^{-1}\,_X\sigma^2\,[\,1 + (r-1)\ _X\rho] \tag{4.2.101}$$

c') stationary in covariance <u>always</u> with stationary covariance

$$_{X^*}\gamma = {_X\gamma} = {_X\rho_X\sigma^2} \tag{4.2.102}$$

When the individual-process is locally covariant the bivariate process $\{X^*Y^*\}$
d) stationary in cross-covariance if r_i=r and A_i=A (a constant) for each i with cross-covariance

$$ {}_{X^*Y^*}\gamma = r^{-1}{}_X\sigma_Y\sigma[{}_{XY}\rho + A\,r^{-1}\,{}_{XY}\rho'] \qquad (4.2.103) $$

When the individual-process is uniformly covariant $\{X^*Y^*\}$ is
d') stationary in cross-covariance if $r_i=r$ with stationary cross-covariance

$$ {}_{X^*Y^*}\gamma = r^{-1}{}_X\sigma_Y\sigma[{}_{XY}\rho + (r-1)\,{}_{XY}\rho'] \qquad (4.2.104) $$

Having obtained the group-process distribution in terms of the individual-process distribution for Gaussian processes we can now move to extend these results to a wider class of processes.

4.2.4. Moments of linear transformations of a process

In the previous paragraphs we derived the group-process distribution when the individual-process has a known multivariate normal distribution. In particular we examined the stationary case.
When we cannot use the Gaussian hypothesis either (a) we must be ready to accept that the individual-process distribution at least tends to normality, or (b) we have to confine our attention to obtaining the lower moments of the group-process given the moments of the individual-process and, if possible, try to fit one of the most common tabulated distributions. In this section the second approach will be followed in order to derive the first four univariate moments, the covariance and the cross-covariance of the group-process given the lower moments of the individual-process distribution.

Suppose we are given a random process $\{X_j\}, j=1,\ldots,n$, which is stationary up to fourth order and has the stationary moments

$$ E(X_j) = {}_X\mu \qquad (4.2.105) $$

$$ E[(X_j - {}_X\mu)^2] = {}_X\sigma^2 \qquad (4.2.106) $$

$$ E[(X_j - {}_X\mu)(X_k - {}_X\mu)] = {}_X\gamma_{jk} = {}_X\rho_X\sigma^2 \qquad (4.2.107) $$

The process may be either locally or uniformly covariant. Consider then the m real-valued functions, defined for short:

$$ x_i^* = x_i^*(X_1,\ldots X_n) = g(\mathbf{X}) \qquad (4.2.108) $$

If the function g has finite derivatives we have

$$ g_j'({}_X\mu) = \partial g(\mathbf{X})/\partial X_j \qquad j=1,\ldots,n \qquad (4.2.109) $$

evaluated at the point ${}_X\mu$. If we now expand $g(x)$ around the mean according to the Taylor's series expansion we have

$$g(\mathbf{X}) = g({}_X\mu) + \sum g_j'(\mu)(X_j - {}_X\mu) + \sum g_j''({}_X\mu)(X_j - {}_X\mu)^2 + \ldots \\ \ldots + O(n^{-1}) \qquad (4.2.110)$$

where $O(n^{-1})$ are the terms of order n^{-1} (Kendall & Stuart, 1969; Vol.I; p.231).
In the case in which we are most interested the functions are first order polynomials. Therefore

$$g'' = g''' = \ldots = 0 \qquad (4.2.111)$$

and the previous Taylor series formula yields

$$g(\mathbf{X}) \approx g({}_X\mu) + \sum g_j'({}_X\mu)(X_j - {}_X\mu) \qquad (4.2.112)$$

This formula allows us to derive all the univariate moments of the group-process in terms of the moments of the individual-process simply by observing that

$$E\{X^{*r}\} = E\{[g(\mathbf{X})]^r\} = E\{[g({}_X\mu) + \sum g_j'({}_X\mu)(X_j - {}_X\mu)]^r\} \qquad (4.2.113)$$

Similarly for the joint moments we can define the two real functions

$$x_i^* = x_i^*(X_1, \ldots, X_n) = g(\mathbf{X}) \\ x_l^* = x_l^*(X_1, \ldots, X_n) = h(\mathbf{X}) \qquad (4.2.114)$$

and find the covariance (Kendall & Stuart, 1969; p.232)

$$\mathrm{Cov}\{g(\mathbf{X}), h(\mathbf{X})\} = {}_{X*}\gamma_{il} \\ = \sum g_j'({}_X\mu) h_j'({}_X\mu)\, {}_X\sigma_j^2 + \sum_{(2)} g_j'({}_X\mu) h_k'({}_X\mu)\, {}_X\gamma_{jk} + O(n^{-1}) \qquad (4.2.115)$$

This approach will be now exploited to obtain lower moments of the group-process in terms of the moments of the individual-process. The two cases of grouping through sums and through averaging will be developed separately.

AGGREGATION THROUGH SUMS

Let us start by considering the case of aggregating the individual-process variables $\{X_j\}$, defined above, into the group-process $\{X^*_i\}$ through a simple sum, that is to say

$$X_i^* = g(\mathbf{X}) = \sum_{j \in G(i)} X_j \qquad (4.2.116)$$

with all the symbols previously introduced. In this case, following Formula (4.2.113), we have for the **mean**

$$ {}_{X*}\mu_i = E(X_i^*) = E[g(\mathbf{X})] = \sum_{j \in G(i)} {}_X\mu_j \\ = r_i\, {}_X\mu \qquad (4.2.117)$$

For the **second moment**, putting ${}_{X}\mu=0$ without loss of generality, we have according t Formula (4.2.113)

$$
\begin{aligned}
{}_{X^*}\sigma^2 &= E(X_i^{*2}) = E\,[g(\mathbf{X})^2] = E\{[\Sigma\ g_j'({}_X\mu)X_j]^2\} \\
&= \Sigma\ \{g_j'({}_X\mu)^2\}\ E(X_j^2) + \Sigma_{(2)}\ g_j'({}_X\mu)g_k'({}_X\mu)\ E(X_jX_k) \\
&= \Sigma\ \{g_j'(\mu)^2\}\ {}_X\sigma_j^2 + \Sigma_{(2)}\ g_j'({}_X\mu)\ g_k'({}_X\mu)\ {}_X\gamma_{jk}
\end{aligned}
\qquad (4.2.118
$$

But in the case of aggregating through sums we have that

$$
g_j' = \begin{cases} 1 & \text{if } j \in G(i) \\ 0 & \text{otherwise} \end{cases} \qquad (4.2.119)
$$

so that

$$
\begin{aligned}
{}_{X^*}\sigma^2 &= \Sigma_{j \in G(i)}\ {}_X\sigma_j^2 + \Sigma_{(2)\ j\neq k \in G(i)}\ {}_X\gamma_{jk} \\
&= r_i\ {}_X\sigma^2 + r_i(r_i - 1)\,{}_X\gamma_{jk}
\end{aligned}
\qquad (4.2.120)
$$

If the individual-process is uniformly covariant we have that ${}_X\gamma_{jk}={}_X\rho\,{}_X\sigma^2$ and

$$
{}_{X^*}\sigma^2{}_i = r_i\ {}_X\sigma^2\,[\,1 + (r_i - 1)\ {}_X\rho] \qquad (4.2.121)
$$

If alternatively the process is locally covariant we have

$$
\begin{aligned}
{}_{X^*}\sigma^2 &= \Sigma_{j \in G(i)}\ {}_X\sigma^2{}_j + \Sigma_{(2)\ j\neq k \in G(i)\ ,\ j \in N(k)}\ {}_X\gamma_{jk} \\
&= r_i\ {}_X\sigma^2 + A_i\ {}_X\gamma
\end{aligned}
\qquad (4.2.121.
$$

For the **third moment** of the univariate distribution we go back to Formula (4.2.113) now setting r=3

$$
E\{[X_i^*]^3\} = E\{[\,g(\mathbf{X})]^3\} = E\{\,[\,\Sigma_{j \in G(i)}g_j'({}_X\mu)\ X_j]^3\}
$$

$$
\begin{aligned}
=E[\,&\Sigma_{j \in G(i)}g_j'^3({}_X\mu)X_j^3 + 3\Sigma_{(2)j\neq k \in G(i)}g_j'^2({}_X\mu)X_j^2\ g_k'({}_X\mu)X_k + \\
&+ \Sigma_{(3)\ j\neq k\neq l \in G(i)}g_j'({}_X\mu)X_jg_k'({}_X\mu)X_k\ g_l({}_X\mu)X_l\ ]
\end{aligned}
$$

$$
\begin{aligned}
=&\Sigma_{j \in G(i)}g_j'^3({}_X\mu)E(X_j^3) + \\
&+3\ \Sigma_{(2)j\neq k \in G(i)}g_j'^2({}_X\mu)g_k'({}_X\mu)E(X_j^2X_k) + \\
&+ \Sigma_{(3)\ j\neq k\neq l \in G(i)}g_j'({}_X\mu)\ g_k'({}_X\mu)\ g_l'({}_X\mu)\ E(X_jX_kX_l)
\end{aligned}
$$

(4.2.122)

But, since $g_j' = g_j'^2 = 1$

$$= \Sigma_{j\,\varepsilon\,G(i)} E(X_j^3) + 3\ \Sigma_{(2)\, j\neq k\,\varepsilon\,G(i)} E(X_j^2 X_k) + \Sigma_{(3)\, j\neq k\neq l\,\varepsilon\,G(i)} E(X_j X_k X_l) \tag{4.2.123}$$

As we said the individual-process is stationary up to the fourth moment. Thus we have

$$E(X_j^3) = E(X^3) = {}_x\mu_{300}$$

$$E(X_j^2 X_k) = E(X^2 X) = {}_x\mu_{210}$$

$$E(X_j X_k X_l) = E(XXX) = {}_x\mu_{111} \tag{4.2.124}$$

and hence

$$E\{[x_i^*]^3\} = r_i\,{}_x\mu_{300} + 3\binom{r_i}{2}2\,{}_x\mu_{210} + \binom{r_i}{3}\,{}_x\mu_{111}$$

$$= r_i\,{}_x\mu_{300} + 3\,r_i\,(r_i-1)\,{}_x\mu_{210} + 6^{-1}\,r_i(r_i-1)(r_i-2)\,{}_x\mu_{111} \tag{4.2.125}$$

This expresses the skewness of the i-th component of the group-process in terms of the lower moments of the individual-process. Note here, incidentally, that in the Gaussian hypothesis ${}_x\mu_{300} = {}_x\mu_{210} = {}_x\mu_{111} = 0$ so that $E(X_i^{*3}) = E(X_j^3) = 0$ which confirms the previous findings. (See § 4.2.3). Note also that $E(X^{*3}) \geq E(X^3)$ (that is the skew is emphasized by grouping) when $\mu_{300} \leq 3r_i\,\mu_{210} + [r_i(r_i-2)/6]\,\mu_{111}$.
In particular the distribution is skewed when $3r_i\,\mu_{210} + [r_i(r_i-2)/6]\,\mu_{111} \geq 0$.
For the **fourth moment** (kurtosis), setting r=4 in Formula (4.2.113) we have

$$E\{[X^*_i]^4\} = E\{[g(\mathbf{X})]^4\} = E\{[\Sigma_{j\,\varepsilon\,G(i)} g_j'({}_x\mu) X_j]^4\}$$

$$\begin{aligned}
&= E\{\Sigma_{j\,\varepsilon\,G(i)}\, g_j'^4({}_x\mu) X_j^4 + \\
&+ 6\,\Sigma_{(2)\, j\neq k\,\varepsilon\,G(i)}\, g_j'^2({}_x\mu) g_k'^2({}_x\mu) X_j^2 X_k^2 + \\
&+ 4\,\Sigma_{(2)\, j\neq k\,\varepsilon\,G(i)}\, g_j'^3({}_x\mu) g_k'({}_x\mu)\, X_j^3 X_k + \\
&+ 12\,\Sigma_{(3)\, j\neq k\neq l\,\varepsilon\,G(i)}\, g_j'^2({}_x\mu) g_k'({}_x\mu) g_l'({}_x\mu)\, X_j^2 X_k X_l + \\
&+ 4\,\Sigma_{(4)\, j\neq k\neq l\neq p\,\varepsilon\,G(i)}\, g_j'({}_x\mu) g_k'({}_x\mu) g_l'({}_x\mu) g_p'({}_x\mu)\, X_j X_k X_l X_p
\end{aligned} \tag{4.2.126}$$

Since $g_j' = g_j'^2 = g_j'^3 = 1$ and, furthermore $E(X^4{}_j) = E(X^4) = {}_x\mu_{4000}$, $E(X_j^2 X_k X_l) = {}_x\mu_{2110}$, $E(X_j^2 X_k^2) = {}_x\mu_{2200}$, $E(X_j^3 X_k) = {}_x\mu_{3100}$, $E(X_j X_k X_l X_m) = {}_x\mu_{1111}$, then from the stationarity of the individual-process, it follows that

$$E\{[x_i^*]^4\} = r_i\, {}_x\mu_{4000} + 6\binom{r_i}{2} 2\, {}_x\mu_{2200} + 8\binom{r_i}{2} {}_x\mu_{3100} +$$

$$+ 12 r_i \binom{r_i-1}{2} 2\, {}_x\mu_{2110} + 4\binom{r_i}{4} {}_x\mu_{1111}$$

$$= r_i\, {}_x\mu_{4000} + 3 r_i (r_i - 1)\, {}_x\mu_{2200} + 4 r_i (r_i - 1)\, {}_x\mu_{3100} +$$
$$+ 6 r_i (r_i - 1)(r_i - 2)\, {}_x\mu_{2110} + 6^{-1} r_i (r_i - 1)(r_i - 2)(r_i - 3)\, {}_x\mu_{1111}$$

(4.2.127)

This expresses the kurtosis of the group-process in terms of the lower moments of the individual-process. Note that the kurtosis is emphasized when ${}_x\mu_{4000} \geq$ $\geq 3 r_i {}_x\mu_{2200} + 4 r_i {}_x\mu_{3100} + 6 r_i (r_i-2) {}_x\mu_{2110} + 6^{-1} r_i (r_i-2)(r_i-3) {}_x\mu_{1111}$.
In particular the process has a positive kurtosis when $3 r_i {}_x\mu_{2200} + 4 r_i {}_x\mu_{3100} + 6 r_i (r_i-2) {}_x\mu_{3110} \leq {}_x\sigma^2$. For the covariance between two random variables of the group-process we have through Formula (4.2.115)

$$_{x^*}\gamma_{i1} \approx \Sigma_j\, g_j'({}_x\mu) h_j'({}_x\mu)\, {}_x\sigma^2_j + \Sigma_{(2) j \neq k\, \varepsilon\, G(i)} g_j'({}_x\mu)\, h_k'({}_x\mu)\, {}_x\gamma_{jk} \qquad (4.2.128)$$

In the case of sums we have

$$g_j'({}_x\mu) = \begin{cases} 1 & \text{if } j\, \varepsilon\, G(i) \\ 0 & \text{otherwise} \end{cases} \qquad (4.2.129)$$

and

$$h_k'({}_x\mu) = \begin{cases} 1 & \text{if } k\, \varepsilon\, G(1) \\ 0 & \text{otherwise} \end{cases} \qquad (4.2.130)$$

If the groups are not partially overlapping, which is the case we are most interested in, we also have

$$g_j'({}_x\mu) h_k'({}_x\mu) = \begin{cases} 1 & \text{if } j\, \varepsilon\, G(i) \text{ and } k\, \varepsilon\, G(1) \\ 0 & \text{otherwise} \end{cases} \qquad (4.2.131)$$

Therefore

$$_{x^*}\gamma_{i1} = \Sigma_{j\, \varepsilon\, G(i)} \Sigma_{k\, \varepsilon\, G(i)}\, {}_x\gamma_{jk} \qquad (4.2.132)$$

and (as in the Gaussian hypothesis, see § 4.2.3) the result is that the spatial autocorrelation between two random variables of the group-process equals the sum of

covariances between the pair of random variables in the individual-process taken one from group i and the other from group l.
If the individual-process is uniformly covariant with ${}_{x}\gamma_{jk} = {}_{x}\gamma = {}_{x}\rho_{x}\sigma^2$ we have

$$ {}_{x^*}\gamma_{il} = r_i r_l \, {}_{x}\rho_{x}\sigma^2 \qquad (4.2.133)$$

If, alternatively the local covariance property holds we have

$$ {}_{x^*}\gamma_{il} = t_{il} \, {}_{x}\rho_{x}\sigma^2 \qquad (4.2.134)$$

where t_{il}, $(t_{il} \leq r_i r_l)$ (as in § 4.2.3) is the number of non-zero covariances at the individual-process level.
Consider now a second individual stationary process $\{Y_j\}$, j = 1,...,n such that $\{X_j Y_j\}$ is a bivariate process jointly stationary up to fourth order, with stationary cross-covariance ${}_{xy}\gamma = {}_{xy}\rho_{x}\sigma_{y}\sigma$ and stationary lagged cross-covariance ${}_{xy}\gamma' = {}_{xy}\rho'_{x}\sigma_{y}\sigma$.
Furthermore consider for Y* the same grouping role as for X* that is

$$ \mathbf{Y^*} = \mathbf{GY} \qquad (4.2.135)$$

the cross-covariance between the group-process $\{X_i^*\}$ and the group-process $\{Y_i^*\}$ i = 1,...,m, is given by Formula (4.2.115)

$$ {}_{x^*y^*}\gamma_{ii} = \Sigma_{j \in G(i)} \, {}_{xy}\gamma_{jj} + \Sigma_{(2)\, j \neq k \in G(i)} \, {}_{xy}\gamma_{jk} \qquad (4.2.136)$$

Again if the individual-process is jointly uniformly covariant we have

$$ {}_{x^*y^*}\gamma_{ii} = r_i \, {}_{xy}\gamma + r_i(r_i - 1) \, {}_{xy}\gamma' \qquad (4.2.137)$$

If we have, instead, a local covariant process, Formula (4.2.115) becomes

$$ {}_{x^*y^*}\gamma_{ii} = r_i \, {}_{xy}\gamma + A_i \, {}_{xy}\gamma' \qquad (4.2.138)$$

where A_i (see § 4.2.3 and § 2.3) is the number of non-zero cross-covariances involved in the sum i.e. the total number of neighbours of all the j ε G(i).

AGGREGATION THROUGHT AVERAGING

Let us now consider, following the lines of the previous section, the case in which a group-process arises from an averaging rather than a sum of the individual-process. Going back to Formula (4.2.113) we have for the **mean**

$$ {}_{x^*}\mu_i = E(X^*_i) = E[g(\mathbf{X})] = \Sigma_{j \in G(i)} (r_i)^{-1} \, {}_{x}\mu_i = {}_{x}\mu \qquad (4.2.139)$$

For the **second moment** we go back to Formula (4.2.113) where now

$$g_j' = \begin{cases} r_i^{-1} & \text{if } j \in G(i) \\ 0 & \text{otherwise} \end{cases} \tag{4.2.140}$$

so that

$$_X{*}\sigma_i^2 = (r_i)^{-2} \Sigma_{j \in G(i)} {}_X\sigma_j^2 + (r_i)^{-2} \Sigma_{(2)\, j \neq k \in G(i)} {}_X\gamma_{jk} \tag{4.2.141}$$

If all the pairs of random variables are equally correlated within the group i we hav $_X\gamma_{jk} = {}_X\gamma = {}_X\rho\, {}_X\sigma^2$, and hence

$$_X{*}\sigma_i^2 = r_i^{-1}\ {}_X\sigma^2\ [\,1 + (r_i - 1)\, {}_X\rho] \tag{4.2.142}$$

If alternatively the process is locally covariant we have:

$$_X{*}\sigma^2_i = r_i^{-1}\ {}_X\sigma^2\, [\,1 + r_i^{-1} A_i\ {}_X\rho] \tag{4.2.143}$$

For the **skewness** starting from Formula (4.2.113) we have now that $g_j' = r_i^{-1}$; $g_j'^2 = r_i^{-2}$; $g_j'^3 = r_i^{-3}$; $g_j'^4 = r_i^{-4}$ so that

$$E(X_i^{*3}) = (r_i^{-3})[\Sigma_{j \in G(i)} E(X_j^3) + 3\ \Sigma_{(2)\, j \neq k \in G(i)} E(X_j^2 X_k) + \Sigma_{(3)\, j \neq k \neq l \in G(i)} E(X_j X_k X_l)\,] \tag{4.2.144}$$

and, from the stationarity of $\{X_i\}$ up to fourth-order, we get

$$r_i^{-2}\, {}_X\mu_{300} + 3 r_i^{-2}(r_i - 1)\, {}_X\mu_{210} + 6^{-1} r_i^{-2}(r_i - 1)(r_i - 2)\, {}_X\mu_{111} \tag{4.2.145}$$

which is positive when

$$_X\mu_{300} > 3(r_i + 1)^{-1}\, {}_X\mu_{210}\ 6^{-1}(r_i - 2)(r_i + 1)^{-1}\, {}_X\mu_{111}$$

Finally for the **kurtosis** of the group-process, going back to Formula (4.2.113) substituting the values of $g_j'^r$, and from the stationarity of $\{X_i\}$,we have

$$\begin{aligned} E(X_i^{*4}) = {} & r_i^{-3}\, {}_X\mu_{4000} + 3\, r_i^{-3}\, (r_i - 1)\, {}_X\mu_{2200} + \\ & + 4\, r_i^{-3}\, (r_i - 1)\, {}_X\mu_{3100} + 6\, r_i^{-3}\, (r_i - 1)(r_i - 2)\, {}_X\mu_{2110} + \\ & + 6^{-1}\, r_i^{-3}\, (r_i - 1)(r_i - 2)(r_i - 3)\, {}_X\mu_{1111} \end{aligned} \tag{4.2.146}$$

which is positive when

$$3(r_i^3-1)^{-1}(r_i-1)_x\mu_{2200}+4(r_i-1)(r_i^3-1)^{-1}{}_x\mu_{3100}+$$
$$+6(r_i-1)(r_i^3 1)^{-1}(r_i-2)_x\mu_{2110}$$
$$+6^{-1}(r_i-1)(r_i^3-1)^{-1}(r_i-2)(r_i-3) \leq 3_x\sigma^4$$

For the covariance between the two random variables of the group-process we have, from Formula (4.2.115)

$$\begin{aligned} &{}_{x^*}\gamma_{il} \\ &=\Sigma_{j\,\varepsilon\, G(i)} g_j'({}_x\mu)h_j'({}_x\mu){}_x\sigma_j^2 \\ &+\Sigma_{(2)\, j\neq k\,\varepsilon\, G(i)}\, g_j'({}_x\mu)\, h_k'({}_x\mu){}_x\gamma_{jk} \end{aligned} \qquad (4.2.147)$$

In this case

$$g_j'({}_x\mu) = \begin{cases} r_i^{-1} & \text{if } j\ \varepsilon\ G(i) \\ 0 & \text{otherwise} \end{cases} \qquad (4.2.148)$$

and

$$h_k'({}_x\mu) = \begin{cases} r_i^{-1} & \text{if } j\ \varepsilon\ G(i) \\ 0 & \text{otherwise} \end{cases} \qquad (4.2.149)$$

and from the hypothesis of non-overlapping between the groups

$$g_j'({}_x\mu)h_k'({}_x\mu) = \begin{cases} (r_i r_l)^{-1} & \text{if } j\ \varepsilon\ G(i) \text{ and } k\ \varepsilon\ G(l) \\ 0 & \text{otherwise} \end{cases} \qquad (4.2.150)$$

Hence

$${}_{x^*}\gamma_{il} = (r_i r_l)^{-1}\, \Sigma_{(2)\, j\neq k\,\varepsilon\, G(i)}\, {}_x\gamma_{jk} \qquad (4.2.151)$$

In the case of uniform covariance ${}_x\gamma_{jk}={}_x\gamma={}_x\rho_x\sigma^2$ so that

$${}_{x^*}\gamma_{il} = {}_x\rho_x\sigma^2 \qquad (4.2.152)$$

In the alternative hypothesis, of local covariance, we have

$${}_{x^*}\gamma_{il} =(r_i r_l)^{-1}\, t_{il}\, {}_x\rho_x\sigma^2 \qquad (4.2.153)$$

where t_{il} has the known meaning of the number of non-zero covariances between random variables taken one in group i and the other in group l.

Finally, considering the bivariate jointly stationary individual-process $\{X_jY_j\}$ $j=1,\dots,n$, the cross-covariance between the group-process $\{X_i*\}$ and the group-process $\{Y_i*\}$ $i=1,\dots,m$, is given by

$$
\begin{aligned}
&{}_{x*y*}\gamma_{ii} \\
&= \Sigma_{j\varepsilon G(i)}\, g_j'({}_x\mu)\, h_j'({}_x\mu)\, {}_x\sigma_j{}^2 \\
&+ \Sigma_{(2)j \neq k\varepsilon G(i)}\, g_j'({}_x\mu)\, h_k'({}_x\mu)\, {}_x\gamma_{jk}
\end{aligned}
\qquad (4.2.154)
$$

In our case $g_j'h_j'=0$ always, and

$$
g_j'({}_x\mu)h_k'({}_x\mu) = \begin{cases} r_i{}^{-2} & \text{if } j \text{ and } k\ \varepsilon\ G(i) \\ 0 & \text{otherwise} \end{cases} \qquad (4.2.155)
$$

so that

$$
{}_{x*y*}\gamma_{ii} = r_i{}^{-2}\, \Sigma\, \Sigma_{\ j \neq k\ \varepsilon\ G(i)}\ {}_{xy}\gamma_{jk} \qquad (4.2.156)
$$

This factors into

$$
{}_{x*y*}\gamma_{ii} = r_i{}^{-2}\ \{\Sigma_{j\ \varepsilon\ G(i)}\ {}_{xy}\gamma_{jj}\ +\ \Sigma_{(2)\ j \neq k\ \varepsilon\ G(i)}\ {}_{xy}\gamma_{jk}\} \qquad (4.2.157)
$$

In the case where the individual-process is stationary and locally covariant with ${}_{xy}\gamma_{jk}={}_{xy}\rho\, {}_x\sigma\, {}_y\sigma$ if $j\ \varepsilon\ N(k)$ and zero otherwise

$$
{}_{x*y*}\gamma_i = r_i{}^{-1}\ {}_{xy}\gamma + A_i\, r_i{}^{-2}\ {}_{xy}\gamma' \qquad (4.2.158)
$$

where A_i ($A_i \leq r_i{}^2$) is now a known quantity. In the case of uniform covariance within the group we have instead

$$
{}_{x*y*}\gamma_i = r_i{}^{-1}\,{}_{xy}\gamma + (r_i-1)\, r_i{}^{-1}\ {}_{xy}\gamma' \qquad (4.2.159)
$$

With the results of this section we conclude the study of the group-process characteristic in terms of the individual-process characteristic.
The next section is devoted to dealing with inference in the case of stochastic spatial processes.

4.3 INFERENCE ON STOCHASTIC SPATIAL PROCESSES

4.3.1 Random sampling and non-random sampling

We stated at the beginning of this chapter that our aim is to describe a set of spatial data as a finite realization of a process of dependent random variables. Having formally defined in **S** 4.1 a random process in two-dimensions, we have to face the problem of inferring its unknown parameters given one drawing of a sample from its joint probability distribution. For the case of classical inference random sampling allows a sample to be drawn from a very special stationary stochastic process i.e. one in which the random variables are mutually independent. In general, however, the random variables of a stochastic process of the kind we are most interested in are not independent. This is the reason why we need a framework for analysing non-random samples. This is the task of this section (The general references for this paragraph may be found in Yaglom, 1962; Hannan, 1970; Bartlett, 1966; Spanos, 1986; Grenader, 1950).

In the **random sample** case it is typically assumed that the generating process $\{X_i\}$ $i=1,\dots,n$, is constituted by random components which are

(a) Normal (see Section 4.2.3)
(b) Independent (see Section 4.1.2)
(c) Identical (i.e. their moments are all equal)

For this case we may specify a reference situation as the following **SCHEME I** [assumptions (a), (b), (c)]:

$$\{X_i\} = \begin{pmatrix} X_1 \\ X_2 \\ \\ \\ X_n \end{pmatrix} \approx \left(\begin{matrix} \mu \\ \mu \\ .. \\ .. \\ \mu \end{matrix} \quad ; \quad \begin{matrix} \sigma^2 \;\; 0 \;\ldots\ldots\ldots\ldots 0 \\ 0 \;\; \sigma^2 \;\; 0 \ldots\ldots\ldots 0 \\ \ldots\ldots\ldots\ldots\ldots\ldots\ldots \\ \ldots\ldots\ldots\ldots\ldots\ldots 0 \\ 0 \ldots\ldots\ldots\ldots\ldots 0 \;\; \sigma^2 \end{matrix} \right) \qquad (4.3.1)$$

It may sometimes be enough to maintain the random scheme that only hypothesis (c) of identical distribution is relaxed. This allows the variance to vary from one random variable to another (heteroskedastic case). In this case we have the following **SCHEME II** [assumptions (a), (b)]:

$$\{X_i\} = \begin{pmatrix} X_1 \\ X_2 \\ \\ \\ X_n \end{pmatrix} \approx \left(\begin{matrix} \mu \\ \mu \\ .. \\ .. \\ \mu \end{matrix} \quad ; \quad \begin{matrix} \sigma_1^2 \;\; 0 \;\ldots\ldots\ldots\ldots 0 \\ 0 \;\; \sigma_2^2 \;\; 0 \ldots\ldots\ldots 0 \\ \ldots\ldots\ldots\ldots\ldots\ldots\ldots \\ \ldots\ldots\ldots\ldots\ldots\ldots 0 \\ 0 \ldots\ldots\ldots\ldots\ldots 0 \;\; \sigma_n^2 \end{matrix} \right) \qquad (4.3.2)$$

However in a general **non-random** scheme we have to relax all three hypotheses. If we retain the assumption of normality, for the sake of simplicity, we have **SCHEME III** [assumptions (a)]:

$$\{X_i\} = \begin{pmatrix} X_1 \\ X_2 \\ \\ \\ X_n \end{pmatrix} \approx \begin{pmatrix} \mu_1 & & \sigma_1^2 \ \gamma_{12} \cdots\cdots \gamma_{1n} \\ \mu_2 & & \gamma_{21} \ \sigma_2^2 \ \gamma_{23} \cdots \gamma_{2n} \\ \cdot\cdot & ; & \cdots\cdots\cdots\cdots \\ \cdots & & \cdots\cdots\cdots \gamma_{n-1\,n} \\ \mu_n & & \gamma_{n1} \cdots\cdots \gamma_{nn-1} \ \sigma_n^2 \end{pmatrix} \tag{4.3.3}$$

When we have only a single sampling experiment at our disposal, as happens almost invariably in geographical analysis, we are forced to assume stationarity in order to have a way out of the impasse of estimating $(n^2 + n)$ unknown moments with only n observations. So retaining now hypothesis (a) and (c) we have **SCHEME IV** [assumptions (a) and (c)]:

$$\{X_i\} = \begin{pmatrix} X_1 \\ X_2 \\ \\ \\ X_n \end{pmatrix} \approx \begin{pmatrix} \mu & & \sigma^2 \ \gamma_{12} \cdots\cdots \gamma_{1n} \\ \mu & & \gamma_{21} \ \sigma^2 \ \gamma_{23} \cdots \gamma_{2n} \\ & ; & \cdots\cdots\cdots\cdots \\ \cdots & & \cdots\cdots\cdots \gamma_{n-1\,n} \\ \mu & & \gamma_{n1} \cdots\cdots \gamma_{nn-1} \ \sigma^2 \end{pmatrix} \tag{4.3.4}$$

Again as in the rest of the book, we may face two types of stationarity
(1) In the local covariance case we have that in the previous scheme

$$\gamma_{ij} = \begin{cases} \gamma & , \text{ if } j \in N(i) \\ 0 & , \text{ otherwise} \end{cases} \tag{4.3.5}$$

with N(i) the previously defined set of neighbours of site i.
(2) In the case of uniform covariance (individuals or totally connected lattices) we have simply

$$\gamma_{ij} = \gamma \qquad \text{each } i,j \tag{4.3.6}$$

Since a sample is one drawing from a joint probability distribution, a sample statistic (e.g. the sample mean) is a random variable whose values vary across samples.
We will now consider the properties of the estimators of the moments of the process when the sample is drawn from a spatial process.
In spite of some exact results, the sampling theory of discrete spatial series, as generated by stochastic processes, is still largely in an early stage of development, and in what follows it will be necessary to present some asymptotic results. Furthermore the restriction to the Gaussian stationary case appears the only viable possibility, since the treatment of processes such as in scheme II, or, even, non-Gaussian processes, requires well specified *ad hoc* models.

It should be noted that studies concerning processes recorded on continuous space (Matern, 1960) as well as the studies concerned with processes laid on regular lattices (Whittle, 1954; Martin, 1979; Haining, 1977) which are at a considerably more advanced stage of development, are not taken into account because they do not contribute to the central concern of this book.

THE PROPERTY OF ERGODICITY

All the methods we employ to estimate the mean, the variance and the covariance of a stationary process using observations from a single realization are derived from the basic assumption of **ergodicity**, a concept borrowed from statistical mechanics. Ergodicity is a property of a process which enables us to replace the ensemble averages with the corresponding spatial averages. Ergodicity implies strong stationarity, although the contrary is not always true.
All the results that follow are valid only if the process under consideration is ergodic (For details on ergodicity see for example Doob, 1978).

4.3.2. Estimation of the mean

Let $\{X_i\}$,$i=1,..,n$, be a stationary process with

$$E(X_i) = {}_X\mu$$

$$E[(X_i - {}_X\mu)^2] = {}_X\sigma^2 \qquad (4.3.7)$$

$$E[(X_i - {}_X\mu)(X_j - {}_X\mu)] = \gamma = \sigma^2 \rho$$

Let also $x_1,....,x_n$ be a set of observations of the process. The sample mean is

$${}_Xm = n^{-1} \sum x_i \qquad (4.3.8)$$

We have

$$E({}_Xm) = E(n^{-1} \sum x_i) = n^{-1} \sum E(x_i) = n^{-1} n \mu = \mu \qquad (4.3.9)$$

which shows that ${}_Xm$ is an **unbiased** estimate of μ.
Furthermore we have

$$E[({}_Xm - {}_X\mu)^2] = E[n^{-1}\sum (x_i - {}_X\mu)]^2 = n^{-2} E[\sum (x_i - {}_X\mu)]^2$$

$$= n^{-2} E[\sum (x_i - {}_X\mu)^2 + \sum_{(2)} (x_i - {}_X\mu)(x_j - {}_X\mu)]$$

$$= n^{-2}[\sum E(x_i - {}_X\mu)^2 + \sum_{(2)} E(x_i - {}_X\mu)(x_j - {}_X\mu)] \qquad (4.3.10)$$

and, for the hypothesis of stationarity

$$n^{-2}\ [n\ {}_X\sigma^2 + \Sigma_{(2)}\ {}_X\gamma] \quad (4.3.11)$$

In the case of uniform covariance the summation in (4.3.11) extends to n(n-1) cross-products , so that

$$E[\ ({}_Xm - {}_X\mu)^2] = {}_X\sigma^2\ [n^{-1} + n^{-1}(n-1)\ {}_X\rho\ ] \quad (4.3.12)$$

Contrastingly, in the case of local covariance we have

$$E[\ ({}_Xm - {}_X\mu)^2] = {}_X\sigma^2\ [n^{-1} + n^{-2}A\ {}_X\rho\ ] \quad (4.3.13)$$

where, as already stated elsewhere in this book, A is the connectedness of the system a a whole (See § 3.3.2).
Thus the sample mean, although an unbiased estimate of μ, has a variance now given b (4.3.12) or (4.3.13) rather then by $n^{-1}{}_X\sigma^2$ as in the case of random sampling (se Kendall and Stuart, 1969; Vol I; p.230). This value is obviously attained when ${}_X\rho = 0$.

For the **consistency** of ${}_Xm$ (remembering that an unbiased estimator is consistent i its variance goes to zero as the sample size goes to infinity) we have, in the uniform covariance hypothesis :

$$\lim_{n\to\infty}\ E[\ ({}_Xm - {}_X\mu)^2] =$$
$$\lim_{n\to\infty}\ {}_X\sigma^2\ [n^{-1} + n^{-1}(n-1)\ {}_X\rho\ ] \simeq {}_X\gamma \quad (4.3.14)$$

The estimator ${}_Xm$ is, therefore, inconsistent.
In contrast, in the case of local covariance

$$\lim_{n\to\infty}\ E[\ ({}_Xm - {}_X\mu)^2]$$
$$\lim_{n\to\infty}\ {}_X\sigma^2\ [n^{-1} + n^{-2}A\ {}_X\rho\ ] = 0 \quad (4.3.15)$$

since $A \le n^2$ always (See § 3.3.2). The rate of convergence depends on how large A i compared with n^2 or, in other words it depends on the average connectedness of th spatial system (see § 3.3.2).
For example in the *line transect case* (see § 3.3.2) we have that A = 2 (n - 1)
Therefore

$$An^{-2} = 2\,(n-1)\,n^{-2} \simeq 2n^{-1} \quad (4.3.16)$$

that converges rapidly to zero. Therefore the lower the connectedness of the spati system, the more reliable is the estimate of the mean in terms of efficiency an consistency.
Let us now set

$$\lambda = E[\ ({}_Xm - {}_X\mu)^2] \quad (4.3.17)$$

This term embodies the effect of the spatial configuration of data on the estimate of the mean. When ${}_x\rho = 0$, of course, no spatial effect occurs and we are again in the classical scheme I (see 4.3.1) as $\lambda = {}_x\sigma^2 n^{-1}$.

4.3.3. Estimation of the variance and the covariance

If we have as a known that $E(X_i) = \mu$, we can define the sample variance by

$$ {}_x s^2 = n^{-1} \Sigma x_i^2 \tag{4.3.18}$$

and the sample covariance by

$$ {}_x c_u = [n(n-1)]^{-1} \Sigma_{(2)} x_i x_j \tag{4.3.19}$$

for the case of uniform covariance. For the case of local covariance we have

$$ {}_x c_L = A^{-1} \Sigma_{(2)} w_{ij} x_i x_j \tag{4.3.20}$$

where w_{ij} are the elements of the connectivity matrix of the spatial system (See § 2.3.2).

It is easy to see that in both cases ${}_x s^2$, c_u and c_L are unbiased estimates of σ^2 and γ. However if we do not know the value of the mean of the process, the estimators are all biased. This can be demonstrated as follows:

In the hypothesis of Formula 4.3.7 we define the **sample variance** as

$$ {}_x\hat{s}^2 = (n-1)^{-1} \Sigma (x_i - {}_x m)^2 \tag{4.3.21}$$

where the symbol ^ refers to sample statistics.

This can also be written as

$$ {}_x\hat{s}^2 = (n-1)^{-1} \Sigma (x_i - {}_x\mu)^2 - (n-1)^{-1} n ({}_x m - {}_x\mu)^2 \tag{4.3.22}$$

whence

$$ \begin{aligned} E({}_x\hat{s}^2) &= (n-1)^{-1} \Sigma [E(x_i - {}_x\mu)^2] - n(n-1)^{-1} E[({}_x m - {}_x\mu)^2] \\ &= (n-1)^{-1} n\, {}_x\sigma^2 - n(n-1)^{-1} E[({}_x m - {}_x\mu)^2] \end{aligned} \tag{4.3.23}$$

and, recalling Formula (4.3.12) we have in the uniform covariance case

$$E({}_X\hat{S}^2) = {}_X\sigma^2[1 - {}_X\rho] \qquad (4.3.24)$$

which is biased, the bias depending on the absolute level of the spatial autocorrelation ${}_X\rho$ (when ${}_X\rho = 0$, of course $E({}_X\hat{S}^2) = \sigma^2$ as in the random case).
In the local covariance hypothesis, from (4.2.23) and recalling (4.3.13) we have

$$E({}_X\hat{S}^2) = {}_X\sigma^2 [\ 1 - A\, n^{-1} (n - 1)^{-1}\, {}_X\rho\,] \qquad (4.3.25)$$

and although biased ${}_Xs^2$ is in this case at least asymptotically unbiased (see Spanos, 1986; p.247) as

$$\lim_{n\to\infty} \{[\,{}_X\sigma^2 - An^{-1}(n-1)^{-1}{}_X\gamma\,] - {}_X\sigma^2\}\sqrt{n} = 0 \qquad (4.3.26)$$

We now consider the **sample autocovariance** which, in the case of uniform covariance and E(X) not known, is defined by

$${}_X\hat{C}u = [n(\ n - 1)]^{-1}\ \Sigma_{(2)}\,(x_i - {}_Xm)(x_j - {}_Xm) \qquad (4.3.27)$$

Consider the identity

$$\Sigma_{(2)}\ (x_i - {}_X\mu)(x_j - {}_X\mu)$$

$$= \Sigma_{(2)}\ [\ (x_i - {}_Xm) + ({}_Xm - {}_X\mu)]\ [\ (x_j - {}_Xm) + ({}_Xm - {}_X\mu)]$$

$$= \Sigma_{(2)}\ (x_i - {}_Xm)\ (x_j - {}_Xm) + n\,(n - 1)\,({}_Xm - {}_X\mu)^2 \qquad (4.3.28)$$

Thus

$$E({}_X\hat{C}u)$$

$$= [n(n-1)]^{-1}E[\Sigma_{(2)}(x_i - {}_Xm)(x_j - {}_Xm) - n(n-1)({}_Xm - {}_X\mu)^2] \qquad (4.3.29)$$

and, recalling (4.3.12)

$$E({}_x\hat{c}_U) = {}_x\gamma - {}_x\sigma^2 n^{-1} - (n-1) n^{-1} {}_x\gamma = {}_x\sigma^2 n^{-1} [{}_x\rho - 1] \tag{4.3.30}$$

Define now the sample autocovariance in the case of local covariance as (Whittle, 1954)

$${}_x\hat{c}_L = A^{-1} \Sigma_{(2)} w_{ij} (x_i - {}_xm)(x_j - {}_xm) \tag{4.3.31}$$

With an argument similar to the case of $\hat{c}_U$ we have

$$E({}_x\hat{c}_L) = A^{-1} E[\Sigma_{(2)} w_{ij} (x_i - {}_x\mu)(x_j - {}_x\mu) - A({}_xm - {}_x\mu)^2]$$

$$= {}_x\gamma - E({}_xm - {}_x\mu)^2 \tag{4.3.31.a}$$

Recalling (4.3.13) this is equal to

$${}_x\gamma - {}_x\sigma^2 n^{-1} - A n^{-2} {}_x\gamma =$$
$${}_x\sigma^2 n^{-1}[(n^2 - A)n^{-1} {}_x\rho - 1] \tag{4.3.32}$$

so that, although biased, ${}_x\hat{c}_L$ is at least asymptotically unbiased being

$$\lim_{n\to\infty} \sqrt{n}[(n^2 - A) n^{-2} {}_x\gamma - {}_x\gamma - {}_x\sigma^2 n^{-1}] = 0 \tag{4.3.33}$$

VARIANCE AND COVARIANCE OF THE s^2 c_U AND c_L

For the calculation of the variance and covariances of s^2 and c in the uniform and the local covariance hypothesis, we need to take into consideration fourth order moments of X_i. Hence it is worthwhile, at this stage, remembering that in a Gaussian process :

$$E[(X_i - {}_x\mu)^3] = 0$$

$$E[(X_i - {}_x\mu)^4] = 3\,{}_x\sigma^4$$

$$E[(X_i - {}_x\mu)^2 (X_i - {}_x\mu)^2] = (1 + 2\,{}_x\rho^2)\,{}_x\sigma^4 \tag{4.3.34}$$

Since the concern of this section is with second order properties of the estimates, we will simplify the notation by assuming that the mean μ is known a priori and set to zero. As a consequence we now have in the case of uniform covariance, the unbiased estimate of the variance given in (4.3.18)

$$ {}_{x}s^2 = n^{-1} \Sigma x_i{}^2 \tag{4.3.35}$$

We have also

$$E({}_{x}s^4) = n^{-2}\, E\,[\,(\,\Sigma x_i{}^2)^2]$$

$$= n^{-2}\, E\,[\,\Sigma\; x_i{}^4 + \Sigma_{(2)}\, x_i{}^2 x_j{}^2]$$

$$= n^{-2}\,[\,\Sigma\, E(x_i{}^4) + \Sigma_{(2)}\, E(x_i{}^2 x_j{}^2)] \tag{4.3.36}$$

and, recalling (4.3.34) we have

$$n^{-2}\,[\,3n\, {}_{x}\sigma^4 + n\,(n-1)(1+2\,{}_{x}\rho^2)\,{}_{x}\sigma^4\,]$$

$$= 3n^{-1}\, {}_{x}\sigma^4 + n^{-1}\,(n-1)(1+2\,{}_{x}\rho^2)\,{}_{x}\sigma^4 \tag{4.3.37}$$

Thus the **variance of $_{x}s^2$** is

$$E\,[\,({}_{x}s^2 - {}_{x}\sigma^2)^2] = E({}_{x}s^4) - {}_{x}\sigma^4$$

$$= n^{-1}\, {}_{x}\sigma^4\,[\,3 + (n-1)\,(1+2\,{}_{x}\rho^2) - n\,]$$

$$= 2\,n^{-1}\, {}_{x}\sigma^4\,[\;1 + (n-1)\,{}_{x}\rho^2\,] \tag{4.3.38}$$

In the local covariance hypothesis, we have analogously

$$E({}_{x}s^4) = n^{-2}\,[\,\Sigma\, E(x_i{}^4) + \Sigma_{(2)}\, w_{ij}\, E(x_i{}^2 x_j{}^2)]$$

$$= n^{-2}\,[\,3n\, {}_{x}\sigma^4 + A\,(1+2\,{}_{x}\rho^2)\,{}_{x}\sigma^4\,] \tag{4.3.39}$$

And, as a consequence

$$E\,[\,({}_{x}s^2 - {}_{x}\sigma^2)^2] = E({}_{x}s^4) - {}_{x}\sigma^4$$

$$= n^{-1}\, {}_{x}\sigma^2\,[3-n + A\,n^{-1}\,(1+2\,{}_{x}\rho^2)] \tag{4.3.40}$$

For the **variance of c_u**, we have that from (4.3.19)

$${}_{x}c_u = [n\,(n-1)]^{-1}\, \Sigma_{(2)}\, x_i x_j$$

is an unbiased estimate of γ in the uniform covariance case, and

$$E({}_xc_u{}^2) = [\, n\,(n - 1)]^{-2}\, E\,[\, \Sigma_{(2)}\, x_ix_j]^2$$

$$= [n\,(n - 1)\,]^{-2}\; E\,[\Sigma_{(2)}\, x_i{}^2x_j{}^2 + \Sigma_{(4)}\, x_ix_jx_kx_l\,]$$

$$= [n\,(n - 1)\,]^{-2}\; [\Sigma_{(2)}\, E(\, x_i{}^2x_j{}^2) + \Sigma_{(4)}\; E(x_ix_jx_kx_l\,)]$$

(4.3.41)

We now apply an exact result for quadrivariate distributions (See Isserlis, 1918; p.137)

$$E(X_iX_jX_kX_l)=E(X_iX_j)E(X_kX_l) + E(X_iX_l)E(X_kX_j) + E(X_iX_k)E(X_jX_l) + \\ + \kappa_4\,[(l - i),(j - i),(i + k - l - j)] \qquad (4.3.42)$$

where $\kappa_4[(l-i)\,,(i-j),(i+k-l-j)]$ is the fourth cumulant of the distribution of $X_iX_jX_kX_l$ (Kendall and Stuart, 1969). However in a Gaussian process all the joint distributions are multivariate normal (see § 4.2.3) hence

$$\kappa_4[(l-i)\,,(i-j),(i+k-l-j)] \;=\; 0 \qquad (4.3.43)$$

Furthermore for the uniform stationarity assumption

$$E(X_iX_jX_kX_l\,) \;=\; 3\; E(X_iX_j)^2 = 3\;{}_x\gamma^2 \qquad (4.3.44)$$

Whence

$$[n\,(n-1)]^{-2}\left[n\,(n-1)\,(1+2\;{}_x\rho)\,{}_x\sigma^4 + 3\binom{n(n-1)}{2}\,{}_x\gamma^2\right]$$

(4.3.45)

Being $\quad [n(n-1)]^2=\binom{n(n-1)}{1}+2\binom{n(n-1)}{2}\quad$ the terms involved in the summation in Formula (4.3.41). Hence

$$E({}_xc_u{}^2)$$

$$=[n(n-1)]^{-2}[n(n-1)(1+2\;{}_x\,\rho^2)_x\,\sigma^4+3n(n-1)(n^{\,2}-n-1)_x\,\gamma^2]$$

$$= [n\,(n - 1)]^{\,-1}[(1 + 2\,{}_x\,\rho^2)\,{}_x\,\sigma^4 + 3\;(n^{\,2} - n - 1)\,{}_x\,\gamma^2]$$

(4.3.46)

Thus the variance of c_u is

$$E[({}_xc_u - {}_x\gamma)^2] = E({}_xc_u^2) - {}_x\gamma^2$$

$$=[n(n-1)]^{-1}\,{}_x\sigma^4\,[1 + 2\,{}_x\rho^2 + 3\,(n^2-n-1)\,{}_x\rho^2 - n(n-1)\,{}_x\rho^2\,]$$

$$=[n(n-1)]^{-1}\,{}_x\sigma^4[1 + 2\,{}_x\rho^2 + 3n^2\,{}_x\rho^2 - 3n\,{}_x\rho^2 - 3\,{}_x\rho^2 - n^2\,{}_x\rho^2 + n\,{}_x\rho^2]$$

$$=[n(n-1)]^{-1}\,{}_x\sigma^4\,[1 + (2n^2 - 2n - 1)\,{}_x\rho^2] \quad (4.3.47)$$

which is approximately equal to

$${}_x\sigma^4\,\{\,[n\,(n-1)]^{-1} + 2\,{}_x\rho^2\,\} \quad (4.3.48)$$

With analogous reasoning we now consider the unbiased estimate of γ in the local covariance hypothesis that recalling (4.3.20) is

$${}_xc_L = A^{-1}\,\Sigma_{(2)}w_{ij}\,x_ix_j \quad (4.3.49)$$

We have

$$E({}_xc_L^2) = A^{-2}\,E(\,\Sigma_{(2)}w_{ij}\,x_ix_j\,)$$

$$= A^{-2}\;E\,[\Sigma_{(2)}\,w_{ij}\,x_i^2x_j^2 + \Sigma_{(4)}\;w_{ij}w_{kl}x_ix_jx_kx_l\,]$$

$$= A^{-2}\;[\Sigma_{(2)}\;w_{ij}\,E(\,x_i^2x_j^2) + \Sigma_{(4)}\,w_{ij}w_{kl}\,E(x_ix_jx_kx_l\,)]$$

$$= A^{-2}\,[\,A\,(\,1 + 2\,{}_x\rho^2)\,{}_x\sigma^4 + 3\,{}_x\gamma^2\,\Sigma_{(4)}\,w_{ij}w_{kl}] \quad (4.3.50)$$

And noting that

$$\Sigma_{(4)}\,w_{ij}w_{kl} = \Sigma_{(2)}\;w_{ij}\,\Sigma_{(2)}\;\;w_{kl} = A^2 \quad (4.3.51)$$

we have

$$E\,({}_xc_L{}^2\,) = A^{-1}\,(\,1 + 2\,{}_x\rho^2)\,{}_x\sigma^4 + 3\,{}_x\gamma^2 \quad (4.3.52)$$

Thus the **variance of c_L** is

$$E[({}_xc_L - {}_x\gamma)^2] = E({}_xc_L{}^2) - {}_x\gamma^2$$

$$= {}_x\sigma^4\,[A^{-1}(1 + 2\,{}_x\rho^2) + 3\,{}_x\rho^2 - {}_x\rho^2\,]$$

$$= {}_x\sigma^4\,[A^{-1} + 2A^{-1}\,{}_x\rho^2 + {}_x\rho^2\,]$$

$$= {}_x\sigma^4\,A^{-1}\,[\,1 + (1 + A)\,2\,{}_x\rho^2\,] \qquad (4.3.53)$$

which approximately yields

$$ {}_x\sigma^4\,[\,A^{-1} + 2\,{}_x\rho^2\,] \qquad (4.3.54)$$

Finally for the **covariance between s² and c** we have the approximate results (Priestley, 1981; p.326)

$$\mathrm{Cov}\,[\,{}_xs^2, {}_xc_U] \approx 2\,n^{-1}\,{}_x\sigma^2{}_x\gamma + 2\,(\,n - 1)\,{}_x\gamma^{\,2} \qquad (4.3.55)$$

and

$$\mathrm{Cov}\,[\,{}_xs^2, {}_xc_L] \approx 2\,n^{-1}\,{}_x\sigma^2{}_x\gamma + 2\,A\,n^{-1}\,{}_x\gamma^{\,2} \qquad (4.3.56)$$

4.3.4. Estimation of the spatial autocorrelation

The sampling properties of the estimate of ρ are complicated, but, for large samples, we may obtain some approximate expressions. Let us define the estimate of ρ in the uniform covariance hypothesis as

$$ {}_xR_u = (n-1)^{-1}\Sigma_{(2)}\,x_ix_j\,(\Sigma x_i{}^2)^{-1} \qquad (4.3.57)$$

assuming once again that μ is known and set to zero.
We have for the **expected value of R**

$$E({}_xR_u) = E[(n-1)^{-1}\Sigma_{(2)}x_ix_j(\Sigma x_i{}^2)^{-1} \qquad (4.3.58)$$

We now recall a standard result for ratios of random variables (Yule and Kendall, 1957; p.329)

$$E(UW^{-1})$$
$$= E(U)[E(W)]^{-1}\{1 - \mathrm{Cov}(U,W)[E(U)E(W)]^{-1} + \mathrm{Var}(W)^2\,E(W)^{-2}\}$$

$$(4.3.59)$$

Applying (4.3.59) to (4.3.58) we have

$$E({}_xR_u) = {}_x\gamma\,{}_x\sigma^{-2}\{1 - {}_x\gamma^{-1}{}_x\sigma^{-2}\,Cov({}_xc_u,{}_xs^2) + {}_x\sigma^{-4}\,Var({}_xs^2)^2\} \tag{4.3.60}$$

and, assuming that c_u and s^2 are at least asymptotically uncorrelated, this approximately gives

$$E({}_xR_u) \approx {}_x\rho\,\{1 - 2n^{-1}[{}_x\rho^2(n-1)+1]\} \tag{4.3.61}$$

For the **variance of R_u** we remember that (Yule and Kendall, 1957; p.329)

$$Var(UW^{-1})$$
$$= Var(U)\,E(U)^{-2} + Var(W)\,E(W)^{-2} - 2\,Cov\,(U,W)\,E(U)^{-1}E(W)^{-1} \tag{4.3.62}$$

and, assuming again that $Cov\,(s^2,c_u)$ is asymptotically zero, we have

$$Var({}_xR_u) = Var\,({}_xs^2)\,{}_x\sigma^{-4} + Var({}_xc_u)\,{}_x\gamma^{-2}$$

$$= 2n^{-1}[{}_x\rho^2(n-1)+1] + {}_x\rho^{-2}[n(n-1)]^{-1} + 2 \tag{4.3.63}$$

using the approximation of Formula (4.3.48). This is asymptotically equal to

$$Var({}_xR_u)\ \underline{\alpha}\ 2\,({}_x\rho^2 + 1) \tag{4.3.64}$$

In the case of local covariance the estimator of ${}_x\rho$ is

$${}_xR_L = nA^{-1}\Sigma_{(2)}w_{ij}\,x_ix_j\,(\Sigma x_i^2)^{-1} \tag{4.3.65}$$

with expectation approximately given by

$$E({}_xR_L) = n\,A^{-1}\ E[\Sigma_{(2)}w_{ij}\ x_ix_j\,(\Sigma x_i^2)^{-1}]$$

$$= nA^{-1}E[\Sigma_{(2)}w_{ij}\,x_ix_j]E[(\Sigma x_i^2)^{-1}]\,[1 + Var(\Sigma x_i^2)^2\ E(\Sigma x_i^2)^{-2}]$$

$$= n\,A^{-1}{}_x\rho\ [1 + 2\,n^{-1}\,{}_x\sigma^2\,({}_x\rho^2\ A + 1)] \tag{4.3.66}$$

For the **variance of R_L** we have, analogously to (4.3.63)

$$Var({}_XR_L) = Var\,({}_Xs^2)\,{}_X\sigma^{-4} + Var({}_Xc_L)\,{}_X\gamma^{-2} =$$

$$2\,n^{-1}\,[\,A\,{}_X\rho^2 + 1\,] + {}_X\rho^{-2}\,A^{-1} + 2 \qquad (4.3.67)$$

using the approximation of (4.3.54). This is asymptotically equal to the constant 2.

4.3.5. Estimation of the moments of bivariate processes

Discussion has been confined so far to the analysis of a single process, but simultaneous relations can also be considered. This allows the cross-correlations between processes to be investigated. These processes give rise to similar problems to those for a univariate process. However because of their higher complexity, the moments of the bivariate processes are not derived here. (See Koopmans, 1950 for the time series analogue ; See also Wold, 1953).

Examples of the approximate moments of the estimates of the cross-covariance and of the lagged cross-covariance of a process of dependent random components can be found in the literature in the special case of a time series (See Bartlett, 1966; p.362; Koopmans, 1950; Wold, 1953).

4.3.6. Conclusion

In this paragraph we derived some properties of the estimates of the moments of spatial Gaussian processes in the hypothesis of local and of uniform covariance (See § 4.2.3). The general conclusion that can be drawn is that the reliability of the estimates in terms of unbiasedness, efficiency and consistency, depends on the degree of connectedness of the spatial system (see § 2.3.2). The lower the connectedness the higher is the reliability of the estimates. This can be seen heuristically by considering that the classical inference random sampling case can be thought as an hypothetical scheme where the connectedness between the observations is zero.

4.3 SUMMARY AND CONCLUSION

In this Chapter we have described a spatial series as a finite realization of a bidimensional stochastic process. Furthermore we have given a formal description of the case in which we have data aggregated at two different levels of spatial resolution (e.g. towns and counties, or also individuals and counties). In these cases we are usually interested in knowing the characteristics of what we call the *individual-process* having at our disposal only observations drawn from the *group-process*. This is the case, for instance, of the *ecological fallacy* problem in which we are interested in drawing inference on the individuals' behaviour, which is not observable, having in hand only spatially grouped data. Moreover for the case of the *scale problem*, we are interested in explaining the reason why the pattern of a geographical distribution changes when we adjust the level of resolution. Finally when we want to perform a *zoning* of a spatial system we desire to choose, among different alternatives, that zoning method which maintains the closest approximation, with the highest level of information, of the original ungrouped data.

In all these cases the interest is to establish a relationship from the group-process observations which leads to estimates of the individual-process characteristics. In this chapter we have established the inverse relationship that leads, from a certain individual-process and a grouping method to a group-process.
The analysis of the effects of shifting the level of spatial resolution (or, which is formally the same, shifting from individuals to areas) has been made with regard to:
1) the probability density function of the two processes when the distribution of the individual-process is completely known (§ 4.2.2),
2) In particular when the distribution of the processes is Gaussian (§ 4.2.3), and
3) the lower moments of the process without specifying the distributional form (§ 4.2.4).
We have seen in this way that the major problems which arises are that
a) Stationarity of the individual-process does not imply stationarity of the group-process.
b) The problem of loss of the stationarity by shifting level is more serious in the case where we aggregate through sums rather than through averages .
c) In contrast, it is less serious when we group with an even number of individuals in each group, for example when dealing with regular square lattice grid.
d) The problem is more serious in the case of *uniform covariance* that in the case of *local covariance* processes.
e) The variance is more seriously affected by grouping than the mean.
f) The covariance between the random components of the same process and the cross-covariance between the two processes increases with the size of the groups and with the level of connectedness of the study-area.

When we accept stationarity of the individual-process and when we can specify a plausible pattern of spatial dependence at the individual-process level, the analysis of this chapter enables us to establish a way to use more efficiently the observations drawn from the group-process to draw inferences on the individual-process. These properties will be used in the following chapters. Finally, the last section of this chapter was devoted to discussing the properties of statistical estimate of non-random samples.

5. Univariate problems: the modifiable areal unit problem

5.1. INTRODUCTION

We have already discussed in Chapters 1-3 the problem of the modifiable unit. The difficulties created by modifiable units are noted by Yule and Kendall (1957; p.310) and for spatial problems have been termed, following Openshaw (1977) the "modifiable areal unit problem". It is worth recalling here that the spatial problem consists of two aspects: the first concerns the different results obtained with the same set of data grouped at different scale levels (e.g. individuals, counties, regions). This is referred to as *scale problem*. The second considers the variability of results not due to variations in the size of the areas, but rather to their shape and it is therefore referred to as *aggregation problem*. In Chapter 4 we put forward a methodological framework that enables us to discuss the modifiable areal unit problem in the context of the theory of stochastic processes. In the present chapter we introduce the detailed analysis of the problem.

We will keep the distinction between scale (which is analysed in § 5.2 and 5.3) and aggregation problems (§ 5.4). The problem of grouping individuals in areal units is not considered here and is put off to chapter 7 where we deal with the ecological fallacy problem. For this reason we will assume uniformly throughout this chapter that the "local covariance" hypothesis applies. (see § 4.2).

Finally the concern of this chapter is restricted to univariate spatial series. The problem of the modification to the correlation between two or more processes, as the result of changing the unit of analysis is left to the last chapters of this book (See Chapters 6 - 7).

5.2 THE SCALE PROBLEM : REGULAR CASE

5.2.1. Introduction

The scale problem in geography may arise for many different reasons. A particular instance occurs when analysing settlement pattern by superimposing over the study area regular grid of contiguous quadrats (Greig-Smith, 1952). The problem then arises of the choice of quadrat size. In fact it is recognised that "Changing the quadrat size will usually affect the degree of spatial dependence between quadrats and the larger the quadrat the weaker the dependence will be " (Cliff and Ord, 1981; p.92, p.99).

More generally when analysing maps in human geography, we have the problem that the observations are recorded in irregular collecting areas of different size and shape and at different level of resolution. In these conditions the results of any statistical analysis depend very much on our choice of the level of resolution, while a certain degree of objectivity is required especially when we are interested in inter-regional comparison.

The aim of this section, and of the following (§ 5.3), is to examine the scale problem in both the regular and the irregular case in order to a) give it a formal description in terms of the analysis of Chapter 4, b) describe formally the relationship between scale and spatial dependence, and c) to propose different approaches.
It is perhaps necessary to remark here that our approach differs substantially from the one adopted by Moellering and Tobler (1970) to study hierarchical variances. In fact Moellering and Tobler studied the variance of a spatial series by assuming that the series itself generated by the convolution of more than one process each exerting its influence at a different level of spatial resolution or wave length. In contrast, we consider the spatial data as generated by a single process of which we want to study the modifications when we change the level of resolution.

5.2.2. Regular square lattice grid

Let us start by considering the case in which we are given a geographical map of objects or individuals, such as , for instance, the distribution of firms in a region.
In order to investigate the spatial arrangement of the objects one common procedure is to superimpose over the study area a grid of regular lattices and then to count the number of individuals for each lattice. A problem with this approach is the choice of the grid size. As already stated in this book the empirical findings of many authors (notably Cliff and Ord, 1981) show that the level of spatial dependence between cells is related to the size of the cells themselves. In particular "the larger the areas, the weaker the dependence will be". The common sense explanation is that the elements of interaction tend to cancel out at a regional scale where the elements of reaction to common factors tend to prevail.
In this section we will try and give a formal explanation to this size-dependence relationship (for a different but related approach see Whittle, 1962).
We will not consider here the first stage of the cell count when we count the number of individuals in each area. To do so we could follow two different approaches. Following a first approach we should assume the number of individuals in each cell as given and attach to each of them a certain discrete distribution incorporating some contagion effect (see Feller, 1943; Neyman, 1939) to indicate, for example, the presence or the absence of the characteristic under study. In this way, using the framework depicted in Chapter 4 and in particular in Section 4.2.4, it is possible to derive the areal distribution given the individuals' distribution. For instance we could derive the areal distribution of unemployed people given the probability of being unemployed for the single individual and given the spatial distribution of individuals.
Alternatively we could assume that the number of individuals or objects in each cell is itself a random variable so that the areal distribution of a certain variable would be the outcome of two compounded random effects: (1) A first effect which embodies the uncertainty we have about the number of individuals in each cell. This number should follow some discrete contagious distribution such as the negative binomial (See Fisher, 1941; Ord, 1972). (2) A second effect which embodies the uncertainty about the value assumed by the variable under study by each of the individuals. In this case we could again exploit the framework of Section 4.2.4, but with the further complexity involved by the fact that the summation index follows a probability distribution.
This approach (although promising of fruitful results) is not undertaken here because it goes beyond the scope of the book.

In contrast we will consider a simpler situation in which we are already given a cell counts map, for which we assume a known joint distribution, and we want to study the modification of the moments of the process as a function of the size of the cells.
In rather formal terms, following the notation of Chapter 4, we define an *individual-process* $\{X_i\}$ $i=1,....,n$ laid down on a regular grid of $\sqrt{n} \times \sqrt{n}$ and such that

$$E(X_i) = \mu$$
$$E[(X_i - \mu)^2] = \sigma^2$$
$$E[(X_i-\mu)(X_j-\mu)] = \gamma \quad \text{when } j \in N(i) \text{ and 0 otherwise} \qquad (5.2.1)$$

Only the local covariance hypothesis will be considered here since the case of totally connected lattices has little practical relevance. We will also assume that the individual-process is Gaussian (this is a simplification as in most of the cases, the distribution is likely to be discrete). As a result second-order properties will describe the process fully and second-order stationarity implies strong stationarity.
Let us further consider a grouping of the process $\{X_i\}$ at a higher hierarchical level to produce a "group-process" $\{X_i^*\}$ such that

$$X_i^* = \Sigma_{j \in G(i)} X_j \qquad (5.2.2)$$

To obtain the moments of the group-process in terms of the moments of the individual-process using the results of Chapter 4, we need to obtain some characteristic values of the lattice. (See § 3.3). First of all we suppose that the grouping is performed in such a way that at each stage each group contains the same number of cells r (the "quadtree" structure shown in Figure 5.2.1). Therefore we have

$$r_i = r = n/m \qquad \text{for each } i \qquad (5.2.3)$$

where m is the number of groups formed and r is such that $r \geq 2$.
For the study of the connectedness of the lattice in hand (see § 3.3.2) we have to assume a certain definition of neighbours. We will assume in the remainder of the discussion the "rook's case" definition of neighbours (See Cliff and Ord, 1981), which is shown in Figure 5.2.2.
It is easy to see in a regular square lattice (like the one in Figure 5.2.1) with the rook's case definition of neighbours, that the level of connectedness is

$$A = 4n - 4\sqrt{n} \qquad (5.2.4)$$

where the second term in the right hand side considers the joins disregarded because of the "boundary-effect" (Griffith, 1985).
Analogously the connectedness within group i (see § 3.3.3) is given by

$$A_i = 4r_i - 4\sqrt{r_i} = 4r - 4\sqrt{r} \qquad (5.2.5)$$

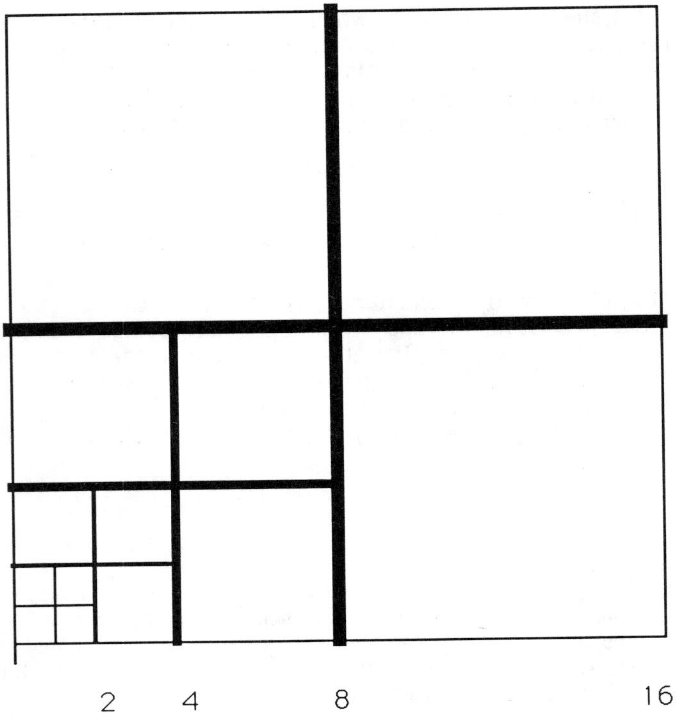

Figure 5.2.1: A "quadtree" structure: Higher order levels are defined as a function of lower order levels (Cliff & Ord, 1981; p.123).

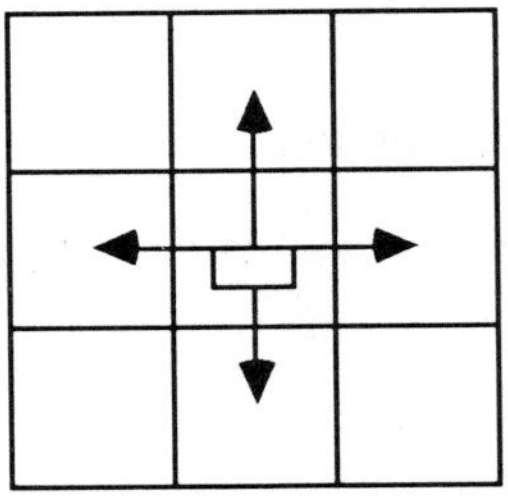

Figure 5.2.2 : Rook's case definition of neighbours (Cliff-Ord ,1981)

and the total "within group" connectedness of the system is

$$\Sigma A_i = m\, A_i = m\,(4r - 4\sqrt{r}) = 4n - 4m\sqrt{r} \quad , \quad \text{each } i \qquad (5.2.6)$$

Hence the total "between groups" connectedness at an individual-process level, remembering Formula (3.3.21), is given by

$$\begin{aligned} \Sigma_{(2)}\, t_{il} &= A - \Sigma A_i \\ &= 4n - 4\sqrt{n} - (4n - 4m\sqrt{r}) \\ &= 4m\sqrt{r} - 4\sqrt{n} \end{aligned} \qquad (5.2.7)$$

Finally the value of t_{il} (as defined in § 3.3.3) is the number of non zero-covariances at the individual-process level between two adjacent groups i and l. In our case this is equal to

$$t_{il} = 2\sqrt{r} \qquad \text{each } i \text{ and } l \qquad (5.2.8)$$

This is easy to see from Figure 5.2.3.
The previous conditions of constancy in the values of r_i, A_i, and t_{il} are enough to ensure that the group-process is still stationary if the individual-process is stationary (see §. 4.2.3). We now have all the elements required to investigate the modification of the moments of the joint distribution of the process as a function of the size of the areas. Consistently with the rest of the book we will examine separately the case in which we simply <u>sum</u> the cells into larger cells, and the case in which we <u>average</u> among them to obtain a higher level of hierarchy.

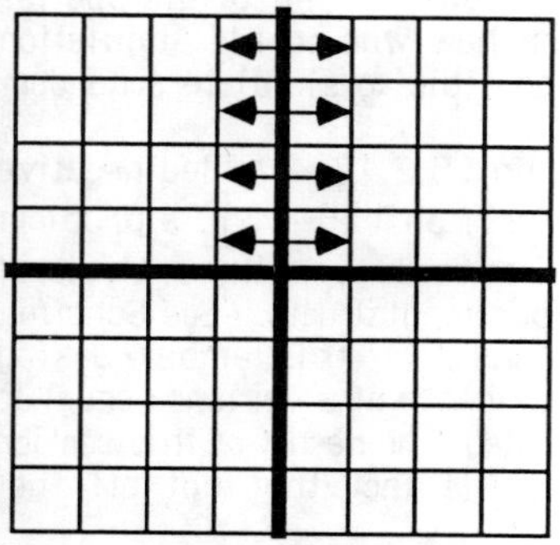

Figure 5.2.3 : Between groups connectedness. Arrows indicate the value of t_{il}. In this case t_{il}=8.

CASE OF SUMS

In the most usual situation of aggregation through sums we have for the mean of the resulting group-process $\{X_i^*\}$ defined as in (5.2.2):

$$_{X^*}\mu = r\ _X\mu \qquad (5.2.9)$$

Thus the mean increases proportionally to the size of the areas. For the variance of the group-process we have

$$_{X^*}\sigma^2 = {}_X\sigma^2\ r\ [\ 1 + r^{-1}\ A_i\ _X\rho\ ] \qquad (5.2.10)$$

and, if the rook's case definition of neighbours holds,we have

$$_{X^*}\sigma^2 = {}_X\sigma^2\ r\ [\ 1 + r^{-1}\ (4r - 4\sqrt{r})\ _X\rho\ ] \qquad (5.2.11)$$

First of all we need to obtain a non-negativity condition on $_{X^*}\sigma^2$ which implies

$$1 + r^{-1}\ (4r - 4\sqrt{r})\ _X\rho \ \geq 0 \qquad (5.2.12)$$

$$_X\rho \ \geq -(4r - 4\sqrt{r})^{-1}\ r \qquad (5.2.13)$$

This provides a lower bound to the value of $_X\rho$. (Note incidentally that when r= 4, as in the example, the lower bound is equal to −0.5). The spatial configuration of data, therefore, imposes a constraint on the maximum negative value of ρ (see Arbia, 1988a). We stated elsewhere in this book (see Section 3.3.2) that an alternative way of describing the spatial configuration of data can be obtained by looking at the principal eigenvector of the connectivity matrix instead of at its connectedness. If we adopt this approach an analogous constraint to that obtained in this section has been found by de Jong, Sprenger and Van Veen (1984). The presence of a lower bound to the spatial autocorrelation has also been found empirically by Openshaw who in his simulation study (Openshaw, 1977; p.18) observed that it was impossible to simulate a random surface with values less than a certain threshold.
The non fulfillment of the constraint expressed in Equation (5.2.13) has led negative estimates of $_X\sigma^2$ in empirical studies (Cliff and Ord, 1981; pp.125-131) a problem which also occurs when applying the standard statistical procedure of the analysis of variance in the estimation of variance components for experimental data. (See Scheffe', 1959; Searle, 1971; p.406-8). When the statisticians face this embarrassing situation the result is usually interpreted as either the evidence of a variance equal to zero, or as the indication that a wrong model has been selected. The result of this section suggest that these nonsense results could be due to the fact that not all the characteristics of the data have been taken into account.
We can now obtain the conditions under which $_{X^*}\sigma^2 \ \geq \ _X\sigma^2$ that is

$$r + (4r - 4\sqrt{r})\ _X\rho \ \geq 1 \qquad (5.2.14)$$

or

$$_X\rho \geq (1-r)(4r-4\sqrt{r})^{-1} \tag{5.2.15}$$

Thus, when (5.2.15) is satisfied the variance increases with r; in contrast, when

$$-r\,(4r-4\sqrt{r})^{-1} \leq {}_X\rho \leq (1-r)(4r-4\sqrt{r})^{-1} \tag{5.2.16}$$

the variance decrease with r. Notice that if r is large $(1-r) \approx -r$ so that the variance increases for each value of $_X\rho$.

As an example consider the case of r=4. In this case the variance of the group-process overcomes the variance of the individual-process when $_X\rho \geq -0.375$. The theoretical behaviour of $_{X*}\sigma^2$ as a function of r is plotted in Figure 5.2.4 for various values of ρ which shows that, when the individual-process possesses a positive autocorrelation, the group-process has a variance higher than in the case of observations generated by a independent process. In contrast, when the autocorrelation in the individual-process is negative the values of the variance are smaller than those obtained in the case of the independent process.

For the definition of the spatial autocovariance we have

$$_{X*}\gamma = 2\sqrt{r}\ {}_X\gamma \tag{5.2.17}$$

Also $_{X*}\gamma \geq {}_X\gamma$, provided that $2\sqrt{r} \geq 1$. This is always true provided that $r > 1$.

Finally for the definition of the spatial autocorrelation coefficient we have

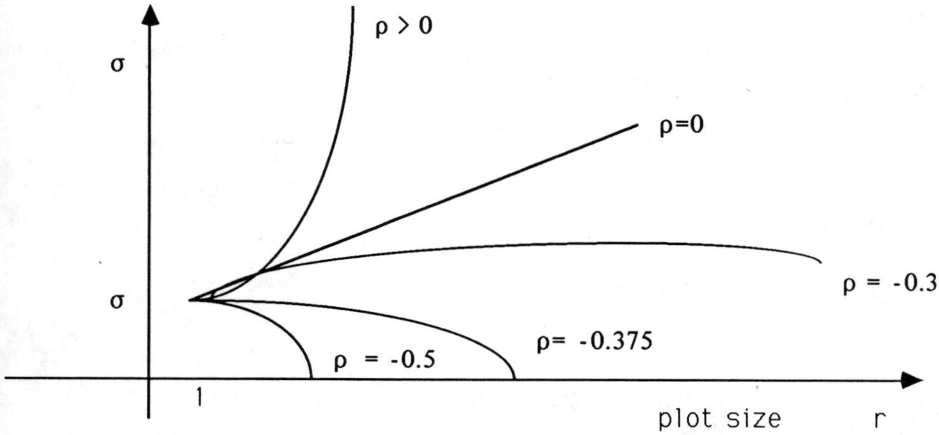

Figure 5.2.4 : Theoretical variance/plot-size relationship for various values of the spatial autocorrelation in the individual process.

$$_{X*}\rho = {}_{X*}\gamma \; {}_{X*}\sigma^{-2} = (2\sqrt{r}\; {}_X\gamma)\{{}_X\sigma^2[r + (4r - 4\sqrt{r})\; {}_X\rho]\}^{-1} \tag{5.2.18}$$

Thus $_{X*}\rho \geq {}_X\rho$ when

$$(2\sqrt{r}\; {}_X\gamma)\; \{{}_X\sigma^2\, [\, r + (4r - 4\sqrt{r})_X\rho]\; \}^{-1} \geq {}_X\gamma\, {}_X\sigma^{-2}$$

$$2\sqrt{r}\;\; [r + (4r - 4\sqrt{r})\, {}_X\rho]^{-1} \;\geq\; 1$$

$$_X\rho \;\leq\; (2\sqrt{r} - r)(4r - 4\sqrt{r})^{-1} \tag{5.2.19}$$

As a result $_X\rho$ increases with the size of the quadrats when (5.2.19) is satisfied. As an example consider again the grouping scheme of Figure 5.2.1 where $r=4$ at each stage of the grouping procedure. In this case the spatial autocorrelation increases when $_X\rho \leq 0$ Thus we have the result that the spatial autocorrelation in the group-process increases if $_X\rho$ is negative and decreases if $_X\rho$ is positive. In other words the spatial autocorrelation is always damped in absolute value by grouping through sums.
This result gives a possible formal explanation of the empirical evidence. For example that given in Cliff and Ord (1981; p. 92; p.125; p.133).

CASE OF AVERAGES

Let us now turn to the case in which we operate a grouping of cells by averaging them into larger zones. Analogously to the previous section we have

$$_{X*}\mu = {}_X\mu \tag{5.2.20}$$

so that the mean of the process is unaffected by shifting the level of resolution of the lattice. For the variance of the process we have now

$$_{X*}\sigma^2 = {}_X\sigma^2 r^{-1}\, [1 + A_i r^{-1}\, {}_X\rho] = {}_X\sigma^2 r^{-1}\, [1 + r^{-1}\, (4r - 4\sqrt{r})\, {}_X\rho] \tag{5.2.21}$$

Similarly to the discussion of the previous section, we have, first of all, to impose a restriction to guarantee the non-negativity of $_{X*}\sigma^2$; thus we have

$$1 + r^{-1}\, (4r - 4\sqrt{r})\, {}_X\rho \;\geq 0$$

$$_X\rho \;\geq\; - r\, (4r - 4\sqrt{r})^{-1} \tag{5.2.22}$$

which provides the negative autocorrelation with the same lower bound as in the case of grouping through sums.
Furthermore the group-process variance is greater or equal to the individual-process variance when

$$r^{-1} + r^{-2}(4r - 4\sqrt{r})\, {}_X\rho \;\geq\; 1$$

or

$$_X\rho \geq r(r-1)(4r-4\sqrt{r})^{-1} \qquad (5.2.23)$$

This is never true as $A_i \leq r_i(r_i - 1)$ (See § 3.3.2). So we have the property that, in grouping through averages, the variance of the process always decreases its value. This is a more general result of the one discussed in Arbia (1986a) for totally connected lattices.

For the covariance we have

$$_{X^*}\gamma = 2\sqrt{r}\, r^{-2}\, {_X\gamma} \qquad (5.2.24)$$

where $r > 1$. Then $_{X^*}\gamma \leq {_X\gamma}$ always.

Finally for the spatial autocorrelation between adjacent zones, we have:

$$_{X^*}\rho = {_{X^*}\gamma}\ {_{X^*}\sigma^{-2}} = 2\sqrt{r}\, r^{-2}\, {_X\gamma}\ \{{_X\sigma^2}\, r^{-2}[r + (4r-4\sqrt{r})\, {_X\rho}]\}^{-1} \qquad (5.2.25)$$

that is $_{X^*}\rho \geq {_X\rho}$ when

$$2\sqrt{r}\,[r + (4r-4\sqrt{r})\, {_X\rho}]^{-1} \geq 1 \qquad (5.2.26)$$

which is the same condition we found in the case of grouping through sums.
So, if we group hierarchically a regular square lattice in equal size groups and we assign to each group the average of the cells contained in it, we have the property that the variance and the covariance of the process behave as monotonic inverse functions of the plot size, and the spatial autocorrelation decreases in absolute value.

The following Table 5.2.1 summarizes the theoretical findings of this section.

Moments	Grouping through sums	Grouping through averages
μ	increase	unaffected
σ^2	increase unless $-0.5 \leq \rho \leq -0.375$	decrease
γ	increase	decrease
ρ	decrease in absolute value	decrease in absolute value

Table 5.2.1: Variation in the moments of a Gaussian stationary process at each step of a hierarchical grouping when four cells are grouped at each level and the rook's case definition of neighbours is assumed.

5.2.3. Data analysis: Matui analysis of settlement pattern

A classic set of data in the analysis of regular grids of contiguous quadrats is the one collected by Matui (1932) and then reanalysed by several authors (Ginsberg, 1952 Moellering and Tobler, 1972; Cliff, Haggett and Frey, 1977; Cliff and Ord, 1973; 1981). In the original work the author counted the number of houses in Hokuno Town Japan, and then divided the map into quadrats each having a side measuring 100 meters by superimposing a regular 30-by-40 grid lattice. Moellering and Tobler (1972), an the authors who subsequently analysed the data, reduced the original lattice to a 32-by-32 regular grid by deleting the last eight columns of the original data and repeating the first two rows at the bottom of the scheme. (See Appendix A.3). This operation is similar to the procedure of mapping a surface onto a torus to correct for edge-effects (See Griffith, 1983). In both cases when the data are generated by a stationary process the operation is permissible in that it does not modify the characteristics of the process. For our purpose we consider, as a starting point, the 32-by-32 version of the lattice. We then aggregate four neighbouring cells at each stage in order to form four more lattices of dimension respectively 16-by-16, 8-by-8, 4-by-4 and 2-by-2 (See Figure 5.2.1). At each level of the hierarchy the variance of the process is estimated (see § 4.3). The value of σ^2 expected after grouping in the case of zero spatial autocorrelation is also computed to allow a comparison. The results are shown in Table 5.2.2 separately for the case of aggregation through sums and aggregation through averages (see also Figure 5.2.5).

It appears that the expected values in the hypothesis of no spatial autocorrelation are always below the empirical values. This indicates the presence in the lattice of a distinctive positive autocorrelation at each level of hierarchy (this result is consistent with the analysis of Cliff and Ord , 1981, p.98).

The analysis can now be taken a step further. In this case we are considering the size of each group is constant (r = 4). Therefore, in the rook's case, if we aggregate through sums we have, recalling Formula (4.2.58) and (5.2.10),

$$_{x^*}\sigma^2 = 4\,_x\sigma^2\ [1 + 2\,\rho] \tag{5.2.27}$$

Let us now call $_{(h)}\sigma^2$ the variance at the h-th level of the hierarchy and, analogously $_{(h)}\rho$ the autocorrelation at the same level of hierarchy. The previous Formula (5.2.27) can be rewritten in a recursive fashion as

Plot size	Number of observations	Grouping through sums		Grouping through averages	
		Empirical $_{x^*}S^2$	Theoretical $_{x^*}\sigma^2=4_x\sigma^2$	Empirical $_{x^*}S^2$	Theoretical $_{x^*}\sigma^2=0.25_x\sigma^2$
1	1024	0.865	0.865	0.865	0.865
4	256	4.273	3.460	0.267	0.216
16	64	21.434	13.840	0.084	0.054
64	16	90.813	55.360	0.022	0.013
256	4	407.000	221.440	0.005	0.003

Table 5.2.2 : Empirical and theoretical values of the variance at various hierarchical levels for Matui data. The theoretical values refer to the case of no spatial autocorrelation (ρ=0.0)

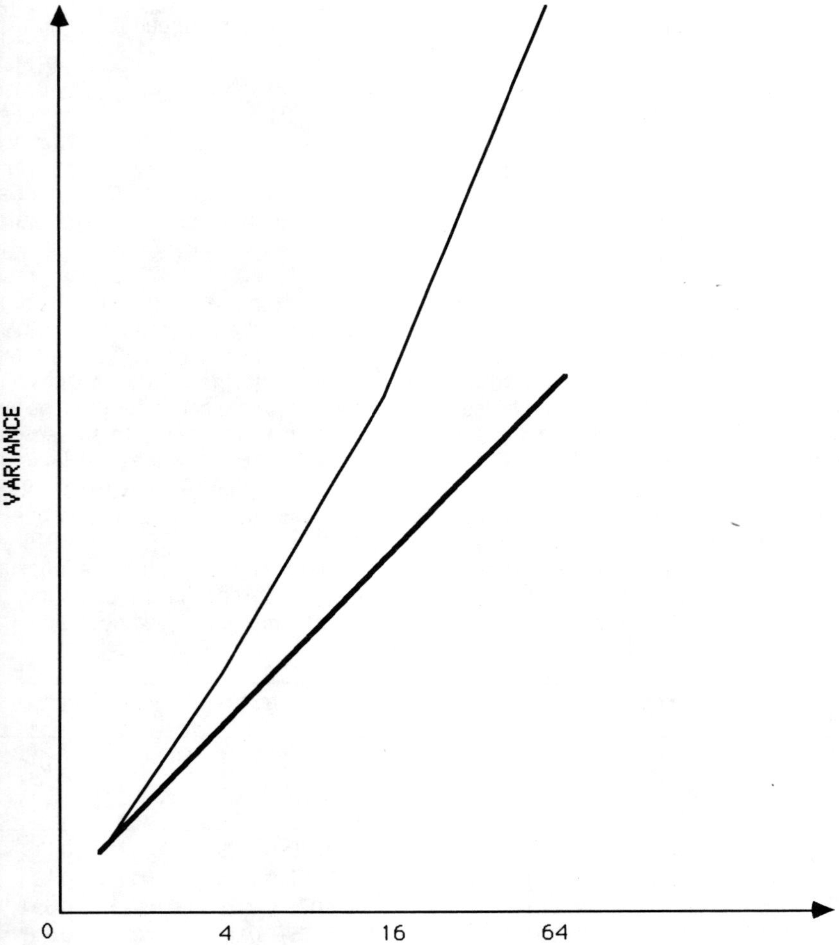

'igure 5.2.5 : Variance / plot-size relationship in the case of grouping through sums, or the Matui data. The bold line indicates the theoretical expectation if no spatial utocorrelation occurs. (Logarithmic scale on both axes).

$$ {}_{(h)}\sigma^2 = 4\,{}_{(h-1)}\sigma^2\,[1 + 2\,{}_{(h-1)}\rho\,] \qquad (5.2.28) $$

it follows that the spatial autocorrelation at the various levels can be approximated by equating the theoretical variance calculated by (5.2.28) and the empirical variance through the formula

$$ {}_{(h-1)}\rho = 0.5\,[0.25\,{}_{(h-1)}\sigma^{-2}\,{}_{(h)}\sigma^2 - 1\,] \qquad (5.2.28.a) $$

An analogous computation can be made in the case of aggregation through averages to give:

$$ {}_{(h)}\sigma^2 = 0.25\,{}_{(h-1)}\sigma^2\,[1 + 2\,{}_{(h-1)}\rho\,] \qquad (5.2.29) $$

and

$$ {}_{(h-1)}\rho = 0.5\,[4\,{}_{(h-1)}\sigma^{-2}\,{}_{(h)}\sigma^2 - 1\,] \qquad (5.2.29.a) $$

The results of the above approach are shown in Table 5.2.3 for the Matui data.
The autocorrelation is positive at each level as expected from the previous analysis and is consistent with the findings of Cliff and Ord (1981, p.98). Furthermore Table 5.2.3 shows the expected tendency of the spatial autocorrelation to diminish in absolute value as the size of the quadrats increases. The approximations of ρ are consistent in the two cases of aggregation through sums and averages. The larger fluctuations in the case of aggregation through averages is due to the computer approximation when, for large r, σ^2 becomes very small. Furthermore the estimate of the variance, and hence of ρ, become more and more unreliable when the number of observations diminishes due to the reduction in the number of degrees of freedom.
The analysis of Table 5.2.3 is an attempt of estimating the value of the spatial autocorrelation of processes examined at different scales by observing the behaviour of the variances at each level showing more explicitly the information already contained in Table 5.2.2.

		Aggregation through sums			Aggregation through averages		
Level (h)	Number of observ.	Theoretical $_{(h)}\sigma^2$	Empirical $_{(h)}\sigma^2$	$_{(h)}\rho$	Theoretical $_{(h)}\sigma^2$	Empirical $_{(h)}\sigma^2$	$_{(h)}\rho$
1	1024	3.46+6.92ρ	4.237	0.117	0.216+0.432ρ	0.267	0.118
2	256	17.092+34.18ρ	21.434	0.127	0.067+0.133ρ	0.084	0.127
3	64	85.736+171.47ρ	90.813	0.029	0.021+0.042ρ	0.022	0.024
4	16	363.252+726.50ρ	407.000	0.060	0.0055+0.011ρ	0.005	0.018

Table 5.2.3: Approximation of the spatial autocorrelation at various scales of the quadrat count of houses in Hokuno Town, Tonami Plain, Japan (Source Matui, 1932).

ıe results of the analysis appear comforting in confirming our theoretical pectations. It has to be emphasized, however, that the procedure gives a good proximation only when the individual-process is stationary.

2.4. Data analysis: Mercer and Hall plots of grain

second set of data that we want to examine is the one collected and studied by Mercer d Hall (1911) (See Appendix A.4). This set of data has been reanalysed several times different authors (Whittle, 1954; Patankar, 1954; Ripley, 1981)
ercer and Hall collected the weight of the yields of grain and straw, expressed in ɔunds, as they occurred in a field divided into 500 approximately regular cells each ot measuring 11 ft by 10.82 ft. There were 25 plots in the West-East direction and 0 plots in the South-North direction.
ɔr the purpose of the present analysis we consider only the plots of grain. ɹrthermore we delete the last 4 columns and the last 9 rows in order to obtain a 16-y-16 grid. We then aggregate four neighbouring cells at each stage following the ouping scheme of Figure 5.2.1 and obtain three extra lattice grid of dimension 8-by-, 4-by-4 and 2-by-2. The previously described approach is then followed by ɔmputing the variance of the plots at each stage of the hierarchy, aggregating the plots ɔth through summation and through averages. The empirical variances is then ɔmpared with the theoretical variance computed in the case of independence between ɜlls. The results of this analysis are displayed in Table 5.2.4 and in Figure 5.2.6.
nere is a substantial difference between the empirical variance and the variance xpected in the case of independence, the former being always higher then the latter. nis indicates the presence of a high level of positive spatial autocorrelation between ıe cells at each level of the hierarchy. This is consistent with the studies of Whittle 1954), Patankar (1954) and Ripley (1981). In order to estimate the level of spatial ɹtocorrelation we then apply the recursive Formulae (5.2.28 to 5.2.29.a) and obtain ıe results displayed in in Table 5.2.5.

lot size	Number of observations	Grouping through sums		Grouping through averages	
		Empirical $_{x*}\sigma^2$	Theoretical $_{x*}\sigma^2=4_x\sigma^2$	Empirical $_{x*}\sigma^2$	Theoretical $_{x*}\sigma^2=0.25_x\sigma^2$
	256	20.616	20.616	20.616	20.616
	64	149.601	82.464	9.350	5.154
6	16	1245.475	329.856	4.865	1.288
4	4	14284.13	1319.424	3.487	0.322

ɔle 5.2.4 : Empirical and theoretical values of the variance at various hierarchical els for Mercer and Hall data. The theoretical values refer to the case of no spatial tocorrelation (ρ=0.0).

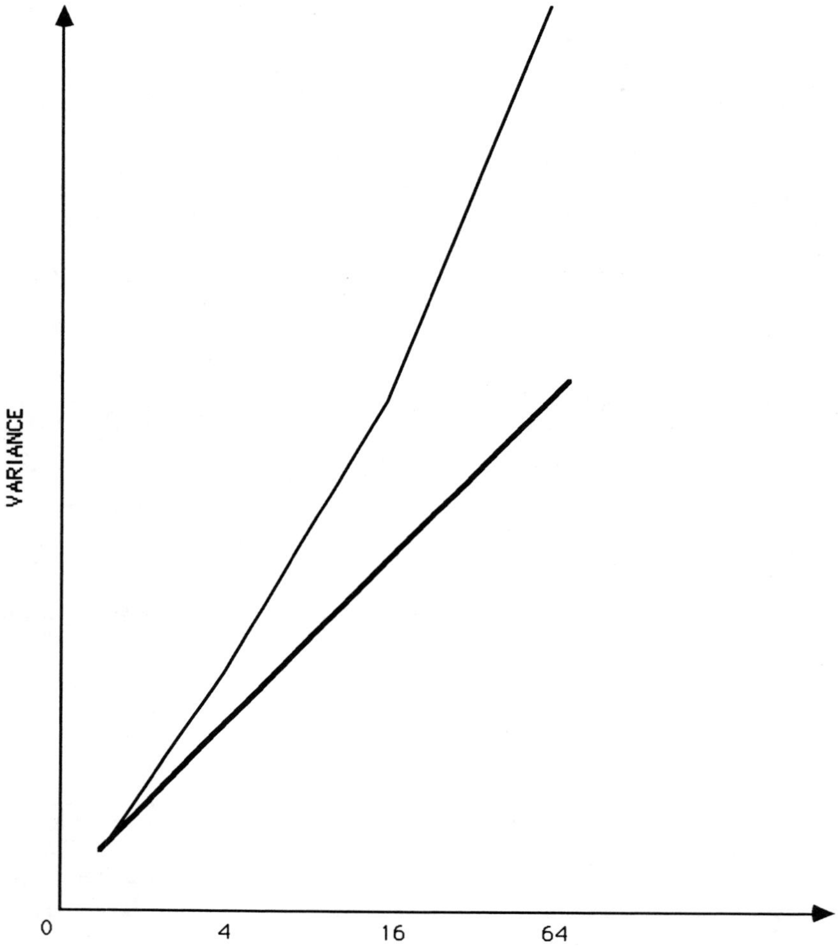

Figure 5.2.6 : Variance / plot-size relationship in the case of grouping through sums, for the Mercer and Hall data. The bold line indicates the theoretical expectation if no spatial autocorrelation occurs. (Logaritmic scale on both axes).

		Aggregation through sums			Aggregation through averages		
evel (h)	Number of observ.	Theoretical $(h)\sigma^2$	Empirical $(h)\sigma^2$	$(h)\rho$	Theoretical $(h)\sigma^2$	Empirical $(h)\sigma^2$	$(h)\rho$
1	256	$82.464+164.328\rho$	149.601	0.407	$5.154+10.308\rho$	9.350	0.407
2	64	$598.404+1196.808\rho$	1245.475	0.541	$2.337+4.675\rho$	4.865	0.541
3	16	$4981.901+9963.8\rho$	14284.130	0.933	$1.216+2.432\rho$	3.487	0.933

able 5.2.5: Approximation of the spatial autocorrelation at various scales of the plots of rain for Mercer and Hall data.

he autocorrelation is positive and high as expected from Table 5.2.4. It is worth noting ere that Whittle (1954) estimated the spatial autocorrelation when cells are isaggregated at the finest level of resolution and found an autocorrelation of 0.29 if measured along the columns and an autocorrelation of 0.52 if measured along the rows. his results, although based upon the 20-by-25 version of the grid shows that our pproximation of the spatial autocorrelation at level one falls within the range (0.29-).52). The increase of the spatial autocorrelation at the higher level of aggregation, which is against the theoretical expectation, could be due to the lack of degrees of reedom and/or to the presence of non-stationarity at the individual-process level.

5.3. THE SCALE PROBLEM: IRREGULAR CASE

5.3.1. Introduction

In the previous paragraph we have shown the consequences of the modifiable areal unit problem in the regular case, i.e. when, starting from a regular lattice of squared cells, higher-order maps are obtained by combining an even number of cells into larger zones.

Even if there are some examples of countries (notably Sweden and USA, See Hågerstrand, 1955 and Passoneau and Wurman, 1966) that record some population data on regular grid, the far more common situation is to have to cope with spatial data which are irregularly nested, each unit at one level of the hierarchy containing a different number of units of the previous level. As an example consider the hierarchy of districts-counties-regions in England or the hierarchy of comuni-provincie-regioni in Italy (see Appendix A.1).

When the spatial hierarchy is specified exogenously and prior to geographical enquiry (as in the case of administrative partition of a country) we have the scale problem. In contrast when the aim of the analysis is to form a hierarchy we have the aggregation problem.

Since we restrict our present concern only to univariate statistical analysis, we face the problem of scale basically when dealing with

a) the spatial distribution of a variable as measured by its variance (e.g. in the study of spatial inequality)

b) spatial dependence or (which is the same when we are dealing with Gaussian processes) spatial autocorrelation.

It has long been recognized that, if we are studying a spatial distribution usin irregular collecting areas, the results will be "affected by the sizes and shapes c territorial units" (Cliff, Haggett and Frey, 1977; p.348). Yule and Kendall (1957 p.311) also inferred, but did not prove formally, that we measure "not only th variation of the quantity under consideration, but the properties of the unit-mes which we have imposed on the system in order to measure it".

The problem of taking the size of census tracts into account in the statistical analysis a spatial distribution has long been recognized in the literature (Robinson, 1956 Thompson, 1957; Robinson Lindberg and Brinkman, 1961; Thomas and Anderson 1965) and the solution of weighting the areas by their size (or by their population although not completely satisfactory, appears the most widely accepted (Bachi, 1957 Gaile, 1985; Williamson, 1970; Bartels, 1976).

However a number of critiques have been made of this approach. Perhaps the mos radical is that the area-weighting solution works only for spatially uncorrelate observations. On the contrary, as Haggett, Cliff and Frey (1977; p.352) cautioned " have generality any weighting procedure must take into account the form of th autocorrelation function among observations".

The aim of this section is

a) To show that the problem of scale in irregular collecting areas is basically a proble of non-stationarity of the underlying process.

b) To show formally how the results of statistical analysis are dependent on the "size and shapes" of the areas (or on the "unit-mesh") imposed.

c) That it is possible to extend the area-weighting solution to take into account not onl the size of the areas, but also their shape and the form of their spatial autocorrelation.

NON-STATIONARITY

From the analysis of Chapter 4 we know that if an individual-process $\{X_i\}$ is Gaussia and stationary with mean ${}_x\mu$, variance ${}_x\sigma^2$ and covariance ${}_x\gamma$, the group-process resulting after summation is still Gaussian but with mean

$$r_i\ {}_x\mu \qquad (5.3.1)$$

variance

$$r_i\ {}_x\sigma^2\ (1 + r_i^{-1}\ A_i\ {}_x\rho) \qquad (5.3.2)$$

autocovariance

$$t_{il}\ {}_x\gamma \qquad (5.3.3)$$

and autocorrelation

$$t_{il}\ {}_x\rho\{r_i(1 + r_i^{-1}A_i\ {}_x\rho)\ r_l(1 + r_l^{-1}A_l\ {}_x\rho)\}^{-1/2} \qquad (5.3.4)$$

Analogously the group-process resulting after averaging is Gaussian with mean

$${}_x\mu \qquad (5.3.5)$$

ariance

$$r_i^{-1} \times \sigma^2 (1 + r_i^{-1} A_i \times \rho) \tag{5.3.6}$$

utocovariance

$$t_{il}\, r_i^{-1} r_l^{-1} \times \gamma \tag{5.3.7}$$

nd autocorrelation

$$t_{il}\, r_i^{-1} r_l^{-1} \times \rho \{ r_i^{-1}(1 + r_i^{-1} A_i \times \rho)\, r_l^{-1}(1 + r_l^{-1} A_l \times \rho) \}^{-1/2} \tag{5.3.8}$$

ormulae (5.3.1) to (5.3.8) show that even if we deal with an individual-process hich is stationary, in the case of irregular collecting areas, the derived group-process s not stationary. Its moments depends on the site i. In other words we have that tationarity at one level of a spatial hierarchy does not imply stationarity at another evel. (A remarkable exception is with grouping in pairs. In this case $r_i^{-1} A_i = 1$).
ormally, therefore, we can no longer refer to the "variance of the group-process" or the "spatial autocorrelation in the group-process" because we have now to deal with s many variances as the number of zones at a group-process level and as many utocorrelations as the square of the number of zones at the group-process level .
ormulae (5.3.1) to (5.3.8) also show that non-stationarity of the process depends on hree elements
) the number of zones in each group (r_i),
) the configuration of the spatial system or its connectedness (reflected in the values f A_i and t_{il}),
) the level of spatial autocorrelation (ρ)
he procedure for estimating the moments of the group-process (e.g. the variance), ithout weighting them, corresponds to the case in which the observation are stationary nd independent, that is to say all the observations are identically and independently istributed (Scheme I in § 4.3.1)
he attempt to estimate the moments of the group-process by weighting the bservations with the size of the areas (Robinson, 1956; Bachi, 1958; Gaile, 1985) orresponds to the case in which only non-stationarity in variance (heteroskedasticity) s assumed together with independence (Scheme II in § 4.3.1).
n the next paragraph we prove that this method does not remove completely the roblem of scale and we propose a revised area weighting solution that takes into ccount not only the size of the areas, but also their shape and the level of dependence mong them.

.3.2. A revised area-weighting solution

s the problem of scale in irregular collecting areas is a consequence of non-tationarity of the generating process, a sensible solution is to try and reduce the rocess to stationarity with some appropriate transformations.

The traditional area-weighting solution, using the size of the areas as weights, leads to computation of the variance as (Gaile, 1985)

$$n^{-1} \sum r_i(x_i - {}_x m)^2 \qquad (5.3.9)$$

This represent an implicit attempt to try to reduce the group-process to stationarity through the transformation:

$$z_i = \sqrt{(r_i)}\, x^*_i \qquad (5.3.10)$$

The transformed process now has the expected value

$$E(z_i) = E(X^*_i \sqrt{r_i}) = \sqrt{r_i}\, E(x^*_i) = 0 \qquad (5.3.11)$$

and variance:

$$E(z_i^2) = E\,[(x^*_i \ \sqrt{r_i})^2] = r_i\, E(X^*_i{}^2) \qquad (5.3.12)$$

However, in the case in which we are aggregating through averages, we have

$$E(z_i^2) = r_i\, {}_x\sigma^2 r_i^{-1} (1 + A_i r_i^{-1}\, {}_x\rho) = {}_x\sigma^2 (1 + A_i r_i^{-1}\, {}_x\rho) \qquad (5.3.13)$$

This shows that the procedure is successful in removing the non-stationarity only for the case in which no spatial autocorrelation is present ($\rho = 0.0$).
Analogously in the case of aggregation through sums we have

$$E(z_i^2) = r_i^2\, {}_x\sigma^2 (1 + A_i r_i^{-1}\, {}_x\rho) \qquad (5.3.14)$$

Alternatively if the weighting procedure is undertaken by employing densities (see Robinson, Lindberg and Drinkman, 1961) we have:

$$z_i = x^*_i\, r_i^{-1} \qquad (5.3.15)$$

so that the variance is now estimated through

$$m^{-1} \sum (x^*_i r_i^{-1} - {}_x m\, r_i^{-1})^2 \qquad (5.3.16)$$

The transformed process has now expectation

$$E(z_i) = E(x^*_i\, r_i^{-1}) = r_i^{-1}\, E(x^*_i) = 0 \qquad (5.3.17)$$

and variance

$$E(z_i^2) = E[(x^*_i\, r_i^{-1})^2] = r_i^{-2} E(x^*_i{}^2) \qquad (5.3.18)$$

From these equations we now have the following variances, for aggregation through averages

$$E(z_i^2) = r_i^{-2}\ {}_x\sigma^2\ r_i^{-1}\ (1 + A_i\ r_i^{-1}\ {}_x\rho)$$

$$= r_i^{-3}\ {}_x\sigma^2\ (1 + A_i\ r_i^{-1}\ {}_x\rho) \qquad (5.3.19)$$

ıd, in the case of aggregation through sums:

$$E(z_i^2) = r_i^{-2}\ {}_x\sigma^2\ r_i\ (1 + A_i\ r_i^{-1}\ {}_x\rho)$$

$$= {}_x\sigma^2\ r_i^{-1}\ (1 + A_i\ r_i^{-1}\ {}_x\rho) \qquad (5.3.20)$$

ɔte that the traditional area-weighting solution, can sometimes be successful in ɘducing the bias in the variance due to the different size of the areas (as in Formula 3.13), but it is unable to remove completely the problem of scale. The transformed ·ocess is still non-stationary.

ɘt us now consider a different set of weights defined by

$$_a w_i = [r_i^{-1}\ (1 + r_i^{-1}\ A_i\ {}_x\rho)\ ]^{-1/2} \qquad (5.3.21)$$

we then apply the transform

$$z_i = {}_a w_i\ X^*_i \qquad (5.3.22)$$

e have that

$$E(z_i) = {}_a w_i\ E(X^*_i) = 0 \qquad (5.3.23)$$

ıd

$$E(z_i^2) = {}_a w_i^2\ E(X^*_i)$$

$$= [\ r_i^{-1}\ (1 + A_i\ r_i^{-1}\ {}_x\rho)]^{-1}\ \ {}_x\sigma^2\ \ [r_i^{-1}\ (1 + A_i\ r_i^{-1}\ {}_x\rho)]$$

$$= {}_x\sigma^2 \qquad (5.3.24)$$

ıe transformed process now has a stationary variance which equals the variance of the dividual-process.
ıalogously, in the case of aggregation through sums, we set

$$_s w_i = [r_i\ (1 + A_i r_i^{-1}\ {}_x\rho)\ ]^{-1} \qquad (5.3.25)$$

ıd

$$z_i = {}_s w_i\ X^*_i \qquad (5.3.26)$$

ading to the same result as in Formula (5.3.24).

Therefore, since r_i and A_i are derived from the physical characteristics of the observed map, and provided that we can hypothesize a plausible value for the spatial autocorrelation ρ, we are able to compute a set of weights that takes into account all the relevant elements. The choice of the value of ρ can be done completely on conjectural basis. However we have to remember that

$$ {}_{X^*}\sigma^2{}_i = {}_X\sigma^2\, r_i\,(1 + A_i\, r_i^{-1}\, {}_X\rho) \qquad (5.3.27)$$

and therefore for ${}_{X^*}\sigma^2 \geq 0$ to be satisfied we must have

$$ {}_X\rho \geq -r_i\, A_i^{-1} $$

for each i. As a consequence

$$ {}_X\rho \geq \max\,(-r_i\, A_i^{-1}) \qquad (5.3.28)$$

This lower bound for the spatial autocorrelation is analogous to the one found in the regular case in § 5.2.2.
Following this approach we give up any attempt to measure the spatial variation of a variable at the observed group-process level, because of its heterogeneity. Instead we describe the spatial variation of the phenomenon through its variance at that level at which the originating process is stationary.
If it is required by the problem in hand that the variance at an individual-process level be estimated, we can then go back to the various non stationary "variances" at the group-process level through Formulae (5.3.2) and (5.3.6).

Let us further consider the case in which we are interested for which the autocovariance of the process is known to be non-stationary. We can proceed in an analogous fashion assuming that there exists a more disaggregated level in which the process is stationary. In the case in which aggregation is made through averaging we then consider the quantity

$$ {}_Xc = A^{-1}\Sigma_{(2)}\, w_{il}(\, r_i r_l\, t_{il}^{-1})x^*{}_i x^*{}_l \qquad (5.3.29)$$

This quantity estimates the individual-process autocovariances making use of group-process observations. In fact:

$$ E({}_Xc) = E\,[\,A^{-1}\Sigma_{(2)}\, w_{il}(\, r_i r_l\, t_{il}^{-1})x^*{}_i x^*{}_l\,] $$

$$ = A^{-1}\Sigma_{(2)}\, w_{il}(\, r_i r_l\, t_{il}^{-1})\; E(x^*{}_i x^*{}_l) \qquad (5.3.30)$$

and, following Formula (5.3.7)

$$ = A^{-1}\Sigma_{(2)}\, w_{il}(\, r_i r_l\, t_{il}^{-1})\,(r_i^{-1} r_l^{-1} t_{il})\, {}_X\gamma = {}_X\gamma \qquad (5.3.31)$$

Analogously in the case of aggregation through sums

$$ {}_{x}c = A^{-1}\Sigma_{(2)}\, w_{il}\, t_{il}^{-1}\, x^{*}_{i} x^{*}_{l} \qquad (5.3.32)$$

nd

$$E({}_{x}c) = A^{-1}\Sigma_{(2)}\, w_{il}\, t_{il}^{-1}\, E(x^{*}_{i} x^{*}_{l})$$

$$= A^{-1}\Sigma_{(2)}\, w_{il}\, t_{il}^{-1}\, t_{il}\, {}_{x}\gamma = {}_{x}\gamma \qquad (5.3.33)$$

gain, as in the case in which we are interested in the variance, once we have obtained he individual-process autocovariance, we can go back to the group-process non-tationary "autocovariances" making use of Formula (5.3.3) or (5.3.7).

.3.3. Data analysis:The distribution of labour force in Italy

o illustrate the revised area weighting solution let us now examine some data taken rom the Italian population Census 1981 (see Appendix A1). In particular we will start onsidering the problem of computing the inter-regional variance of the employed opulation.

able 5.3.1 summarizes all the data we need as inputs to compute the weighted ariance. The table shows the total number of employed people in the 20 Italian dministrative regions in 1981 (ISTAT, 1982) together with a standardized z-score ersion which is obtained by subtracting the mean from the raw data and dividing by the tandard deviation in order to have a data series which has zero mean and variance equal) unity.

 columns four and five of Table 5.3.1 are also listed the values of r_i and A_i. These are, espectively, the number of provincie (the lower level of the administrative hierarchy Italy) in each region, and the within region connectedness (see § 3.3.3), measured y the number of neighbouring provincie in each region (See the map in Appendix .1).

ive sets of weights are then computed under the set of hypotheses that the spatial utocorrelation assumes two moderate values (ρ = 0.1 and ρ= -0.1), one high positive alue (ρ = 0.5), and one high negative value (ρ=-0.29). The value of ρ equal to -0.29 as chosen because it is very close to the lower bound. In fact remembering Formula 5.3.28) we have

$$\rho \geq \max\,(\, r_i A_i^{-1})$$

hich in this case is -0.299. The values of $r_i A_i^{-1}$ are listed column five of Table 5.3.1. inally the value of ρ=0.0 corresponds to the case in which we weight simply with the ize of the areas.

he values of the weights in the five hypotheses are shown in Table 5.3.2.

 we compute the variance of the transformed data we now have the inter-regional ariance of the employed under the various hypotheses of spatial autocorrelation. This displayed in Table 5.3.3.

Regions	Number of employed population	Standardized number of employed	N. of provincie in each region r_i	Regional connectedness A_i	$-r_iA_i^-$
Piemonte	1829253	0.939	6	16	-0.375
Valle d'Aosta*	45265	-1.102	1	0	$-\infty$
Lombardia	3685405	3.062	9	28	-0.321
Friuli Ven-Giu	475530	-0.610	4	6	-0.666
Trentino A-A	346045	-0.758	2	2	-1.000
Veneto	1696160	0.787	7	24	-0.291
Liguria	637789	-0.424	4	6	-0.666
Emilia Romagna	1713270	0.807	8	18	-0.444
Toscana	1341231	0.381	9	24	-0.375
Umbria	328566	-0.788	2	2	-1.000
Marche	564483	-0.508	4	6	-0.666
Lazio	1684923	0.775	5	12	-0.416
Abruzzo	406094	-0.689	4	10	-0.400
Molise	108852	-1.028	2	2	-1.000
Campania	1499053	0.562	5	12	-0.416
Puglie	1205035	0.225	5	12	-0.416
Basilicata	196293	-0.929	2	2	-1.000
Calabria	564868	-0.473	3	4	-0.750
Sicilia	1332625	0.371	9	30	-0.300
Sardegna	475007	-0.610	3	4	-0.750
ITALY		0.000	94	220	

Table 5.3.1: Labour forces from the Italian population Census 1981. (Source: ISTAT, 1982). * Valle d'Aosta has the administrative status of being a single region and a provincia. Therefore $A_i = 0$ and the theoretical lower bound in $-\infty$. However its regional average connectedness has the finite value of zero.

ρ	σ^2
-0.29	1.67589
-0.1	0.29409
0.0	0.24144
0.1	0.29087
0.5	0.15057

Table 5.3.3 : Weighted estimate of the inter-regional variance under various hypotheses of spatial autocorrelation.

The value of σ^2 varies a lot, ranging from 1.67 to 0.15. All values differ from the unweighted variance (which, we remember, was set equal to unity) and from the variance weighted with the size of the areas, which is equal to 0.24.
Finally the non-stationary regional "variances" at the group-process level are obtained by multiplying the variance under the different hypotheses by the term

$$r_i(1+A_i r_i^{-1} {}_X\rho)$$

in each region. The results (shown in Table 5.3.4) reveal a marked heterogeneity of the variance.
Let us now turn to the problem of computing a weighted autocovariance between the observed data. Table 5.3.5 shows the connectivity matrix **W** and the matrix **T** of the between group links (see § 3.3.3) for the map of the Italian regions and provincie (see Appendix A1).
If we apply the formula in Equation (5.3.32) we have the covariance at the individual-process level ${}_X\gamma$ = -0.02937412. This indicates the presence of a negative autocorrelation among the Italian provincie for the variable "employed".

Regions	ρ = -0.29	ρ =-0.1	ρ =0.0	ρ =0.1	ρ =0.5
Piemonte	0.85749	0.47637	0.40825	0.36274	0.26726
Valle d'Aosta	1.00000	1.00000	1.00000	1.00000	1.00000
Lombardia	1.06600	0.40161	0.33333	0.29111	0.20851
Friuli Ven.-Giu.	0.66519	0.54233	0.50000	0.46625	0.37796
Trentino A.-A.	0.83918	0.74536	0.70711	0.67420	0.57735
Veneto	4.99994	0.46625	0.37796	0.32616	0.22942
Liguria	0.65519	0.54233	0.50000	0.46625	0.37796
Emilia Romagna	0.59976	0.40161	0.35355	0.31944	0.24254
Toscana	0.70014	0.38925	0.33333	0.29617	0.21822
Umbria	0.83918	0.74536	0.70711	0.67420	0.57735
Marche	0.66519	0.54233	0.50000	0.46625	0.37796
Lazio	0.81111	0.51299	0.44721	0.40161	0.30151
Abruzzo	0.95346	0.57735	0.50000	0.44721	0.33333
Molise	0.83918	0.74536	0.70711	0.67420	0.57735
Campania	0.81111	0.51299	0.44721	0.40161	0.30151
Puglie	0.81111	0.51299	0.44721	0.40161	0.30151
Basilicata	0.83918	0.74536	0.70711	0.67420	0.57735
Calabria	0.73721	0.62017	0.57735	0.54233	0.44721
Sicilia	1.82574	0.40825	0.33333	0.28868	0.20412
Sardegna	0.73721	0.62017	0.57735	0.54233	0.44721

Table 5.3.2 : Weights for the calculation of the inter-regional labour force variance for different values of spatial autocorrelation.

Region	$\rho = -0.29$ $\sigma^2 = 1.67589$	$\rho = -0.1$ $\sigma^2 = 0.24144$	$\rho = 0.0$ $\sigma^2 = 0.29087$	$\rho = 0.1$ $\sigma^2 = 0.29409$	$\rho = 0.5$ $\sigma^2 = 0.15057$
1.Piemonte	2.279	1.448	2.210	1.293	2.108
2. Valle d'Aosta	1.675	0.241	0.290	0.294	0.150
3. Lombardia	1.474	2.173	3.492	1.823	3.463
4.Friuli V.G.	3.787	0.965	1.338	1.352	1.054
5. Trentino A.A.	2.237	0.483	0.639	0.529	0.452
6.Veneto	0.067	1.690	2.734	1.353	2.860
7. Liguria	2.815	0.965	1.338	1.352	1.064
8. Emilia Rom.	4.658	1.931	2.850	1.823	2.559
9. Toscana	3.418	2.173	3.316	1.940	3.162
10. Umbria	2.379	0.483	0.639	0.529	0.452
11. Marche	5.681	0.965	1.338	1.352	1.054
12. Lazio	2.547	1.207	1.803	1.117	1.656
13. Abruzzo	1.843	0.965	1.454	0.882	1.355
14. Molise	2.379	0.438	0.639	0.529	0.452
15. Campania	2.547	1.207	1.803	1.117	1.656
16. Puglie	2.547	1.207	1.803	1.117	1.656
17. Basilicata	2.379	0.483	0.639	0.529	0.452
18. Calabria	3.083	0.724	0.989	0.764	1.003
19. Sicilia	1.676	2.172	3.490	1.764	3.614
20. Sardegna	3.083	0.724	0.989	0.764	1.003

Table 5.3.4: Non-stationary variance of the group-process for different values of the individual-process spatial autocorrelation ρ.

	1	2	3	4	5	6	7	8	9	10	11	12	13	14	15	16	17	18	19	20	A
emonte	0	1	1	0	0	0	1	1	0	0	0	0	0	0	0	0	0	0	0	0	4
l d'Aosta	1	0	0	0	0	0	0	0	0	0	0	0	0	0	0	0	0	0	0	0	1
mbardia	1	0	0	0	1	1	0	1	0	0	0	0	0	0	0	0	0	0	0	0	4
iuli Ven-Giu	0	0	0	0	0	1	0	0	0	0	0	0	0	0	0	0	0	0	0	0	1
entino A-A	0	0	1	0	0	1	0	0	0	0	0	0	0	0	0	0	0	0	0	0	2
neto	0	0	1	1	1	0	0	1	0	0	0	0	0	0	0	0	0	0	0	0	4
juria	1	0	0	0	0	0	0	1	1	0	0	0	0	0	0	0	0	0	0	0	3
n Romagna	1	0	1	0	0	1	1	0	1	0	1	0	0	0	0	0	0	0	0	0	6
scana	0	0	0	0	0	0	1	1	0	1	1	1	0	0	0	0	0	0	0	0	5
Jmbria	0	0	0	0	0	0	0	0	1	0	1	1	0	0	0	0	0	0	0	0	3
Marche	0	0	0	0	0	0	0	1	1	1	0	1	1	0	0	0	0	0	0	0	5
.azio	0	0	0	0	0	0	0	0	1	1	1	0	1	1	1	0	0	0	0	0	6
Abruzzo	0	0	0	0	0	0	0	0	0	0	1	1	0	1	0	0	0	0	0	0	3
Molise	0	0	0	0	0	0	0	0	0	0	0	1	1	0	1	1	0	0	0	0	4
Campania	0	0	0	0	0	0	0	0	0	0	0	1	0	1	0	1	1	0	0	0	4
Puglie	0	0	0	0	0	0	0	0	0	0	0	0	0	1	1	0	1	0	0	0	3
Basilicata	0	0	0	0	0	0	0	0	0	0	0	0	0	0	1	1	0	1	0	0	3
Calabria	0	0	0	0	0	0	0	0	0	0	0	0	0	0	0	0	1	0	0	0	1
Sicilia	0	0	0	0	0	0	0	0	0	0	0	0	0	0	0	0	0	0	0	0	0
Sardegna	0	0	0	0	0	0	0	0	0	0	0	0	0	0	0	0	0	0	0	0	0

	1	2	3	4	5	6	7	8	9	10	11	12	13	14	15	16	17	18	19	20
emonte	0	4	10	0	0	0	8	2	0	0	0	0	0	0	0	0	0	0	0	0
l d'Aosta	4	0	0	0	0	0	0	0	0	0	0	0	0	0	0	0	0	0	0	0
mbardia	10	0	0	0	6	6	0	14	0	0	0	0	0	0	0	0	0	0	0	0
iuli Ven-Giu	0	0	0	0	0	10	0	0	0	0	0	0	0	0	0	0	0	0	0	0
entino A-A	0	0	6	0	0	8	0	0	0	0	0	0	0	0	0	0	0	0	0	0
neto	0	0	6	10	8	0	0	2	0	0	0	0	0	0	0	0	0	0	0	0
juria	8	0	0	0	0	0	0	6	4	0	0	0	0	0	0	0	0	0	0	0
n Romagna	2	0	14	0	0	2	6	0	20	0	2	0	0	0	0	0	0	0	0	0
scana	0	0	0	0	0	0	4	20	0	6	2	4	0	0	0	0	0	0	0	0
Jmbria	0	0	0	0	0	0	0	0	6	0	8	6	0	0	0	0	0	0	0	0
Marche	0	0	0	0	0	0	0	2	2	8	0	2	2	0	0	0	0	0	0	0
.azio	0	0	0	0	0	0	0	0	4	6	2	0	8	2	4	0	0	0	0	0
Abruzzo	0	0	0	0	0	0	0	0	0	0	2	8	0	6	0	0	0	0	0	0
Molise	0	0	0	0	0	0	0	0	0	0	0	2	6	0	6	2	0	0	0	0
Campania	0	0	0	0	0	0	0	0	0	0	0	4	0	6	0	4	4	0	0	0
Puglie	0	0	0	0	0	0	0	0	0	0	0	0	0	2	4	0	8	0	0	0
Basilicata	0	0	0	0	0	0	0	0	0	0	0	0	0	0	4	8	0	8	0	0
Calabria	0	0	0	0	0	0	0	0	0	0	0	0	0	0	0	0	4	0	0	0
Sicilia	0	0	0	0	0	0	0	0	0	0	0	0	0	0	0	0	0	0	0	0
Sardegna	0	0	0	0	0	0	0	0	0	0	0	0	0	0	0	0	0	0	0	0

able 5.3.5 : Connectivity matrix (a) and matrix of the between group cross-links b) of the 20 Italian administrative regions.

5.3.4. Simultaneous estimation of σ^2 and ρ

A weakness of the revised area weighting solution to the scale problem which has been advanced is that, in order to compute the weights to estimate the variance, we need to know the spatial autocorrelation ρ. Furthermore, even if the weights for the estimation of the autocovariance γ can be easily derived from the physical characteristics of the map, to have an estimate of ρ we need the value of σ^2 because $\rho = \gamma\,\sigma^{-2}$. We come therefore to a point in which, in order to compute ${}_X\sigma^2$ we need to know ρ and in order to compute ρ we need to know σ^2. This circularity suggest a iterative approach. This is now presented for the two cases of aggregation through sums and aggregation through averages.

In the case of aggregation through sums, we start by assuming a certain value for the autocorrelation at the individual-process level, say ${}_{(1)}\rho$, simply on a conjectural basis, but remembering the constraint expressed in Formula (5.3.28) that, ${}_{(1)}\rho \geq \max(-r_i A^{-1})$.

Having chosen a value for ${}_{(1)}\rho$ within the admissible range, we can then set

$$ {}_{(1)}w_i = [\, r_i\,(1 + A_i r_i^{-1}\,{}_{(1)}\rho)\,]^{-1/2} \qquad (5.3.34) $$

and

$$ {}_{(1)}z_i = {}_{(1)}w_i \;\; x^*_i \qquad (5.3.35) $$

We then compute

$$ {}_{(1)}\sigma^2 = m^{-1} \sum (\, {}_{(1)}z_i - {}_{(1)}\bar{z}\,)^2 \qquad (5.3.36) $$

where ${}_{(1)}\bar{z} = m^{-1} \sum {}_{(1)}z_i$. Furthermore we set

$$ u_{il} = r_i r_l (t_{il})^{-1} \qquad (5.3.37) $$

and compute the weighted autocovariance:

$$ c = A^{-1} \sum\nolimits_{(2)} \; w^*_{il}\, u_{il}\, (x_i^* x_l^*) \qquad (5.3.38) $$

where w^*_{il} is the element of the connectivity matrix $\mathbf{W}^*$ at the group-process lev (see § 3.3.3). As a consequence we have:

$$ {}_{(2)}\rho = c\; {}_{(1)}\sigma^{-2} \qquad (5.3.39) $$

This value is then substituted into the previous Formula (5.3.34). This then yields second, more accurate, set of weights

$$ {}_{(1)}w_i = [\, r_i\,(1 + A_i r_i^{-1}\,{}_{(2)}\rho)\,]^{-1/2} \qquad (5.3.40) $$

which in turn provides a second approximation for σ^2, say ${}_{(2)}\sigma^2$.
The process is then iterated κ times until we satisfy a convergence limit

$$_{(\kappa)}\rho \approx {}_{(\kappa-1)}\rho \tag{5.3.41}$$

and

$$_{(\kappa)}\sigma^2 \approx {}_{(\kappa-1)}\sigma^2 \tag{5.3.42}$$

It can be shown that the process converges after a finite number of iterations. This can be proved as follows.
Consider the quantity $\Delta_{(\kappa)}\rho = ({}_{(\kappa)}\rho - {}_{(\kappa-1)}\rho)$, and suppose that ${}_{(\kappa)}\rho > {}_{(\kappa-1)}\rho$. This implies

$$_{(k)}w_i=[r_i(1+A_i r_i^{-1}{}_{(\kappa)}\rho)]^{-1/2}<[r_i(1+A_i r_i^{-1}{}_{(\kappa-1)}\rho)]^{-1/2}={}_{(k-1)}w_i \tag{5.3.43}$$

and hence

$$_{(\kappa)}\sigma^2=E[({}_{(k)}w_i X_i^*)^2]={}_{(k)}w_i^2 E(X_i^{*2})<{}_{(k-1)}w_i^2 E(X_i^{*2})={}_{(\kappa-1)}\sigma^2 \tag{5.3.44}$$

so that

$$_{(\kappa+1)}\rho = c\,{}_{(\kappa)}\sigma^{-2} < c\,{}_{(\kappa-1)}\sigma^{-2} = {}_{(\kappa)}\rho \tag{5.3.45}$$

With an analogous reasoning we have

$$_{(\kappa)}\rho < {}_{(\kappa-1)}\rho \rightarrow {}_{(\kappa+1)}\rho > {}_{(\kappa)}\rho \tag{5.3.46}$$

hence

$$|\Delta_{(\kappa)}\rho| < |\Delta_{(\kappa-1)}\rho| \tag{5.3.47}$$

which, by Cauchy criterion (Apostol, 1974) is a necessary and sufficient condition for the series of ${}_{(\kappa)}\rho$ to converge.
The iterative calculation for the case of aggregation through averages follows exactly the same lines except for the fact that we now set ${}_{(1)}w_i = [r_i^{-1}(1 + A_i r_i^{-1}{}_{(1)}\rho)]^{-1/2}$.

5.3.5. Data analysis: The spatial distribution of labour force in Italy

To illustrate the iterative procedure let us consider again the example of regional employment in Italy already examined in § 5.3.3.
To test for the presence of possible multiple points of convergence five different starting points are chosen for ρ, that is $\rho = -0.29$; $\rho = 0.0$; $\rho = 0.1$; $\rho = 0.5$; $\rho = 0.9$.
The process is then iterated until the values of ρ and σ^2 are equal up to the fifth decimal figure. (The FORTAN program used is listed in Appendix 5.1).

Table 5.3.6 shows that the estimation procedure converges quite rapidly (after 10 iterations) in all the five experiments (see also Figures 5.3.1) with stable results of

$$\rho = -0.10409$$

$$\sigma^2 = 0.28220$$

Moreover the solutions do not depend upon the initial value of ρ. Notice that the average size of the regions is

$$94 / 20 = 4.7$$

and the average connectedness of the spatial system as a whole is

$$220/94 = 2.3$$

(a) Values for ${}_X\rho$

	Starting values				
	−0.29000	**0.00000**	**0.10000**	**0.50000**	**0.90000**
Iterations					
1	-0.01845	-0.12807	-0.14733	-0.20536	-0.05615
2	-0.12417	-0.09771	-0.09226	-0.07340	-0.05615
3	-0.09878	-0.10572	-0.10709	-0.11171	-0.11577
4	-0.10545	-0.10367	-0.10331	-0.10211	-0.10103
5	-0.10374	-0.10420	-0.10429	-0.10460	-0.10487
6	-0.10418	-0.10406	-0.10404	-0.10396	-0.10489
7	-0.10407	-0.10410	-0.10410	-0.10412	-0.10414
8	-0.10410	-0.10409	-0.10409	-0.10408	-0.10408
9	-0.10409		-0.10409	-0.10409	

(b) Values for ${}_X\sigma^2$

Iterations	1.59210	0.22936	0.19938	0.14303	0.11905
2	0.23657	0.30062	0.31837	0.40018	0.52315
3	0.29737	0.27785	0.27428	0.26294	0.25372
4	0.27856	0.28334	0.28432	0.28768	0.29073
5	0.28315	0.28190	0.28166	0.28082	0.28009
6	0.28195	0.28227	0.28234	0.28255	0.28275
7	0.28226	0.28218	0.28216	0.28211	0.28206
8	0.28218	0.28220	0.28221	0.28222	0.28223
9	0.28220	0.28220	0.28219	0.28219	
10			0.28220	0.28220	

Table 5.3.6: Convergence of the recursive estimation of (a) ρ and (b) σ with different starting values.

If we construct a relationship like the one in Formula (5.3.2), but based on the assumption that all the regions have the same size and connectedness equal to their average we have

$$_{X*}\sigma^2 \approx 4.7\, _X\sigma^2 (1 + 2.3\, _X\rho)$$

and, in our case

$$_{X*}\sigma^2 \approx 4.7 \ (0.2822) [1 - 2.3 \ (0.10409)]$$
$$= 1.009$$

which is very close to the empirical value of the variance that was set to 1. This demonstrates that the link between individual-process moments and group-process moments approximately holds if applied to the average at least when $_X\rho$ is not too large. Having assessed the values of σ^2 and ρ at the stationary individual-process level, the non-stationary moments of the group-process can be easily evaluated from Formulae (5.3.1) to (5.3.8). The non-stationary regional variances are displayed in Figure 5.3.2.

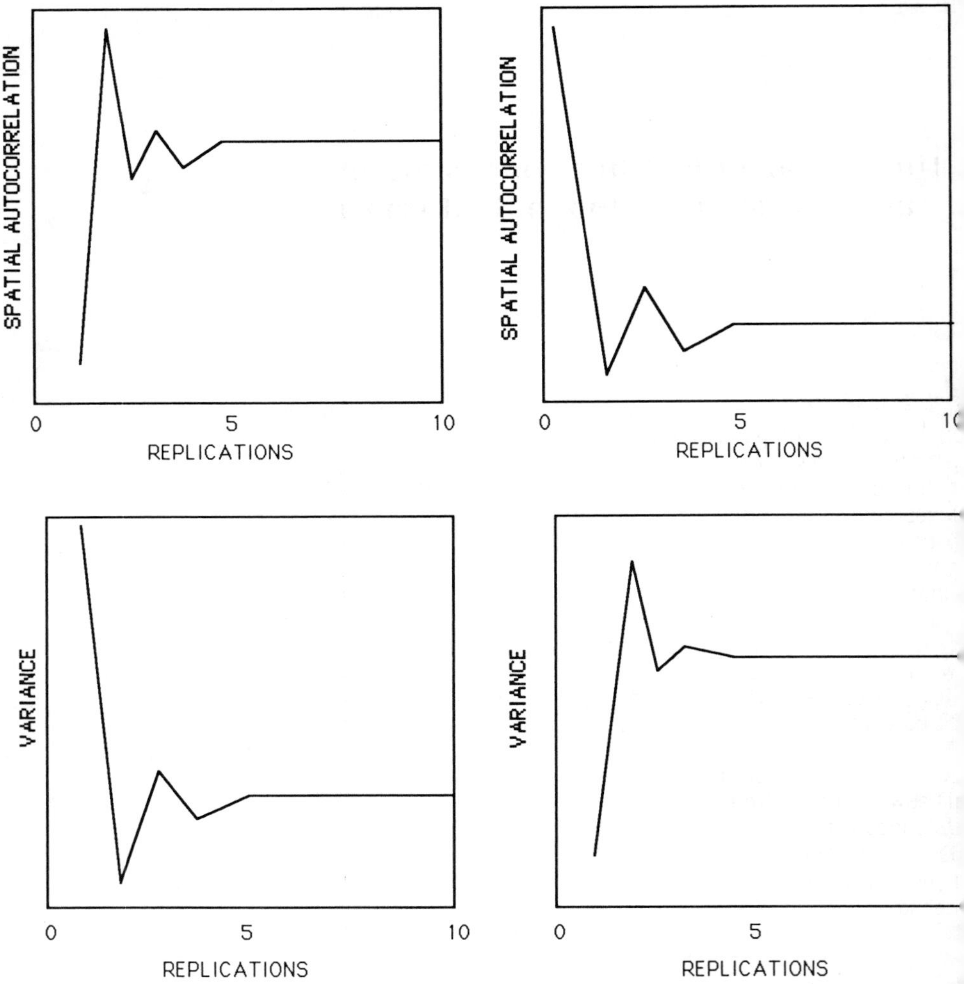

Figure 5.3.1: Convergence of the spatial autocorrelation and of the variance in the recursive procedure. The starting values is $\rho = -0.29$ in the diagrams on the left and $\rho = 0.1$ in the diagrams on the right.

Figure 5.3.2: Non-stationary variances of the regional employment in Italy. Recursive estimation

5.4 THE AGGREGATION PROBLEM

5.4.1. Introduction

This chapter is devoted to analysis of the problems that arise in univariate statistical analysis of spatial data when the sites of the study area are different in size and shape. In § 5.2 we dealt with zones equal in shape, but of different sizes (scale problem in regular grid lattice). Section 5.3 was devoted to dealing with zones that differ in both size and shape. In this section we complete the discussion of the modifiable area unit problem by considering the case in which the difference between the zones is not due to their size, which is held constant, but to the way in which they connect with one another in the study area. This is what is usually termed *aggregation* problem. It is also the *zoning* problem if the aggregation has to be performed incorporating a contiguity constraint. We restrict our attention, as before, to the univariate case.

5.4.2. Grouping, zoning and regular zoning

Let us start by considering n random components of a process $\{X_i\}$; i = 1,...n observed in a study area and suppose that we want to aggregate them into m fewer and larger zones in such a way that $nm^{-1} = r$ for each r. Of course given a certain spatial scale (that is given a value of r) there are a number of alternative aggregations that can be performed (for practical examples see Tooze, 1976; Kirby and Taylor, 1976). The moments of the group-process depend on the way in which the original observations are combined together. The $\binom{n}{r}$ possible alternatives are termed *grouping systems* (Openshaw, 1977c; p.128) and the distribution of the moments of the group-process, when changing the grouping criterion, is termed the *grouping distribution* (See figure 5.4.1). Since we are interested in geographical processes it is sensible to consider in our analysis only a particular subclass of grouping systems which incorporates a contiguity constraint in its formation. A grouping with contiguity constraint is termed (Openshaw, 1977c) a *zoning* of the study area. The set of all possible zonings is called the set of *zoning systems*. We will use the term *zoning distribution* to indicate the distribution of the moments of the group-process obtained by changing the zoning criterion.
We now wish to introduce the further constraint that the group-process has to be stationary if the individual-process is stationary. This is obtained (see Chapter 4) when the between group connectedness and the within group connectedness are both constant in all groups. A zoning which incorporates this regularity constraint will be referred to as *regular zoning* of the study area and, with an obvious extension of the previous concepts, we will refer to a *regular zoning system* and to a *regular zoning distribution* (See Figure 5.4.1). As the various moments of the group-process depend in a functional form on the level of connectedness of the spatial scheme (see § 5.2 and 5.3), it follows that the zoning distribution of the moments of the group-process can be studied on a theoretical basis by simply allowing the degree of connectedness of the regular zoning system to vary in all possible ways. The analysis of these permutations will be the subject of the remainder of this chapter. Following a tradition of previous studies on the subject (Openshaw and Taylor, 1979) we will consider first the theoretical limits of the group-process moments imposed by the configuration of the spatial system under study. Secondly we will examine the complete *regular zoning distribution* of the moments of the group-process .

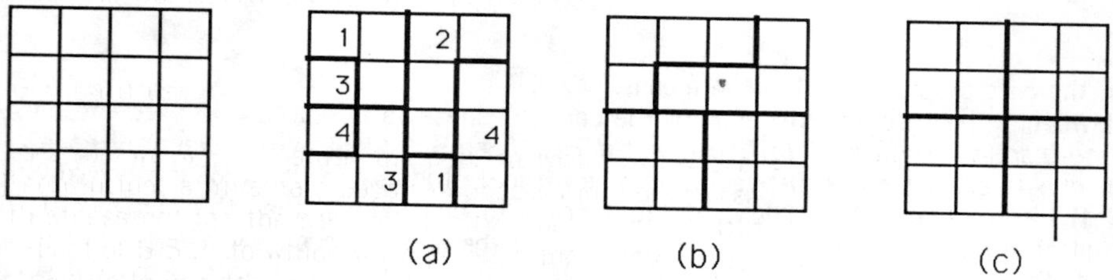

Figure 5.4.1 : Grouping (a), Zoning (b) and Regular zoning (c) of a 4-by-4 regular square lattice grid

5.4.3. Zoning range of the variance

THEORY

From the analysis of Chapter 4 we know that the mean of the group-process is equal to ${}_X\mu^* = r\,{}_X\mu$ in the case of grouping through sums, and ${}_X\mu^* = {}_X\mu$ in the case of grouping through means. It is clear therefore that, although there is a scale effect in the first case, no aggregation effect occurs on the mean.
From the definition of the group variance we now have

$$ {}_{X^*}\sigma^2 = {}_X\sigma^2\, r\,(1 + A_i r_i^{-1}\, {}_X\rho) \qquad (5.4.1)$$

in the case of grouping through sums. It is

$$ {}_{X^*}\sigma^2 = {}_X\sigma^2\, r^{-1}\,(1 + A_i r_i^{-1}\, {}_X\rho) \qquad (5.4.2)$$

in the case of grouping through means. It follows that the range of the zoning distribution of ${}_{X^*}\sigma^2$ is determined by the within group average connectedness, given ${}_X\rho$. Let us now recall the theoretical limits of the average within group connectedness (See § 2.2). These are

$$ 2\,(r-1)\,r^{-1} \le v_i^* \le r-1 \qquad (5.4.3)$$

where, from § 3.3.2, $v_i^* = A_i r_i^{-1}$.
It follows that in different regular zoning systems the variance can vary within the range

$$ {}_X\sigma^2 r\,[1 + 2(r-1)r^{-1}\,{}_X\rho] \le {}_{X^*}\sigma^2 \le {}_X\sigma^2 r\,[1 + (r-1)\,{}_X\rho] \qquad (5.4.4)$$

in the case of grouping through sums, and within the range

$$ {}_X\sigma^2 r^{-1}[1+2(r-1)r^{-1}{}_X\rho] \leq {}_{X^*}\sigma^2 \leq {}_X\sigma^2 r^{-1}[1+(r-1){}_X\rho] \tag{5.4.5} $$

in the case of grouping through means.
However, the theoretical range of the connectedness is based on two extreme cases, the *line transect* and the *totally connected* case (See § 3.3..2), which are only rarely found in practice. As a consequence in most empirical studies the range of the group variance will be much smaller. The important point to be made is that the configuration of a spatial system imposes a limit to the range of the group-process variance and this limit does not depend on the variable under study, but it is a property of the spatial system in itself. For this reason we will now examine the limits of the group-process variance in some particular cases.

EXAMPLE 5.1: 4-BY-4 REGULAR LATTICE GRID

Consider first the simple case in which 16 observations on the individual-process are recorded on a 4-by-4 regular lattice grid and we want to perform a regular zoning of 4 cells. (See the example of § 5.2) In this case the minimum of the within group connectedness is reached when the cells in each group lie on a line. In contrast the maximum of the within group connectedness is achieved when the groups form a larger 2-by-2 quadrat (See Figure 5.4.2).
The range of v_i^* is therefore

$$ 1.5 \leq v_i^* \leq 2 \tag{5.4.6} $$

Note that in this case 1.5 and 2 are the only admissible values of v_i^* under the regularity constraint. As a consequence of Formula (5.4.6) the range of the variance at the group-process level is

$$ 4\,{}_X\sigma^2\,[1 + 1.5\,{}_X\rho] \leq {}_{X^*}\sigma^2 \leq 4\,{}_X\sigma^2\,[1 + 2\,{}_X\rho] \tag{5.4.7} $$

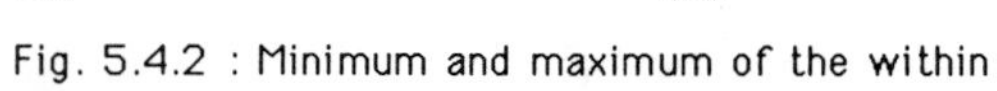

(a) (b)

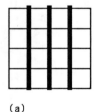

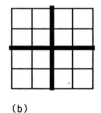

Fig. 5.4.2 : Minimum and maximum of the within group average connectedness of a 4 cells zoning in a 4-by-4 regular lattice grid. In the case (a) A = 6, v* = 1.5 and t = 8. In the case (b) A = 8, v* = 2 and t = 4.

in the case of grouping through sums. It is

$$0.25\,{}_X\sigma^2\,[1 + 1.5\,{}_X\rho] \leq {}_{X^*}\sigma^2 \leq 0.25\,{}_X\sigma^2\,[1 + 2\,{}_X\rho] \qquad (5.4.8)$$

in the case of grouping through means.

The range of ${}_{X^*}\sigma^2$ for different values of the spatial autocorrelation is reported in Table 5.4.1 (case of sums) and in Table 5.4.2 (case of means). In both cases the variance of the individual-process is set equal to 1 and the values of the spatial autocorrelation are such that ${}_X\rho \geq -0.5$, for the reasons explained in § 5.2.2.

From the analysis of the two tables it is possible to see that the range of the variance increases with the absolute value of the spatial autocorrelation. Furthermore the range degenerates to zero when ${}_X\rho = 0.0$. This is to be expected because in this case no effect of the spatial configuration occurs and the results are not affected by the different zoning systems.

Individual process spatial autocorrelation ${}_X\rho$	Group process variance Minimum	Maximum
-0.1	3.2	3.4
0.0	4.0	4.0
0.1	4.6	4.8
0.5	7.0	8.0
0.9	9.4	11.2

Table 5.4.1 Theoretical limits of the group-process variance for different values of the spatial autocorrelation in a 4-by-4 regular square lattice grid when the group size is is r=4 (case of aggregation through sums).

Individual process spatial autocorrelation	Group process variance Minimum	Maximum
-0.1	0.20	0.21
0.0	0.25	0.25
0.1	0.28	0.30
0.5	0.44	0.50
0.9	0.59	0.70

Table 5.4.2 Limits of the group-process variance for different values of the spatial autocorrelation in a 4-by-4 regular square lattice grid when the group size is r = 4 (case of aggregation through means.)

EXAMPLE 5.2: 9-BY-9 REGULAR LATTICE GRID

As a second example consider now a 9-by-9 regular lattice grid ($n = 81$) with a group size $r = 9$. Also in this case the minimum of the within group connectedness is reached in the *line transect* case, and the maximum when each group form a 3-by-3 quadrat (see Figure 5.4.3).
Therefore the range of v_i^* is now

$$1.78 \le v_i^* \le 2.67 \tag{5.4.9}$$

as it is easy to see. As a consequence the range of the group-process variance is

$$9\,{}_X\sigma^2\ [1 + 1.78\,{}_X\rho] \le {}_{X*}\sigma^2 \le 9\,{}_X\sigma^2\ [1 + 2.67\,{}_X\rho] \tag{5.4.10}$$

in the case of grouping through sums and

$$0.11\,{}_X\sigma^2\ [1 + 1.78\,{}_X\rho] \le {}_{X*}\sigma^2 \le 0.11\,{}_X\sigma^2\ [1 + 2.67\,{}_X\rho] \tag{5.4.11}$$

in the case of grouping through means.
In Tables 5.4.3 and 5.4.4 different values of the spatial autocorrelation are considered and, analogously to Table 5.4.1 and 5.4.2, the range of the group-process variance is computed in the case of grouping through sums and, respectively, through means.
Tables 5.4.3 and 5.4.4 confirm the results of Example 5.1 showing that the range is wider when the spatial autocorrelation at a individual-process level is larger in absolute value. Furthermore the joint consideration of Example 5.1 and Example 5.2 shows that, when all the other elements are held constant, the range of the variance is directly related to the group size.

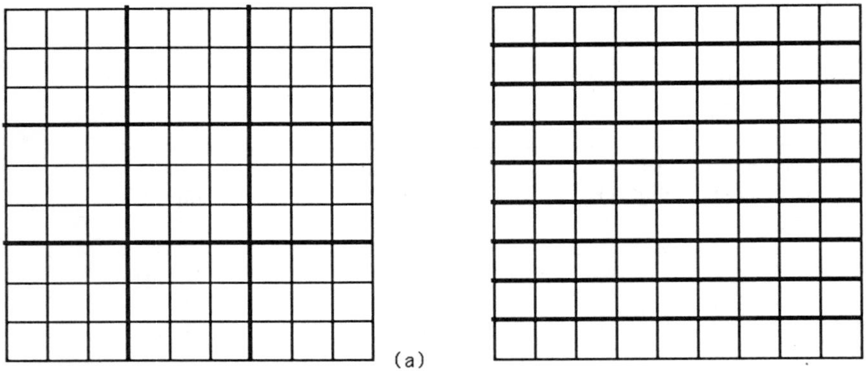

(a) (b)

Fig. 5.4.3: Minimum and Maximum of the within group connectedness in a 9-by-9 regul grid lattice. In the case (a) $A_i = 24$, $v^*_i = 2.67$ and $t_{i1} = 6$. In the case (b) $A_i = 16$, v^*_i 1.78 and $t_{i1} = 18$.

Individual process spatial autocorrelation $_x\rho$	Group process variance Minimum	Maximum
-0.1	6.6	7.4
0.0	9.0	9.0
0.1	10.6	11.4
0.5	17.1	21.0
0.9	23.4	30.6

Table 5.4.3 Limits of the group-process variance for different values of the spatial autocorrelation in a 9-by-9 regular square lattice grid when the group size is r = 9 (case of aggregation through sums.)

Individual process spatial autocorrelation $_x\rho$	Group process variance Minimum	Maximum
-0.1	0.0807	0.0903
0.0	0.1100	0.1100
0.1	0.1297	0.1393
0.5	0.2085	0.2565
0.9	0.2873	0.3737

Table 5.4.4 Limits of the group-process variance for different values of the spatial autocorrelation in a 9-by-9 regular square lattice grid when the group size is r = 9 (case of aggregation through means.)

EXAMPLE 5.3: THE MAP OF THE PROVINCIA OF AREZZO (ITALY)

Let us now consider the case of a system of irregular collecting areas (See § 3.3). The spatial system we want to study is the administrative *provincia* of Arezzo (Tuscany, Italy) (See Appendix A2). The *provincia* of Arezzo is divided into 39 smaller administrative units called *comuni*; however for the purpose of producing regular zoning systems of the area an extra *comune* is obtained by splitting in two the area of the *comune* n.31 (see Appendix A.2). Our aim is to examine the range of the within group average connectedness when the group size is 4. The minimum of the within group connectedness is obtained, as usual, in the *line transect* case when $A_i=6$ and, consequently $v_i^* = A_i r_i^{-1} = 1.5$. The theoretical maximum of the within group average connectedness is, instead, obtained in the *totally connected* case. However, by examining the results of a permutation study of the 40 zones (see Section 5.4.5 for details), it was seen that it is not possible to produce a regular zoning system of the area with an average within group connectedness higher than 2. Two typical configurations of the area in the case of $v_i^* = 1.5$ and $v_i^* = 2.0$ are displayed in Figure 5.4.4. As a consequence of the range of the connectedness, the range of the variance of the group-process is

$$4\ {}_X\sigma^2\ [1 + 1.5\ {}_X\rho] \leq {}_{X^*}\sigma^2 \leq 4\ {}_X\sigma^2\ [1 + 2.0\ {}_X\rho]$$

in the case of grouping through sums. For the case of grouping through averages, we have instead,

$$0.25\ {}_X\sigma^2\ [1 + 1.5\ {}_X\rho] \leq {}_{X^*}\sigma^2 \leq 0.25\ {}_X\sigma^2\ [1 + 2.0\ {}_X\rho]$$

It is easy to see that the range of the variance in this irregular lattice is the same as in the 4-by-4 regular lattice studied in Example 5.1 to which we refer for the theoretical limits on the value of the spatial autocorrelation ${}_X\rho$ under different hypotheses (See Tables 5.4.1 and 5.4.2).

For the purpose of illustration we now consider the zoning range of ${}_X\sigma^2$ in an empirical case. We refer to the data of ENEL (Italian Electric Energy National Company) about the electricity consumption in Tuscany (See Appendix A2) and we consider the variable "worked hours" of the medium-sized manufacturing industry in the first semester of 1985 recorded by ENEL in the 40 *comuni* of Arezzo. The data are displayed in Table 5.4.5. The variance at the individual level is 4891.24.

Code number	Comune	Worked hours
1	Anghiari	172.176
2	Arezzo	161.837
3	Badia tebalda	0.0
4	Bibbiena	284.173
5	Bucine	129.381
6	Capolona	166.842
7	Caprese Michelangiolo	53.841
8	Castel Focognano	159.800
9	Castelfranco di Sopra	114.386
10	Castel San Niccolo'	121.884
11	Castiglione Fibocchi	177.547
12	Castiglion Fiorentino	344.325
13	Cavriglia	258.632
14	Chitignano	0.0
15	Chiusi della Verna	126.295
16	Civitella in Val di Chiana	160.342
17	Cortona	154.950
18	Foiano della Chiana	185.245
19	Laretina	181.019
20	Loro Ciuffenna	172.245
21	Lucignano	151.503
22	Marciano della Chiana	154.340
23	Montemignaio	0.0
24	Monterchi	86.759
25	Monte San Savino	227.173
26	Montevarchi	189.076
27	Ortignano Raggiolo	205.000
28	Pergine Valdarno	93.332
29	Pian di Sco	117.722
30	Pieve Santo Stefano	296.164
31	Poppi	111.344
31.a	Poppi	111.344
32	Pratovecchio	260.094
33	San Giovanni Valdarno	327.947
34	Sansepolcro	173.553
35	Sestino	250.000
36	Stia	318.328
37	Subbiano	159.976
38	Talla	0.0
39	Terranuova Bracciolini	202.355

Table 5.4.5 : Worked hours of the medium-sized manufacturing industry in 40 *comuni* of Arezzo (Tuscany) in the first semester of 1985 . Source : See Appendix A.2.

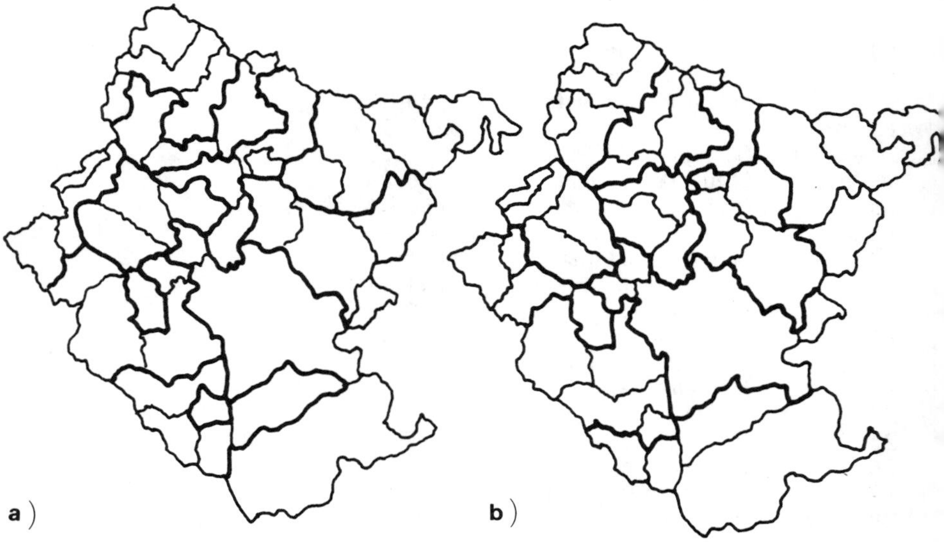

Figure 5.4.4: Two regular zoning systems of the provincia of Arezzo (Italy). In the case (a) v_i*= 1.5. In the case (b) v_i*= 2.0.

We now group the observations according to the two schemes of Figure 5.4.4 i.e. in the case of minimum and maximum average within group connectedness. The resulting observations are displayed in Table 5.4.6 for the cases of aggregation through sums .

In the case of grouping through sums the resulting range of the variance is

$$24161.2 \le {}_{X^*}\sigma^2 \le 26343.5$$

This can also be expressed as

$$4.939\ {}_X\sigma^2 \le {}_{X^*}\sigma^2 \le 5.508\ {}_X\sigma^2$$

The range of the variances lies above the value of $4\ {}_X\sigma^2$ which is the value expected in the case of independence between the observations (See § 5.2.2). Therefore the analysis of this example suggests the presence of a moderate positive spatial autocorrelation among the original data (See the theory of this chapter and Table 5.4.1)
Furthermore, in the case of grouping through averages we have

$$1506.50 \le {}_{X^*}\sigma^2 \le 1683.81$$

or

$$0.308\ {}_X\sigma^2 \le {}_{X^*}\sigma^2 \le 0.344\ {}_X\sigma^2$$

which confirms the previous conclusions.

Group number	Within group average connectedness Minimum $v_i^* = 1.5$	 Maximum $v_i^* 2.0$
1	689.766	700.306
2	722.401	711.861
3	818.687	452.937
4	383.932	719.717
5	452.937	385.993
6	600.005	607.162
7	592.464	911.693
8	648.674	595.566
9	908.246	868.987
10	659.818	606.708
Variance	24161.200	26343.500

Table 5.4.6: Worked hours of the medium-sized manufacturing industry in two zoning systems of the *provincia* of Arezzo (Tuscany, Italy) in the first semester of 1985.

5.4.4. Zoning range of the autocovariance and of the autocorrelation functions

THEORY

Following the lines of the previous section let us now consider, for the case of regular zoning, the range of the spatial autocovariance ${}_{X*}\gamma$ and of the spatial autocorrelation ${}_{X*}$ of the group-process.
From the analysis of Chapter 4 we know that

$$ {}_{X*}\gamma = t_{il}\ {}_{X}\gamma \qquad (5.4.12)$$

in the case of grouping through sums. It is

$$ {}_{X*}\gamma = t_{il}\,(r_i r_l)^{-1}\ {}_{X}\gamma \qquad (5.4.13)$$

if we are grouping through means. It is therefore necessary to recall the theoretical range of the between groups connectedness, that is (See § 3.3.2)

$$ 2 \le t_{il} \le r_i r_l \qquad (5.4.14)$$

In our case, since $r_i = r_l = r$, we have

$$ 2 \le t_{il} \le r^2 \qquad (5.4.15)$$

It follows that the theoretical range of the spatial autocovariance in a regular zoning system is

$$ 2\ {}_{X}\gamma \le {}_{X*}\gamma \le r^2\ {}_{X}\gamma \qquad (5.4.16)$$

in the case of grouping through sums. It is

$$ 2\,r^{-2}\ {}_{X}\gamma \le {}_{X*}\gamma \le {}_{X}\gamma \qquad (5.4.17)$$

in the case of grouping through means.
The theoretical range of ${}_{X*}\rho$ is obtained by considering that

$$ \mathrm{Min}\,|{}_{X*}\rho| = \mathrm{Min}\,|{}_{X*}\gamma|\ \{\mathrm{Max}\ {}_{X*}\sigma^2\}^{-1} \qquad (5.4.18)$$

and

$$ \mathrm{Max}\,|{}_{X*}\rho| = \mathrm{Max}\,|{}_{X*}\gamma|\ \{\mathrm{Min}\ {}_{X*}\sigma^2\}^{-1} \qquad (5.4.19)$$

ubstituting the values of ${}_{x*}\gamma$ and ${}_{x*}\sigma^2$ we have that

$$2r^{-1}\,{}_x\rho\{1+(r-1)\,{}_x\rho\}^{-1} \le |{}_{x*}\rho| \le r\,{}_x\rho\{1+2(r-1)r^{-1}\,{}_x\rho\}^{-1} \tag{5.4.20}$$

n both the case of sums and the case of means, since ${}_{x*}\rho$ is a standardized moment.
et us now examine the empirical range of ${}_{x*}\gamma$ and ${}_{x*}\rho$ in some particular spatial chemes.

XAMPLE 5.4: A 4-BY-4 REGULAR LATTICE GRID

o start with let us go back to the previous example of a 4-by-4 regular grid lattice. We ow have the property that, when the within group average connectedness attains its ninimum ($v_i^*=1.5$), the between group average connectedness is at its maximum level $t_{il} = 8$). Conversely when v_i^* is at its maximum ($v_i^* = 2$), t_{il} has the minimum value f 4 (See Figure 5.4.2). As a consequence the spatial autocovariance of the group-rocess is

$$4\,{}_x\gamma \le |{}_{x*}\gamma| \le 8\,{}_x\gamma \tag{5.4.21}$$

n the case of grouping through sums, and

$$0.25\,{}_x\gamma \le |{}_{x*}\gamma| \le 0.5\,{}_x\gamma \tag{5.4.22}$$

n the case of grouping through means. Hence for the spatial autocorrelation of the roup-process we have

$$4\,{}_x\gamma\{4\,{}_x\sigma^2(1+2\,{}_x\rho)\}^{-1} \le |{}_{x*}\rho| \le 8\,{}_x\gamma\{4\,{}_x\sigma^2(1+1.5\,{}_x\rho)\}^{-1} \tag{5.4.23}$$

r simply

$$ {}_x\rho\{1+2\,{}_x\rho\}^{-1} \le |{}_{x*}\rho| \le {}_x\rho\{1+1.5\,{}_x\rho\}^{-1} \tag{5.4.24}$$

or both the cases of grouping through sums and of grouping through means.
he limits of ${}_{x*}\rho$ for different values of ${}_x\rho$ (within the admissible range ${}_x\rho \ge -0.5$) are eported in Table 5.4.7.
rom Table 5.4.7 it is possible to see that, analogously to the range of the variance, the ange of ${}_{x*}\rho$ increases with the absolute value of ${}_x\rho$.

Individual process spatial autocorrelation $_X\rho$	Group process spatial autocorrelation Minimum	Maximum
-0.1	-0.125	-0.117
0.0	0.000	0.000
0.1	0.083	0.174
0.5	0.250	0.571
0.9	0.320	0.766

Table 5.4.7 Limits of the group-process spatial autocorrelation for different values of the individual-process spatial autocorrelation in a 4-by-4 regular square lattice grid when the group size is r = 4.

EXAMPLE 5.5: A 9-BY-9 REGULAR LATTICE GRID

As a second example let us examine again the 9-by-9 regular grid lattice and observ that the minimum of v_i^*, which is 1.78, corresponds to the line transect case when th between group connectedness is at its maximum (t_{i1} = 18). Conversely, at the maximu of the between group average connectedness, (v_i^*=2.67) corresponds the minimum o t_{i1}, which is now 6 (See Figure 5.4.3).

In this spatial scheme, therefore, the range of the spatial autocovariance, at a group-process level, is

$$6 \;_X\gamma \leq {}_{X*}\gamma \leq 18 \;_X\gamma \qquad (5.4.25)$$

in the case of grouping through sums, and

$$(6/81) \;_X\gamma \leq {}_{X*}\gamma \leq (18/81) \;_X\gamma \qquad (5.4.26)$$

in the case of grouping through means.
As a consequence we have for the spatial autocorrelation of the group-process

$$6_X\gamma \{ 9_X\sigma^2 (1 + 2.67_X\rho)\}^{-1} \leq |_{X*}\rho| \leq 18_X\gamma \{9_X\sigma^2 (1 + 1.78_X\rho)\}^{-1} \qquad (5.4.27)$$

or

$$0.66_X\rho\{ 1 + 2.67_X\rho\}^{-1} \leq |_{X*}\rho| \leq 2_X\rho \{1 + 1.78_X\rho\}^{-1} \qquad (5.4.28)$$

for both the case of sums and the case of means. The range of ${}_X*\rho$ for different values of ${}_X\rho$ (${}_X\rho \geq 0.374$) is reported in Table 5.4.8.
Table 5.4.8 confirms the results of Example 5.4, that the range of the group-process spatial autocorrelation increases with the absolute value of the individual-process spatial autocorrelation. Furthermore when the other elements are held constant, the indeterminacy of ${}_X*\rho$ is higher with r = 9 than with r = 4.

5.4.5. Zoning distribution of the moments of the group-process

THEORY

In the previous section we have considered the maximum and the minimum value of the moments of the group-process. These limits can be interpreted as the extreme values of the distribution of the various moments for alternative regular zonings at each scale. Along the lines of the foregoing analysis we can now study the complete *regular zoning distribution* of the moments of the group-process.
As already stated the distribution of the various moments can be studied by simply looking at the distribution of the connectedness of alternative regular zoning systems. A zoning distribution of the connectedness arises from the fact that we can have more than one regular zoning which yields the same level of connectedness. If we consider for example a 4-by-4 regular grid lattice, there are various configurations of the spatial system (some of which are reported in Figure 5.4.5) that give rise to the same value of the average within group connectedness $v_i^*=1.5$. In contrast there is a single regular zoning system that produces a level of the average within group connectedness $v_i^* = 2$.
In this simple case the zoning distribution of the within group average connectedness is the one shown in Figure 5.4.6(a).

Individual process spatial autocorrelation ${}_X\rho$	Group process spatial autocorrelation Minimum	Maximum
-0.1	-0.240	-0.090
0.0	0.000	0.000
0.1	0.052	0.169
0.5	0.142	0.529
0.9	0.175	0.692

Table 5.4.8 Limits of the group-process spatial autocorrelation for different values of the individual-process spatial autocorrelation in a 9-by-9 regular square lattice grid when the group size is r = 9 .

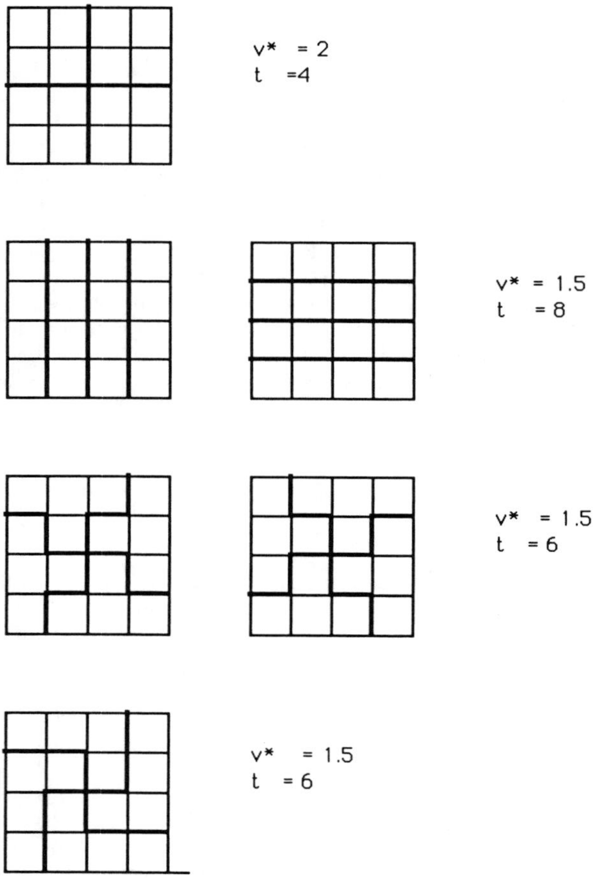

Fig 5.4.5 : Different "regular zoning systems of 16 cells on a 4-by-4 regular lattice grid with various levels of connectedness for r= 4.

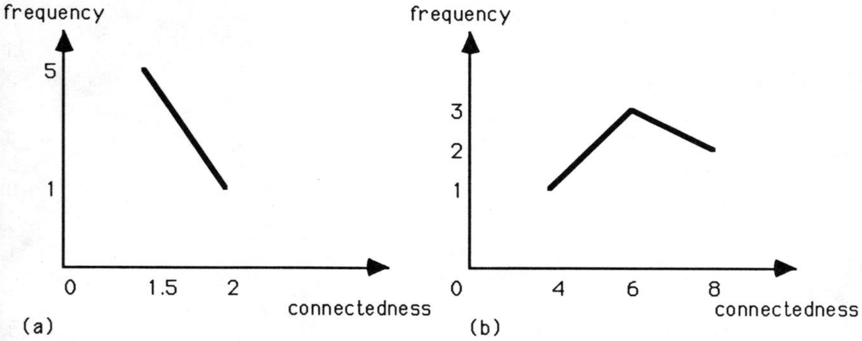

Fig .5.4.6: Frequency distribution of the possible levels of the (a) within group and (b) between group connectedness in a 4-by-4 regular square lattice grid with the group size r= 4.

Analogously we can derive the distribution of the between group connectedness which is isplayed in Figure 5.4.6(b). It follows that in this simple lattice, if we aggregate through sums of the observations, the variance of the group-process will show the ollowing frequency distribution

value of ${}_X{*}\sigma^2$	frequency
$4\ {}_X\sigma^2\ (1 + 1.5\ {}_X\rho)$	5
$4\ {}_X\sigma^2\ (1 + 2\ {}_X\rho)$	1

with a similar distribution in the case of aggregation through means.
imilarly the spatial autocovariance of the group-process will be distributed in the ollowing way

value of ${}_X{*}\gamma$	frequency
$4\,{}_X\gamma$	1
$6\,{}_X\gamma$	3
$8\,{}_X\gamma$	2

with analogous distributions in the case of grouping through means. Finally the spatial utocorrelation at a group-process level will be distributed as follow

value of ${}_{x}*\rho$	frequency
${}_{x}\rho\,(1 + 2{}_{x}\rho)$	1
$1.5{}_{x}\rho\,(1 + 1.5{}_{x}\rho)$	3
$2{}_{x}\rho\,(1 + 1.5{}_{x}\rho)$	2

In general we expect that when n is large, if compared with r, there is a great number possible alternatives for regular zoning systems. Hence the distribution of th connectedness can be approximated by a continuous function. Furthermore the with group connectedness is a measure of the internal cohesion of a group. Therefore it can argued that the higher the cohesion, the stronger are the constraints when the areas a combined into larger groups. Hence the number of configurations that it is possible obtain with a given level of within group connectedness decreases with the within gro connectedness itself (See Figure 5.4.6.a). As a consequence the frequency distribution the within group average connectedness will be a monotonically decreasing function. contrast, for the between group connectedness we can expect that the values close to th limits are attained less frequently than other values. This gives rise to a unimod Gaussian distribution of the between groups connectedness and hence of the spati autocorrelation in various zoning systems. (See Figure 5.4.6.b).
With such a premise the study of the zoning distribution of ${}_{x}*\sigma^2$ coincides with the stu of the zoning distribution of the within group connectedness v_i* and the study of th distribution of the autocovariance coincides with the study of the zoning distribution the between group connectedness t_{il}. When the number of cells is large, compared wi the group size, we have to consider a large number of zoning systems so that computational study appears to be the only possible approach. We take this as th approach to be followed .

PERMUTATIONAL STUDY

In developing a computational approach to the study of the connectedness distribution different lattices we adopt the following steps (the FORTRAN program used in th simulation is listed in Appendix 5.2):
1) The areas at an individual-process level are coded with an integer j=1,.......,n.
2) A series of pseudo-random permutations of the first n integers are performed and th groups are formed by considering at each permutation the first r areas to be in the fir group, the areas from r + 1 to 2r to be in the second group and so on. This procedur produces a series of grouping systems with no particular constraint.
3) Among the grouping systems obtained only those that fulfill the contiguity constrai (zoning systems) are retained.
4) The connectivity within groups is computed in each zoning system and the zonings th do not fulfill the regularity requirement are eliminated.

(AMPLE 5.6

; a first example we consider a 6-by-6 regular square lattice grid and different random ·rangements of the 36 areas into groups of 6 cells each. A number of pseudo-random ·rmutations of the first 36 integers were performed using the subroutine G05EJF of e Nag library on the IBM 3081 of the University of Cambridge, in order to produce)0 regular zoning systems. Some of the regular zoning systems produced are displayed Figure 5.4.7.
ıe resulting frequency distribution of the within group average connectedness is splayed in Table 5.4.8.
ıble 5.4.8 shows that in this case we obtain the monotonically decreasing frequency stribution which was expected by the theory. Note that in the case of $v_i^* = 2.33$, the two ses found after 200 permutations are the only possible configurations.
; a consequence of Table 5.4.8, in the case of grouping through sums, we derive the llowing empirical distribution of ${}_{x}{*}\sigma^2$ in a 6-by-6 regular square lattice grid :

value of ${}_{x}{*}\sigma^2$	frequency
$4\ {}_{x}\sigma^2\,(1 + 1.67\ {}_{x}\rho)$	113
$4\ {}_{x}\sigma^2\,(1 + 2.00\ {}_{x}\rho)$	85
$4\ {}_{x}\sigma^2\,(1 + 2.33\ {}_{x}\rho)$	2

ith an analogous distribution in the case of grouping through averages. The same stribution is displayed in Figure 5.4.8.

'alue of the within group ıverage connectedness	frequency
1.67	113
2.00	85
2.33	2

ıble 5.4.8: Empirical frequency distribution of the possible levels of the average within oup connectedness in a 6-by-6 regular square lattice grid with a group size r = 4.

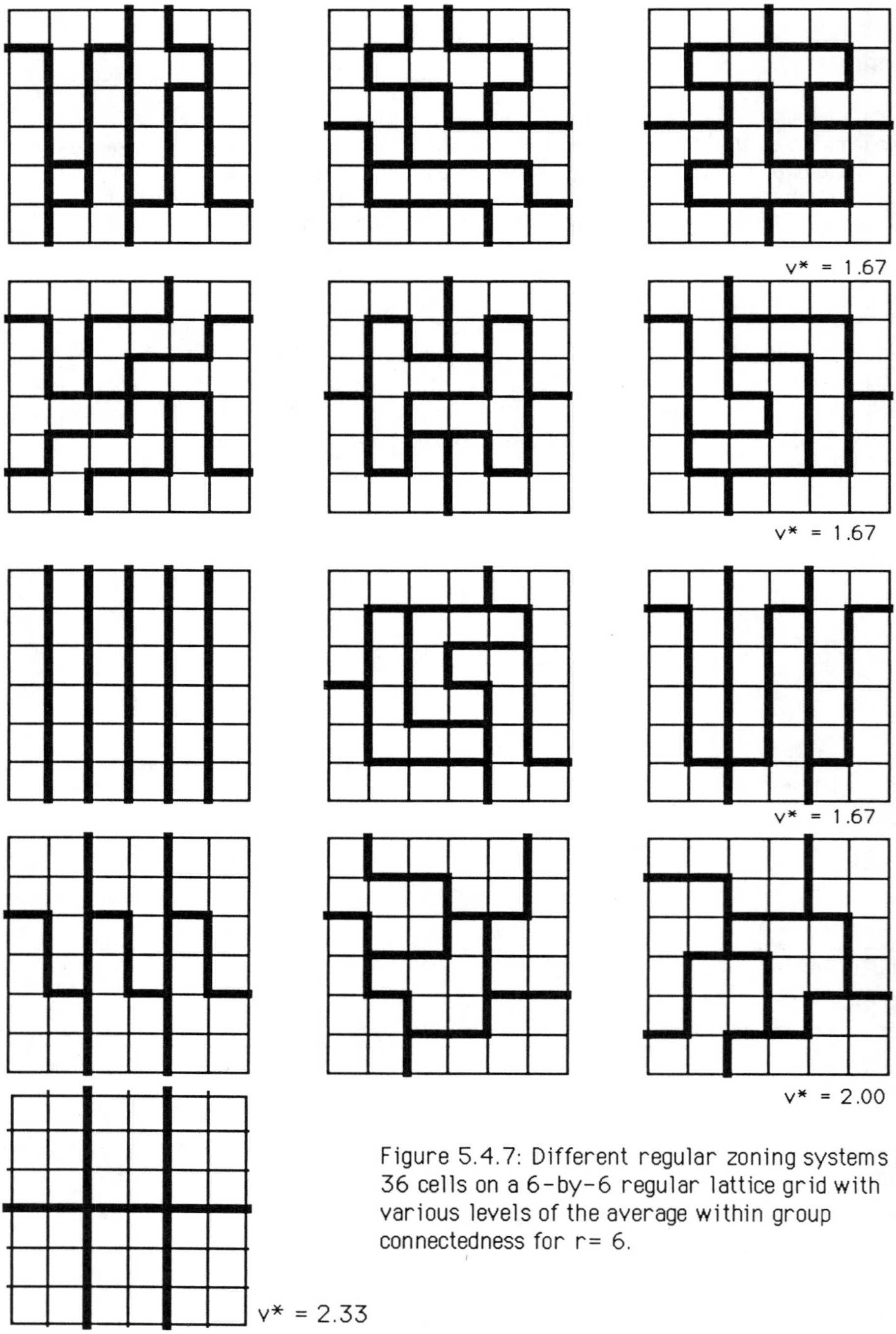

Figure 5.4.7: Different regular zoning systems of 36 cells on a 6-by-6 regular lattice grid with various levels of the average within group connectedness for r= 6.

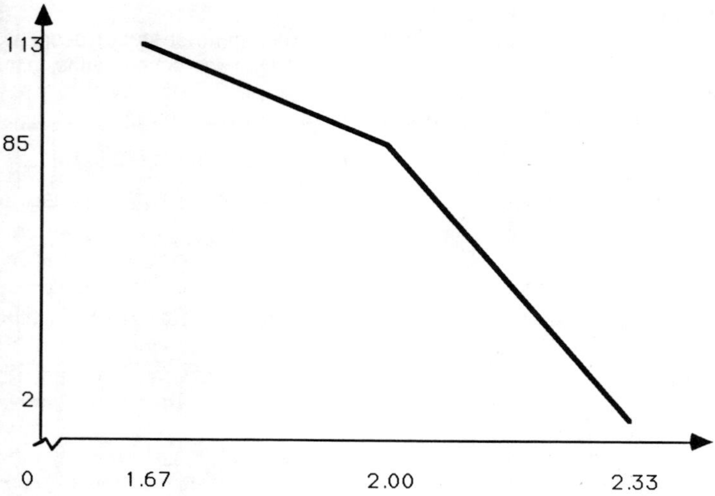

Figure 5.4.8 : Empirical frequency distribution of the possible levels of within group average connectedness after 200 permutations of a 6-by-6 regular square lattice grid with group size r = 4.

XAMPLE 5.7

second and larger 9-by-9 regular lattice is now considered employing the same rocedure. A wider range of configurations is now possible. In fact the within group verage connectedness can assume the values of 1.78, 2.00, 2.22, 2.44 and 2.67. In this omputational study a lot more of pseudo-random permutations had to be considered in rder to produce 200 regular zoning systems. Some of the regular zonings produced by he pseudo-random procedure are displayed in Figure 5.4.9.

n this case the empirical frequency distribution of v_i^* is displayed in Table 5.4.9.

s a consequence we can derive the following frequency distribution of ${}_X\sigma^2$ in a 9-by-9 egular square lattice grid:

value of ${}_{X*}\sigma^2$	frequency
$9\ {}_X\sigma^2\,(1 + 1.78\ {}_X\rho)$	165
$9\ {}_X\sigma^2\,(1 + 2.00\ {}_X\rho)$	23
$9\ {}_X\sigma^2\,(1 + 2.22\ {}_X\rho)$	8
$9\ {}_X\sigma^2\,(1 + 2.44\ {}_X\rho)$	3
$9\ {}_X\sigma^2\,(1 + 2.67\ {}_X\rho)$	1

The same distribution is also shown in Figure 5.4.10 .
The results of this second permutation study confirms the monotonically decreasi character of the frequency distribution of the within group average connectedness fou in the previous example.
The two examples of this section will be taken a stage further in the next chapter.

Value of the within group average connectedness	frequency
1.78	165
2.00	23
2.22	8
2.44	3
2.67	1

Table 5.4.9 : Empirical frequency distribution of the possible levels of the avera within group connectedness in a 9-by-9 regular square lattice grid with a group size r 9.

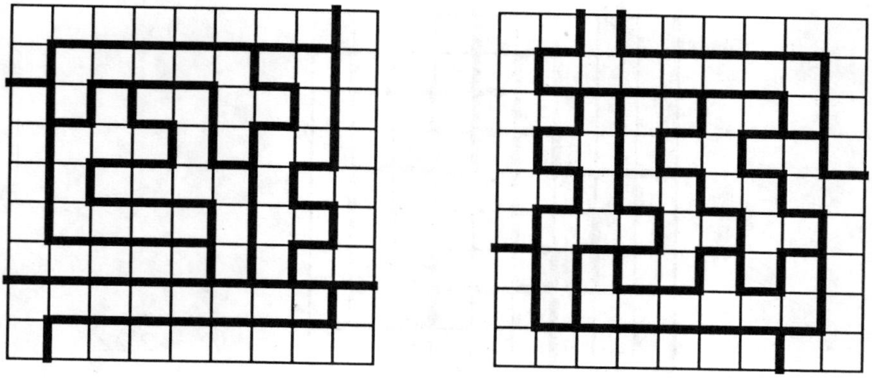

v* = 1.78

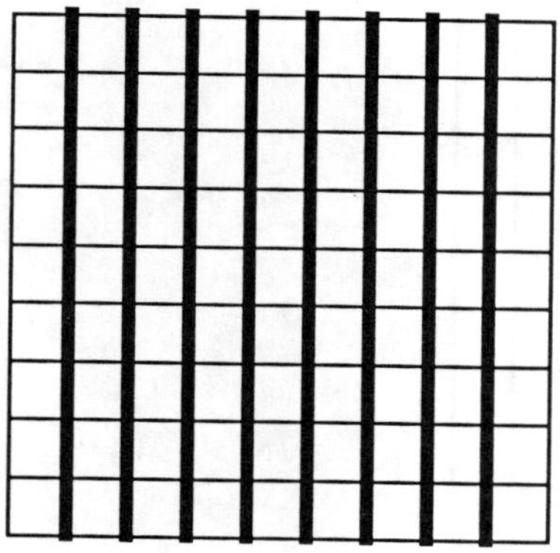

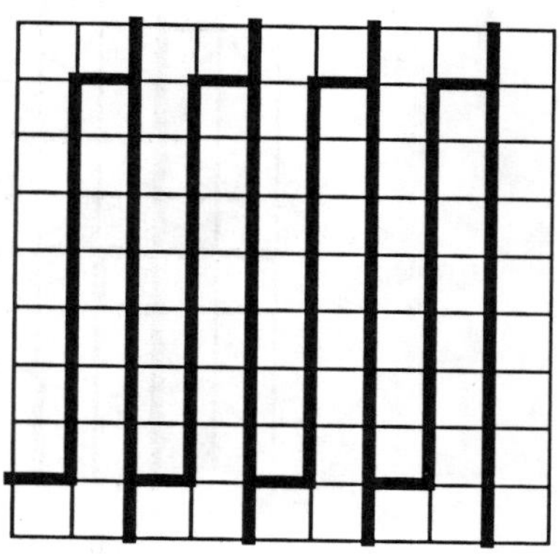

v* = 2.00

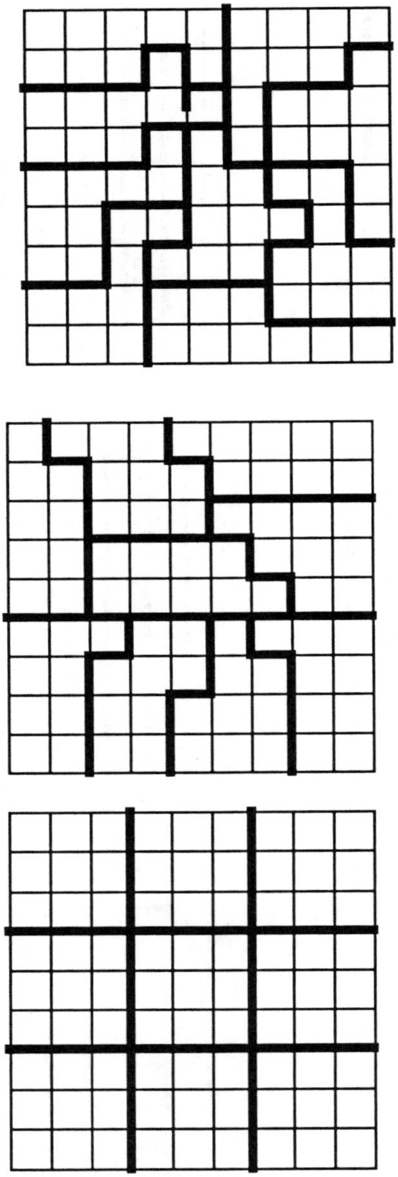

v* = 2.22

v* = 2.44

v* = 2.67

Figure 5.4.9: Different regular zoning systems of 81 cells on a 9-by-9 regular square lattice grid with various levels of the within group connectedness for r = 9.

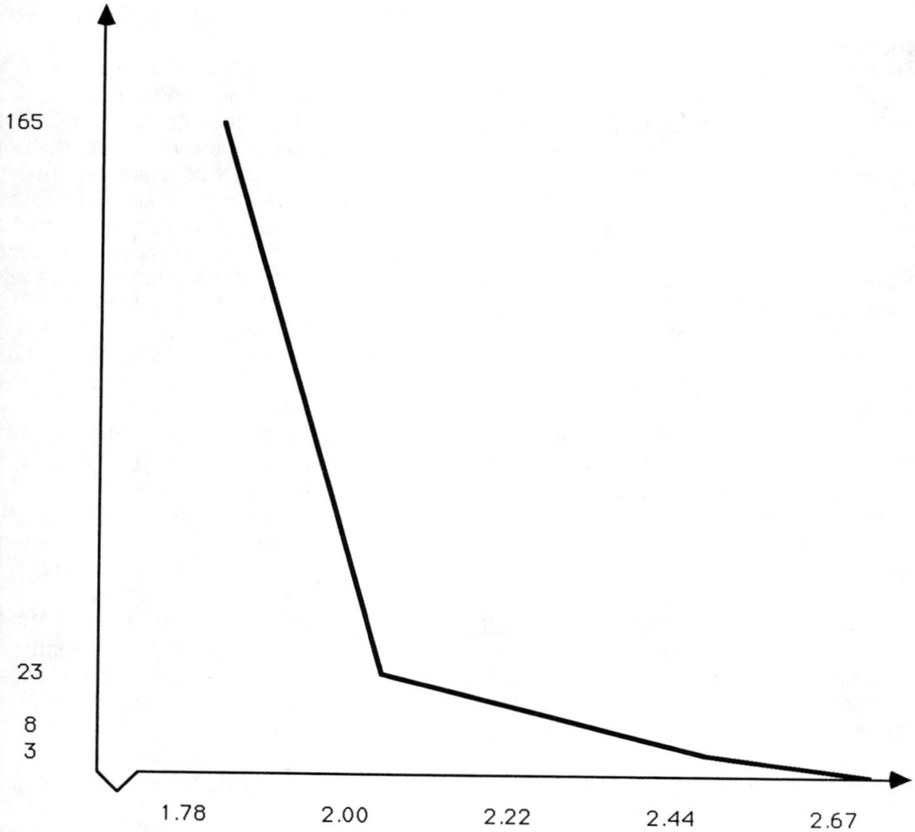

'igure 5.4.10: Empirical distribution of the possible levels of within group average onnectedness in a 9-by-9 regular square lattice grid with group size r=9.

5.5 SUMMARY AND CONCLUSION

This chapter has applied the theory developed in Chapter 4 to the modifiable areal un problem in univariate statistical analysis. In particular we have analysed the effects shifting from an individual-process level to a group-process level when:
(a) the groups are equal shape, but of different size (scale problem in regula lattices § 5.2)
(b) the groups differ both in size and shape (scale problem in irregular lattices § 5.3 and
(c) the groups are equal in size, but they differ in their shape (aggregatio problem § 5.4)
Concerning the scale problem in regular lattices we have found that the variation of th various moments by shifting from the individual-process to the group-process lev depends upon the spatial configuration of the data and that this dependence can b expressed through a functional form. This has led us to provide a theoretical explanatic of the empirical evidence of the decrease (increase) of the variance when we shift th level of resolution by averaging (summation), and of the dampening in absolute value the spatial autocorrelation as we increase the group size (Cliff and Ord, 1981 Furthermore we have proved that the spatial autocorrelation of a process at differe scales can be studied by observing the rate of decrease (increase) of the variance whe we pass from the finest to a coarser level of resolution. Finally we have found (for bo regular and irregular lattices) that there is a minimum achievable value of the spati autocorrelation imposed by the configuration of the spatial system. This limit empirically found by other authors (Openshaw and Taylor, 1979), is inversely relat to the average within group connectedness of the spatial system.
Dealing with the scale problem in irregular lattices we have proposed an area-weighti solution which is corrected to take into account not only the size of the areas, as in th traditional theory (Robinson, 1956), but also the connectedness and the level o dependence among the observations. Furthermore we have proposed a recursiv procedure to estimate the moments of the individual-process when only the group process is observed. The performance of the revised area-weighting solution and of th iterative estimation procedure is tested through empirical examples.
Finally focusing on the aggregation problem, we have studied the theoretical limit within which the moments of the group-process are free to range when we modify th zonal boundaries. The complete zoning distribution of the variance and of the spati autocorrelation was also studied both theoretically and practically in some regular a irregular spatial systems, by exploiting a computational approach.

The set of results obtained in the present chapter will be extended in the next chapter deal with bivariate spatial series.

APPENDIX 5.1

FORTRAN PROGRAM FOR THE RECURSIVE ESTIMATION OF σ^2 AND ρ

```
C
C          ESTIMATE THE INDIVIDUAL-PROCESS MOMENTS WITH THE GROUP C
C          PROCESS OBSERVATIONS
C
           PARAMETER(NZONES=20,NOBS=200,NLINKS=62)
C
           REAL X( NZONES ), R( NZONES),A( NZONES),W( NZONES, NZONES)
           REAL T( NZONES, NZONES), RHO(NOBS),M(NZONES,NOBS)
           REAL Z( (NZONES,NOBS),AV(NOBS).S( (NZONES,NOBS)
           REAL SS( (NZONES,NOBS),VAR(NOBS),V(NZONES,NZONES)
           REAL C(NZONES,NZONES),COV
           REAL B, XS(NZONES),COVP(NZONES)
C
C          NOW READS THE STARTING VALUE OF RHO
C
           READ(5,*) RHO(1)
C
C          NOW READS THE VECTOR OF OBSERVATIONS ON THE GROUP-PROCESS
C
           DO 103 I=1,NZONES
103        READ(5,*) X(I)
C
C          NOW READS THE DIMENSIONS OF THE GROUPS (ri) AND THEIR WITHIN
C          GROUP CONNECTEDNESS (Ai)
C
           DO 2 I=1,NZONES
           READ (5,*) R(I)
2          CONTINUE
           DO 3 I=1,NZONES
           READ(5,*)A(I)
3          CONTINUE
C
C          NOW READS THE CONNECTIVITY MATRIX W
C
           DO 20 I=1,NZONES
           READ(5,*) (W(I,J),J=1,NZONES)
20         CONTINUE
C
C          NOW READS THE MATRIX OF THE BETWEEN GROUPS LINK T
C
           DO 11 I=1,NZONES
           READ (5,*)(T(I,J),J=1,NZONES
11         CONTINUE
C
C          COMPUTES THE MEAN OF THE VECTOR OF OBSERVATIONS X
```

```
C
      B=0.0
      DO 30 I=1,NZONES
      B=B +X(I)
30    CONTINUE
      B = B/7
      DO 80 I=1,NZONES
      XS(I)=X(I)-B
80    CONTINUE
C
C     MAIN LOOP OF RECURSIVE ESTIMATION BEGINS
C
      DO 2200 K=1, NOBS
C
C     COMPUTES THE WEIGHTS FOR THE VARIANCE
C
      DO 5 I=1,NZONES
      M(I,K) =0.0
      M(I,K)=M(I,K)+((RHO(K)*A(I)/R(I))+1)*R(I))
      M(I,K)=M(I,K)**0.5
      M(I,K)=1/M(I,K)
5     CONTINUE
C
C     NOW COMPUTES THE WEIGHTED VARIANCE
C
      DO 6 I=1,NZONES
      Z(I,K)=0.0
      Z(I,K)=Z(I,K)+M(I,K)*X(I))
6     CONTINUE
      AV(K)=0.0
      DO 7 I=1,NZONES
      AV(K)=AV(K)+Z(I,K)
7     CONTINUE
      AV(K)=AV(K)/NZONES
      DO 8 I=1,NZONES
      S(I,K)=0.0
      S(I,K)=S(I,K)+(Z(I,K)-AV(K))
      SS(I,K)=S(I,K)**2
8     CONTINUE
      VAR(K)=0.0
      DO 9 I=1,NZONES
      VAR(K)=VAR(K)+SS(I,K)
9     CONTINUE
      VAR(K)=VAR(K)/NZONES
C
C     NOW COMPUTES THE WEIGHTS FOR THE SPATIAL AUTOCOVARIANCE
C
      DO 12 I=1,NZONES
      DO 13 J=1,NZONES
      Y(I,J)=W(I,J)/(T(I,J)+0.00001)
13    CONTINUE
```

```
12        CONTINUE
C
C         WHEN T(I,J)=0 ALSO W(I,J)=0. THE INCLUSION OF 0.00001 ENSURES
C         THAT THE RATIO T(I,J)/W(I,J) = 0 AS IT IS NEEDED RATHER THAN BEING
C         AN UNDETERMINED QUANTITY. WHEN W(I,J)≠0 ALSO T(I,J)≠0 AND THEIR
C         RATIO □ W(I,J)/T(I,J)+0.00001
C
C         NOW COMPUTES THE WEIGHTED SPATIAL AUTOCOVARIANCE
C
          COV=0.0
          DO 60 I=1,NZONES
          COVP=0.0
          DO 70 I=1,NZONES
70        COVP(J)=COVP(J)+Y(I,J)*XS(I)
60        COV=COV+COVP(J)*XS(J)
          COV=COV/NLINKS
C
C         NOW ADJUSTS THE ESTIMATE OF THE SPATIAL AUTOCORRELATION
C
          RHO(K+1)=COV/VAR(K)
C
C         NOW WRITES THE RESULTS
C
          WRITE(6,*) RHO(K),VAR(K)
C
C         MAIN LOOP ENDS
C
2200      CONTINUE
C
C         END OF THE PROGRAM
C
          STOP
          END
```

APPENDIX 5.2

FORTRAN PROGRAM TO PRODUCE PSEUDO-RANDOM REGULAR ZONING SYSTEMS

```
C
C         GENERATES PSEUDO-RANDOM PERMUTATIONS
C
          INTEGER I,IFAIL, J ,K, M, N, NOUT, INDEX,
C
          PARAMETER(NZONES=36,NOBS=200)
C
          REAL W(NZONES,NZONES)
C
C         READS THE CONNECTIVITY MATRIX
C
          DO 50 I=1,NZONES
          READ (5,*)(W(I,J),J=1,NZONES)
50        CONTINUE
C
C         NOW CALL THE NAG ROUTINE WHICH PERMUTES THE FIRST (NZONES)
C         INTEGERS
C
          DATA NOUT/6/
          N= NZONES
          M= NOBS
          CALL G05CBF (0)
          WRITE (NOUT,99997) M, N
          DO 40 J= 1,M
                DO 20 I=1,N
                INDEX(I) = I
20        CONTINUE
          IFAIL =0
          CALL G05EHF(INDEX,N,IFAIL)
C
C         NOW INTRODUCE THE CONTIGUITY CONTRAINT IN THE FIRST GROUP
C
          IF (((W(INDEX(1),INDEX(2)).EQ.1.OR.W(INDEX(1),INDEX(3)).EQ.1
     *      .OR.W(INDEX(1),INDEX(4)).EQ.1.OR.W(INDEX(1),INDEX(5))
     *      .EQ.1.OR. W(INDEX(1),INDEX(6)) .EQ. 1)) .AND.
     *      ((W(INDEX(1),INDEX(2)).EQ.1 .OR. W(INDEX(3),INDEX(2)).EQ.1
     *      .OR. W(INDEX(2),INDEX(4)).EQ.1.OR.W(INDEX(2),INDEX(5))
     *      .EQ. 1.OR. W(INDEX(2),INDEX(6)).EQ.1)) .AND.
     *      ((W(INDEX(1),INDEX(3)).EQ.1.OR.W(INDEX(3),INDEX(2)).EQ.1
     *      .OR.W(INDEX(3),INDEX(4)).EQ.1.OR.W(INDEX(3),INDEX(5))
     *      .EQ.1.OR. W(INDEX(3),INDEX(6)).EQ.1)).AND.
     *      ((W(INDEX(1),INDEX(4)).EQ.1.OR.W(INDEX(4),INDEX(2)).EQ.1
     *      .OR. W(INDEX(3),INDEX(4)).EQ.1.OR. W(INDEX(4),INDEX(5))
     *      .EQ.1 .OR. W(INDEX(4),INDEX(6)) .EQ.1)) .AND.
     *      ((W(INDEX(1),INDEX(5)).EQ.1. OR. W(INDEX(5),INDEX(2)) .EQ.1
```

```
     *    .OR. W(INDEX(3),INDEX(5)) .EQ.1.OR. W(INDEX(4),INDEX(5))
     *    .EQ.1 .OR.(W(INDEX(5),INDEX(5)),EQ,1)).AND
     *    ((W(INDEX(1),INDEX(6)).EQ.1. OR. W(INDEX(6),INDEX(2)) .EQ.1
     *    .OR. W(INDEX(3),INDEX(6)) .EQ.1.OR. W(INDEX(4),INDEX(6))
     *    .EQ.1 .OR.(W(INDEX(5),INDEX(6)),EQ,1))) THEN
C
C         NOW INTRODUCE THE CONTIGUITY CONSTRAINTS FOR THE SECOND
C         GROUP
C
          ..................
C
C         NOW INTRODUCE THE CONTIGUITY CONSTRAINTS FOR THE LAST GROUP
C
          ................
C
C
C         NOW WRITE THE OBSERVATIONS
C
          WRITE (NOUT, 99998)(INDEX(K),K=1,N)
          ENDIF
99998     FORMAT( 1X,36I3)
99997     FORMAT(I3,23H,PERMUTATIONS OF THE FIRST,I2,9H INTEGERS/1X)
40        CONTINUE
C
C         END OF THE PROGRAM
C
          STOP
          END
```

6. Bivariate problems: The modifiable areal unit problem and correlation between processes

6.1 INTRODUCTION

In Chapter 5 we looked at a number of problems arising in the statistical analysis of a single variable measured in a cross-section such as a map, using the methodological framework put forward in Chapter 4. In this chapter, and in the next, we are interested in an extension of the previous results to the case of statistical analysis of spatial data with more than one variable. In particular the aim of this chapter is to consider the different results obtained when measuring the dependence between processes recorded at different level of spatial resolution, while in the next chapter we will deal with the *ecological fallacy* problem. For this reason throughout this chapter we will uniformly assume the *local covariance* hypothesis, as employed in Chapter 5. Furthermore we will restrict ourselves, consistent with the rest of the book, to Gaussian processes, so that the focus will be on the cross-correlations between processes. Finally, we will consider only bivariate spatial processes; the more general multivariate case involves a more complicated notation and theory beyond the scope of the present discussion (See Mardia, 1988; Wartenberg, 1985).

Historically it was for the analysis of the correlation between variables in data grouped at different levels of spatial resolution that the modifiable areal unit problem was first noticed. Yule and Kendall (1950; p.312) observed that "the magnitude of a correlation will, in general, depend on the unit chosen if that unit is modifiable"; as a result correlation measures "not only the variation of the quantities under consideration, but also the properties of the unit-mesh which we have imposed on the system in order to measure it". Similarly Cliff and Ord (198; p.130) observed that "the degrees of correlation between variables is a function of the size of the areas considered"; as a result they argued that a "suitable functional form describing the change in correlation with size" should be sought.

The aim of this chapter is to investigate the functional form linking the change in correlation between two variables with the size and the shape of the given spatial areas. Firstly, we will examine the case of observations laid on a regular square lattice grid (§ 6.2); secondly, we will investigate the aggregation problem where we modify not only the size, but also the shape of the areas (§ 6.3).

Before examining these problems in detail it is necessary, first, to make a classification of the different kinds of dependence that may occur when dealing with bivariate spatial processes.

6.1.1. Typologies of spatial dependence

Cliff and Ord (1981) distinguished two kinds of spatial dependence in a multivariate context.

First, it may happen that the realization of a process in one area depends on the realization of another process in the same area. This reflects a form of dependence referred to as *reaction*. This is what we normally look at in a standard regression analysis. It describes the whole pattern of possible dependence if we assume that the observations are drawn from a process with independent random components. However, if we consider a spatial series as the realization of a random process constituted by mutually dependent components, as is the object of this book, a second form of spatial dependence is involved which embodies the *interaction* between areas (Cliff and Ord, 1981; p.141).

This interaction is itself divided into two subcomponents. First there is the dependence between neighbouring random variables belonging to the same process; this is the spatial autocorrelation of the process, referred to in the regional economic literature as the *spill over* effect (See Paelinck and Nijkamp, 1975; p.450). The second subcomponent is the dependence between random variables recorded in neighbouring areas, but belonging to two different processes. This is sometimes referred to as the *spin off* effect (Paelinck and Nijkamp,1975; p.450).

Dealing with bivariate processes we can identify these different elements of dependence by looking at the variance-covariance matrix.

Consider the matrix $\mathbf{V}$ defined as in (4.2.72)

$$\mathbf{V} = \begin{pmatrix} {}_x\mathbf{V} & {}_{xy}\mathbf{V} \\ {}_{yx}\mathbf{V} & {}_y\mathbf{V} \end{pmatrix}$$

The off-diagonal elements of the sub-matrices ${}_x\mathbf{V}$ and ${}_y\mathbf{V}$, typically equal to ${}_x\rho$ ${}_y\rho$ or zero, represent the spatial autocorrelation displayed, respectively, by $\{X_i\}$ and $\{Y_i\}$. The submatrices ${}_{xy}\mathbf{V}$ and ${}_{yx}\mathbf{V}$, in contrast, contain the information about the cross-links between the two processes. In particular the diagonal elements of ${}_{xy}\mathbf{V}$ and ${}_{yx}\mathbf{V}$ represent the *reaction* term, or cross-covariances which are equal to ${}_{xy}\rho$. In contrast the off-diagonal elements represent the *interaction* term or lagged cross-covariance (or the spin off effect) between the two processes which is symbolized by ${}_{xy}\rho'$.

In economic geography we typically have

$$|{}_{xy}\rho| \geq |{}_{xy}\rho'| \qquad (6.1.1)$$

in that the dependence between the two processes $\{X\}$ and $\{Y\}$ is usually stronger within an area than between an area and its neighbours. Furthermore we will assume throughout this chapter that the two kinds of dependence are in the same direction, that is

$$\text{Sign}\,({}_{xy}\rho) = \text{Sign}\,({}_{xy}\rho') \qquad (6.1.2)$$

(For a fuller discussion see Paelinck and Nijkamp, 1975, p.451).
In the remainder of this chapter it will often be useful to refer to the ratio between the two kinds of cross-links , that is ${}_{xy}\rho' {}_{xy}\rho^{-1}$. From Formulae (6.1.1) and (6.1.2) we have the range of this ratio; that is

$$0 \leq {}_{xy}\rho' {}_{xy}\rho^{-1} \leq 1 \qquad (6.1.3)$$

Similarly, concerning the relationship between spill over and spin off effects we have typically

$$|{}_{x}\rho| \geq |{}_{xy}\rho'|$$
and
$$|{}_{y}\rho| \geq |{}_{xy}\rho'| \qquad (6.1.4)$$

Thus, as before, it is assumed that the dependence between the areas is stronger with respect to the same variable than to different variables. The relationships between ${}_{x}\rho$, ${}_{y}\rho$, ${}_{xy}\rho$ and ${}_{xy}\rho'$ are displayed diagrammatically in Figure 6.1.1.
In the analysis that follows we are interested in studying the change of the genuine reaction between two processes when we modify the size or the shape of the areas which constitute the spatial system.

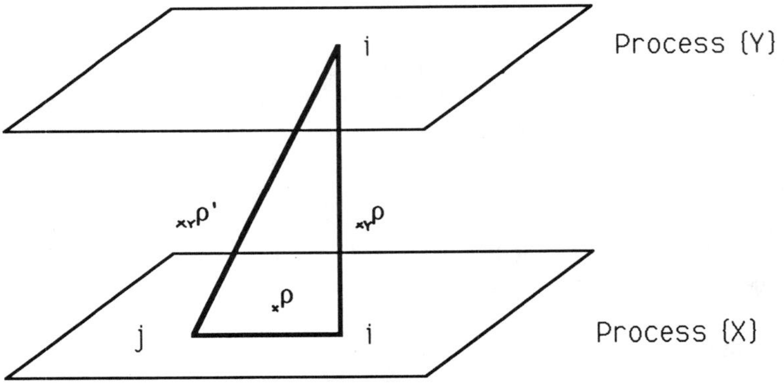

Figure 6.1.1 Typologies of dependence in a bivariate spatial process .

6.2 SCALE AND CORRELATION BETWEEN PROCESSES

6.2.1. Generalities

In this section we will consider the case in which we observe, at different levels of spatial resolution, a bivariate Gaussian process laid on a regular square grid lattice. It is worth stressing, for the sake of clarity, that this section represents the bivariate counter-part of § 5.2, to which we will refer for symbols and results.
The restriction to regular lattices allows us to deal with processes that are stationary at both the individual and the group level (with moments given by Formulae 4.2.93 to 4.2.104 in Chapter 4) so that we can concentrate on the "functional form" which links the individual-process cross-correlation with the group-process cross-correlation.
Cliff and Ord (1981) noticed that as adjacent areas are aggregated this causes an increase in correlation. This is consistent with the results obtained in the literature (Yule & Kendall, 1950; Openshaw and Taylor, 1979; Curry, 1972).
In this paragraph we will study the change in cross-correlation as a function of the size of the groups.
From Formulae 4.2.93 to 4.2.104 we have for the group-process cross-correlation of group i

$$ {}_{x^*y^*}\rho_i = {}_{x^*y^*}\rho = {}_{x^*y^*}\gamma\, {}_{x^*}\sigma^2\, {}_{y^*}\sigma^2 $$

$$ = \{[(1 + A_i r_i^{-1}\, {}_x\rho)(1 + A_i r_i^{-1}\, {}_y\rho)]^{-1/2}\}\{{}_{xy}\rho(1 + A_i r_i^{-1}\, {}_{xy}\rho'\, {}_{xy}\rho^{-1})\} $$

(6.2.1)

This applies both for the case when we aggregate through sums and through means.
In a regular lattice, like the one examined in § 5.2 (See also Figure 5.2.1) we know that the average within group connectedness is constant and equal to
$A_i r_i^{-1} = r_i^{-1}\,[\,4r - 4\sqrt{r}\,]$ (See 5.2.4).
Therefore we have

$$ {}_{x^*y^*}\rho $$

$$ =\{[(1 +(4r-4\sqrt{r})r_i^{-1}\, {}_x\rho)(1 +(4r-4\sqrt{r})r_i^{-1}\, {}_y\rho)]^{-1/2}\} $$
$$ \{{}_{xy}\rho[1 +(4r-4\sqrt{r})r_i^{-1}\, {}_{xy}\rho'\, {}_{xy}\rho^{-1}]\} $$

(6.2.2)

Formula (6.2.2) expresses the change in the cross-correlation between the process {X} and the process {Y} as a function of four elements :
(i) the size of the group r (the connectedness being held constant).
(ii) the spatial autocorrelation of the two processes ${}_x\rho$ and ${}_y\rho$.
(iii) the spin off effect between the process {X} and the process {Y} measured by ${}_{xy}\rho'$.

(iv) the value of the cross-correlation at the individual-process level measured by ${}_{xy}\rho$.

Before discussing the effect of shifting the level of spatial resolution (i.e. of increasing r) it is useful to discuss some relationships between the elements appearing in Formula (6.2.1).
First of all, let us set for the denominator of (6.2.1)

$$H = [(1 + A_i r_i^{-1}\, {}_x\rho)(1 + A_i r_i^{-1}\, {}_y\rho)]^{-1/2} \qquad (6.2.3)$$

From the discussion of the change in variance with changing levels of resolution (§ 5.2) we know that both ${}_x\rho$ and ${}_y\rho$ have a lower bound which equals minus the inverse of the average connectedness $-A_i^{-1} r_i$. Therefore we have that

$$H \geq 0 \qquad (6.2.4)$$

which holds always. This also gives a meaning to the expression under square root in Formula (6.2.1).
Secondly let us consider the sign of ${}_{x*y*}\rho$. Remembering that ${}_{xy}\rho' {}_{xy}\rho^{-1} \geq 0$ always (see Formula 6.1.3), it follows that

$$1 + A_i r_i^{-1}\, {}_{xy}\rho' {}_{xy}\rho^{-1} \geq 0 \qquad (6.2.5)$$

always. And , since H is also a positive expression, the sign of ${}_{x*y*}\rho$ is determined only by ${}_{xy}\rho$. We have, therefore, under our assumptions that the sign of the cross-correlation does not change as a result of changing the scale of analysis.
Finally let us consider the restriction imposed in Formula (6.2.1) by the fact that the admissible range of ${}_{x*y*}\rho$ has to be specified by:

$$-1 \leq {}_{x*y*}\rho \leq 1 \qquad (6.2.6)$$

As a result of this restriction it follows that:

$$-1 \leq \{{}_{xy}\rho + A_i r_i^{-1}\, {}_{xy}\rho'\} H^{-1} \leq 1 \qquad (6.2.7)$$

This holds since

$$-H - A_i r_i^{-1}\, {}_{xy}\rho' \leq {}_{xy}\rho \leq H - A_i r_i^{-1}\, {}_{xy}\rho' \qquad (6.2.8)$$

Thus when ${}_{xy}\rho \geq 0$ (and consequently when ${}_{xy}\rho' \geq 0$)

$${}_{xy}\rho \geq -H - A_i r_i^{-1}\, {}_{xy}\rho' \qquad (6.2.9)$$

always. Conversely when ${}_{xy}\rho \leq 0$ (and when ${}_{xy}\rho' \leq 0$)

$${}_{xy}\rho \leq H - A_i r_i^{-1}\, {}_{xy}\rho' \qquad (6.2.10)$$

always . Therefore the constraints (6.2.7) can also be written as

$$ {}_{xy}\rho \le H - A_i r_i^{-1}\, {}_{xy}\rho' \qquad \text{if } {}_{xy}\rho \ge 0 \tag{6.2.11}$$

and

$$ {}_{xy}\rho \ge -H - A_i r_i^{-1}\, {}_{xy}\rho' \qquad \text{if } {}_{xy}\rho \le 0 $$

This set of properties define formally the constraints imposed by the configuration of the spatial system under consideration to the group-process cross-covariance. As such they represent the bivariate extension of the lower bound to the spatial autocorrelation considered in § 5.2.2.

6.2.2. Change of the cross-correlation with the size of the areas

Let us now go back to Formula (6.2.1) We have that $| {}_{x*y*}\rho | \ge | {}_{xy}\rho |$ when

$$ | {}_{xy}\rho | \, (1 + A_i r_i^{-1}\, {}_{xy}\rho'\, {}_{xy}\rho^{-1})\, H^{-1} \ge | {}_{xy}\rho | \tag{6.2.12}$$

or

$$ (1 + A_i r_i^{-1}\, {}_{xy}\rho'\, {}_{xy}\rho^{-1})\, H^{-1} \ge 1 \tag{6.2.13}$$

First of all observe that when ${}_{xy}\rho'\, {}_{xy}\rho^{-1} = {}_{x}\rho = {}_{y}\rho$ the expression is exactly equal to one. Thus when ${}_{x}\rho = {}_{y}\rho = \rho$ the cross-covariance increases when we change the level of resolution provided that, in addition

$$ {}_{xy}\rho'\, {}_{xy}\rho^{-1} \ge \rho \tag{6.2.14}$$

This is a condition which is always met if $\rho \le 0$.
Another sufficient (although still not necessary) condition for the increase of the cross-correlation with grouping can be easily obtained by considering that $1 + A_i r_i^{-1}\, {}_{xy}\rho'\, {}_{xy}\rho^{-1} \ge 1$ since $A_i r_i\, {}_{xy}\rho'\, {}_{xy}\rho^{-1} \ge 0$.
Therefore for $| {}_{x*y*}\rho |$ to be greater than $| {}_{xy}\rho |$ it suffices that

$$ H \le 1 $$

or that

$$ [(1 + A_i r_i^{-1}\, {}_{x}\rho)(1 + A_i r_i^{-1}\, {}_{y}\rho)]^{1/2} \le 1 \tag{6.2.15}$$

Being H always positive, we can square both members of (6.2.15) which gives

$$ 1 + A_i r_i^{-1}\, {}_{x}\rho + A_i r_i^{-1}\, {}_{y}\rho + A_i^2 r_i^{-2}\, {}_{x}\rho\, {}_{y}\rho^{-1} \le 1 \tag{6.2.16}$$

And, dividing by the positive value $A_i r_i^{-1}$ yields

$$ {}_{x}\rho + {}_{y}\rho + A_i r_i^{-1}\, {}_{x}\rho\, {}_{y}\rho \le 0 \tag{6.2.17}$$

This provides a sufficient condition on ${}_x\rho_y\rho$. Furthermore if we consider that min $({}_x\rho)$ = min$({}_y\rho)$ = $-A_i^{-1}r_i$ (see § 5.2) we have two particularizations of (6.2.17)

$$_x\rho \leq -2\,{}_y\rho$$

and

$$_y\rho \leq -2\,{}_x\rho \qquad (6.2.18)$$

So far we have confined our attention only to the combinations of values of the spatial autocorrelation of the two processes, for which we get an increase in the cross-correlation shifting from one level of resolution to another. To obtain a sufficient and necessary condition which describes the effect of aggregation we need also to discuss the values of the cross-correlation and of the spatially lagged cross-correlation.
Going back to Formula (6.2.13) because both the denominator and the numerator are positive, it can be shown to be equivalent to

$$(1 + A_i r_i^{-1}\,{}_{xy}\rho'\,{}_{xy}\rho^{-1})^2\, H^{-2} \geq 1 \qquad (6.2.19)$$

or

$$(1 + A_i r_i^{-1}\,{}_{xy}\rho'\,{}_{xy}\rho^{-1})^2 \geq (1 + A_i r_i^{-1}\,{}_x\rho)(1 + A_i r_i^{-1}\,{}_y\rho)$$

Hence

$$1 + 2A_i r_i^{-1}\,{}_{xy}\rho'\,{}_{xy}\rho^{-1} + A_i^2 r_i^{-2}\,{}_{xy}\rho'^2\,{}_{xy}\rho^{-2}$$
$$\geq 1 + A_i r_i^{-1}\,{}_x\rho + A_i r_i^{-1}\,{}_y\rho + A_i^2 r_i^{-2}\,{}_x\rho\,{}_y\rho \qquad (6.2.20)$$

and, since $A_i r_i^{-1}$ is a positive expression

$$2\,{}_{xy}\rho'\,{}_{xy}\rho^{-1} + A_i r_i^{-1}\,{}_{xy}\rho'^2\,{}_{xy}\rho^{-2} \geq {}_x\rho + {}_y\rho + A_i r_i^{-1}\,{}_x\rho\,{}_y\rho \qquad (6.2.21)$$

Formula (6.2.21) expresses the necessary and sufficient condition to be fulfilled for the cross-correlation to increase when we pass from an individual to a group-process level. Unfortunately the formula is not immediately suggestive since the inequality condition depends on various combinations of six elements: the two spatial autocorrelations, the two cross-correlations, as well as the size and the connectedness of the two group-processes under consideration. As a result insights depend upon the circumstances of each individual empirical study. For this reason, in the next section, we will re-examine some examples found in the literature and interpret them in the light of the foregoing results.

6.2.3. Yule & Kendall data and other examples

YULE & KENDALL YIELDS OF WHEAT AND POTATOES

As a first example let us now consider the case examined by Yule and Kendall (1950; p.311). These two authors considered the yields per acre of wheat and potatoes in each of the 48 agricultural counties of England (See Chapter 2) in 1936, and found a correlation between the two variables of + 0.2189. They then grouped the counties in pairs and determined for each of the 24 resulting pairs the arithmetic mean yield. (Notice, however, that the contiguity constraint is not respected in all the groups). The correlation was then +0.2963. The process of grouping in pairs was then repeated to obtain 12 larger areas for which the value of the correlation was 0.5757. The process was then taken a step further to obtain 6 and 3 groups, but the results were not significant due to the lack of degrees of freedom.

The spatial map of the English counties is irregular but the connectedness is $A_i r_i^{-1} = 1$ for each group. This condition is sufficient to ensure that the process generating the observations is stationary at the group-process level provided that it is stationary at the individual-process level. From the analysis of § 6.2.2 we know that the cross-correlation increases with the size of the areas if

$$2\,{}_{xy}\rho'\,{}_{xy}\rho^{-1} + A_i r_i^{-1}\,{}_{xy}\rho'^{2}\,{}_{xy}\rho^{-2} \geq {}_x\rho + {}_y\rho + A_i r_i^{-1}\,{}_x\rho\,{}_y\rho$$

so that, in this case we have

$$2\,{}_{xy}\rho'\,{}_{xy}\rho^{-1} + {}_{xy}\rho'^{2}\,{}_{xy}\rho^{-2} \geq {}_x\rho + {}_y\rho + {}_x\rho\,{}_y\rho \qquad (6.2.22)$$

If we assume that the level of spatial autocorrelation is approximately the same for the two variables considered, and there is no strong reason to question this for wheat and potatoes yields, then we can make use of the sufficient condition (6.2.14) and assert that the cross-correlation increases if

$${}_{xy}\rho'\,{}_{xy}\rho^{-1} \geq \rho$$

where $\rho = {}_x\rho \approx {}_y\rho$. In our case, therefore, at the three levels of aggregation ${}_{xy}\rho'$ and ρ have to respect the inequalities:

$$\rho \leq 4.56\,{}_{xy}\rho'$$
$$\rho \leq 3.40\,{}_{xy}\rho'$$
$$\rho \leq 1.73\,{}_{xy}\rho'$$

This is consistent with the hypothesis (6.1.4) for ρ and ${}_{xy}\rho'$. These a priori results are consistent with, and provide explanation for the empirical findings of Yule and Kendall. Thus the theory developed in § 6.2.2 is demonstrated in this case.

OPENSHAW & TAYLOR ARTIFICIAL IOWA DATA

As a second example consider the data examined by Openshaw and Taylor (1979). These authors (as already shown in Chapter 2) describe a procedure for generating two sets of artificial data for 99 IOWA counties which satisfy the properties of zero skewness and kurtosis as in the normal distribution, have a cross-correlation between the two variables of 0.34, and have a specified spatial autocorrelation for the two variables. Three different levels of spatial autocorrelation were considered: (a) a maximum negative autocorrelation (for which the authors empirically specified the lower bound derived in § 5.2) which was defined at the values of −0.71 and −0.57 for the two variables, (b) a maximum positive autocorrelation which was empirically determined at the values of +0.82 and +0.92, and (c) zero autocorrelation. The authors then computed the cross-correlation between the two variables after simulating a number of alternative zoning systems. They found a general increase in cross-correlation as a result of shifting from a lower to a higher level of resolution.

In theory the results of this chapter should not be applied to the Openshaw and Taylor example because their case considers a number of zoning systems which yield non-stationary group-processes. Furthermore the analysis can be only partial because the effect of the lagged cross-covariance is not controlled for. However the analysis of this example is useful for illustrative purposes.

In the case of maximum positive autocorrelation for both variables let us set ${}_x\rho \approx {}_y\rho \approx \rho \approx +0.86$ (that is the mean between the empirical values of 0.82 and 0.92). Furthermore we consider ${}_{xy}\rho = +0.34$ as in the artificial IOWA data. Therefore

$$ {}_{x^*y^*}\rho \approx {}_{xy}\rho\,[1 + A_i r_i^{-1}\, {}_{xy}\rho'\,(0.34)^{-1}]\,[1 + A_i r_i^{-1}\, 0.86]^{-1} $$

so that $|{}_{x^*y^*}\rho| \geq |{}_{xy}\rho|$ if ${}_{xy}\rho' \geq 0.29$, which is consistent with the hypothesis concerning ${}_{xy}\rho'$ in § 6.1.1.

In the case of zero spatial autocorrelation we have simply

$$ {}_{x^*y^*}\rho = {}_{xy}\rho\,[1 + A_i r_i^{-1}\, {}_{xy}\rho'\,(0.34)^{-1}] \geq {}_{xy}\rho $$

always.

Finally in the case of maximum negative spatial autocorrelation we have that the sufficient condition stated in (6.2.14) is met and the cross-correlation always increases. Furthermore the denominator of (6.2.1) is now close to zero and, as a result, ${}_{x^*y^*}\rho$ increases towards its more extreme values.

Thus we have the property that the increase in cross-correlation when data are aggregated, must be sharper in the case of negative spatial autocorrelation case, must be moderated in the case of positive spatial autocorrelation and must assume an intermediate value in the random zoning case. This explains why Openshaw and Taylor (1979) found the more extreme values of cross-correlation when ρ is negative and less extreme values when ρ is positive. This example will be considered again in the next Section 6.3.

CLIFF & ORD LAND USE IN LONDON

As a final example we will consider some data drawn from the *Atlas of London* (Jones & Sinclair, 1968; sheets 43-45) and analysed by Cliff and Ord (1981; p.131). The data (as already shown in Chapter 2) give the area of floor space in office, commercial and industrial land use in London in 1962, recorded on a 24-by-24 regular square lattice. Cliff and Ord considered the cross-correlations between commerce and offices (regression 1) and between industry and offices (regression 2). They employed five different levels of successive aggregation of the original data, considering at each stage 4, 4, 4 and 3 cells of the previous level. This is summarized in Table 6.2.1.

They found that at the lower scales (level 1 and 2) the competitive influence between land uses dominates (negative autocorrelation). As a result the sufficient condition (6.2.14) is met and the cross-correlation increases when shifting from level 1 to 2 and from level 2 to 3.

In contrast, at the higher scales a positive autocorrelation was detected due to the dominance of neighbourhood effects. As a consequence the full relationship (6.2.21) applies. However Cliff and Ord noticed that the cross-correlation does not increase as sharply as before. In fact it flattens out from level 3 onwards or even decays (p.133). The less precise conclusions for aggregation from level 4 onwards, however, are also due to the reduced degrees of freedom.

CONCLUSION

As a result of the discussion of these examples it is possible to conclude that the theoretical results developed in paragraph 6.2.2 are confirmed by empirical examples. Moreover, the theory which has been developed gives explanation for results which were previously interpretable only as empirical "rules of thumb". We now move on to expand these results for the aggregation effect on bivariate analysis.

LEVEL	LATTICE DIMENSION	NUMBER OF ORIGINAL CELLS IN EACH GROUP	OBSERVED CORRELATION	
			Regression 1	Regression 2
1	24-by-24 = 576		0.19	0.09
2	12-by-12 = 144	r= 4	0.36	0.16
3	6-by-6 = 36	r= 4	0.67	0.33
4	3-by-3 = 9	r= 4	0.71	0.34
5	3-by-1 = 3	r= 3	0.97	0.32

Table 6.2.1 : Groupings used in the Cliff and Ord analysis of land use in London. (Source: Cliff and Ord, 1981; p.131).

6.3. AGGREGATION AND CORRELATION BETWEEN PROCESSES

6.3.1. Generalities

In § 6.2 we considered the effects of shifting the level of resolution on the measures of cross-correlation of a bivariate process. Following the lines of Chapter 5, where we dealt with the effects of the modifiable areal unit problem in univariate statistical analysis, we now have to face the problem of the variability of the cross-correlation not due just to changes in the size of the areas, but also due to changes in their shape. We referred to this problem as the aggregation (or zoning) problem (See § 5.4). It will often be necessary throughout this section to report results obtained in § 5.4.3 to which we also refer for notation and definitions. It is worth recalling here that in § 5.4.3 we established that the variability of the univariate moments, at the group-process level when we change the zoning system, is due to the fact that the configuration of the spatial system is also changed when we change the zoning criterion. In an analogous fashion we can now study the variability of the cross-correlation in alternative regular zoning systems (for the definition of regular zoning systems, see § 5.4.2) as a function of the connectedness at the group-process level. We will uniformly assume that the process is stationary at the individual level. Again, as in Chapter 5 and following the example of previous studies in the field (Openshaw and Taylor, 1979) we will first study the limits to the aggregation effect, that is the lowest and the highest value of the cross-correlation that it is possible to achieve changing the zones boundaries of a given spatial system. This aim is pursued in § 6.3.2. Secondly the complete regular zoning distribution of the cross-correlation in the group-process will be investigated theoretically and through examples (§ 6.3.3).

6.3.2. Zoning range of the cross-correlation

In this section we wish to study the theoretical limits of the cross-correlation between the process $\{X_i\}$ and the process $\{Y_i\}$ in alternative zoning systems. In other words given a bivariate individual-process we want to establish the minimum and the maximum level of the cross-correlation that it is possible to obtain in the group-process by changing the zone boundaries.
Let us start by observing that, from Formula (6.2.1), we have

$$
\begin{aligned}
{}_{x^*y^*}\rho &= \{{}_{xy}\gamma + v_i^* \, {}_{xy}\gamma'\}\{{}_x\sigma^2 \, {}_y\sigma^2\}^{-1/2} \\
&= \{{}_{xy}\rho + v_i^* \, {}_{xy}\rho'\}\{(1 + v_i^* \, {}_x\rho)(1 + v_i^* \, {}_y\rho)\}^{-1/2} \qquad (6.3.1)
\end{aligned}
$$

Formula (6.3.1) shows that the range of ${}_{x^*y^*}\rho$ in different zoning systems depends on the range of v_i^* given the values of ${}_{xy}\rho$, ${}_{xy}\rho'$, ${}_x\rho$ and ${}_y\rho$.
We already know (see § 5.4.3) that the theoretical range of the average within group connectedness is

$$2(r-1)r^{-1} \leq v_i^* \leq r - 1$$

The theoretical limits of the cross-correlation therefore are :

$$\text{Min}\,|{}_{x*y*}\rho| = |{}_{xy}\rho|\{1 + 2(r-1)r^{-1}\,{}_{xy}\rho'\,{}_{xy}\rho^{-1}\}\{[1 + 2(r-1)r^{-1}\,{}_{x}\rho][1 + 2(r-1)r^{-1}\,{}_{y}\rho]\}^{-1/2} \qquad (6.3.2)$$

and

$$\text{Max}\,|{}_{x*y*}\rho| = |{}_{xy}\rho|\{1 + (r-1)\,{}_{xy}\rho'\,{}_{xy}\rho^{-1}\}\{[1 + (r-1)\,{}_{x}\rho][1 + (r-1)\,{}_{y}\rho]\}^{-1/2} \qquad (6.3.3)$$

since (6.3.1) is an increasing function of v_i^*.

However we have already remarked (see § 5.4.3) that the theoretical limits of the average within group connectedness are of little practical relevance. In fact they are based on two very extreme cases, the *line transect* case and the *totally connected* case (see § 3.3.2), both of which are only rarely found in empirical studies. As a consequence the actual range of the connectedness is likely to be much smaller in most empirical cases. For this reason, consistently with Chapter 5, in the remainder of this section we will consider the actual limits imposed on ${}_{x*y*}\rho$ by the spatial configuration of data in some particular lattices.

EXAMPLE 6.1

First of all consider the fairly simple case of a 4-by-4 regular square lattice grid and the variability of ${}_{x*y*}\rho$ when groups are made by aggregating 4 cells. We know from the discussion of § 5.4.3 that in this case the range of the average within group connectedness is

$$1.5 \le v_i^* \le 2$$

Therefore for the cross-correlation of the group-process we have

$${}_{x*y*}\rho \ge {}_{xy}\rho\{1 + 1.5\,{}_{xy}\rho'\,{}_{xy}\rho^{-1}\}\{(1 + 1.5\,{}_{x}\rho)(1 + 1.5\,{}_{y}\rho)\}^{-1/2}$$

and

$${}_{x*y*}\rho \le {}_{xy}\rho\{1 + 2\,{}_{xy}\rho'\,{}_{xy}\rho^{-1}\}\{(1 + 2\,{}_{x}\rho)(1 + 2\,{}_{y}\rho)\}^{-1/2}$$

The range of ${}_{x*y*}\rho$ for different combinations of the values of ${}_{x}\rho$, ${}_{y}\rho$ and ${}_{xy}\rho'\,{}_{xy}\rho^{-1}$ is reported in Table 6.3.1. In all cases the values of the spatial autocorrelation of both $\{X_i\}$ and $\{Y_i\}$ are such that ${}_{x}\rho \ge -0.5$ and ${}_{y}\rho \ge -0.5$, as in the discussion of § 5.2.2. To determine the actual range of ${}_{x*y*}\rho$ the entries of Table 6.3.1 have to be multiplied by ${}_{xy}\rho$.

Table 6.3.1 shows that the range of ${}_{x*y*}\rho$ decreases as we move from left to right, that is when the *spin off* effect is reduced. Furthermore when the other elements are held constant, the range of ${}_{x*y*}\rho$ is emphasized by a negative spatial autocorrelation and reduced by a positive spatial autocorrelation. (See also the comments on the exampl taken from Openshaw and Taylor 's data in § 6.2.3). Note that in some cases the entrie are less than zero, which means that the cross-correlation decreases with grouping. I the three cases marked with (†) this is because the sufficient condition stated ir Formula (6.2.14) is not met; in the other cases marked with (††), the necessary an sufficient condition of Formula (6.2.21) is not fulfilled . Finally when ${}_x\rho = {}_y\rho =$ ${}_{xy}\rho' \, {}_{xy}\rho^{-1}$ from the theory developed in § 6.2.2 (and, in particular from Formul 6.2.14) only one value is given because no spatial configuration effect occurs.

EXAMPLE 6.2

A second larger 9-by-9 regular square lattice grid is now considered where 81 observations are grouped in various ways to form groups of 9 cells each. In this case th limits for v_i^* are (see § 5.4.3)

$$1.78 \leq v_i^* \leq 2.67$$

Individual-process spatial autocorrelation	${}_{xy}\rho'{}_{xy}\rho^{-1}=1$		Individual-process ${}_{xy}\rho'{}_{xy}\rho^{-1}=0.5$		cross-correlation ${}_{xy}\rho'{}_{xy}\rho^{-1}=0.1$	
	Min	Max	Min	Max	Min	Max
${}_x\rho={}_y\rho= -0.1$	2.94	3.75	2.06	2.50	1.35	1.5
${}_x\rho={}_y\rho= 0.0$	2.50	3.00	1.75	2.00	1.15	1.20
${}_x\rho={}_y\rho = 0.1$	2.17	2.50	1.52	1.67	1.00	1.00
${}_x\rho={}_y\rho = 0.5$	1.42	1.50	1.00	1.00	0.60 †	0.66 †
${}_x\rho={}_y\rho = 0.9$	1.06	1.07	0.71 †	0.74 †	0.43 †	0.49 †
${}_x\rho= 0.1\ {}_y\rho = -0.1$	2.53	3.06	1.77	2.04	1.16	1.22
${}_x\rho= 0.5\ {}_y\rho = -0.1$	2.05	1.37	1.43	1.58	0.94 ††	0.95 ††
${}_x\rho= 0.1\ {}_y\rho = 0.0$	2.33	2.74	1.63	1.82	1.07	1.09
${}_x\rho= 0.5\ {}_y\rho = 0.0$	1.89	2.12	1.32	1.14	0.85 ††	0.87 ††
${}_x\rho= 0.9\ {}_y\rho = 0.0$	1.63	1.79	1.14	1.19	0.72 ††	0.75 ††

Table 6.3.1: Range of the group-process cross-correlation ${}_{x*y*}\rho$ in a 4-by-4 regular square lattice grid, for different combinations of the values of the spatial correlation $({}_x\rho, {}_y\rho)$ and of the cross-correlation $({}_{xy}\rho' \, {}_{xy}\rho^{-1})$ in the individual-process, and the group size is equal 4.

so that we now have

$$_{x*y*}\rho \geq {}_{xy}\rho\{1+1.78\,{}_{xy}\rho'{}_{xy}\rho^{-1}\}\{(1+1.78\,{}_{x}\rho)(1+1.78\,{}_{y}\rho)\}^{-1/2}$$

and

$$_{x*y*}\rho \leq {}_{xy}\rho\{1+2.67\,{}_{xy}\rho'{}_{xy}\rho^{-1}\}\{(1+2.67\,{}_{x}\rho)(1+2.67\,{}_{y}\rho)\}^{-1/2}$$

Table 6.3.2 displays the limits of $_{x*y*}\rho$ when various combination of $_x\rho$, $_y\rho$ and $_{xy}\rho'$ $_{xy}\rho^{-1}$ are considered.

Table 6.3.2 confirms the findings of the previous example with the range directly related to the *spin off* effect and inversely with the spatial autocorrelation in the two processes. Furthermore, when all the other elements are held constant, the ranges of $_{x*y*}\rho$ of Table 6.3.2 are wider than those of Table 6.3.1 showing that they are directly related to the level of within group connectedness.

EXAMPLE 6.3

As a third example let us consider again the simulation study performed by Openshaw and Taylor (1979) that we have already analysed in § 6.2.3. There are various reasons why the analysis of this chapter applies only approximately to this case. First of all we are interested in processes that are stationary at both the

Individual-process spatial autocorrelation	$_{xy}\rho'{}_{xy}\rho^{-1}=1$		Individual-process $_{xy}\rho'{}_{xy}\rho^{-1}=0.5$		cross-correlation $_{xy}\rho'{}_{xy}\rho^{-1}=0.1$	
	Min	Max	Min	Max	Min	Max
$_x\rho={}_y\rho=-0.1$	3.38	5.01	2.30	3.18	1.43	1.73
$_x\rho={}_y\rho=0.0$	2.78	3.67	1.89	2.33	1.18	1.22
$_x\rho={}_y\rho=0.1$	2.36	2.90	1.60	1.84	1.00	1.00
$_x\rho={}_y\rho=0.5$	1.47	1.57	1.00	1.00	0.54	0.62
$_x\rho={}_y\rho=0.9$	1.07	1.08	0.68	0.73	0.37	0.45
$_x\rho=0.1\ {}_y\rho=-0.1$	2.82	3.83	1.92	2.42	1.19	1.31
$_x\rho=0.5\ {}_y\rho=-0.1$	2.23	2.80	1.15	1.78	0.94	0.96
$_x\rho=0.1\ {}_y\rho=0.0$	2.56	3.26	1.74	2.07	1.08	1.12
$_x\rho=0.5\ {}_y\rho=0.0$	2.02	2.40	1.37	1.52	0.83	0.86
$_x\rho=0.9\ {}_y\rho=0.0$	1.72	1.98	1.17	1.26	0.69	0.73

Table 6.3.2 : Range of the group-process cross-correlation $_{x*y*}\rho$ in a 9-by-9 regular square lattice grid for different combinations of the values of the spatial autocorrelation ($_x\rho$, $_y\rho$) and of the cross-correlation ($_{xy}\rho'$ $_{xy}\rho^{-1}$) in the individual-process , and the group size is equal 9.

individual and the group level. For this reason we consider only *regular zonir systems,* that is zoning systems that do not affect the property of stationarity (See 5.4.2). In fact we know from the analysis of Chapter 4 that only in this case is i meaningful to deal with a single cross-correlation of the group-process. In contras Openshaw and Taylor considered all the possible zoning systems (only with th contiguity constraint) including those that give rise to non-stationary group-processe where the estimation of the cross-correlation assumes a more dubious meaning (See 4.3). Secondly the effect of the lagged cross-covariance (or the "spin off" effect. See 6.1) is not controlled for in the Openshaw and Taylor analysis. Thirdly we assume th the lagged cross-covariance exerts its effect in the same direction in the cross-covariance so that the aggregation produces changes in the magnitude of $_{x^*y^*}\rho$, but n in its sign. In contrast in the study of Openshaw and Taylor $_{x^*y^*}\rho$ is allowed to rang between -1 and 1.
The main results of Openshaw and Taylor concerning the range of the cross-correlatior already shown in Table 2.10 (Chapter 2) are repeated for convenience in Table 6.3.3 . The general feature of these results is that, at a given spatial scale, the range of th cross-correlation is larger if the two variables show a negative spatial autocorrelatior In contrast the range is smaller when both the variables display a positive spatia autocorrelation. Finally in the case of no spatial autocorrelation the range assumes a intermediate value. The results of Openshaw and Taylor, therefore, are consistent wit those of the previous examples and with the theory developed in this chapter. In the nex paragraph we will consider again this example when dealing with the complete zonin distribution of $_{x^*y^*}\rho$.

EXAMPLE 6.4

As a final example let us go back to the map of the *provincia* of Arezzo already considered in Example 5.3 in § 5.4.3. For the borders of the 40 *comuni* of the

number of zones	average group size	spatial autocorrelation $_x\rho=-0.57$ $_y\rho=-0.71$		$_x\rho=$ $_y\rho=0.0$		$_x\rho=0.82$ $_y\rho=0.92$	
		Min	Max	Min	Max	Min	Max
6	16.5	-.99	.99	-.99	.99	-.99	.99
12	8.2	-.97	.99	-.99	.99	-.99	.99
18	5.5	-.97	.99	-.97	.99	-.92	.99
24	4.1	-.98	.99	-.90	.99	-.89	.98
30	3.3	-.93	.98	-.86	.98	-.78	.95
36	2.7	-.93	.98	-.80	.98	-.61	.93
42	2.4	-.92	.97	-.79	.96	-.52	.93
48	2.0	-.87	.96	-.66	.95	-.39	.89
54	1.8	-.85	.95	-.52	.91	-.32	.88

Table 6.3.3: Some approximate limits of the cross-correlation in different zoning systems. Source: Openshaw (1981). p.22.

rovincia of Arezzo see Appendix A.2. We want to study the zoning range of the cross-orrelation when groups are made by aggregating 4 *comuni*. We know from the analysis § 5.4.3 that the range of the within group average connectedness is

$$1.5 \leq v_i^* \leq 2.0$$

s a consequence, the theoretical range of the cross-correlation is, in this case, the ame as that reported in Example 6.1 (See in particular Table 6.3.1). In Example 5.3 e considered the effect of grouping observations on the variable "worked hours" of the edium-sized manufacturing industry in the 40 *comuni* of Arezzo. We now consider as second variable the "unitary consumption", expressed in kilowatts, of the same firms. For definitions see Appendix A.2). We then postulate a linear specification of the echnical relationship between "worked hours" and "unitary consumption". The value of he two variables recorded at the communal level are displayed in Table 6.3.4.
he cross-correlation at this level of spatial resolution is

$${}_{xy}\rho = 0.772167$$

Ve now group the observations according to the two regular zoning systems displayed in igure 5.4.5 that is in two cases in which the within group average connectedness ssumes its minimum and maximum value.
Ve now have that the cross-correlation at the group-process level assumes the two alues

$${}_{x^*y^*}\rho = 0.76622$$

nd

$${}_{x^*y^*}\rho = 0.68864$$

his can also be expressed as

$$0.8918296\ {}_{xy}\rho \leq {}_{x^*y^*}\rho \leq 0.9923091\ {}_{xy}\rho$$

hich confirms the theoretical findings of this section. Note that in this particular case e condition for the increase of ${}_{x^*y^*}\rho$ is not met (See § 6.2 and Table 6.3.1).

3.3. Zoning distribution of the cross-correlation

As we observed in § 5.3 the zoning distribution of the moments of the group-process arises from the fact that, by changing the zone boundaries of a spatial system, we produce a change in its connectedness to which the moments are functionally related. In particular in the case we are analysing the value of the cross-correlation depends functionally on the within group average connectedness so that the study of the distribution of v_i^* coincides with the study of the distribution of ${}_{x^*y^*}\rho$.

Code number	Comune	Worked hours	Unitary consumption
1	Anghiari	172.176	114210
2	Arezzo	161.837	76114
3	Badia tebalda	0.0	0
4	Bibbiena	284.173	176454
5	Bucine	129.381	51062
6	Capolona	166.842	139328
7	Caprese Michelangiolo	53.841	14860
8	Castel Focognano	159.800	93003
9	Castelfranco di Sopra	114.386	54677
10	Castel San Niccolo'	121.884	49810
11	Castiglione Fibocchi	177.547	132766
12	Castiglion Fiorentino	344.325	239811
13	Cavriglia	258.632	225320
14	Chitignano	0.0	0
15	Chiusi della Verna	126.295	78265
16	Civitella in Val di Chiana	160.342	75014
17	Cortona	154.950	93865
18	Foiano della Chiana	185.245	129417
19	Laretina	181.019	118438
20	Loro Ciuffenna	172.245	161462
21	Lucignano	151.503	130898
22	Marciano della Chiana	154.340	63897
23	Montemignaio	0.0	0
24	Monterchi	86.759	29705
25	Monte San Savino	227.173	137667
26	Montevarchi	189.076	75459
27	Ortignano Raggiolo	205.000	61500
28	Pergine Valdarno	93.332	47343
29	Pian di Sco	117.722	39639
30	Pieve Santo Stefano	296.164	195646
31	Poppi	111.344	58627
31.a	Poppi	111.344	58627
32	Pratovecchio	260.094	339266
33	San Giovanni Valdarno	327.947	139312
34	Sansepolcro	173.553	86169
35	Sestino	250.000	78000
36	Stia	318.328	270124
37	Subbiano	159.976	59143
38	Talla	0.0	0
39	Terranuova Bracciolini	202.355	66170

Table 6.3.4: Worked hours and electricity unitary consumption in kilowatts per hour of the medium-sized manufacturing industry in 40 *comuni* of Arezzo (Tuscany) in the first semester of 1985. Source: See Appendix A2.

oreover we can have more than one regular zoning system which yields the same level connectedness. This fact produces a frequency distribution of the connectedness and, nce of the cross-correlation. Finally we can expect that the maximum of the within oup connectedness (which is realized in the *totally connected* case, see § 3.3.2) can obtained only in a small number of zoning systems while the minimum value of v^*_i, rresponding to the *line transect* case is more likely to occur (See Figure 5.4.7). This creasing shape of the within group average connectedness produces a frequency stribution of the cross-correlation which is also decreasing when ${}_{xy}\rho$ is negative. It is, stead, increasing when ${}_{xy}\rho$ is positive. Let us now examine the distribution of ${}_{x^*y^*}\rho$ some particular lattices.

AMPLE 6.5

n the simple case of a 4-by-4 regular square lattice grid we have shown in § 5.3 hat, if the groups are made by aggregating 4 cells the within group average onnectedness has the following distribution (See also Figure 5.4.5).

Average within group connectedness	Frequency
1.5	5
2.0	1

s a consequence the cross-correlation in different zoning systems assumes the ollowing values:

Group-process cross-correlation	Frequency
${}_{xy}\rho\{1 + 1.5\,{}_{xy}\rho'\,{}_{xy}\rho^{-1}\}\{(1+1.5\,{}_{x}\rho)(1+1.5\,{}_{y}\rho)\}^{-1/2}$	5
${}_{xy}\rho\{1 + 2\,{}_{xy}\rho'\,{}_{xy}\rho^{-1}\}\{(1+2\,{}_{x}\rho)(1+2\,{}_{y}\rho)\}^{-1/2}$	1

XAMPLE 6.6.

et us now examine the case of a 6-by-6 regular square lattice grid. From the results f the computational study made in § 5.4 we know that in the case in which the group ize is 6 the within group average connectedness has the following empirical istribution:

Average within group connectedness	Frequency
1.67	113
2.00	85
2.33	2

herefore the empirical zoning distribution of the cross-correlation is the following:

Group-process cross-correlation	Frequency
$_{xy}\rho\{1 + 1.67\,_{xy}\rho'_{xy}\rho^{-1}\}\{(1+1.67_x\rho)(1+1.67_y\rho)\}^{-1/2}$	113
$_{xy}\rho\{1 + 2.00\,_{xy}\rho'_{xy}\rho^{-1}\}\{(1+2.00_x\rho)(1+2.00_y\rho)\}^{-1/2}$	85
$_{xy}\rho\{1 + 2.33\,_{xy}\rho'_{xy}\rho^{-1}\}\{(1+2.33_x\rho)(1+2.33_y\rho)\}^{-1/2}$	2

The same results are also displayed in Figure 6.3.1 under different hypotheses of t values of $_{xy}\rho$ $_{xy}\rho'$, $_x\rho$ and $_y\rho$.

EXAMPLE 6.7

Let us further consider the larger 9-by-9 regular square lattice grid alreac examined in the permutational study of § 5.4.5 and in example 6.3. When th observations are grouped in various ways to form groups of 9 cells each, the followi empirical distribution of the within group average connectedness was found.

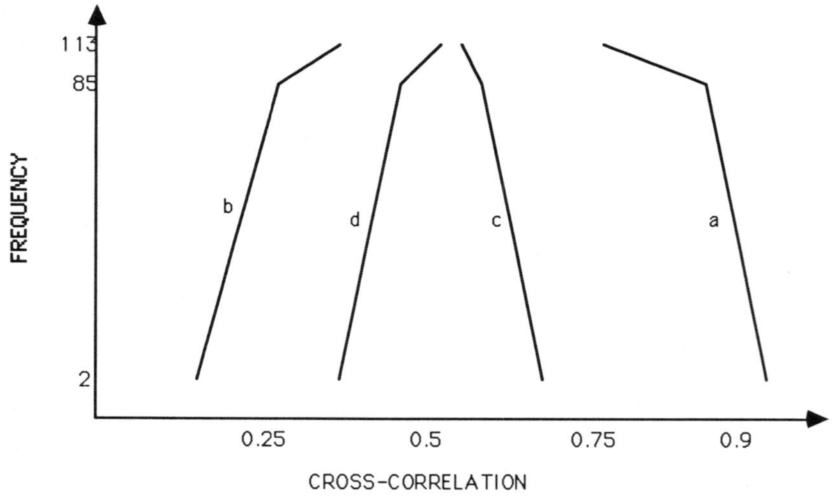

Figure 6.3.1: Zoning distribution of the group-process cross-correlation in a 6-by 6 regular square lattice grid with the group size r = 6. In all cases $_{xy}\rho = 0.5$ a) $_{xy}$ $_{xy}\rho^{-1} = 0.5$, $_x\rho = _y\rho = 0.1$; b) $_{xy}\rho'\ _{xy}\rho^{-1} = 0.1$, $_x\rho = _y\rho = 0.5$; c) $_{xy}\rho'\ _{xy}\rho^{-1} = 0.$, $_x\rho = _y\rho = 0.0$; d) $_{xy}\rho'\ _{xy}\rho^{-1} = 0.1$, $_x\rho = 0.9$, $_y\rho = -0.1$. (Logarithmic scale c vertical axis).

Average within group connectedness	Frequency
1.78	82.5
2.00	11.5
2.22	4.0
2.44	1.5
2.67	0.5

'his produces the distribution of the group-process cross-correlation displayed in 'igure 6.3.2 .

XAMPLE 6.8

As a final example let us go back to examine the results of Openshaw and Taylor (1979) nd Openshaw (1981) in the light of the theory developed in the previous section eeping in mind what has already been observed in example 6.3 about the possibility of pplying the theory of this chapter to this particular case.
he main conclusions from the experiments of Openshaw and Taylor about the zoning istribution of the cross-correlation are displayed in Table 6.3.4 for three levels of the patial autocorrelation in the two variables (See example § 6.2.3).

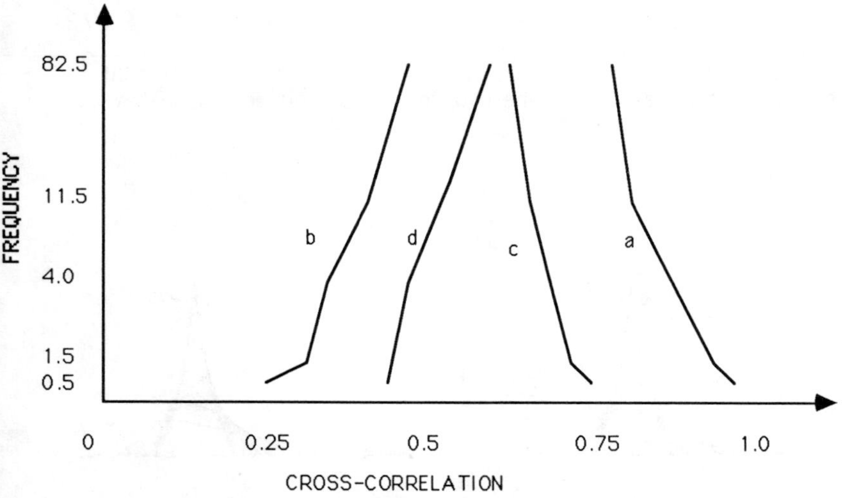

igure 6.3.2 : Zoning distribution of the group-process cross-correlation in a 9-by- regular square lattice grid with the group size r = 9.In all cases $_{xy}\rho = 0.5$) $_{xy}\rho'\,_{xy}\rho^{-1} = 0.5$, $_{x}\rho = {}_{y}\rho = 0.1$; b) $_{xy}\rho'\,_{xy}\rho^{-1} = 0.1$, $_{x}\rho = {}_{y}\rho = 0.5$; c) $_{xy}\rho'\,_{xy}\rho^{-1}$ = 0.1 , $_{x}\rho = {}_{y}\rho = 0.0$; d) $_{xy}\rho'\,_{xy}\rho^{-1} = 0.1$, $_{x}\rho = 0.9$, $_{y}\rho = -0.1$. Logarithmic scale on vertical axis).

Useful insights on the zoning distribution of $_{x*y*}\rho$ are also provided by Figure 6.3.: (Table 6.3.4 and Figure 6.3.3 already appeared Chapter 2, but they are repeated her for convenience).
From Table 6.3.4 and Figure 6.3.2 the following conclusions can be drawn:
1) The zoning distribution of the sample cross-correlation has an approximate Gaussia shape.

number of zones	average group size	zoning distribution of the cross-correlation $_x\rho=-0.57$ $_y\rho=-0.71$		$_x\rho=$ $_y\rho=0.0$		$_x\rho=0.82$ $_y\rho=0.92$	
		Mean	Standard deviation	Mean	Standard deviation	Mean	Standard deviation
6	16.5	.31	.443	.61	.294	.60	.247
12	8.2	.30	.370	.47	.263	.52	.176
18	5.5	.29	.350	.42	.227	.48	.142
24	4.1	.31	.309	.40	.192	.44	.121
30	3.3	.32	.277	.39	.166	.42	.108
36	2.7	.32	.242	.38	.146	.40	.098
42	2.4	.33	.209	.37	.128	.39	.087
48	2.0	.33	.183	.36	.112	.38	.080
54	1.8	.33	.160	.36	.100	.34	.072

Table 6.3.4 : Zoning distribution of the cross-correlation for three different levels of spatial autocorrelation in the two variables. Source : Openshaw (1981) p.18.

a) b)

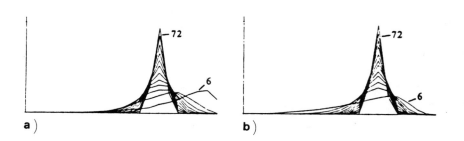

Figure 6.3.3 : Zoning distribution of the cross-correlation in the simulation study of Openshaw and Taylor(1979; p.138). (a) $_x\rho={}_y\rho=0.0$. (b) $_x\rho=0.82$ $_y\rho=0.92$.

) The variance of the zoning distribution increases with the scale or, in other words, t is directly related to the group size r.

oncerning the Gaussian shape of the distribution of $_{x*y*}\rho$ we have to remember that penshaw and Taylor, by not making any explicit assumption on the lagged cross-ovariance, allowed it to vary from one experiment to another. We know from the heory of this chapter that the group-process cross-correlation increases or ecreases if compared with the individual-process cross-correlation, depending on he value of $_{xy}\rho'$. The Gaussian shape found by Openshaw and Taylor may well derive, herefore, by the fact that they considered jointly the increasing section of the requency distribution of $_{xy}\rho$, and its decreasing section. (See, for example, Figure .3.1 and 6.3.2).

oncerning the variance of the zoning distribution of $_{xy}\rho$, the analysis of § 6.3.2 shows hat the zoning range of $_{x*y*}\rho$ increases with r. We know that the range of a istribution is a measure of dispersion and, as such, is related to the variance of the istribution itself, so that the theory is consistent with the findings of Openshaw and aylor.

he reason for the more dispersed distribution when r is large is that in this case the ites of a spatial system can be combined in groups in a large number of different ways nd this produces the more extreme values of the connectedness. In contrast, when r is mall only few combinations of the sites are possible (See § 5.4.3). This point can also e demonstrated by observing that the theoretical lower limits of the within group onnectedness v_i^* in the *line transect* case is $2(r-1)r^{-1}$, and it tends to 2 as r ncreases towards infinity. In contrast the upper limit of v_i^* in the *totally connected* ase is $(r-1)$, which is not bounded by any upper limit as r increases to infinity. As a onsequence the range of v_i^* also increases towards infinity when r increases. Finally igure 6.3.3 shows that the assumption that $_{x*y*}\rho$ does not change sign with ggregation (see Formula 6.1.2 in § 6.1.1) is not a strong restriction since most of he sample cross-correlations are positive when the value of $_{xy}\rho$ at the individual-rocess level is positive (in the case analysed $_{xy}\rho$ was equal to 0.3466).

.4. SUMMARY AND CONCLUSION

n this chapter we have extended the results of Chapter 5 to deal with the modifiable real unit problem for the case of bivariate statistical analysis. We have shown that the heory developed here gives an explanation for the increase in the correlation between wo variables when we increase the level of aggregation. This has previously been nterpreted only as an empirical "rule of thumb".

n § 6.2 dealing with the <u>scale problem</u>, we have shown that that the increase of $_{xy}\rho$ hen we increase the level of aggregation depends upon the various combinations of six lements which derive from the spatial configuration of the data: the two spatial utocorrelations, the cross-covariance, the lagged cross-covariance, the size of the reas, and their connectedness.

he same elements also determine the theoretical range and the zoning distribution of $_{*y*}\rho$ when we change the zonal boundaries, as we shown in § 6.3 in dealing with the <u>ggregation problem</u>.

n particular we have proved that the range of $_{x*y*}\rho$,and hence the variance of its oning distribution, is directly related to the *spin off* effect. Furthermore the range is

wider if a negative spatial autocorrelation occurs in both variables; it is smaller if there is a positive spatial autocorrelation in the variables. Finally the range of the zoning distribution increases as the level of the within group average connectedness increases.
The theory developed in this chapter has been tested in a number of empirical examples concerned with regular lattices as well as irregular collecting areas. Furthermore the results concerning the aggregation problem have been tested by performing a series of pseudo-random permutations of the study area.

In this chapter we conclude the discussion, started in Chapter 5, of the modifiable area unit problem in univariate and bivariate statistical analysis. The next chapter is devoted to examining a special case derived from the results of this chapter which occurs when the units on which the individual-process is observed are actual individuals interacting in a study area and not zones; this is the so called "ecological fallacy" problem.

7. Bivariate problems: The ecological fallacy

7.1 INTRODUCTION

In all the foregoing chapters we considered various forms of a model linking what we called the "individual-process", that is the process generating the observations at the finest level of resolution, to the "group-process", that is the process resulting after aggregating the observations into larger areal units. The present chapter is devoted to considering the case in which the individual-process is constituted by non-modifiable individuals (see § 2.3) instead of areas. We encounter this case when we study the individual behaviour of economic agents, such as families, firms, labour unions or governmental units, interacting in a study area. In particular the concern of this chapter is with the mechanism through which the individual agents' behaviour gives rise to spatial relationships.

We know from the discussion of Chapter 2 that at all the times when we want to infer individual relationships from correlations based on areal observations our conclusions are fallacious. The term *ecological fallacy* which describes this problem is due to a seminal paper by Robinson (1950) in which the author showed, using examples based on socio-economical variables, that the value of the cross-correlation based on spatial observations is always greater in absolute value than the value of the cross-correlation based on individuals. He also concluded that "there needs to be no correspondence between the individual correlation and the ecological correlation " (Robinson, 1950; p.354).

The problem of ecological fallacy, which has been recognized as "an inescapable one in all statistical geography" (Duncan et al., 1961), represents the geographical counterpart of analogous statistical problems encountered in other fields, like, for example, the possible inconsistency between micro-economic theories and macro relationships (Klein, 1946; Theil, 1954; Modigliani and Brumberg, 1959; Pesaran et al., 1986) and, in general, the problem of creating class intervals for statistical observations.

In the next section (§ 7.2.1) a stochastic formulation of individual behaviour in the space economy will be presented (See Curry, 1978). This will allow us to extend the results of Chapter 4 to deal with ecological fallacy problems in the context of regional economics.

We will assume , as in earlier discussion, that the individual behaviour is the outcome of a Gaussian stochastic process. This requires us to specify a plausible structure for the variance-covariance matrix. We will assume throughout the chapter that the "uniform covariance" hypothesis applies (See § 4.2) . Furthermore a slightly different hypothesis will be exploited in § 7.2.3 to deal with the existence of *Cliques* in the study area. Finally the theoretical results of this chapter will be tested by exploiting a microsimulation approach.

7.2 THE ECOLOGICAL FALLACY PROBLEM

7.2.1. A stochastic formulation of the ecological fallacy problem

Let us start by considering a random spatial economy (Orcutt, 1957; Curry, 1978; Hildenbrand, 1971) constituted by n interacting individuals indexed by j (j=1,...,n). These individuals can be each elemental decision-making entities "such as, for example, firms, families, labour unions or governmental units" (Orcutt, 1957). If we consider for example individual consumption we can attach to each household a random variable X(i). In this way each consumer is assumed to possess his own probability distribution in that certain levels of consumption are more likely than others. Furthermore each consumer is assumed to be "behaviourally responsible to the decision of other consumers" (Rosenblatt, 1956). It follows than that the joint probability distribution of the n random variables attached to the n individuals describes fully their joint behaviour and that the whole spatial economy can be described as a random process . Following this approach the observed spatial economy is viewed as a finite realization of such a process.

If we restrict ourselves, consistently with the rest of the book, to Gaussian stochastic processes, a central role is played by the variance-covariance matrix which embodies all the information about the dependence between individuals. Here the autocovariance between pairs of individuals indicates a similarity in their economic behaviour. A positive autocovariance indicates, for example, that if a certain level of consumption is observed in the j-th consumer, we are likely to observe similar levels in other individuals that interact with him (e.g. individuals living in the same area).

Let us now consider an aggregation of the individual economic agents into territorial units. The individual behaviour in a given area produces as a consequence the emergence of spatial relationships among the areas (Curry, 1978). The analysis of Chapter 4 together with the foregoing description of a random spatial economy now enables us to investigate formally the links existing between the behaviour of individuals and spatial relationships.

In particular we are interested in analysing the formal links between the *individual correlation* and the *ecological correlation* (the correlation found at an aggregate level). For this reason in the analysis of the effects of grouping on the moments of the process we will restrict attention to the cross-correlation.

7.2.2. The uniform covariance assumption

When we are dealing with a small spatial economy in which only a few strongly interacting individual economic agents operate, we can postulate that they are all equally pairwise correlated, or, in other words, that the interaction among individuals is not restricted to *Cliques* (Besag, 1974). This is the essence of what we called the "uniform covariance" assumption put forward in § 4.2.3.

In this paragraph we deal with the effects on the cross-correlation of the process of grouping individuals into territorial units, under the hypothesis that the individual-process is uniformly covariant. It is worth noting here that we implicitly mention this case when dealing with the problem of scale in the case of "totally connected lattices" (See Chapter 6).

Let us first recall the result of Section 4.2 which expresses the group-process cross-correlation ${}_{x^*y^*}\rho$ in terms of the individual-process cross-correlation ${}_{xy}\rho$. Assuming that the individual-process $\{X_j, Y_j\}$ is stationary and Gaussian with moments

$$\boldsymbol{\mu} = ({}_x\boldsymbol{\mu}, {}_y\boldsymbol{\mu}) \qquad (7.2.1)$$

and

$$\mathbf{V} = \begin{pmatrix} {}_x\mathbf{V} & {}_{xy}\mathbf{V} \\ {}_{xy}\mathbf{V} & {}_y\mathbf{V} \end{pmatrix} = \begin{pmatrix} {}_x\sigma^2 \; {}_x\gamma \cdots\cdots {}_x\gamma & {}_{xy}\gamma \; {}_{xy}\gamma' \cdots\cdots {}_{xy}\gamma' \\ \cdots\cdots & \cdots\cdots \\ {}_x\gamma \; {}_x\gamma \cdots\cdots {}_x\sigma^2 & {}_{xy}\gamma' \; {}_{xy}\gamma' \cdots\cdots {}_{xy}\gamma \\ {}_{xy}\gamma \; {}_{xy}\gamma' \cdots\cdots {}_{xy}\gamma' & {}_y\sigma^2 \; {}_y\gamma \cdots\cdots {}_y\gamma \\ \cdots\cdots & \cdots\cdots \\ {}_{xy}\gamma' \; {}_{xy}\gamma' \cdots\cdots {}_{xy}\gamma & {}_y\gamma \; {}_y\gamma \cdots\cdots {}_y\sigma^2 \end{pmatrix} \qquad (7.2.2)$$

the cross-correlation of the i-th group is equal to (see Formulae 4.2.98 and 4.2.104):

$${}_{x^*y^*}\rho_i$$

$$= \{r_i\, {}_x\sigma\, {}_y\sigma [{}_{xy}\rho + (r_i - 1)\, {}_{xy}\rho']\}\{r_i\, {}_x\sigma^2[1 + (r_i - 1)\, {}_x\rho]\, r_i\, {}_y\sigma^2[1 + (r_i - 1)\, {}_y\rho]\}^{-1/2}$$

$$= \{{}_{xy}\rho[1 + (r_i - 1)\, {}_{xy}\rho'\, {}_{xy}\rho^{-1}]\}\{[1 + (r_i - 1)\, {}_x\rho][1 + (r_i - 1)\, {}_y\rho]\}^{-1/2}$$

$$(7.2.3)$$

From now on we wish to simplify the discussion by assuming that the autocorrelation is the same in the two processes X and Y, and that it is equal to the value of the lagged cross-correlation. In symbols

$${}_x\rho = {}_y\rho = {}_{xy}\rho' = \rho \qquad (7.2.4)$$

There appear to be no strong reasons against this assumption if we consider that the three elements ${}_x\rho$, ${}_y\rho$ and ${}_{xy}\rho'$, represent the influence of other individuals (or of the "environment") on the individual economic agent, so that they are likely to be of the same sign. Furthermore the three elements in (7.2.4) are likely to be very small in absolute value so that the approximation should not lead to serious biases for the purposes of our discussion. We will further assume, as in Chapter 6

$$|\rho| \leq |{}_{xy}\rho| \qquad (7.2.5)$$

Finally, if we are dealing with a very large number of individuals, we can assume that the group size is constant and equal to r.
As a consequence of these assumptions the cross-correlation at a group-process level simplifies into

$$_{x^*y^*}\rho_i = {}_{x^*y^*}\rho$$

$$= {}_{xy}\rho\,[1 + (r - 1)\,\rho\,{}_{xy}\rho^{-1}]\,[1 + (r - 1)\,\rho]^{-1} \qquad (7.2.6)$$

Before examining in detail the consequence of grouping individuals into territorial units, let us first consider the restrictions imposed on the model by our assumptions. First of all let us recall that, from the discussion of § 5.2.2, the autocorrelation provides a lower bound which ensures the positiveness of the variance in the group-process. The lower bound is

$$\rho \geq -v_i^{*-1} \qquad (7.2.7)$$

where v_i^* is the average within group connectedness of group i (See § 3.3.3). In the case we are considering we have that

$$v_i^* = (r - 1) \qquad (7.2.8)$$

so that now ρ is forced to be

$$\rho \geq -(r - 1)^{-1} \qquad (7.2.9)$$

and, for large r

$$\rho \geq 0 \qquad (7.2.10)$$

Secondly, consider that the group-process cross-correlation has to be less than one in absolute value . As a consequence we have that

$$|{}_{xy}\rho|\,\{1 + (r - 1)\,\rho\,|{}_{xy}\rho|^{-1}\}\,\{1 + (r - 1)\,\rho\}^{-1} \leq 1$$

or

$$|{}_{xy}\rho| \leq 1 \qquad (7.2.11)$$

which is always true. As a consequence no additional constraints are imposed on the model.

We can now obtain the condition under which the cross-correlation increases in absolute value by shifting from the individual to the group level, that is

$$|{}_{x^*y^*}\rho| \geq |{}_{xy}\rho| \qquad (7.2.12)$$

This inequality is satisfied when

$$|{}_{xy}\rho|\,\{1 + (r - 1)\,\rho\,|{}_{xy}\rho|^{-1}\}\,\{1 + (r - 1)\,\rho\}^{-1} \geq |{}_{xy}\rho|$$

or

$$1 + (r - 1)\,\rho\,|_{xy}\rho|^{-1} \geq 1 + (r - 1)\,\rho$$

or also

$$\rho\,|_{xy}\rho|^{-1} \geq \rho \qquad (7.2.13)$$

When ρ is positive the condition becomes

$$|_{xy}\rho|^{-1} \geq 1 \qquad (7.2.14)$$

which is always true. In contrast, when ρ is negative the condition becomes

$$|_{xy}\rho|^{-1} \leq 1 \qquad (7.2.15)$$

which is never true.

As a conclusion, Formula (7.2.14) states that when the autocorrelation is positive the ecological correlation is always greater in absolute value than the individual correlation. This theoretical result is consistent with the empirical finding of Robinson (1950). In contrast when ρ is negative the cross-correlation decreases in absolute value. This second case, however, is of little empirical relevance when the group size is large, as a consequence of the restriction (7.2.9). Furthermore in most socio-economic studies the spatial autocorrelation between individuals is likely to be positive (e.g. in studies on consumer behaviour).

The element that causes the "aggregation effect" is the presence of the interaction term ρ. In fact when $\rho = 0$, no aggregation bias occurs and the group-process cross-correlation equals the individual-process cross-correlation.

Table 7.2.1 shows the value of the group-process cross-correlation $_{x*y*}\rho$ for various values of the individual-process autocorrelation ρ and cross-correlation $_{xy}\rho$, and for various group sizes. The values of ρ are chosen in such a way that $\rho \geq -(r - 1)^{-1}$ as stated in Formula (7.2.9).

The main conclusion that can be drawn from Table 7.2.1 is that the increase of the cross-correlation when we consider groups instead of individuals depends mainly on the value of ρ. Even for very small values of the autocorrelation in the individual-process the group-process cross-correlation increases dramatically as group size increases. Moreover the increase is proportional to the group size with the result that, when r is large, e.g. 10,000, a very small level of autocorrelation in the individual-process can produce a dramatic change in the cross-correlation.

Finally, in the few cases in which ρ can assume a negative value, the cross-correlation decreases in absolute value.

	Group size r = 100			Group size r=10000		
$\lvert {}_{xy}\rho \rvert$	0.10	0.50	0.90	0.10	0.50	0.90
${}_{x}\rho$						
-0.0010	0.01	0.44	0.89			
-0.0005	0.05	0.47	0.89			
-0.0001	0.09	0.49	0.90			
0.0000	0.10	0.50	0.90	0.10	0.50	0.90
0.0001	0.11	0.51	0.90	0.55	0.74	0.95
0.0005	0.14	0.52	0.90	0.85	0.92	0.98
0.0010	0.18	0.54	0.91	0.92	0.95	0.99
0.0050	0.39	0.66	0.93	0.98	0.99	0.99
0.0100	0.55	0.75	0.94	0.99	0.99	0.99
0.0500	0.84	0.91	0.98	0.99	0.99	0.99
0.1000	0.92	0.95	0.99	0.99	0.99	0.99
0.5000	0.98	0.99	0.99	0.99	0.99	0.99

Table 7.2.1: Values of the group-process cross-covariance for various values of the individual-process autocorrelation and cross-covariance and for various group sizes.

7.2.3. The *Clique* assumption

In the previous section we provided a theoretical explanation for the empirically observed increase in the cross-correlation when moving from the individual-process to the group-process level. We must, however, remark that when we want to apply this model to empirical studies the assumption of stationarity at the individual-process level does not seem realistic. If this was the case we would have to accept that the degree of correlation between a variable recorded in any pair of individuals is always the same, no matter their location, profession, age and so on.

There are, however, a number of cases in which the model put forward in this chapter can be applied; for example in geographical studies at a micro scale of analysis as in urban geography. In this case we deal with large number of individuals in a very small area. The idea is that we have to reduce the study-area to small zones where stationarity becomes plausible. Another important case is when we study the behaviour of a limited number of individual economic agents in a given study area. This is the case, for example, of an oligopolistic market as examined by Haining (1983a,1983b)(see also Haining and Bennett, 1985).

In this section an attempt is made to overcome some of the limitations imposed by the uniform covariance hypothesis by introducing an alternative interpretation of the model. Consider the case in which the study area is divided into territorial units that constitute *Cliques* (Besag, 1974; p.197) in the sense that the individuals have a strong interaction within a group, but no interaction occurs between the groups. There are a number of examples in the economic literature where this hypothesis has been considered. For example Quandt (1972), in putting forward a probability theory of consumer behaviour, suggested that there exist sets of consumers who are dependent on one another, although there is no dependence between sets. He derives this conclusion making use of the concept of "separable utility" (Arrow, 1972). (For a spatial interpretation of "separability" see Smith, 1975 and Curry, 1978).

Further theoretical reference to the hypothesis of *Cliques* in economics can be found in Buchanan's theory of *clubs* (Buchanan, 1965) and in Tiebout's "pure" theory of local expenditure (Tiebout, 1956).
In terms of the analysis of this chapter the *Cliques* assumption can be expressed by saying that the individual-process is still uniformly covariant , but only within the groups. As a consequence each of the four blocks of the variance-covariance matrix of the process (see Formula 7.2.2) assumes a block-diagonal structure. In particular for the submatrix ${}_x\mathbf{V}$ we have:

$$
{}_x\mathbf{V} = \begin{pmatrix} {}_x\sigma^2 & {}_x\gamma & \cdots & & & \\ {}_x\gamma & {}_x\sigma^2 & \cdots & & & \\ \cdots & & {}_x\sigma^2 & {}_x\gamma & \cdots & \\ \cdots & & {}_x\gamma & {}_x\sigma^2 & \cdots & \\ \cdots & & & \cdots & {}_x\sigma^2 & {}_x\gamma \\ \cdots & & & \cdots & {}_x\gamma & {}_x\sigma^2 \end{pmatrix} \qquad (7.2.16)
$$

with analogous structure for the submatrices ${}_y\mathbf{V}$ and ${}_{xy}\mathbf{V}$.
It is easy to see that, if this hypothesis holds, the group-process is now constituted by uncorrelated random components. In fact no spill over and spin off occurs between the groups (See § 6.1.1).
If we assume the *Clique* interpretation of a spatial economy the results obtained in the previous section under the uniform covariance hypothesis still hold true. However the resulting formalization is closer to reality and some of the limitations of the previous section are overcome. The crucial point is that we have to be able to specify an aggregation to groups that can be considered as spatial *Cliques*.
A way to achieve this aim is to consider different zoning systems of the study area (§ 5.4) and to choose among them the one in which the spatial autocorrelation between zones is closest to zero, and for which within-zone autocorrelation is maximized.

7.2.4. Microsimulation results

In this section the theoretical results of this chapter will be tested by exploiting a microsimulation approach. The so-called "microsimulation approach" to economics has been introduced by Orcutt (1960) and Orcutt et al. (1976). He constructed a model of household sector in which groups of individual economic agents are delineated as following certain postulated behaviour rules. This kind of model has been used by the federal government of the United States to study the impact of governmental policies on the household sector. Other examples of microsimulation studies in economics can be found in Pechman and Okner (1974) in the analysis of the structure of personal tax, and in Pryor (1973) and Blinder (1974) in the study of income distribution. Finally there are examples in which the performance of the whole economy as the result of individual decisions has been simulated. See for example Eliansson (1976) for the Swedish economy and Bennett and Bergmann (1986) for the United States. Generally these models have been used to simulate the performance of an economy at a national level, although some regional applications can be found in the literature. For example Caldwell et al. (1979) studied a model of household energy consumption for the New York state. Other examples can be found in Clarke, Keys and Williams (1979; 1981) to which we also refer for a more detailed review.

The common feature of these works is that they make use of samples of actual individual households and firms and apply to them the postulated behaviour pattern in order to extrapolate their choices in a future moment of time. The results are then aggregated to obtain the values of the macro-economic variables. Furthermore no explicit attempt is made to introduce interaction between individual economic agents. Finally only a single replication of the model is usually considered.
In contrast, the model we present simulates the economic behaviour of a number of interacting individuals at a given moment of time with an explicit reference to their location in space. In addition, more than one realization of the postulated process is considered.
We will consider two experiments. In the first we simulate the joint behaviour of 160 households evenly distributed in a study area divided into a 4-by-4 regular square lattice grid. The aim is to study the effect of grouping individuals on the consumption function of the household.
In the second experiment, which is more ambitious, we simulate the economic behaviour of 6000 individuals in the 20 Italian administrative regions (See Appendix A.1).

EXAMPLE 7.1: MICROSIMULATION - REGULAR LATTICE.

As a first micro-simulation experiment , we consider the economic behaviour of 160 households living in a study area upon which a 4-by-4 regular square lattice grid is superimposed. We assume that the individuals are evenly distributed in the study area so that each cell contains 10 individuals. A relationship between the consumption and the personal income can be postulated to make the example more concrete. The observations of personal income and personal consumption are supposed to be drawn from a Gaussian process $\{X_j Y_j\}$ $j=1,....,n$, which is stationary with mean

$$\boldsymbol{\mu} = ({}_X\boldsymbol{\mu}, {}_Y\boldsymbol{\mu}) = (\mathbf{0},\mathbf{0})$$

for sake of simplicity, and a variance -covariance matrix of dimension 320-by-320 with typical element σ_{jk} such that:

$$\sigma_{jk} = \begin{cases} {}_X\sigma^2 = {}_Y\sigma^2 = \sigma^2 & \text{if } k = j \\ {}_X\rho_X\sigma^2 = {}_Y\rho_Y\sigma^2 = \rho\sigma^2 & \text{if } k,j \in G(i) \\ {}_{XY}\rho_X\sigma_Y\sigma = {}_{XY}\rho\sigma^2 & \text{if } k = j+160 \text{ or } j = k+160 \\ 0 & \text{otherwise} \end{cases}$$

as in Formula (7.2.16).
For the generation of observations drawn from a Gaussian process with a specified variance-covariance matrix, a number of approaches exist (See Larimore, 1977; Chambers, 1977; Haining, Griffith & Bennett, 1981; Arbia, 1986b; Goodchild, 1980). Some of these are referred to in Appendix A.5.
For the purpose of our experiment we exploit the Cholesky decomposition of the matrix V. (See Appendix A.5), making use of the subroutines G05EAF and G05EZF of the

Fortran - Nag library. The FORTRAN program used to input the covariance matrix and for the generation of observations from the specified process is listed in Appendix 7.1. In the variance-covariance matrix **V** we assumed

$$_{xy}\rho = 0.5$$

Furthermore three different values of the autocorrelation between individuals were assumed for ρ equal to 0.1, 0.01, 0.001. Finally in all the experiments we assumed

$$_{x}\sigma_{y}\sigma = 1$$

The simulation procedure involves the decomposition into a triangular form of a 320-by-320 matrix, hence the computing time and storage required becomes very large (Wilkinson & Reinsh, 1971). The storage required was 2500 kilobites, while 5 seconds are needed to obtain each replication. For these reasons only 50 replications for each experiment are performed, for a total time of approximately 5 minutes. 50 replications are enough to ensure a convergence of the estimates up to the second decimal figure.

The results of the micro-simulation are displayed in Table 7.2.2 to 7.2.4 and in Figure 7.2.1 to 7.2.3.

Tables 7.2.2 to 7.2.4 show the ecological cross-correlation estimated at each run and recursively adjusted after each replication. It is worth stressing that the target value of $_{xy}\rho = 0.5$ for the individual-process cross-correlation is reached in the three experiments only with a certain approximation (see top of the tables). Consequently the value of the ecological cross-correlation expected from the theory is obtained by applying Formula (7.2.6) to the final estimate of the individual cross-correlation after the 50 replications.

The theory of this chapter is confirmed by the results of the three experiments in that the ecological cross-correlation is always greater than the individual cross-correlation. Furthermore the increase is sharper when the autocorrelation ρ is higher. In fact when $\rho = 0.001$ there is only a small increase of the ecological cross-correlation if compared with the individual cross-correlation. In contrast when $\rho = 0.1$, a dramatic change of the value of $_{x^*y^*}\rho$ occur after grouping. It is interesting to note that in all the experiments the empirical values of $_{x^*y^*}\rho$ slightly exceed the theoretical expectations. This is probably due to the fact that the procedure employed fails to generate a value of ρ exactly equal to the one required in 50 replications.

Even if no attempt is made to test statistically the difference between the individual and the ecological cross-correlation in our experiment, the example shows that if we are dealing with few individuals whose economic behaviour is not independent from one another (in our example where the group size is 10 the individuals can be members of the same family) a study of consumer behaviour can lead to very different conclusions if we use data collected into spatial units instead of individuals.

${}_{xy}\rho = 0.51398351$

	O.L.S.	Iterative estimation		OLS	Iterative estimation		OLS	Iterative estimation
1	0.6057	0.6057	18	0.5123	0.5525	35	0.5599	0.5318
2	0.2823	0.4440	19	0.3612	0.5424	36	0.5561	0.5325
3	0.5981	0.4953	20	0.5183	0.5412	37	0.5303	0.5325
4	0.6937	0.5449	21	0.4241	0.5355	38	0.5379	0.5326
5	0.3909	0.5141	22	0.5818	0.5376	39	0.4558	0.5306
6	0.5192	0.5149	23	0.7039	0.5448	40	0.5103	0.5301
7	0.5615	0.5216	24	0.5416	0.5447	41	0.7236	0.5348
8	0.5269	0.5222	25	0.3837	0.5382	42	0.5739	0.5358
9	0.7220	0.5444	26	0.6095	0.5410	43	0.4097	0.5328
10	0.4526	0.5352	27	0.4886	0.5390	44	0.3716	0.5292
11	0.6221	0.5431	28	0.5784	0.5404	45	0.3760	0.5258
12	0.6145	0.5491	29	0.2830	0.5316	46	0.5535	0.5264
13	0.6846	0.5595	30	0.5911	0.5335	47	0.3346	0.5223
14	0.5529	0.5590	31	0.5653	0.5346	48	0.5943	0.5238
15	0.7063	0.5688	32	0.5743	0.5358	49	0.5754	0.5248
16	0.4840	0.5635	33	0.4758	0.5340	50	0.5477	0.5253
17	0.4159	0.5548	34	0.4329	0.5310			

Table 7.2.2 : Ecological correlation in 50 replications of the microsimulation experiment when $\rho = 0.001$.

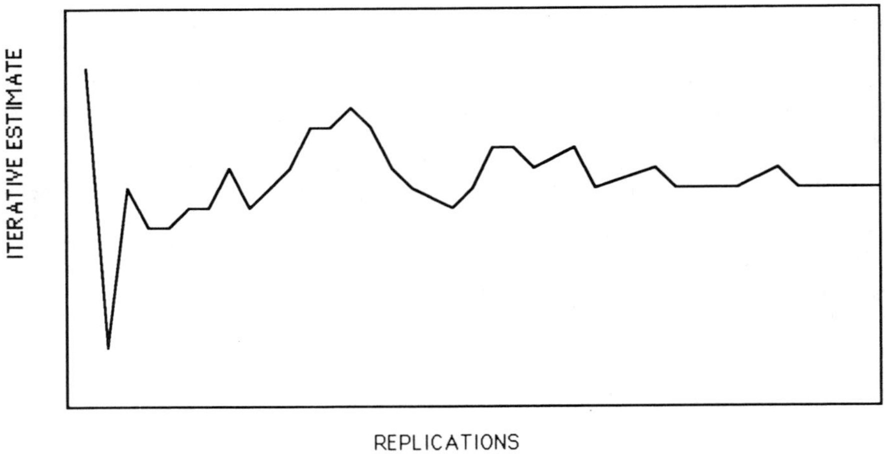

Figure 7.2.1: Convergence of the estimate of ${}_{xy}\rho$ in 50 replications of the microsimulation when $\rho = 0.001$.

$_{xy}\rho$ = 0.5151586

	O.L.S.	Iterative estimation		OLS	Iterative estimation		OLS	Iterative estimation
1	0.6538	0.6538	18	0.5975	0.5572	35	0.7245	0.5795
2	0.7549	0.7043	19	0.7682	0.5682	36	0.6464	0.5814
3	0.7933	0.7339	20	0.5332	0.5665	37	0.6378	0.5829
4	0.5786	0.6951	21	0.4612	0.5615	38	0.6330	0.5842
5	0.3752	0.6311	22	0.7974	0.5722	39	0.5381	0.5830
6	0.3266	0.5803	23	0.6498	0.5756	40	0.4678	0.5811
7	0.6286	0.5872	24	0.6298	0.5778	41	0.5033	0.5783
8	0.4033	0.5642	25	0.5631	0.5772	42	0.6443	0.5798
9	0.6067	0.5689	26	0.7865	0.5853	43	0.6442	0.5814
10	0.4189	0.5539	27	0.5694	0.5847	44	0.5609	0.5809
11	0.6286	0.5607	28	0.6005	0.5829	45	0.7686	0.5850
12	0.4546	0.5519	29	0.3739	0.5780	46	0.4670	0.5825
13	0.4243	0.5413	30	0.6191	0.5793	47	0.6012	0.5829
14	0.7958	0.5595	31	0.5148	0.5772	48	0.5109	0.5814
15	0.5862	0.5612	32	0.5711	0.5771	49	0.4853	0.5794
16	0.4430	0.5538	33	0.4271	0.5725	50	0.7123	0.5821
17	0.5693	0.5548	34	0.6659	0.5753			

Table 7.2.3 : Ecological correlation in 50 replications of the microsimulation experiment when ρ = 0.01.

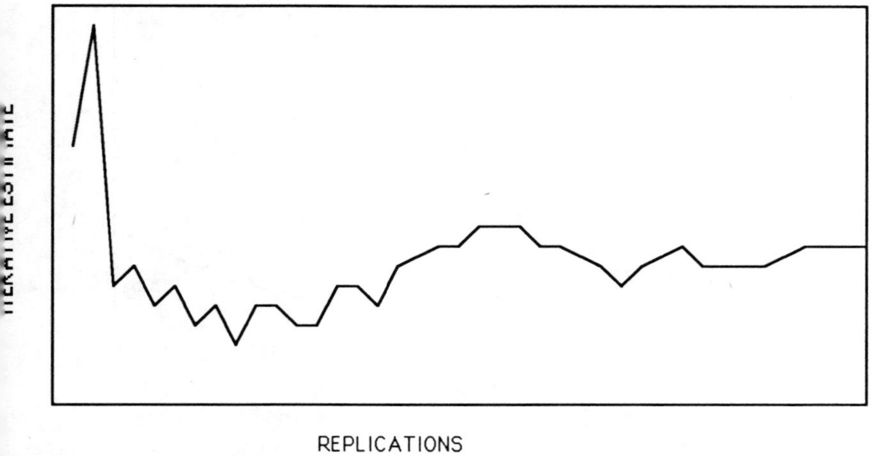

Figure 7.2.2: Convergence of the estimate of $_{xy}\rho$ in 50 replications of the microsimulation when ρ = 0.01

$_{xy}\rho$ = 0.5196913

	O.L.S.	Iterative estimation		OLS	Iterative estimation		OLS	Iterative estimation
1	0.8208	0.8208	18	0.7464	0.7959	35	0.7047	0.7948
2	0.8708	0.8457	19	0.7749	0.7948	36	0.7975	0.7948
3	0.8898	0.8604	20	0.8776	0.7990	37	0.8188	0.7955
4	0.7836	0.8412	21	0.7285	0.7956	38	0.7853	0.7952
5	0.8856	0.8501	22	0.8123	0.7964	39	0.7880	0.7950
6	0.7569	0.8345	23	0.8071	0.7968	40	0.8084	0.7954
7	0.7345	0.8202	24	0.7913	0.7966	41	0.8036	0.7956
8	0.8009	0.8178	25	0.7824	0.7960	42	0.8172	0.7961
9	0.7989	0.8157	26	0.7978	0.7961	43	0.8129	0.7965
10	0.6895	0.8031	27	0.7654	0.7949	44	0.8105	0.7968
11	0.8870	0.8107	28	0.7960	0.7950	45	0.9283	0.7997
12	0.6598	0.7981	29	0.8431	0.7966	46	0.7636	0.7989
13	0.6981	0.7904	30	0.8207	0.7974	47	0.8268	0.7995
14	0.8027	0.7913	31	0.8081	0.7978	48	0.8558	0.8007
15	0.7893	0.7912	32	0.7874	0.7975	49	0.7088	0.7988
16	0.8876	0.7972	33	0.8910	0.8003	50	0.7853	0.7985
17	0.8254	0.7988	34	0.7024	0.7974			

Table 7.2.4: Ecological correlation in 50 replications of the microsimulation experiment when $\rho = 0.1$.

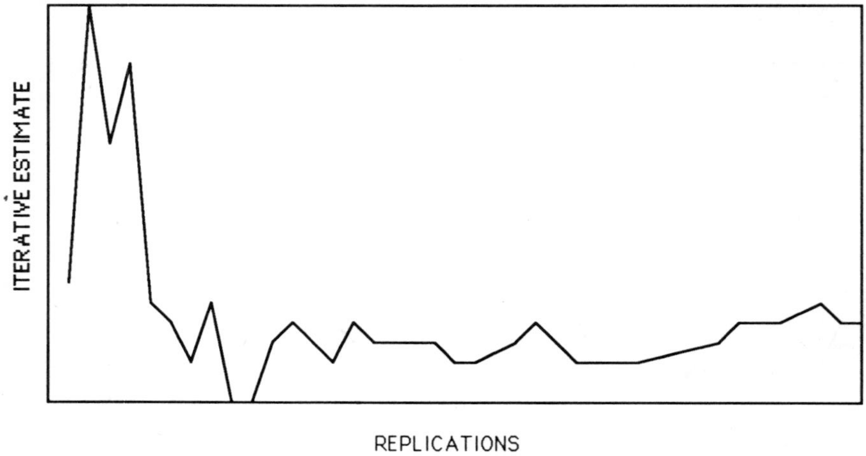

Figure 7.2.3: Convergence of the estimate of $_{xy}\rho$ in 50 replications of the microsimulation when $\rho = 0.1$

EXAMPLE 7.2: MICROSIMULATION - IRREGULAR LATTICE.

A weakness of the first microsimulation experiment is that, due to computer limitations, (the maximum dimension allowed for a matrix is 400-by-400) we have to build up spatial groups constituted by only a small number of individuals (In our case 10).
In an attempt to overcome this limitation we propose here a second microsimulation procedure.
First of all we consider a single process $\{X_j\}$, j=1,....,n, with a variance covariance matrix ${}_X\mathbf{V}$

$$
{}_X\mathbf{V} = \begin{pmatrix} {}_X\sigma^2 \; {}_X\gamma \ldots\ldots\ldots\ldots\ldots \\ {}_X\gamma \; {}_X\sigma^2 \ldots\ldots\ldots\ldots\ldots \\ \ldots\ldots \quad {}_X\sigma^2 {}_X\gamma \ldots\ldots \\ \ldots\ldots \quad {}_X\gamma \, {}_X\sigma^2 \ldots\ldots \\ \ldots\ldots\ldots\ldots \quad {}_X\sigma^2 {}_X\gamma \\ \ldots\ldots\ldots\ldots \quad {}_X\gamma \, {}_X\sigma^2 \end{pmatrix} \tag{7.2.17}
$$

Since ${}_X\mathbf{V}$ has a block diagonal structure, we can perform the Cholesky decomposition separately in each block (See Appendix A.6). This allows us to cope with a very large number of individuals in each block. Formally we have

$$
{}_X\mathbf{V} = \begin{pmatrix} \mathbf{L}_{(1)}\mathbf{L}'_{(1)} & & & \\ & \mathbf{L}_{(2)}\mathbf{L}'_{(2)} & & \\ & & \ldots\ldots\ldots & \\ & & & \mathbf{L}_{(m)}\mathbf{L}'_{(m)} \end{pmatrix} = \mathbf{LL}' \tag{7.2.18}
$$

where $\mathbf{L}$ is a lower triangular matrix n by n, and $\mathbf{L}_{(1)},\mathbf{L}_{(2)},\ldots\ldots,\mathbf{L}_{(m)}$ are lower triangular matrices of dimensions r-by-r. The observations $\mathbf{x}$ drawn from the process $\{X_j\}$ are then obtained by the matrix product (See Appendix A.5):

$$
\mathbf{x} = \mathbf{Le} = \begin{pmatrix} \mathbf{L}_{(1)}\mathbf{e} \\ \mathbf{L}_{(2)}\mathbf{e} \\ \ldots\ldots \\ \mathbf{L}_{(m)}\mathbf{e} \end{pmatrix} \tag{7.2.19}
$$

where $\mathbf{e}$ are i.i.d. N(0,1).
Once the observations of the process $\{X_j\}$ are simulated the observations of the process $\{Y_j\}$ are obtained assuming a linear relationship between the two processes

$$
\mathbf{Y} = \beta\, \mathbf{X} + \mathbf{e} \tag{7.2.20}
$$

where β is an arbitrary value. Through this approximated procedure we can simulate the economic behaviour in space of a large number of individuals.

The objective of our second experiment is to simulate the economic behaviour of 6,000 individuals distributed in the 20 Italian regions (See Appendix A.1). 300 individuals are assumed to live in each region. Let us start by considering the 300-by-300 variance-covariance matrix of one of the blocks in which the matrix ${}_{X}\mathbf{V}$ in Formula (7.2.17) is decomposed. This submatrix has the typical element σ_{jk} such that

$$\sigma_{jk} = \begin{cases} 1 & \text{if } j = k \\ \rho & \text{otherwise} \end{cases} \tag{7.2.21}$$

since the uniform covariance assumption (see § 4.2.3) holds within each block. We can now simulate the behaviour of the individuals included in this block with respect to the process {X} by exploiting the procedure described in Example 7.1 (See also the Appendix A.5). We assume the process {X} to be spatially independent at the level of the 20 regions, as a consequence of the block diagonal structure of ${}_{X}\mathbf{V}$ (See Formula 7.2.16). The assumption of spatial independence between regions can be reasonably accepted here as a consequence of the fact that, as we have repeatedly observed in this book, the larger are the areas, the weaker the dependence will be (see, for example, § 5.2.3). To generate 6,000 observations of the stationary process {X}, it is enough, therefore, to replicate 20 times the simulation procedure described for one block.
In our experiment we considered a very low level of the autocorrelation between individuals (ρ=0.0001) and the process {X} is assumed to have zero mean for the sake of simplicity.
Once the observations from the process {X} are simulated for the 6,000 individuals, we can generate a second variable which is linearly dependent on the first by using Formula (7.2.20). In our experiment we assumed :

$$Y_j = 0.9\, X_j + e_j \qquad j=1,\ldots,6000$$

where e_j are observations generated from an independent distribution N(0,1).
A problem with this approach is that the cross-correlation between {X} and {Y} cannot be perfectly controlled for since it depends on the correlation between the process $\{X_j\}$ and the random shocks $\{e_j\}$.
In fact we have

$$E(Y_j, X_j) = E\,[\,(0.9\, X_j + e_j)\, X_j]$$

$$= 0.9\, E(X_j{}^2) + E(X_j e_j)$$

$$= 0.9 + E(X_j e_j)$$

The individual cross-correlation estimated after 10 replications is found to be

$${}_{xy}\rho = 0.6621938$$

Replications	Individual Correlation O.L.S.	Individual Correlation Recursive estimation	Ecological Correlation O.LS.	Ecological Correlation Recursive estimation
1	0.6182604	0.6182604	0.8617424	0.8617424
2	0.7048496	0.6615550	0.9106296	0.8861860
3	0.6665478	0.6632192	0.8320540	0.8681420
4	0.6148796	0.6511343	0.8382905	0.8606791
5	0.6857361	0.6580547	0.8468794	0.8579191
6	0.7193024	0.6682626	0.9320403	0.8702727
7	0.7209271	0.6757861	0.8878255	0.8727802
8	0.7204734	0.6813720	0.8681004	0.8721952
9	0.5782144	0.6699100	0.7679027	0.8606072
10	0.6012541	0.6630444	0.8719592	0.8617424
Theoretical value				0.6720008

Table 7.2.5 : Individual-process cross-correlation between 6,000 simulated individuals and ecological cross-correlation between the 20 Italian regions.

Finally having now 6000 observations on both $\{X\}$ and $\{Y\}$, we can group the individuals to give the observations at the group-process level, that is the value of X and Y at the regional level. The results of the microsimulation are displayed in Table 7.2.5. The group-process cross-correlation estimated after 10 replications is now

$$_{x*y*}\rho = 0.8617424$$

If we recall Formula (7.2.6), we have that the value of $_{x*y*}\rho$ expected from the theory is $_{x*y*}\rho = 0.6720008$. This shows that, as already noted in Example 7.1, the theory developed in this chapter has the tendency to underestimate the aggregation effect. This fact, however could also be due to the failure of the simulation procedure to produce observations with the required value of the individual autocorrelation ρ in only 10 replications.
The results of this second microsimulation experiment generally confirm the theory and the results of the first microsimulation. Bearing in mind all the limitations which arise from having only 10 replications of the microsimulation, it appears that even a very small amount of the autocorrelation among individuals can produce a dramatic change in the cross-correlation at the regional level. This change is in the direction indicated by the theory developed in this chapter.

7.3 SUMMARY AND CONCLUSION

In this chapter the results of Chapter 6 have been extended to the case in which the individual-process is observed on actual individuals rather then areas. By describing the problem of the *ecological fallacy* in terms of stochastic processes, we have shown formally that it shares a common ground with the modifiable areal unit problem.
Two cases have been examined in particular: when all the individuals in the study area interact with one another (the *uniform covariance* assumption in § 7.2.2), and when

interaction among individuals is restricted to spatial groups (the *Clique* assumption in § 7.2.3). In both cases we have shown that even a very small amount of autocorrelation between the individuals can produce the ecological fallacy effect. Furthermore if the interaction among individuals is positive, as occurs in most socio-economic studies, by grouping we obtain an increase of the cross-correlation between the two processes. Conversely when the interaction among individuals is negative, a decrease of the cross-correlation occurs. Moreover the increase (decrease) of $_{X^*Y^*}\rho$ with grouping is directly related to the number of individuals in each group.
The theory developed in this chapter has been tested through two microsimulation experiments. In the first experiment we simulated with the computer the economic behaviour of 160 households laid in an area divided into 16 adjacent quadrats. In the second experiment, instead, we simulated a *Clique* structure of the behaviour of 6000 individuals living in the 20 administrative regions into which Italy is divided.

APPENDIX 7.1

MICROSIMULATION : FORTRAN PROGRAM LISTING

```
C
C         GENERATES  RANDOM OBSERVATIONS FROM A MULTIVARIATE PROCESS
C
          IMPLICIT REAL *8 (A-H, O-Z)
C
          PARAMETER (MATSIZ=320,NBLKS=16,NOBS =50)
          PARAMETER (NREF=(MATSIZ+1)*(MATSIZ+2)/2)
C
          REAL*8 MEAN(MATSIZ), COV(MATSIZ,MATSIZ), RANVEC(MATSIZ,5)
          REAL*8 REF(NREF)
          INTEGER  GRPSIZ(0:NBLOKS)
          INTEGER  WHERE , DELTA
C
C         NOW THE DATA STATEMENT GIVING THE SIZES OF THE GROUPS
C
          DATA
          *GRPSIZ/0,10,10,10,10,10,10,10,10,10,10,10,10,10,10,10,10/
C
C         NOW GIVE VALUES OF DATA IN THE MATRIX
C
          DATA SIGMA, RHO, RHO2/1.,.0001,.5/
C
          DELTA = MATSIZ/2
          WHERE = 0
C
C         INITIALIZE COVARIANCE MATRIX
C
          DO 5 I=1,MATSIZ
          MEAN(I)=0.0
          DO 5 J=1,MATSIZ
5         COV(I,J) = 0.0
C
          DO 10 NBLOCK = 1, NBLOKS
          WHERE = WHERE + GRPSIZ(NBLOCK-1)
          NSIZBL+GRPSIZ(NBLOCK)
          DO 10 IX=1,NSIZBL
          DO 10 IY=1,NSIZBL
          IF (IX .EQ. IY) THEN
                 COV(WHERE+IX,WHERE+IY) = SIGMA
                 COV(WHERE+IX+DELTA,WHERE+IY) = RHO2
                 COV(WHERE+IX,WHERE+IY+DELTA) = RHO2
                 COV(WHERE+IX+DELTA,WHERE+IY+DELTA) = SIGMA
          ELSE
                 COV(WHERE+IX,WHERE+IY) = RHO
                 COV(WHERE+IX+DELTA,WHERE+IY) = RHO
```

```
                COV(WHERE+IX,WHERE+IY+DELTA) = RHO
                COV(WHERE+IX+DELTA,WHERE+IY+DELTA) = RHO
          ENDIF
10        CONTINUE
C
C         NOW CALL THE NAG ROUTINE TO GENERATE THE MULTIVARIATE RANDOM
C         OBSERVATIONS
C         THE G05EAF NAG PARAMETERS ARE DEFINED AS FOLLOWS:
C         MEAN = REAL ARRAY OF DIMENSION AT LEAST MATSIZ CONTAINING THE
C         VECTOR OF MEANS. MATSIZ = INTEGER. ON ENTRY MATSIZ MUST SPECIFY
C         THE NUMBER OF DIMENSIONS OF THE VARIANCE/COVARIANCE MATRIX.
C         COV = REAL ARRAY OF DIMENSION (MATSIZ,MATSIZ) CONTAINING THE
C         VARIANCE COVARIANCE MATRIX ELEMENTS.  0.0 = SPECIFIES THE
C         MAXIMUM ERROR IN ANY ELEMENT OF COV, RELATIVE TO THE LARGEST
C         ELEMENT OF COV. CAN ASSUME ANY ALTERNATIVE VALUE BETWEEN 0.0
C         AND 0.1/MATSIZ. REF = REAL ARRAY OF DIMENSION (NREF). ON EXIT,
C         REF CONTAINS THE REFERENCE VECTOR FOR SUBSEQUENT USE BY
C         G05EZF.  NREF = INTEGER. ON ENTRY, NREF MUST SPECIFY THE
C         DIMENSION OF REF AS DECLARED IN THE CALLING (SUB)ROUTINE.
C         NREF≥(MATSIZ+1)(N+2)/2. IFAIL = INTEGER. ON ENTRY, IFAIL MUST
C         BE SET TO 0 OR 1 UNLESS THE ROUTINE DETECTS AN ERROR IFAIL
C         CONTAINS 0 ON EXIT.
C         THE GOEZF NAG PARAMETERS ARE DEFINED AS FOLLOWS:
C         RANVEC = REAL ARRAY OF DIMENSION AT LEAST MATSIZ. ON ENTRY
C         RANVEC CONTAINS THE PSEUDO-RANDOM MULTIVARIATE NORMAL
C         VECTOR GENERATED BY THE ROUTINE. MATSIZ = SEE ABOVE. REF = SEE
C         ABOVE. NREF = SEE ABOVE. IFAIL = SEE ABOVE.
C
          DO 40 K=1,NOBS/5
          DO 20 I=1,5
          CALL G05EAF(MEAN,MATSIZ,COV,MATSIZ,0.0,REF,NREF,IFAIL)
20        CALL G05EZF (RANVEC(1,I),MATSIZ,REF,NREF,IFAIL)
C
C         NOW WRITE THE OBSERVATIONS IN FORM 5-BY-MATSIZ
C
          DO 40 I+1,MATSIZ
          WRITE(6,30)(RANVEC(I,J),J=1,5)
30        FORMAT(1X,5(F10.6,1X))
C
C         END OF THE PROGRAM
C
          STOP
          END
```

8. The dampening effect of spatial correlogram

8.1 INTRODUCTION

In foregoing chapters we have analysed some problems that arise in the statistical analysis of spatial data for situations in which the areas under study may differ from one another in size and/or shape. Although the aim of this book is not to give an exhaustive account of all the problems that occur when a statistical analysis is performed making use of data which are geographically dispersed, there is another problem to which the methodological framework put forward in Chapter 4 can be extended, namely the problem of estimating the *spatial correlogram*.
One of the basic assumptions throughout this book is that the dependence among the different random variables of a process is restricted to a small subset of the sites called *neighbours*. In Section 2.4 we relaxed this hypothesis and allowed for the possibility of having, in place of a single set of neighbours, several sets of neighbours which refer to sites that are one, two, or more spatial lags apart where lags refer to analogy with time series analysis.
In this chapter we analyse the problem of estimating a spatial correlogram within the framework put forward in Chapter 4. Our aim is to find theoretical substantiation to the observed pattern for the decreasing shape of most empirical spatial correlograms as discussed in Chapter 2.

8.2. THE DAMPENING EFFECT

8.2.1. Introduction

One of the main difficulties in translating the correlogram, a concept born in time series analysis into spatial terms, is that in space there does not exist a complete and unique ordering of observations as we have in time. Instead ordering must be introduced using some information about the configuration of the map we are analysing. For a Gaussian stationary stochastic process this is usually achieved by defining a set of neighbours for each site j, say N(j). We also define the connectivity matrix **W** already mentioned in Chapter 3, but with the further requirement that the off-diagonal non-zero elements are scaled to sum to unity in each row. With the symbols already introduced we have:

$$w_{jk} \in \mathbf{W} \quad \begin{cases} v_j^{-1} & \text{,if } k \in N(j) \\ 0 & \text{,otherwise} \end{cases} \qquad (8.1.1)$$

and

$$\Sigma_j \; w_{jk} = 1 \tag{8.1.2}$$

Given these definitions, the term

$$L(X_j) = \Sigma_{j \,\varepsilon\, N(k)} \; w_{jk} \, X_j \tag{8.1.3}$$

plays the role of the spatially lagged variable. An extension of Equation (8.1.3) to lags higher than the first is also possible by defining a hierarchical spatial ordering of the neighbours of each site in a sequence of sets ${}_gN(j)$ and, accordingly, a set of g-th order weights matrices **W(g)** of elements $w(g)_{jk}$ scaled to sum to unity in each row. Starting from this spatial lag definition different estimators of the correlogram can be defined . The most common of them are analysed and criticized in the next section.

8.2.2. Some estimates of the spatial correlogram

Suppose we are given j sites ($j=1,\ldots,n$) with a spatial order and a vector of observations $x_1,\ldots,x_n$ that we can consider as a single realization of a discrete stochastic process $X_1,\ldots,X_n$. The process is supposed to be, as usual, stationary and Gaussian, with moments

$$E(X_j) = 0 \qquad ,\text{each } j \tag{8.2.1}$$

$$E(X_j^2) = \sigma^2 \qquad ,\text{each } j \tag{8.2.2}$$

$$E(X_j X_k) = \sigma^2 \, c \; |j - k| \qquad ,\text{each } j \text{ and } k \tag{8.2.3}$$

where c is a function depending on the distance between j and k . If the observations lie on a line and the dependence is unilateral (time-like case, see Chapter 3) the empirical correlogram at lag t^* is given by the sum of the cross-products between the original series expressed in terms of the difference from the sample mean $z_j = x_j - x^*$, and the lagged series $L(z_j) = z_{j+t^*}$, where the data are shifted t^* steps ahead and scaled with the variance of the series itself

$$\rho_{t^*} = (\,\Sigma\; z_i \, z_{i+t^*})\,(\,\Sigma\, z_i^2)^{-1} \tag{8.2.4}$$

This is sometimes corrected by multiplying by the term $[n/(n-t^*)]$ to eliminate the bias due to the observations which have been lost (Priestley, 1981). This alternative estimator is less biased, but a source of bias still remains due to the presence of x^* which is only an estimate. If the observations are laid unto a regular square lattice grid with two time-like axes, the lagged series $L^s L^r (z_{ij}) = z_{i+s\;,\;j+r}$ again can be interpreted as a shift of the original series s and r steps ahead along the two axes. In this case the two-dimensional empirical autocovariance for two time-like axes at lag s and r is defined as

$$C(s,r) = n_1^{-1} n_2^{-1} \sum_{i=1}^{(n_1-s)} \; \sum_{i=1}^{(n_2-r)} z_{ij} \; z_{i+s,\, j+r} \tag{8.2.5}$$

where n_1 and n_2 are the number of rows and columns of the lattice such that $n_1 n_2 = n$ (Whittle, 1954; p.440).
This estimator is also biased. In fact it is based upon the summation of $(n_1 - |s|)(n_2 - |r|)$ cross-products varying at each lag. The alternative

$$C^*(s,r) = (n_1-|s|)^{-1}(n_2-|r|)^{-1} \sum_{i=1}^{(n_1-s)} \sum_{i=1}^{(n_2-r)} z_{ij}\, z_{i+s,\, j+r} \qquad (8.2.6)$$

is obtained by analogy with the time series cases (Ripley, 1981). The empirical correlogram follows immediately by scaling $C(s,r)$ and $C^*(s,r)$ with the variance of the series itself.
Let us now examine a system of irregular collecting areas with no time-like ordering. The sample spatial correlogram is based upon the sample autocovariance between the observed series and the lagged series (Cliff et al., 1975). The g-th order lagged series, say ${}^g z$, expressed in terms of differences from the sample mean, is defined similarly to Formula (8.1.3) by

$${}^g z_i = \Sigma_{j\, \varepsilon\, gN(i)}\, w(g)_{ij}\, z_j \qquad (8.2.7)$$

where $w(g)_{ij}$ are the previously defined g-th order weights. So when dealing with time series and regular lattices the original series is shifted to account for lags, but when dealing with space the lagged series is a moving-average of the original observations.
As a consequence of (8.2.7) and by analogy with (8.2.4), the empirical autocovariance at lag g is given by

$$C(g) = n^{-1} \Sigma\, z_i\, {}^g z_i \qquad (8.2.8)$$

However two different scalings are possible and accordingly we have two estimates for the empirical correlogram. If we scale (8.2.8) with the variance of the series itself, we get

$$I(g) = (\Sigma\, z_i\, {}^g z_i)\, (\Sigma\, z_i{}^2)^{-1} \qquad (8.2.9)$$

Alternatively, we can scale the autocovariance with the geometric average of the variance of the original and of the lagged series, leading to

$$R(g) = (\Sigma\, z_i\, {}^g z_i)\, [\,(\Sigma\, {}^g z_i{}^2)\, (\Sigma\, z_i{}^2)\,]^{-1/2} \qquad (8.2.10)$$

Equation (8.2.9) represents the well-known *Moran coefficient* (Moran, 1954; Cliff and Ord, 1981; Haining, 1978c; Ord, 1975), while (8.2.10) is usually referred to as *modified spatial autocorrelation coefficient* (Bennett, 1979; Hooper and Hewings, 1981; Upton and Fingleton, 1985) and is based on a formula originally due to Whittle (1954). A property that links the two preceding estimates is the inequality (see Cliff and Ord, 1981; p.21)

$$|I(g)| \leq (\Sigma\ gz_i^{\ 2} / \ \Sigma\ z_i^2)^{1/2} \qquad (8.2.11)$$

and therefore the modified spatial autocorrelation coefficient can be viewed as the Moran coefficient divided by its theoretical maximum, namely

$$R(g) = I(g) / \text{Max}\,|I(g)| = I(g)\ (\Sigma\ z_i^2 / \ \Sigma\ gz_i^2)^{1/2} \qquad (8.2.12)$$

This last equation shows why in a time series the two estimators are equal. In fact, for a time series $\Sigma\ z_i^{\ 2} \approx \Sigma\ gz_i$ unless the number of observations is very small. This *identity* is generally false for a spatial series. It can be noted that both the estimates can be seen as the correlation between the sample realization of two processes, the first being the process underlying the series itself ,and the second being constituted by a moving average of the first. We investigate the effects of this phenomenon in the rest of this chapter through theoretical development and calculation, and through simulation studies.

8.2.3. The reduction in variance of the lagged series

In order to investigate the moments of the process underlying the lagged series we can, now, exploit the results of Chapter 4. Consider the variates Z_i corresponding to their observed values z_i. Their expectations are (Cliff and Ord, 1981)

$$E(Z_i) = 0 \qquad (8.2.13)$$

and

$$E(Z_i^2) = [(n-1)/n]\ \sigma^2 \qquad (8.2.14)$$

The corresponding first-order lagged variate $'Z_i$ has expectations

$$E('Z_i) = E(\ \Sigma\ w_{ij}\ Z_j) = \ \Sigma\ w_{ij}\ E(\ Z_j) = \ 0 \qquad (8.2.15)$$

and

$$E('Z^2_i) = E(\ \Sigma\ w_{ij}\ Z_j)^2 = E(\ \Sigma\ w_{ij}^{\ 2} Z^2_j) + 2\,\Sigma_{(2)j,k\,\varepsilon N(i)}\ w_{ij} w_{ik}\ E(\ Z_j Z_k) \qquad (8.2.16)$$

In order to preserve stationarity in the process underlying the lagged series we are, at first, forced to assume that each site has the same number of neighbours, that is that $v_j = v^*$ for each j. This condition is true only for an infinite regular lattice grid; however is not uncommon to find real situations where this assumption approximately holds true. In this case Equation (8.2.16) reduces to

$$E('Z^2_i) = E[\ \Sigma\ v^{*-2} Z^2_j\ ] + 2\,[\ \Sigma_{(2)j,k\,\varepsilon N(i)}\ v^{*\,-2}\ E(\ Z_j Z_k)] \qquad (8.2.17)$$

The first summation contains v* non-zero terms, while the second is defined relative to all pairs of sites j and k that share a common neighbour i.

There are $\binom{n}{v^*}$ such pairs of sites, so that

$$E({}'Z^2_i) = v^{*-1} E(Z^2_j) + [(v^* - 1)/v^*] E(Z_j Z_k) \qquad (8.2.18)$$

where $E(Z_j Z_k)$ is limited to those sites j and k included in N(i).
Let us now define the expected reduction in variance with the ratio

$$H = E({}'Z_i^2) \ / \ E(Z^2) \qquad (8.2.19)$$

The behaviour of this ratio has already been studied in a previous work (Arbia, 1985). In our elementary case we have

$$H = v^{*-1} + (v^* - 1) E(Z_j Z_k) [v^* E(Z_j^2)]^{-1} \qquad (8.2.20)$$

In the simplest case where the process $\{X_i\}$ is constituted of independent random components, we have that $E(Z_j Z_k) = -n^{-1} \sigma^2$ (Cliff and Ord, 1981), so that

$$H = v^{*-1}[1 - (v^* - 1)/(n - 1)] \qquad (8.2.21)$$

This equation shows that H is negatively related to the average number of neighbours v^*. The reason for this negative relationship is that if the number of terms involved in a moving average increases, the steeper will be the decline in the variance of the process. Clearly then, if the number of neighbours increases monotonically as the spatial lag increases,

$$E({}^gZ_i^2) \leq E({}^{g-1}Z_i^2) \leq \ldots\ldots\ldots\ldots \leq E(Z_i^2) \qquad (8.2.22)$$

and, as a consequence,

$$H(g) \leq H(g-1) \leq \ldots\ldots\ldots\ldots\ldots \leq 1 \qquad (8.2.23)$$

where H(g) measures the reduction in variance at lag g.
If this is the case, the lagged series ${}^g z_i, {}^{g-1}z_i, \ldots, {}^1 z_i$ are generated by lagged processes $\{{}^gZ_i\}, \{{}^{g1}Z_i\}, \ldots \{{}^1Z_i\}$, with variances converging to zero when g increases. The effect is shown in Figure 8.2.1.
Formula (8.2.20) also shows that, if the correlation between sites with a common neighbour is positive, H will be inflated and the reduction in variance is moderated compared with the white noise case. In contrast when $E(Z_j Z_k)$ is negative , H will be depressed and hence the reduction in variance is more marked. This happens because, when pairs of sites with a common neighbour are positively correlated, the average will contain values that tend to be similar and the reduction will not be too sharp. In contrast if the same sites are negatively correlated the average will dramatically smooth the surface. This of course does not mean that in a positively autocorrelated surface the reduction is always less than in a negatively autocorrelated surface: the smoothing depends on the order of the relation and on the lattice configuration. For example, in a regular lattice with the rook's case definition (Cliff and Ord, 1981) we have the

property that sites with a common neighbour are second-order neighbours of on another so that, if the first-order autocorrelation is not zero (whatever its sign) th second-order neighbours are positively autocorrelated .

In Section 8.2.5 we will show that the decrease in variance when shifting from th original to the lagged series is responsible for the distortion of the empirical spatia correlogram. Before discussing this effect into detail, however, we want to make a shor digression about the connectedness of systems of irregular collecting areas observed a different spatial lags.

8.2.4. Some consideration about the connectedness of irregular collecting areas

In the previous section we have shown that the average connectedness of a spatial schem one of the major elements in the determination of the *reduction in variance* that occur the variates ${}^{g}Z_i$ corresponding to the observed g-th order spatially lagged value ${}^{g}z_i$.

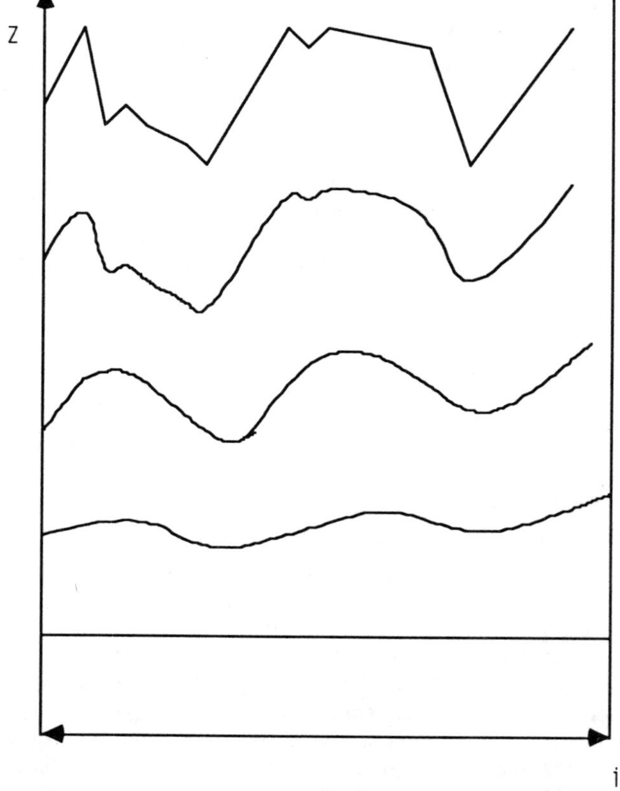

Figure 8.2.1: An hypothetical univariate spatial series (upper figure) and the corresponding lagged values (lower figures).

We have already said elsewhere in this book that there are two possible definitions of g-th order neighbours when we deal with systems of irregular collecting areas (See Chapter 2). We can either (i) consider two sites i and j to be g-th order neighbours if the shortest path from i to j passes through (g - 1) intervening sites, or (ii) we consider two sites i and j to be g-th order neighbours if their distance d_{ij} (or generalized distance) falls within the g-th distance class $a_{g-1} \leq d_{ij} \leq a_g$ with a_g the bounds of the classes. In this second case, to compute the distance between the sites we use the centroids of the areas.
The study of the theoretical number of *distance-based* neighbours at different distance classes (or lags) has been the subject of a large number of studies by that branch of spatial analysis referred to as *point-pattern analysis* (Bartlett, 1975; Ripley, 1977). An attempt at integrating point-pattern analysis with studies on the spatial autocorrelation has been made by Getis (1983; 1985).
In this literature it has been shown that if the centroids of the sites are randomly distributed following a simple Poisson process, the expected number of neighbours within a circle of radius t for each site is (Ripley, 1977):

$$v^*(t) = \pi \; t^2 \qquad (8.2.24)$$

In Formula (8.2.24) $v^*(t)$ is the average number of neighbours falling in the circle of radius t, and π=3.14159265 is the mathematical constant. This result refers to unbounded areas and does not take into account edge effects. So if we confine our attention to short distances that are less sensitive to boundary effects, the number of neighbours increases monotonically with distance, as postulated in (8.2.22), if the points are randomly distributed over space. This pattern is likely to occur also for contiguity-based neighbouring zones. Figure 8.2.2 shows the contiguity-based number of neighbours for the Italian provinces while Figure 8.2.3 displays the same Italian provinces represented by their centroids and the new measure of the distance-based neighbours at each lag.
The plot of the number of neighbours calculated by the two methods shares a close resemblance. In particular note the decrease in the last lags due to the boundaries. Table 8.2.1 displays the average number of neighbours which we calculate for various regular lattice grids of different dimension and edge structure. All lattices are mapped onto a torus.
It can be seen that the average number of neighbours increases up to the maximum of one half of the diameter of the associated graph and then decreases. This shows also that mapping onto a torus does not remove completely the edge effect as, after a certain lag, some neighbours have to be deleted because they already appear as lower order neighbours. The same phenomenon has been noticed by Griffith (1987) who severely criticized the use of toroidal mapping to simulate infinite lattices. The argument on which the author based his criticism is that the spatial correlogram associated to a torus mapping moves cyclically when the lag increases whereas the spatial correlogram of an infinite lattice process should tend to zero as the distance tends to infinity. Figure 8.2.4 shows the same pattern for the average number of neighbours in the rectangular lattice grid of 20-by-25 cells of the Mercer and Hall (1911) data which have been studied several times in the spatial literature.
Remembering the link between v^* and H expressed in Formula (8.2.20) we might therefore expect that the reduction in variance will have a U shape with a minimum at around half of the diameter of the associated graph. However this turning point is likely to be beyond the number of lags the researcher is usually interested in; accordingly the

shape of H will appear in most of empirical cases to be monotonically decreasing. To show this point Figure 8.2.5 displays the expected reduction in variance at various lag in the theoretical case of Figure 8.2.4 (Mercer and Hall data). The H function is computed by assuming the underlying process to be white noise making use of Formula (8.2.21).

8.2.5. The dampening effect on the empirical correlogram

In this section we will examine some of the possible consequences of the reduction in variance discussed in the previous sections. The empirical correlogram based on Formula (8.2.9) at the g-th lag is

$$I(g) = \mathrm{Cov}\,(z, {}^{g}z) \,/\, \mathrm{Var}\,(z) \qquad (8.2.25)$$

However, since ${}^{g}z_i$ tends to have zero variance, also its covariance with z_i tends to zero when g increases. So we might expect

$$|I(g+1)| \leq |I(g)| \qquad (8.2.26)$$

Hence a spurious damping of I, at least in the first lags, is to be expected. Furthermore the already mentioned theoretical maximum of I (Formula 8.2.11) can now be interpreted as an estimate of the H function so that

$$|I(g)| \leq [\, \Sigma {}^{g}z_i{}^2 \,/\, \Sigma z_i{}^2]^{1/2} = \left[\hat{H}(g)\right]^{1/2} \qquad (8.2.27)$$

where $\hat{H}(g)$ is an estimate of H(g). The Moran estimate is therefore dominated by the square root of H and hence is bounded to decline initially. This effect is shown in Figure 8.2.6. This dampening of the correlogram is not a genuine results of a realistic distance decay of spatial interaction, but is due merely to the inadequacy of our estimator and particularly to the definition of spatial lag (Getis, 1985). This phenomenon can perhaps explain the typical shape observed in a number of empirical correlograms.

Spatial lag order	Rook's case 6-by-6	Rook's case 8-by-8	Queen's case 6-by-6	Queen's case 8-by-8
1	4	4	8	8
2	8	8	16	16
3	10	12	11	24
4	8	14	-	15
5	4	12	-	-
6	1	4	-	-
7	-	4	-	-
8	-	1	-	-

Table 8.2.1: Average number of neighbours in different lattices that have been mapped onto a torus.

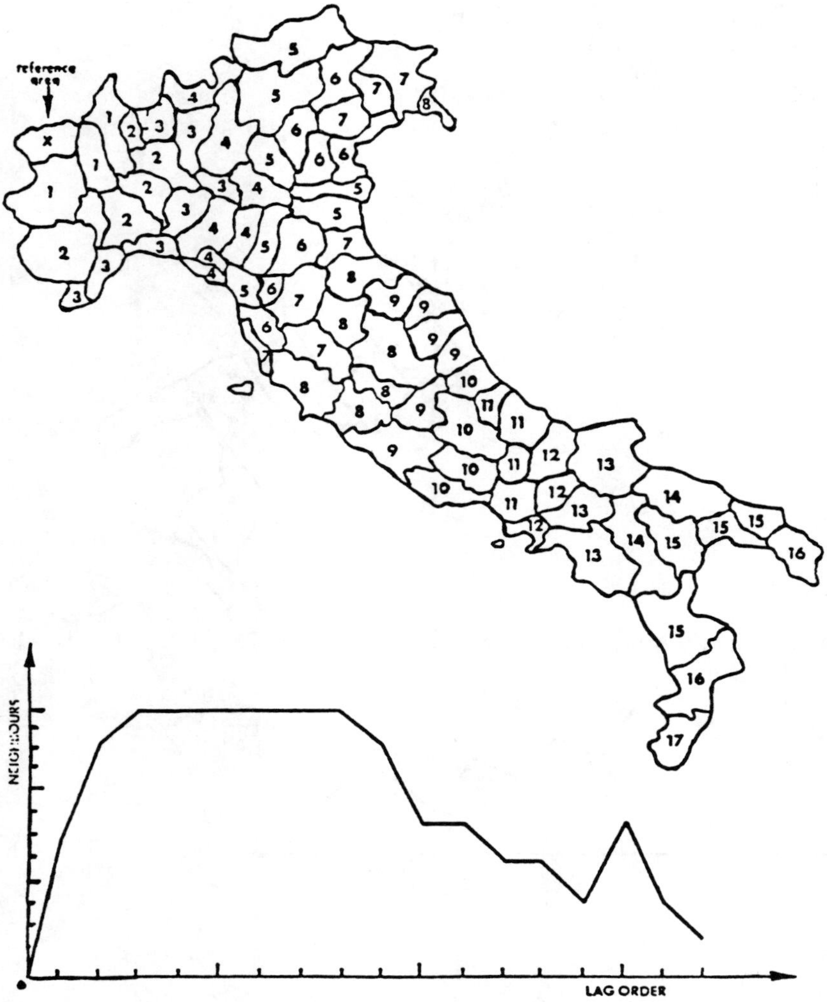

Figure 8.2.2: Various order neighbours of the reference area. Source: Arbia(1985).

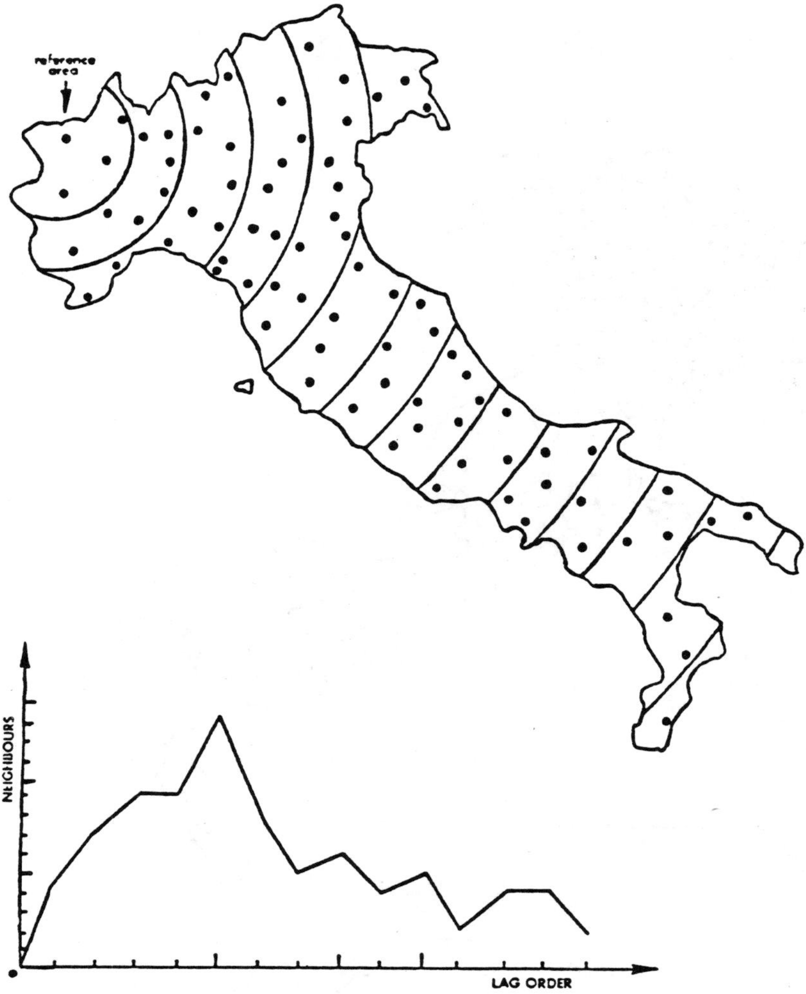

Figure 8.2.3: Various order distance-based neighbours of the reference area. Source: Arbia(1985).

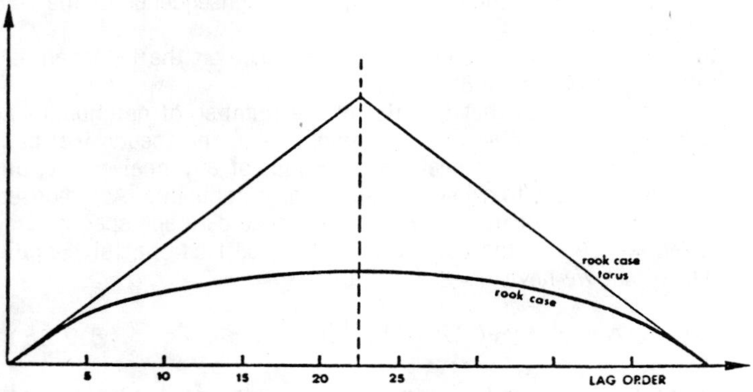

Figure 8.2.4 : Average number of neighbours in a rectangular lattice grid 20-by-25.Source: Arbia (1985).

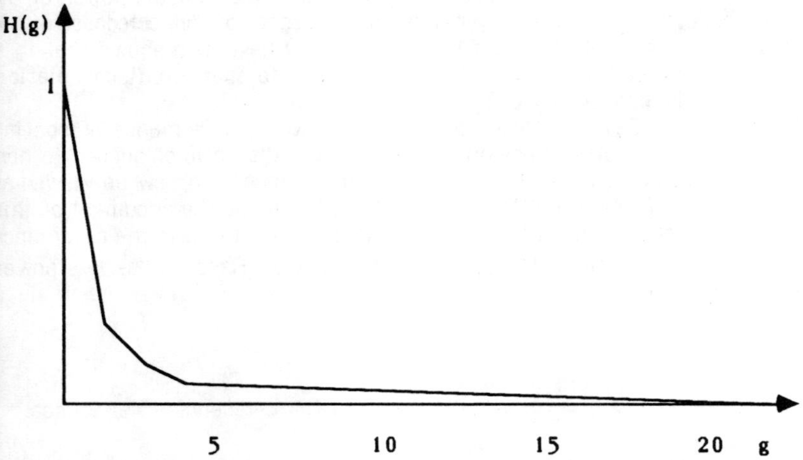

Figure 8.2.5 : Expected reduction in variance for a white noise process on a lattice 20-by-25 (Rook's case definition).

If we look for example at the correlogram for the measles data in the 178 Genera register offices reported in Section 2.4 we notice that the correlogram decreases up to half of the diameter of the associated graph and then it increases again. This particular example, therefore, seems to confirm the theoretical results of this section. The dampening effect, therefore, also explains why in the literature significant autocorrelation beyond the first lag is only very rarely observed.
A second possible consideration is that the decay is likely to be smoother when the correlation between short distance neighbours is high, as a consequence of the smoother decline in variance (See Section 8.2.3).
Another possible distortion induced by the decline in variance on the I-Moran estimate of the correlogram is displayed in Figure 8.2.7.
When the lattice configuration is such that the plot of the number of neighbours against the lag has lags for which there are relatively few neighbours, the theoretical bounds of I are such that the correlogram can show peaks not because of any real effect, but as a result of an increase in variance due to a lower number of neighbours. As a consequence we might erroneously identify significant lags merely because data are sparse.
The situation can be even worse for the estimate of the modified spatial correlogram (See Formula 8.2.10). In fact we have

$$R(g) = [\mathrm{Cov}({}^{g}z, z)/\mathrm{Var}(z)]\,[\mathrm{Var}(z)/\mathrm{Var}({}^{g}z)]^{1/2} \qquad (8.2.28)$$

and Cov $({}^{g}z, z)$ and Var$({}^{g}z)$ both tend to zero as the order of lag increases. The consequence is that the estimates have very large sample variations and are very unreliable except for the first and the very last lags. As a results small variations in the character of the sample can produce considerable differences in empirical estimates (Pfeiffer and Deutsch, 1981). Looking at a series of empirical studies the impression seems to be confirmed that the correlogram is more subject to variations at high lags, as it is to be expected from the behaviour of the H function (Ripley, 1981; p.62).
It is well known that the I-Moran correlation coefficient can also be used as a test to identify the presence of spatial autocorrelation between the observations (Cliff and Ord 1981). With respect to this problem it has already been observed that the power of the tests of spatial autocorrelation is "inversely related to the degree of connectedness of the lattice" (Cliff and Ord, 1981; p.174). Cliff and Ord (1981) have also shown that in a *totally connected lattice* (see Chapter 3) the power of all the spatial autocorrelation tests falls down to equal the probability of Type I error for all levels of ρ.
Furthermore Haining (1978a) has observed that the power performance of spatial autocorrelation tests is "less satisfactory in the case where the ratio of border to non border cells increases" (op.cit.; p.123). The decrease in variance can now be viewed as the cause of the poorest performance of the tests. In fact, following the argument of this section, the greater the decrease in variance of the lagged series, the less the covariance between z and ${}^{g}z$ is a good measure of the spatial autocorrelation. Hence it has less power to discriminate independence.

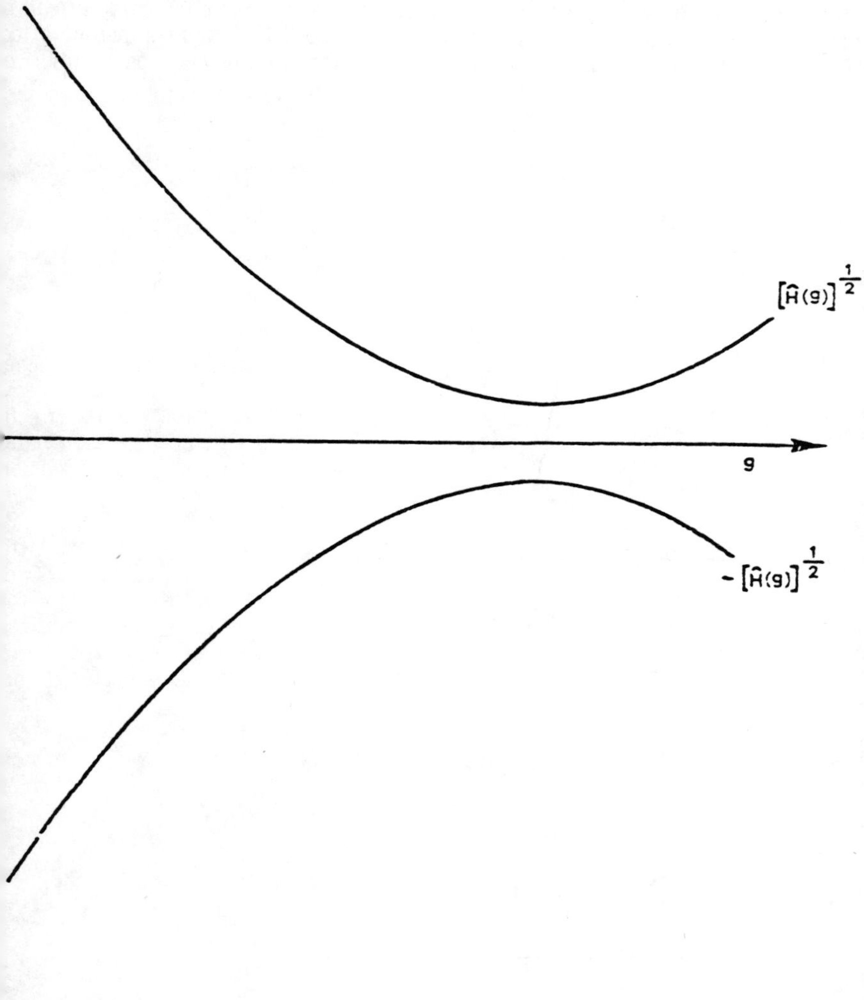

igure 8.2.6: Bounds of the Moran-based correlogram. Source: Arbia(1985).

8.3 SIMULATION STUDY

8.3.1. Introduction

When the spatial system is such that each site has the same number of neighbours an the process is constituted by independent random components, the *dampening effect* o the variance can be computed exactly by use of Formula (8.2.21): the dampening effec is entirely determined by the lattice configuration through the average number o neighbours.

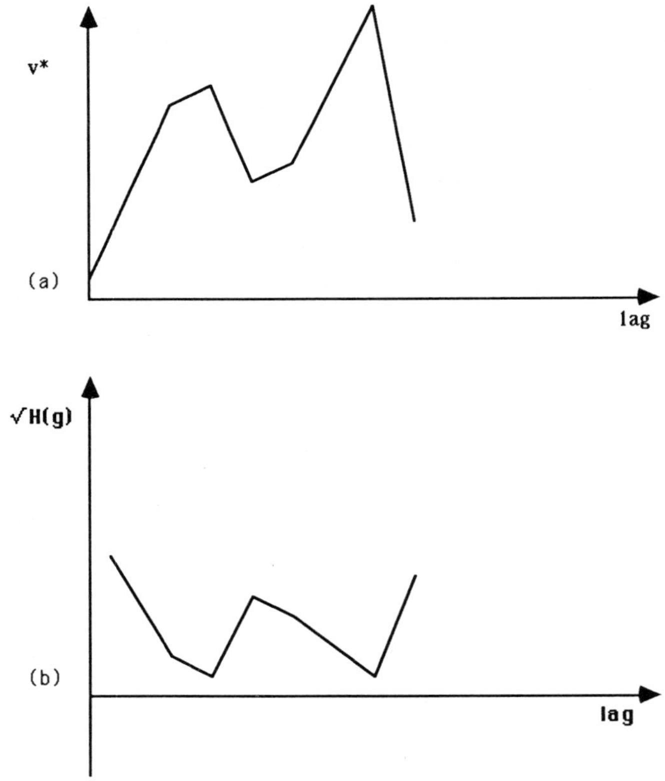

Figure 8.2.7: Number of neighbours at different spatial lags (a) and corresponding bands for the I-Moran estimate (b)

Iowever the value of v^* is only one element in determining H when the spatial system s constituted by irregular collecting areas and the process is constituted by dependent andom variables. In this section we will examine, through a simulation study, the legree to which these other factors also modify the rate of decrease in variance. Because he number of possible configurations is infinite for irregular collecting areas, imulation studies permit the analysis of some of the most common situations.

.3.2. Simulation results

n this section the results of Section 8.2 will be extended to account for the joint effect f three factors: (i) processes constituted by dependent random variables; (ii) rregular collecting areas; (iii) variable number of observations.
o isolate the three effects six different layouts were considered: (a) A 6-by-6 regular attice grid with the rook's case definition, mapped unto a torus. (b) A 6-by-6 regular attice grid with the rook's case definition. (c) An 8-by-8 regular lattice grid with he rook's case definition. (d) A 10-by-10 regular lattice grid with the rook's case efinition. (e) A 6-by-6 regular lattice grid with the queen's case definition. (f) A ystem of 36 irregular collecting areas representing the Southern Italian *provincie*.
n all case standardized binary weights are employed so that stationarity is guaranteed hen $|\rho|<1$. For the generation of observations drawn from stochastic spatial processes ith random dependent component a number of approaches exist (Haining, Griffith and ennett, 1983; Chambers, 1970; Kleijnen, 1987; Johnson, 1987). In our case we onsider the approximate model-based solution described in Appendix A.5 leading to five ifferent levels of first-order autocorrelated surfaces with $\rho = \pm 0.9$; ± 0.5 and 0.0. 00 replications were run for each experiment. The H function is firstly estimated at ach run through the formula

$$\hat{H}_r = \Sigma_i \, gz_{ir}^2 \, / \, \Sigma_i \, z_{ir}^2 \qquad (8.3.1)$$

here the index $r = 1, \ldots, R$ stands for the run number. The estimates at each run are hown in Figure 8.3.1.
The reduction in variance is then iteratively estimated through the formula

$$\hat{H} \quad \Sigma_{(2)} \, gz_{ir}^2 \, / \, \Sigma_{(2)} \, z_{ir}^2 \qquad (8.3.2)$$

n our study 300 replications were enough to ensure a convergence of the value of H up the third decimal figure (See Figure 8.3.2). The main results of the six layouts are ummarized in Tables 8.3.1 and 8.3.2.
s expected the decrease in variance is inversely related to the average number of eighbours v^* in the case of independence ($\rho = 0.0$). In contrast when $\rho \neq 0.0$ the inimum decrease is attained in the case of irregular collecting areas. Furthermore it confirmed that the presence of a first-order positive autocorrelation structure oderates the loss in variance.
n a regular lattice grid, *ceteris paribus*, the torus case is dominated by the non-torus eference data (due to the minor number of neighbours for the boundaries) and in the ueen's case there is a more rapid reduction in variance than in the rook's case. As we ready suggested (see Section 8.2.3), in a regular lattice grid and the rook's case efinition of neighbours the effects of a negatively autocorrelated surfaces are

symmetric to those of a positively correlated one. In contrast, in the queen's case and in the case of irregular collecting areas, the experiments show that the dampening is steeper when $\rho < 0.0$.
The results of layouts (b), (c) and (d) seem to confirm that the size of the lattice affects only marginally the value of H. The case of irregular collecting areas behaves quite differently if compared with the other cases in that the introduction of a positive dependency structure among the observations has a greater moderating effect. In the case of maximum positive autocorrelation the values of H appear unaffected by v^* except in the irregular case. However, this can also be due to the poorest performance of the simulation procedure when ρ is close to one.
Table 8.3.2 compares the simulated values of H with those expected from the theoretical analysis of Section 8.2, when $\rho = 0.0$. As expected, when all sites have the same number of neighbours (that is in the case of a regular lattice grid mapped unto a torus), Formula (8.2.20) provides the exact value of H.
When this condition is not met, the same formula always underestimates H, the error being related to the difference in the number of neighbours as measured by the variance of the distribution of the v_j's (indicated with the symbol σ^2_v).
The analysis of this section has been exploratory. No attempt has been made to develop a distribution theory for H and hence no probabilistic rule is available to test the differences between the results of the various experiments. The derivation of the exact distribution of H is a field that requires further investigation beyond the scope of this book. However the empirical frequency distribution of H has been explored in 10 cases. The results of the skewness and kurtosis test of normality (Spanos, 1986), and of the joint χ^2 test, are reported in Table 8.3.3 showing that the distribution of H appears at least asymptotically normal (See also Figure 8.3.3). Figure 8.3.4 shows the interpolation of the empirical distribution of H and displays five pairwise comparisons which seek to isolate the influence of the autocorrelation structure, the configuration of the spatial system and the spatial system dimension. From the graphs it is possible to argue the value of v^* as a diagnostic (See Figures 8.3.4.c and 8.3.4.e). Contrasting evidence is provided about ρ in Figures 8.3.4.a and 8.3.4.b , while different values of the number of observations do not produce very different distributions of H (As shown in Figure 8.3.4.d).

Spatial system	v^*	$\rho = -0.9$	$\rho = -0.5$	$\rho = 0.0$	$\rho = +0.5$	$\rho = +$[illegible]
(b) 6-by-6 Rook's case	3.3	32.4	29.7	29.6	29.8	3[illegible]
(c) 8-by-8 Rook's case	3.5	34.8	29.9	28.6	30.2	3[illegible]
(d) 10-by-10 Rook's case	3.6	36.8	30.1	28.1	31.0	3[illegible]
(f) 36 irregular collecting areas	3.9	30.4	27.7	26.7	45.3	5[illegible]
(a) 6-by-6 Rook's case on to a torus	4.0	36.1	23.1	22.8	23.0	3[illegible]
(e) 6-by-6 Queen's case	6.1	10.1	10.4	15.9	17.1	3[illegible]

Table 8.3.1: Estimates of the H function from the simulation after 300 replications (H is expressed as a percentage).

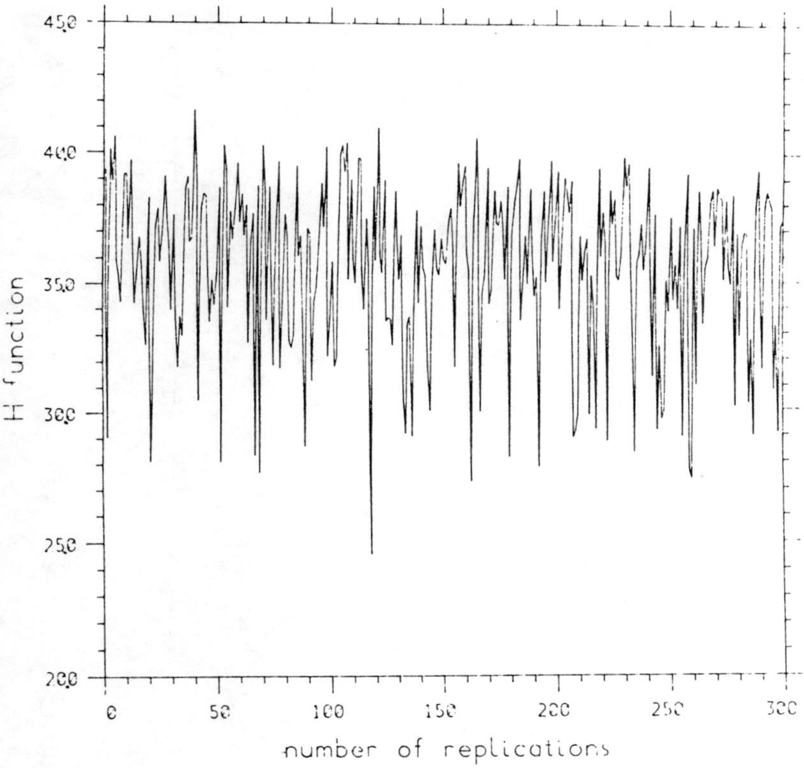

Figure 8.3.1: Estimation of the H function at each of the 300 replications

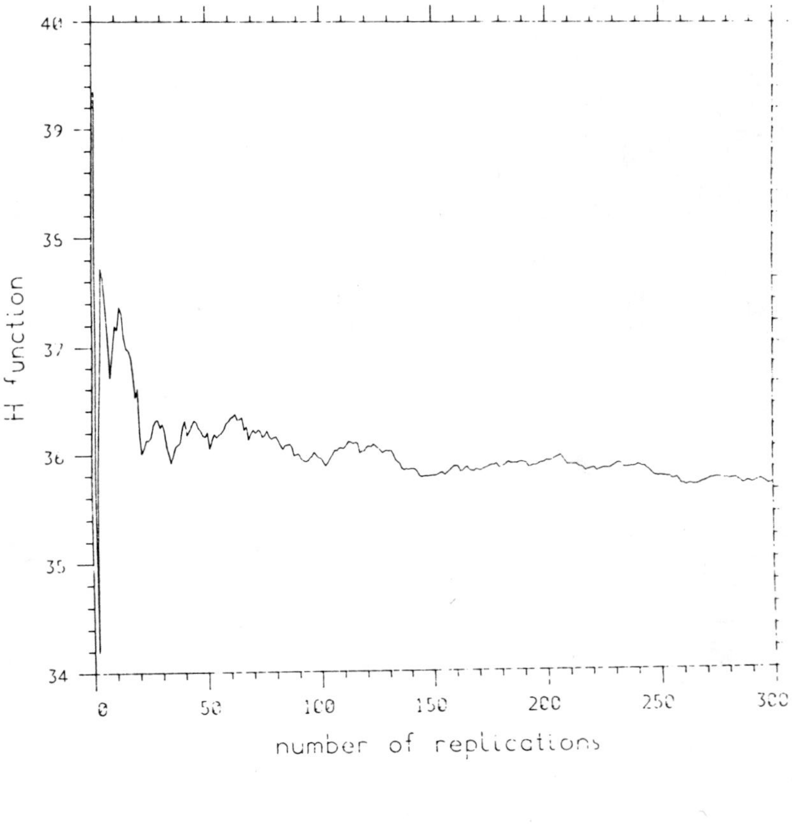

Figure 8.3.2: Iterative estimation of the H function in 300 replications.

Spatial system	V^*	σ^2_V	$\hat{H}$ (ρ=0)	Theoretical H	% Error
b) 6-by-6 rook's case	3.3	0.44	29.6	28.3	4.3
c) 8-by-8 rook's case	3.5	0.37	28.6	27.4	4.2
d) 10-by-10 rook's case	3.6	0.32	28.1	27.0	3.9
f) 36 irregular collecting areas	3.9	1.22	26.7	23.4	12.3
a) 6-by-6 rook's case on a torus	4.0	0.00	22.8	22.8	0.0
e) 6-by-6 queen's case	6.1	3.20	15.9	14.0	11.9

Table 8.3.2 : Values of the H function from the simulation study when ρ = 0 and theoretical values (see Formula 8.2.21).

Spatial system	Mean	Var	Skew	Kurt	Min	Max	γ_1	γ_2	s.k.t.
Irregular ρ=0	26.77	55.34	0.69	0.32	11.8	53.9	1.68	0.39	2.97
6-by-6 rook torus ρ=0.9	35.65	10.65	-0.84	0.18	24.5	41.6	-2.04	-0.22	4.21
6-by-6 rook torus ρ=0	22.81	32.90	0.35	0.06	9.2	42.6	0.85	0.07	0.73
6-by-6 rook ρ=0.9	32.50	62.70	0.39	-0.56	7.1	50.9	0.95	-0.68	1.36
6-by-6 rook ρ=0.5	29.80	61.21	0.41	-0.02	5.3	47.7	1.02	-0.02	1.04
6-by-6 rook ρ=0	29.60	56.00	0.34	0.08	11.7	55.6	0.82	0.09	0.68
6-by-6 queen ρ=0	15.90	23.40	0.54	0.60	5.3	35.1	1.31	0.73	2.24
6-by-6 queen ρ=0.5	17.12	28.13	0.50	0.51	5.8	36.8	1.22	0.62	1.87
8-by-8 rook ρ=0	28.57	32.14	0.58	0.57	13.9	49.2	1.89	0.92	4.41
8-by-8 rook ρ=0.9	34.61	68.50	0.47	-0.40	18.2	53.5	1.54	0.65	2.79

Table 8.3.3: Some characteristics of the empirical distribution of H in the 300 simulations. Note that γ_1=Skew$(n/6)^{1/2}$ and γ_2 = Kurt$(n/24)^{1/2}$ are Normal deviates. The skewness and kurtosis joint test (s.k.t. = $\gamma_1^2 + \gamma_2^2$) is asymptotically a χ^2 with 2 degrees of freedom.

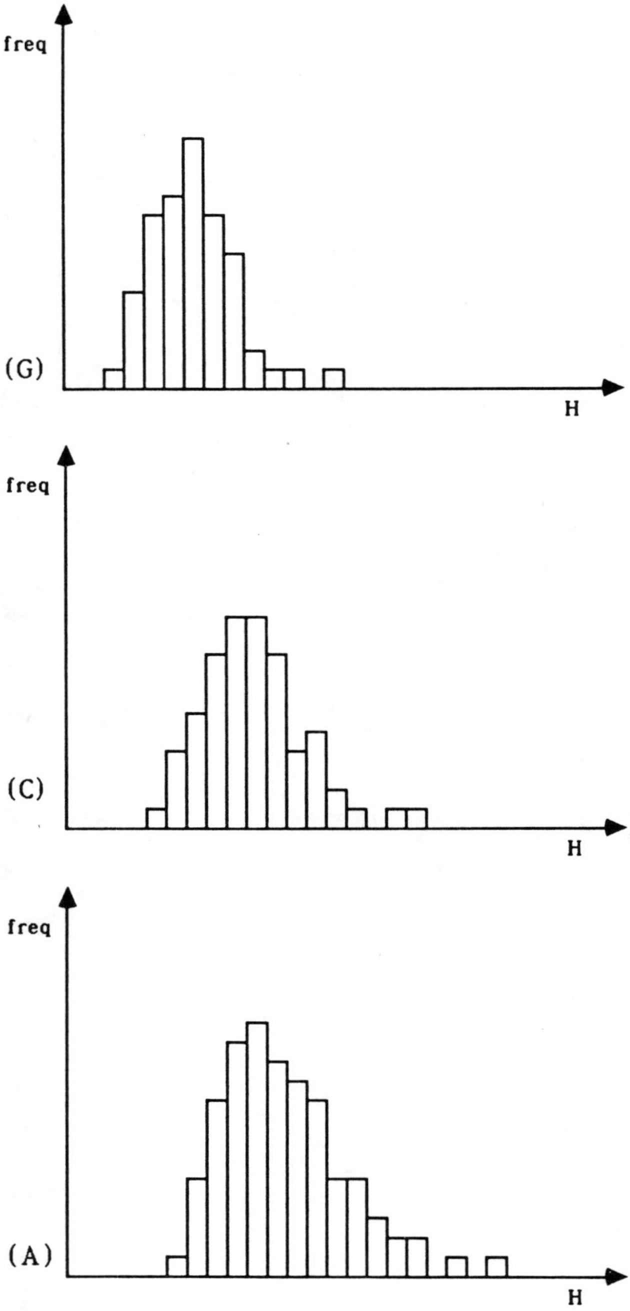

Figure 8.3.3: Empirical distribution of H in ten different layouts (See Table 8.3.3).
Continued

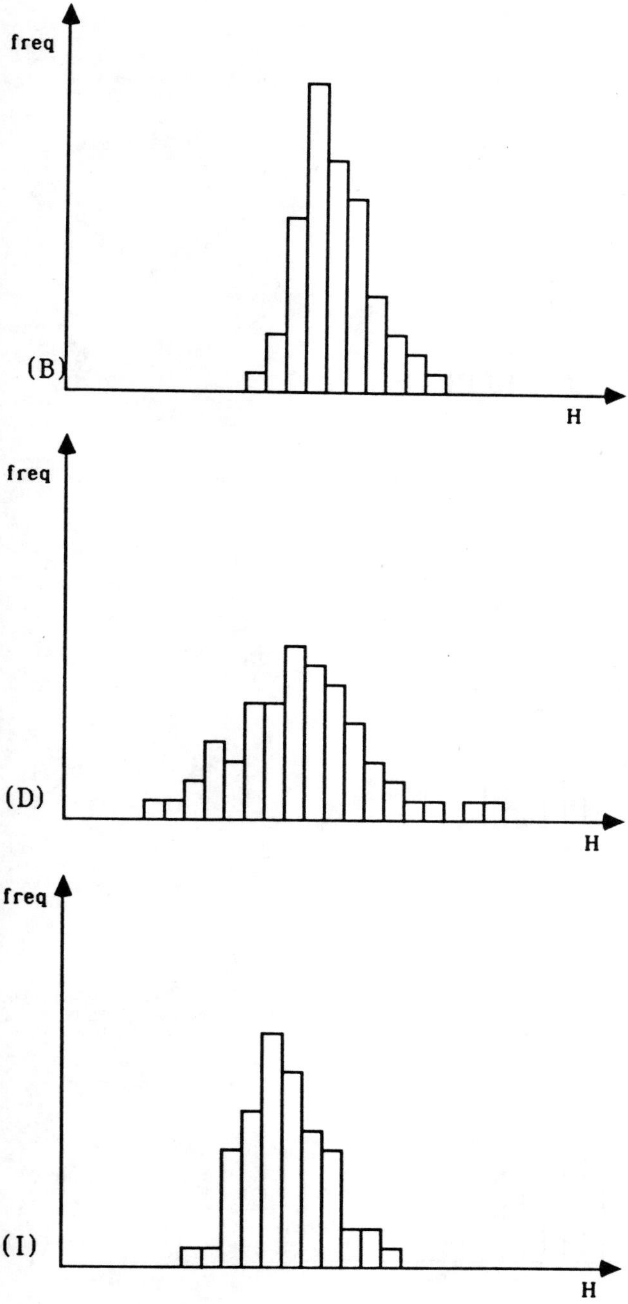

Figure 8.3.3 Empirical distribution of H in ten different layouts (See Table 8.3.3) Continued

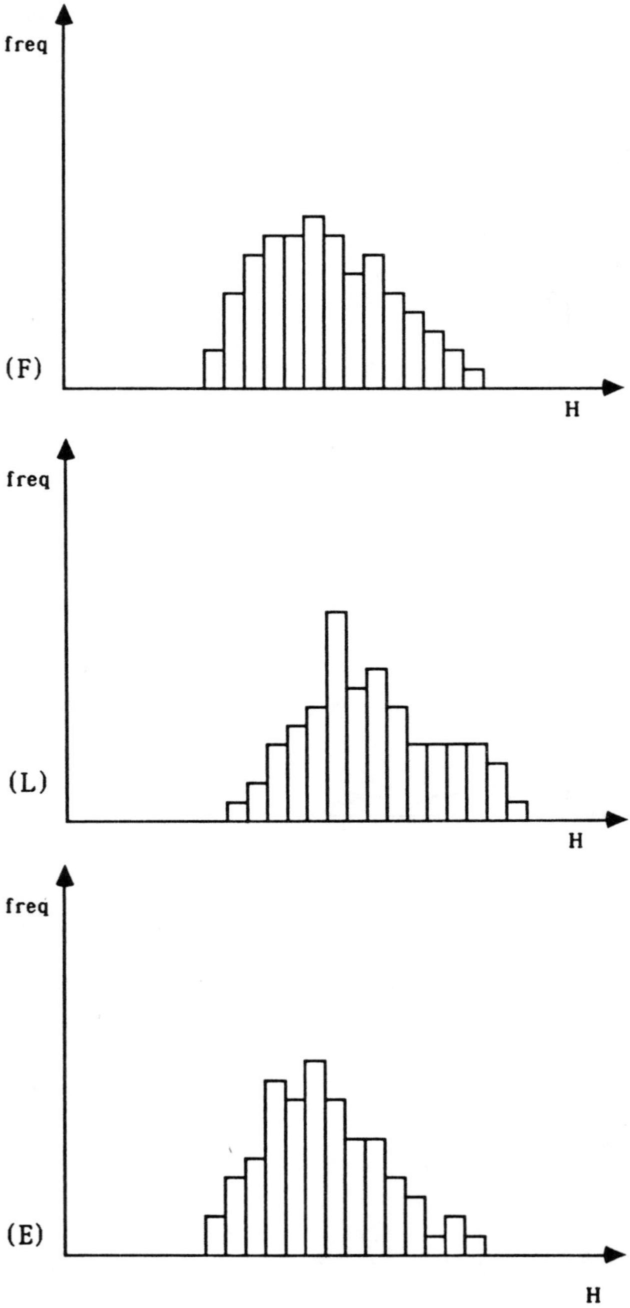

Figure 8.3.3: Empirical distribution of H in ten different layouts. (See Table 8.3.3) Continued

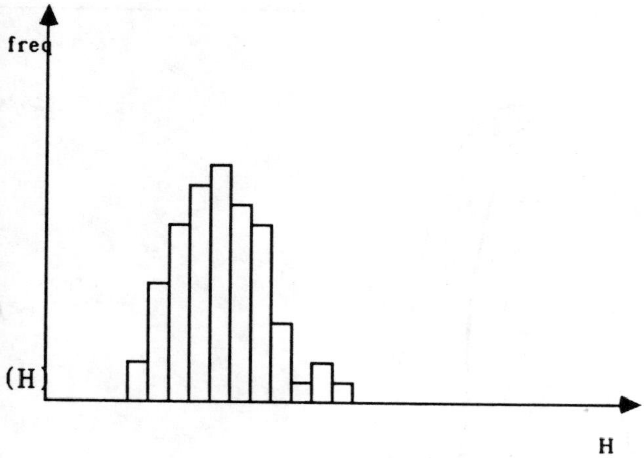

Figure 8.3.3: Empirical distribution of H in ten different dayouts.(See Table 8.3.3)

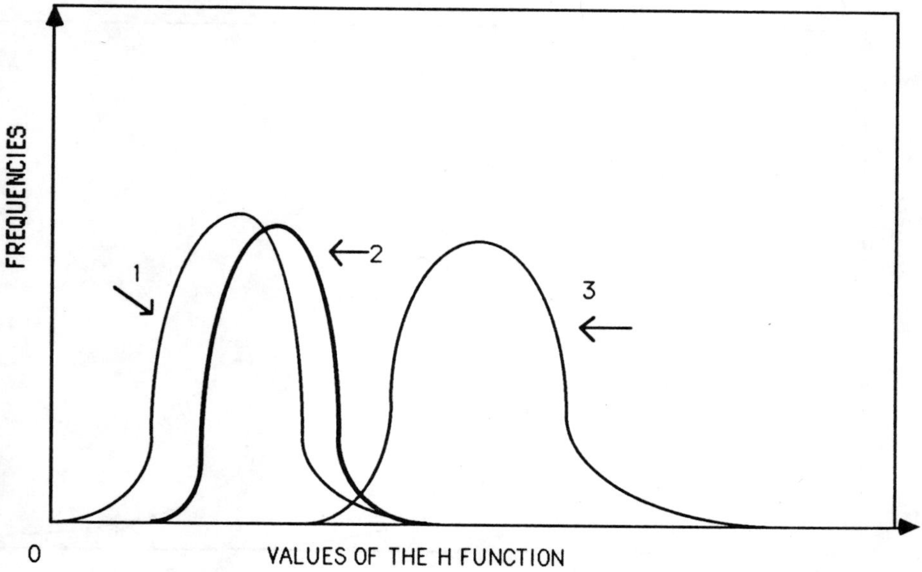

Figure 8.3.4a: Empirical distribution of the H function in a 6-by-6 lattice with the queen's case. Curve (1) $\rho = 0.0$, (2) $\rho = 0.5$, (3) $\rho = 0.9$.

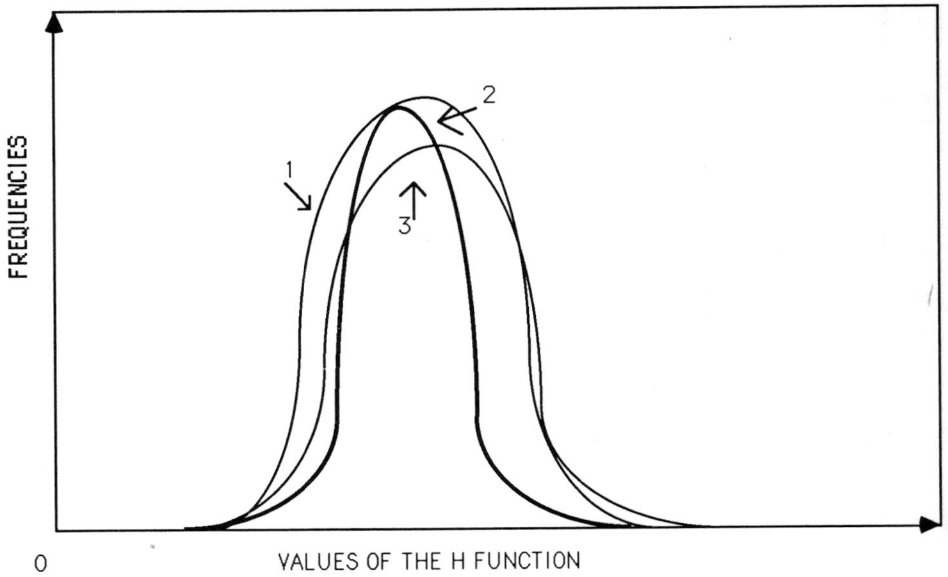

Figure 8.3.4b: Empirical distribution of the H function in a 6-by-6 lattice with the rook's case. Curve (1) $\rho = 0.0$, (2) $\rho = 0.5$, (3) $\rho = 0.9$.

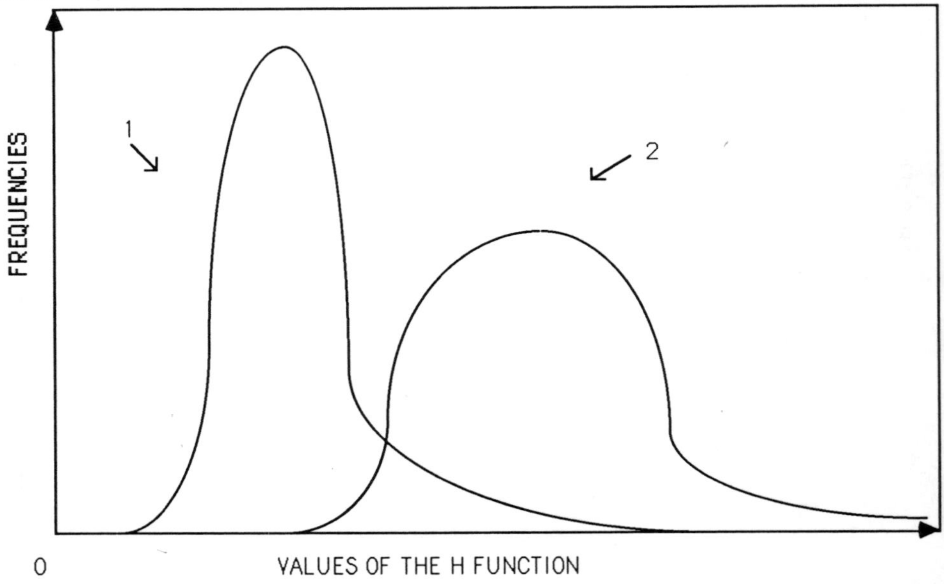

Figure 8.3.4c: Empirical distribution of the H function in a 6-by-6 lattice (1) with the rook's case and (2) with the queen's case. In both cases $\rho = 0.0$.

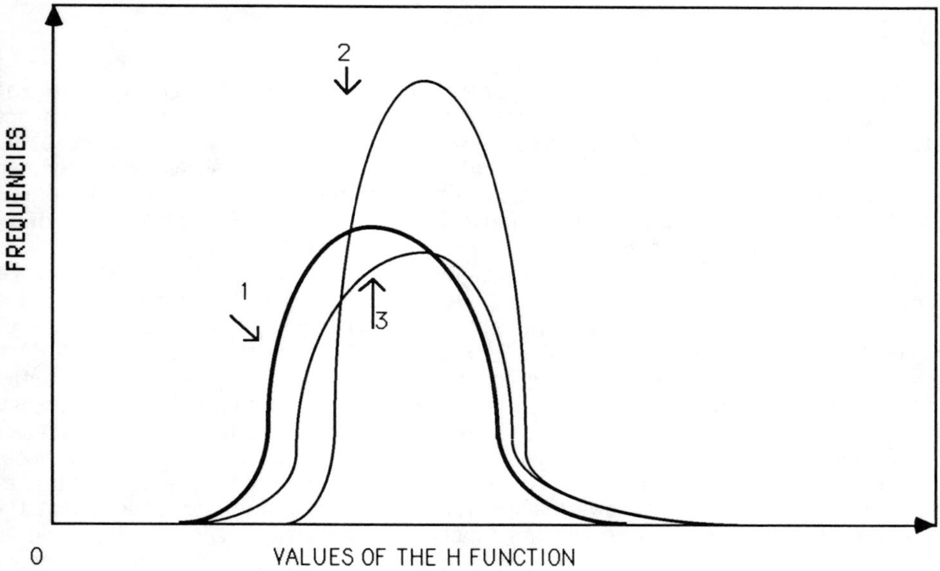

Figure 8.3.4d: Empirical distribution of the H function in various lattices with the rook's case. (1) 6-by-6 lattice, (2) 8-by-8 lattice and (3) 10-by-10 lattice. In all cases $\rho = 0.0$.

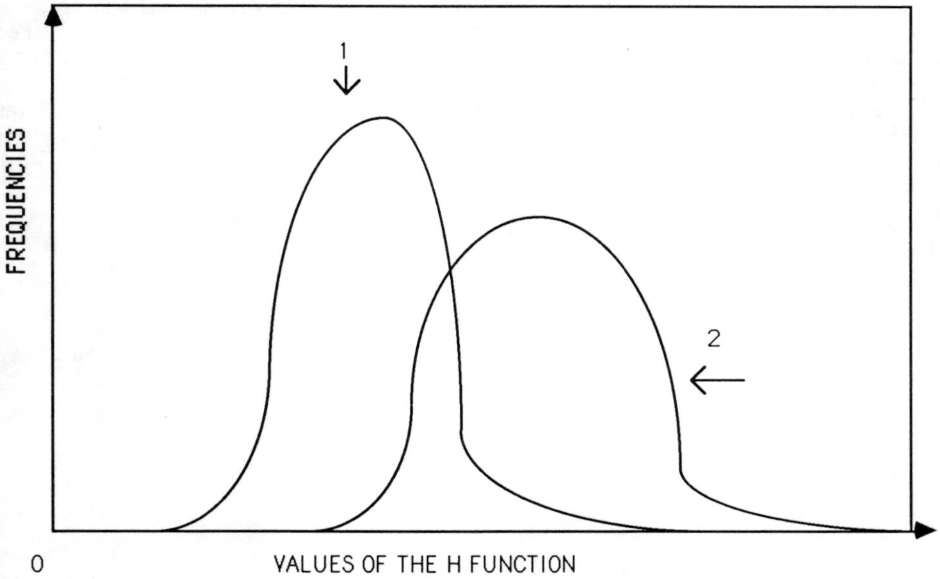

Figure 8.3.4e: Empirical distribution of the H function in a (2) 6-by-6 lattices with the rook's case, and (2) the same mapped on to a torus. In both cases $\rho = 0.0$.

8.4 SUMMARY AND CONCLUSION

In this chapter we examined how the definition of the *spatially lagged variable* can affect the estimation of the spatial correlogram. There is a substantial difference between the *lagged series* definition dealing with time series (or with Cartesian spatial systems) and dealing with spatial systems of irregular collecting areas. In the former case the lagged series is generated by a shift of the original series along the time axis (or along the two axes in a Cartesian lattice). In the latter it is instead, a moving-average of the original series. As a consequence the variance of the lagged series is reduced in comparison with the variance of the original series. This phenomenon has already been observed by Cliff and Ord (1981), Ripley (1981), Besag (1974) and Cliff et al.(1975). However it has never previously received a formal treatment.
Through analytical studies (Section 8.2.2) and Monte Carlo methods (Section 8.2.4) it was possible to state that the rate of decrease of the variance is related to the spatial configuration of the data and to the spatial autocorrelation of the underlying process. With respect to the configuration it was shown that, in general, the higher the number of neighbours for each area, the steeper is the decline of the variance. Since in most empirical cases the average number of neighbours increases with the spatial lag, as shown in Section 8.2.4, it follows that the plot of the decrease in variance against the lag order is likely to be a decreasing function converging to zero. The decline is moderated by the presence of positive spatial autocorrelation between sites which share a common neighbour. It is instead exacerbated when this correlation is negative.
Due to this effect the *I-Moran* based estimate of the spatial correlogram, which is bounded by the decrease in variance function, tends dramatically to zero in absolute value as soon as a lag is introduced. Furthermore peaks in the correlogram can be due to particular configurations of the spatial observations rather than to the presence of real spatial effects. Finally the *modified spatial correlogram* supplies erratic and hence unreliable estimates except for the first and the last lags.
The results of this chapter suggest that great caution should be used in the use of the spatial correlogram for systems of irregular collecting areas and that the substantive meaning of possible peaks should be carefully examined.

9. Conclusion

The aim of this book has been to develop a methodological framework to explain, control for and, eventually, to eliminate some of the difficulties arising from the configuration of data in statistical analysis of geographical problems. Throughout the book we have used the term *spatial data configuration* to describe the set of all the relevant information which specifies the geography of a study area such as neighbourhood links between regions from which the data derive, their size, their shape, and their relative and absolute location. In particular we have discussed four main manifestations of the effects of spatial data configuration: the scale problem, the aggregation problem, the ecological fallacy problem and the problem of estimating the spatial correlogram.
The approach followed throughout the book has been to consider a spatial series as the observed realization of a stochastic process. This approach has allowed the development of a general theoretical framework within which each problem specified above can be treated. The common feature of these theoretical problems is that in each case we operate with a statistical manipulation of the original set of data, either explicitly or implicitly (as is the case in the estimation of the spatial correlogram). The theory of stochastic process has allowed us to study the effects of these manipulations on the moments of the generating process.
The subject matter of the book has been defined in **Chapter 2**. Here we have described the modifiable areal unit problem, the ecological fallacy problem and the spatial correlogram through a review of the previous literature in the field. Some empirical examples were also reported. For the scale problem and the ecological fallacy problem, it emerges that by increasing the scale of analysis, an increase in the absolute value of the correlation coefficient is generally obtained. For the aggregation problem the previous literature seems to agree that aggregation variability is not susceptible to a systematic approach. This book has attempted to provide such an approach. We have also found in the literature that most estimates of the empirical correlogram show a tendency to a sharp decrease in absolute value soon after the first lag. We have demonstrated how spatial data configuration gives rises to this characteristic.
The book deals with each of its main problems as a manifestation of the *configuration of spatial data* . For this reason it was necessary to devote **Chapter 3** to defining and to formalizing this concept. In **Chapter 4** we have derived the formal theoretical results which constitute the backbone of the whole book. In this chapter we have given a formal description, in terms of the theory of stochastic processes, of the situation in which we have data at two different levels of aggregation. Observations at the finest level of resolution were considered as generated by what we called an *individual-process*. In contrast the observations at the coarser level of resolution were considered as drawn from a *group-process*. To simplify the discussion we uniformly assumed throughout the book that the individual-process is always stationary. The aim of this chapter was to establish a relationship leading from a given individual-process and a grouping criterion to a group-process. This aim has been achieved following three different approaches.

Firstly, we derived the probability density function of a group-process in terms of the probability density function of the individual-process that generates it.
Secondly, we have discussed the case of Gaussian processes. In this case a paramount role is played by the variance-covariance matrix of the process. Consequently we have had to introduce an hypothesis about the form of the variance-covariance matrix which embodies a plausible pattern of dependence for the cases under study. We have distinguished two different patterns of dependence. When dealing with individual-processes which refer to actual individuals interacting in the study area, we have postulated that all the random variables are equally pairwise correlated. We have referred to this hypothesis as to the *uniform covariance* assumption. In contrast, when dealing with individual-processes observed on spatial units, the most plausible hypothesis is that correlation exists only within subsets of neighbouring areas. We have referred to this second hypothesis as the *local covariance* assumption. The main results of this analysis has been to show that stationarity of the individual-process does not necessarily imply stationarity of the group-process. The conditions under which this occurs have been considered in detail. Thirdly, without specifying the distributional form of the process, we have derived the moments of the group-process in terms of the moments of the individual-process. The study have been restricted to the lower order univariate moments (mean, variance, skewness and kurtosis), and to the spatial autocorrelation, and cross-correlation between two processes. In the last section of Chapter 4 we have derived some properties of the estimates of the moments of stochastic spatial processes.
In the remainder of the chapters the formal results obtained in Chapter 4 have been employed and adapted to analysing each of the main problems of spatial data configuration confronted in this book. In **Chapter 5** we have analysed the modifiable areal unit problem in univariate statistical analysis. We have considered three relevant cases: (i) the problem of scale in regular lattices; (ii) the problem of scale in irregular collecting areas; and (iii) the aggregation problem.
For the <u>scale problem in regular lattices</u> we have proved that the moments in the group-process can be expressed as a function of the moments of the individual-process and of the spatial configuration of the spatial data. The study of this functional form has led us to provide a theoretical explanation of empirical regularities found in the literature, such as the decrease in absolute value of the spatial autocorrelation as the group size increases. Furthermore we have shown that the spatial autocorrelation at different scales can be studied by observing the plot of the variance of the process against the group size. When dealing with the <u>scale problem in irregular lattices</u> the major result is that, in most cases, the group-process is not stationary even if the individual-process is stationary. This fact suggests that the non-stationarity of spatial processes which is often observed may arise from particular configurations of the data or, in other words, from the way in which data are collected. We have suggested two ways of overcoming this problem of non-stationarity of the group-process:
(i) A revised area-weighting solution which takes into account not only the size of the areas, but also their shape and the level of dependence among them.
(ii) An iterative estimation procedure to estimate the moments of the individual-process when only the group-process is observed.
The performance of the two methods has been tested through a number of empirical examples.
Finally we have found that (in the case of both regular and the irregular lattices) there is a minimum achievable value for the negative spatial autocorrelation which is imposed by the configuration of the spatial system of data collection.

Dealing with the aggregation problem we have demonstrated that, in spite of the sceptical conclusions of the existing literature in this field, the problem is susceptible to a statistical approach. In fact we have derived the theoretical limits within which the moments of the group-process can range when we arbitrarily modify the zonal boundaries. The practical implication of this is that it is possible to estimate the maximum error one can make by using grouped, instead of ungrouped, observations. The whole zoning distribution of the variance and of the spatial autocorrelation was also studied both theoretically and in practical situations by considering regular and irregular lattices and performing a series of pseudo-random permutations of the study area.

The results on the modifiable areal unit problem have been extended in **Chapter 6** to deal with the implications on bivariate statistical analysis. We have shown that the theory developed in Chapter 4 provides an explanation for the increase in the cross-correlation between two processes when we increase the level of aggregation. This phenomenon has been previously interpreted only as an empirical *rule of thumb*. For the scale problem we have obtained a functional form which describes the change in the cross-correlation with the size of the area. Apart from the size of the area this functional form depends also on the level and form of spatial autocorrelation displayed by the two processes, by the cross-correlation at the individual level, and by the average connectedness within the groups. For the aggregation problem we have studied the aggregation variability of the cross-correlation for different levels of spatial autocorrelation at the individual-process level. In particular we have found that the range of the cross-correlation is wider if a negative spatial autocorrelation occurs in both variables. In contrast it is smaller if the two variables display a positive spatial autocorrelation. Furthermore the range of the estimates of the cross-correlation increases as the level of the average within group connectedness increases.

Having exhausted in Chapter 5 and 6 the analysis of the modifiable areal unit problem, in **Chapter 7** we then moved to the ecological fallacy problem. By describing the behaviour at the individual level in terms of stochastic process theory, we have shown formally that the ecological fallacy problem can be treated analytically in the same way as the scale problem. Two particular hypotheses have been examined into detail: when all the individuals are equally pairwise correlated in the study area; and when interaction among individuals is restricted to *Cliques*. In both cases we have demonstrated that the ecological fallacy problem arises as a consequence of the existence of a certain degree of autocorrelation between behaviour at the individual level. The significance of this problem is proved by the fact that even a very small level of autocorrelation between individuals can produce very large ecological fallacies.

The theoretical findings of this chapter have been confirmed by the results of two experiments in which we have simulated the behaviour of, respectively, 160 and 6,000 individuals in a geographical space.

Finally in **Chapter 8** we have considered the problem of the estimation of the spatial correlogram. In this chapter we have shown that the definition of a lagged spatial series differs substantially, from the definition of a lagged time series. A lagged time series is obtained by shifting the original series along the time axis. In contrast a lagged spatial series is a moving-average of the original series. This fact gives rise to a number of disturbing effects. First of all, the estimate of the spatial correlogram tends to zero soon after the first lag not only because of a genuine decay of interaction with distance, but also due to statistical reasons arising from spatial data configuration and the method of calculation. Furthermore particular configurations of the spatial data can produce spurious peaks in the correlogram. For the same reasons the modified spatial correlogram supplies unreliable estimates except in the case of the first and the last lags.

Alongside the analytical results obtained, the whole work suggests that it is possible to treat within the same methodological framework, a number of spatial topics which were previously unconnected, or only loosely connected. Furthermore the approach suggested in this book shows the way in which the physical characteristics of a geographical map can be formally taken into account in the statistical analysis of spatial series.

APPENDIX A.1: Population, employed and activity rates at various spatial scales in Italy in 1981.

Tables A.1.1 contains a spatial disaggregation of data drawn from Italian population Census of 1981. Italy is divided into 20 large administrative areas called "regioni", 95 smaller areas called "provincie" and 8,127 small areas called "comuni". The three levels form a fully nested hierarchy as shown in Figures A.1.1 to A.1.3.
The data reported here are published by ISTAT (the Italian National Statistics Bureau) at a communal level, but here are aggregated into 291 local labour markets grouping contiguous "comuni".
The first column in the tables displays for each local labour market, the name of the main "comune", the "provincia" in which the local labour market lies (into brackets) and its region (in bold at the beginning of every new region). Column two displays the total population aged 15 years or more (15 years being the minimum age to work in Italy) which lived in the area at the time of the Census survey. Column three shows the total number of individuals that at the time of the census survey were employed in a full-time or part-time, permanent or temporary job. Column four is the activity rate given by the ratio between the employed and the population over fifteen at a local labour market level. Column five and six are again the activity rate, but computed at a provincial and, respectively, regional level.

Figure A.1.1: 20 Italian *regioni*

Figure A.1.2: 95 Italian *provincie*

Figure A.1.3: 291 Italian local labour markets.

Local labour market	Population over 15 ys	Employed population	Activity rate	Provinc Act.rate	Regional Act.rate
001 TORINO(TO)**PIEMONTE**	1685587	857359	50.8	50.6	49.8
002 IVREA(TO)	106954	52608	49.2	50.6	49.8
003 PINEROLO(TO)	103842	50712	48.8	50.6	49.8
004 VERCELLI(VC)	116496	56905	48.8	51.0	49.8
005 BIELLA(VC)	164885	85840	52.1	51.0	49.8
006 BORGOSESIA(VC)	50139	26237	52.3	51.0	49.8
007 NOVARA(NO)	261181	133033	50.9	50.3	49.8
008 VERBANIA(NO)	152638	74989	49.1	50.3	49.8
009 CUNEO(CU)	121577	61269	50.4	50.2	49.8
010 SALUZZO(CU)	129115	65118	50.4	50.2	49.8
011 ALBA(CU)	123610	64661	52.3	50.2	49.8
012 MONDOVI'(CU)	76066	35222	46.3	50.2	49.8
013 ASTI(AS)	180883	86181	47.6	47.6	49.8
014 ALESSANDRIA(AL	324907	145478	44.8	45.0	49.8
015 CASALE MONFERRATO(AL)	72018	33504	46.5	45.0	49.8
016 AOSTA(AO)**VAL D'AOSTA**	54732	26681	48.7	49.3	49.3
017 SAINT VINCENT	36978	18584	50.3	49.3	49.3
018 CHIAVENNA(SO)**LOMBARDIA**	48335	23842	49.3	48.9	51.8
019 SONDRIO(SO)	87403	42553	48.6	48.9	51.8
020 ANGOLO TERME(BS)	68057	33716	49.5	51.5	51.8
021 PROVAGLIANO V SABBIA(BS)	44170	22559	51.1	51.5	51.8
022 DESENZANO DEL GARDA(BS)	81109	40084	49.4	51.5	51.8
023 POMPIANO(BS)	123712	67408	54.5	51.5	51.8
024 BRESCIA(BRESCIA)	481986	247842	51.4	53.0	51.8
025 SPINONE AL LAGO(BG)	66665	34455	51.7	53.0	51.8
026 ALBINO(BG)	94083	50656	53.8	53.0	51.8
027 PIAZZA BREMBANA(BG)	34712	17752	51.1	53.0	51.8
028 BERGAMO(BG)	341885	179907	52.6	53.0	51.8
029 TREVIGLIO(BG)	159615	87676	54.9	53.0	51.8
030 LECCO(CO)	209521	107266	51.2	51.8	51.8
031 DONGO(CO)	43480	20945	48.2	51.8	51.8
032 COMO(CO)	245755	127479	51.9	51.8	51.8
033 CANTU'(CO)	116139	62664	53.9	51.8	51.8
034 VARESE(VA)	322879	167959	52.0	53.3	51.8
035 BUSTO ARSIZIO(VA)	302764	165385	54.6	53.3	51.8
036 MILANO(MI)	3017376	1583015	52.5	52.3	51.8
037 CASSANO D'ADDA(MI)	57552	30817	53.5	52.3	51.8
038 LODI(MI)	153131	75234	49.1	52.3	51.8
039 PAVIA(PV)	154248	73939	47.9	47.7	51.8
040 VIGEVANO(PV)	147731	74139	50.2	47.7	51.8
041 VOGHERA(PV)	128989	57750	44.8	47.7	51.8
042 CREMA(CR)	87465	45876	52.4	49.8	51.8
043 SORESINA(CR)	46280	22952	49.6	49.8	51.8
044 CREMONA(CR)	139354	67160	48.2	49.8	51.8
045 CASTIGLIONE DI STIVERE(MA)	69356	36636	52.8	50.0	51.8
046 MANTOVA(MA)	156734	77595	49.5	50.0	51.8

047 SUZZARA(MA)	82553	40144	48.6	50.0	51.8
048 SPILIMBERGO(PD)**FRIULI**	43788	20218	46.2	49.2	46.7
049 PORDENONE(PD)	177066	88365	49.9	49.2	46.7
050 TOLMEZZO(UD)	69124	31579	45.7	47.6	46.7
051 CIVIDALE DEL FRIULI(UD)	75962	36676	48.3	47.6	46.7
052 LATISANA(UD)	80961	38617	47.7	47.6	46.7
053 UDINE(UD)	207565	99398	47.9	47.6	46.7
054 GORIZIA(GO)	120020	55244	46.0	46.0	46.7
055 TRIESTE(TS)	244323	105433	43.1	43.1	46.7
056 ROVERETO(TN)**TRENT.-A.A**	90459	43263	47.8	47.2	50.6
057 BERSONE(TN)	26737	12218	45.7	47.2	50.6
058 CLES(TN)	40405	18806	46.5	47.2	50.6
059 TRENTO(TN)	168898	79341	46.9	47.2	50.6
060 CAPRIANA(TN)	28035	13831	49.3	47.2	50.6
061 BOLZANO(BZ)	155690	82052	52.7	54.0	50.6
062 BRENNERO(BZ)	41220	23124	56.1	54.0	50.6
063 BADIA(BZ)	46591	26214	56.3	47.2	50.6
064 MERANO(BZ)	86024	46731	54.3	54.0	50.6
065 VENEZIA(VE)**VENETO**	519100	236530	45.6	46.2	49.3
066 SAN DONA' DI PIAVE(VE)	76684	37231	48.5	46.2	49.3
067 PORTOGRUARO(VE)	69732	33588	48.2	46.2	49.3
068 MONTEBELLUNA(TV)	144477	76816	53.2	50.6	49.3
069 TREVISO(TV)	256224	126626	49.4	50.6	49.3
070 CONEGLIANO(TV)	167160	83781	50.1	50.6	49.3
071 FELTRE(BL)	47444	21204	44.7	46.7	49.3
072 BELLUNO(BL)	97848	46208	47.2	46.7	49.3
073 S. STEFANO DI CADORE(BL)	34354	16536	48.1	46.7	49.3
074 VICENZA(VI)	213126	109123	51.2	52.4	49.3
075 VALDAGNO(VI)	102629	56294	54.8	52.4	49.3
076 BASSANO DEL GRAPPA(VI)	120296	64160	53.3	52.4	49.3
077 ROTZO(VI)	132121	68388	51.7	52.4	49.3
078 BADIA POLESINE(RO)	69926	34854	49.8	48.8	49.3
079 ROVIGO(RO)	135072	65250	48.3	48.8	49.3
080 CAMPOSANPIETRO(PD)	127685	66474	52.0	49.6	49.3
081 PADOVA(PD)	444687	217982	49.0	49.6	49.3
082 ESTE(PD)	64282	31489	49.0	49.6	49.3
083 GARDA(VR)	117154	59561	50.8	49.2	49.3
084 VERONA(VR)	347188	166004	47.8	49.2	49.3
085 PALU'(VR)	151942	78061	51.4	49.2	49.3
086 SAN REMO(IM)**LIGURIA**	106229	48765	45.9	44.9	41.8
087 IMPERIA(IM)	82244	35918	43.7	44.9	41.8
088 ALBENGA(SV)	93795	42802	45.6	43.6	41.8
089 SAVONA(SV)	120646	51213	42.4	43.6	41.8
090 CAIRO MONTENOTTE(SV)	36597	15551	42.5	43.6	41.8
091 GENOVA(GE)	795845	326470	41.0	41.2	41.8
092 CHIAVARI(GE)	89015	36962	41.5	41.2	41.8
093 LA SPEZIA(SP)	202792	80108	39.5	39.5	41.8
094 RIMINI(FO)**EM-ROMAGNA**	199577	96959	48.6	50.8	54.2
095 CESENA(FO)	140177	74916	53.4	50.8	54.2
096 FORLI'(FO)	143016	73169	51.2	50.8	54.2
097 RAVENNA(RA)	143051	75060	52.5	53.1	54.2

098 LUGO(RA)	89272	48384	54.2	53.1	54.2
099 FAENZA(RA)	65762	34751	52.8	53.1	54.2
100 CASTEL D'AIANO(BO)	45552	21649	47.5	53.1	54.2
101 IMOLA(BO)	65572	34683	52.9	53.1	54.2
102 CREVALCORE(BO)	142745	84319	59.1	53.1	54.2
103 BOLOGNA(BO)	533476	277572	52.0	53.1	54.2
104 PARMA(PR)	233598	117707	50.4	48.8	54.2
105 ALBARETO(PR)	45017	16983	37.7	48.8	54.2
106 FIDENZA(PR)	59044	28999	49.1	48.8	54.2
107 LUGAGNAGO VAL D'ARDA(PC)	59901	28638	47.8	47.0	54.2
108 PIACENZA(PC)	117316	56328	48.0	47.0	54.2
109 BOBBIO(PC)	57533	25464	44.2	47.0	54.2
110 FERRARA(FE)	185612	92088	49.6	50.2	54.2
111 ARGENTA(FE)	131883	67225	50.9	50.2	54.2
112 GUASTALLA(RE)	85939	46438	54.0	53.0	54.2
113 REGGIO NELL'EMILIA(RE)	184947	97223	52.6	53.0	54.2
114 CASTELNOVO NE' MONTI(RE)	69656	36948	53.0	53.0	54.2
115 MIRANDOLA(MO)	121759	71183	58.4	56.6	54.2
116 PAVULLO NEL FRIGNANO(MO)	70142	36909	52.6	56.6	54.2
117 SASSUOLO(MO)	79319	47025	59.3	56.6	54.2
118 MODENA(MO)	218459	122650	56.1	56.6	54.2
119 MASSA(MS)**TOSCANA**	166898	67426	40.4	40.3	45.3
120 BARGA(LU)	55674	23227	41.7	45.2	45.3
121 VIAREGGIO(LU)	130697	57033	43.6	45.2	45.3
122 LUCCA(LU)	130297	62961	48.3	45.2	45.3
123 PISTOIA(PT)	131866	64881	49.2	50.6	45.3
124 PESCIA(PT)	85647	45124	52.7	50.6	45.3
125 PRATO(FI)	239821	132644	55.3	50.8	45.3
126 BORGO SAN LORENZO(FI)	48061	23663	49.2	50.8	45.3
127 FIRENZA (FI)	581179	281288	48.4	50.8	45.3
128 EMPOLI(FI)	125047	67105	53.6	50.8	45.3
129 PISA(PI)	172871	79717	46.1	48.1	45.3
130 PONTEDERA(FI)	117688	61695	52.4	48.1	45.3
131 VOLTERRA(PI)	28841	12162	42.2	48.1	45.3
132 LIVORNO(LI)	199245	85246	42.8	42.9	45.3
133 PIOMBINO(LI)	61407	27008	43.9	42.9	45.3
134 PORTOFERRAIO(LI)	23204	9581	41.3	42.9	45.3
135 GROSSETO(GR)	126790	55147	43.5	42.5	45.3
136 ORBETELLO(GR)	56484	22799	40.3	42.5	45.3
137 SIENA(SI)	148992	70501	47.3	46.9	45.3
138 MONTEPULCIANO(SI)	67223	30824	45.8	46.9	45.3
139 AREZZO(AR)	202441	101398	50.0	49.6	45.3
140 BIBBIENA(AR)	55918	26801	47.9	49.6	45.3
141 CITTA' DI CAST.(PG)**UMBRIA**	89446	43264	48.4	47.1	49.8
142 PERUGIA(PG)	262319	127487	48.6	47.1	49.8
143 FOLIGNO(PG)	123709	53051	42.9	47.1	49.8
144 ORVIETO(TR)	38282	15952	41.7	41.0	49.8
145 TERNI(TR)	146603	59960	40.9	41.0	49.8
146 URBINO(PS)**MARCHE**	61456	28852	46.9	47.6	49.2
147 PESARO(PS)	207047	99055	47.8	47.6	49.2
148 ANCONA(AN)	289164	143194	49.5	49.0	49.2

149 FABRIANO(AN)	63240	29521	46.6	49.0	49.2
150 MACERATA(MC)	198156	102695	51.8	50.5	49.2
151 CAMERINO(MC)	42373	18823	44.4	50.5	49.2
152 FERMO(AS)	189688	99223	52.3	50.0	49.2
153 ASCOLI PICENO(AS)	94875	43120	45.4	50.0	49.2
154 BOLSENA(VT)**LAZIO**	69480	26625	38.3	39.7	42.9
155 VITERBO(VT)	146482	59248	40.4	39.7	42.9
156 MAGLIANO SABINO(RI)	38055	14396	37.8	39.1	42.9
157 RIETI(RI)	61283	25930	42.3	39.1	42.9
158 PESCOROCCHIANO(RI)	16289	4933	30.2	39.1	42.9
159 ROMA(ROMA)	2895681	1264402	43.6	40.3	42.9
160 LATINA(LT)	223438	103326	46.2	44.3	42.9
161 GAETA(LT)	98423	39441	40.1	44.3	42.9
162 ANAGNI(FR)	64388	26243	40.7	40.8	42.9
163 FORSINONE(FR)	133213	55460	41.6	40.8	42.9
164 SORA(FR)	70374	28934	41.1	40.8	42.9
165 CASSINO(FR)	88206	34982	39.6	40.8	42.9
166 PONZA(FR)	3002	1003	33.4	40.8	42.9
167 L'AQUILA(AQ)**ABRUZZO**	79788	32846	41.1	38.8	42.2
168 SULMONE(AQ)	55943	20153	36.0	38.8	42.2
169 AVEZZANO(AQ)	98347	37892	38.5	38.8	42.2
170 CHIETI(CH)	126659	54895	43.3	42.7	42.2
171 VASTO(CH)	72816	30419	41.8	42.7	42.2
172 LANCIANO(CH)	92947	38566	41.5	42.7	42.2
173 PESCARA(PE)	146927	63772	43.4	41.7	42.2
174 PENNE(PE)	35805	14622	40.8	41.7	42.2
175 BUSSI SUL TIRINO(PE)	41894	15347	36.6	41.7	42.2
176 TERAMO(TE)	80374	35111	43.7	46.3	42.2
177 GIULIANOVA(TE)	72077	35397	49.1	46.3	42.2
178 ROSETO DEGLI ABRUZZI(TE)	58395	27074	46.4	46.3	42.2
179 VENAFRO(IS)**MOLISE**	22287	8645	38.7	41.6	42.0
180 ISERNIA(IS)	51194	21948	42.9	41.6	42.0
181 BOJANO(CB)	23461	10180	43.4	42.2	42.0
182 CAMPOBASSO(CB)	88353	37062	41.9	42.2	42.0
183 TERMOLI(CB)	73675	31017	42.1	42.2	42.0
184 VAIRANO PAT.(CE)**CAMPANIA**	57509	24169	42.0	49.5	40.3
185 PIEDIMONTE MATESE(CE)	38984	16746	42.9	49.5	40.3
186 SESSA AURUNCA(CE)	41939	17708	42.2	49.5	40.3
187 CAPUA(CE)	42975	17094	39.7	49.5	40.3
188 CASERTA(CE)	211987	83619	39.4	49.5	40.3
189 AVERSA(CE)	139673	51205	36.7	49.5	40.3
190 TELESE(BE)	68096	27786	40.8	41.1	40.3
191 BENEVENTO(BE)	155001	63952	41.2	41.1	40.3
192 POZZUOLI(NA)	126876	48250	38.0	35.8	40.3
193 NAPLOI(NA)	1472049	505309	34.3	35.8	40.3
194 POMIGLIANO D'ARCO(NA)	265356	107272	40.4	35.8	40.3
195 CASTELLAM. DI STABIA(NA)	241457	92678	38.3	35.8	40.3
196 AVELLINO(AV)	185430	71120	38.3	39.3	40.3
197 ARIANO IRPINO(AV)	73629	29121	39.5	39.3	40.3
198 S.ANGELO DEI LOMBARDI(AV)	74346	30685	41.3	39.3	40.3
199 NOCERA INFERIORE(SA)	163435	68068	41.6	41.1	40.3

200 SALERNO(SA)	240764	93610	38.8	41.1	40.3
201 BATTIPAGLIA(SA)	80254	37030	46.1	41.1	40.3
202 EBOLI(SA)	69892	29758	42.5	41.1	40.3
203 AGROPOLI(SA)	44330	17017	38.3	41.1	40.3
204 ROCCADASPIDE(SA)	30036	12126	40.4	41.1	40.3
205 VALLO DELLA LUCANIA(SA)	39474	15409	39.0	41.1	40.3
206 SALA CONSILINA(SA)	54967	24173	43.9	41.1	40.3
207 SAPRI(SA)	36645	15148	41.3	41.1	40.3
208 APRICENA(FG)**PUGLIA**	40381	14518	35.9	39.2	42.5
209 VIESTE(FG)	35798	14172	39.5	39.2	42.5
210 FOGGIA(FG)	226360	90839	40.1	39.2	42.5
211 MANFREDONIA(FG)	81742	31277	38.2	39.2	42.5
212 CERIGNOLA(FG)	108137	43862	40.6	39.2	42.5
213 TRANI(BA)	223160	90669	40.6	41.7	42.5
214 MODUGNO(BA)	227453	94766	41.7	41.7	42.5
215 BARI(BA)	516694	211509	40.9	41.7	42.5
216 PUTIGNANO(BA)	105683	50981	48.2	41.7	42.5
217 TARANTO(TA)	415787	178577	42.9	42.9	42.5
218 BRINDISI(BR)	287417	135372	47.1	47.1	42.5
219 LECCE(LE)	241676	105116	43.5	44.3	42.5
220 NARDO'(LE)	180295	81920	45.4	44.3	42.5
221 OTRANTO(LE)	137987	61347	44.4	44.3	42.5
222 ISOLE TREMITI(LE)	282	110	39.0	44.3	42.5
223 POTENZA(PZ)**BASILICATA**	125475	55540	44.2	42.9	43.1
224 MELFI(PZ)	77443	32012	41.3	42.9	43.1
225 MOLITERNO(PZ)	32646	13689	41.9	42.9	43.1
226 SENISE(PZ)	30284	13138	43.4	42.9	43.1
227 LAGONEGRO(PZ)	41481	17638	42.5	42.9	43.1
228 MATERA(MT)	57836	25357	43.8	43.7	43.1
229 STIGLIANO(MT)	36357	15478	42.6	43.7	43.1
230 POLICORO(MT)	52966	23441	44.2	43.7	43.1
231 R. CALABRIA(RC)**CALABRIA**	170743	61018	35.7	38.1	38.9
232 BOVA(RC)	36033	11673	32.4	38.1	38.9
233 LOCRI(RC)	56505	20413	36.1	38.1	38.9
234 ROCCELLA IONICA(RC)	41659	13885	33.3	38.1	38.9
235 ROSARNO(RC)	122451	56079	45.7	38.1	38.9
236 CATANZARO(CZ)	132148	49879	37.7	37.7	38.9
237 CIRO'(CZ)	37905	13923	36.7	37.7	38.9
238 CROTONE(CZ)	66392	24995	37.6	37.7	38.9
239 LAMEZIA TERME(CZ)	90108	35301	39.1	37.7	38.9
240 PETILIA POLICASTRO(CZ)	56907	20062	35.2	37.7	38.9
241 SOVERATO(CZ)	51996	18809	36.1	37.7	38.9
242 VIBO VALENTIA(CS)	108632	42743	39.3	40.8	38.9
243 COSENZA(CS)	179188	68462	38.2	40.8	38.9
244 ACRI(CS)	101109	42886	42.4	40.8	38.9
245 CASTROVILLARI(CS)	61163	27369	44.7	40.8	38.9
246 PAOLA(CS)	57787	22621	39.1	40.8	38.9
247 ROSSANO(CS)	78448	32122	40.9	40.8	38.9
248 SCALEA(CS)	50947	21675	42.5	40.8	38.9
249 TREBISACCE)CS)	26047	10953	42.0	40.8	38.9
250 TRAPANI(TP)**SICILIA**	157958	56541	35.8	35.7	36.3

251	MARSALA(TP)	156282	55737	35.7	35.7	36.3
252	PALERMO(PA)	716009	256703	35.8	35.7	36.3
253	CORLEONE(PA)	32654	10985	33.6	35.7	36.3
254	TERMINI IMERESE(PA)	75778	25478	33.6	35.7	36.3
255	CEFALU'(PA)	38628	14232	36.8	35.7	36.3
256	PETRALIA SOPRANA(PA)	30478	11093	36.4	35.7	36.3
257	SCIACCA(AG)	85347	30772	36.0	34.0	36.3
258	AGRIGENTO(AG)	159013	52662	33.1	34.0	36.3
259	LICATA(AG)	103800	35080	33.8	34.0	36.3
260	AGIRA(EN)	66131	22639	34.2	33.4	36.3
261	ENNA(EN)	78590	25720	32.7	33.4	36.3
262	CALTANISSETTA(CL)	108269	36274	33.5	33.2	36.3
263	GELA(CL)	102786	33779	32.8	33.2	36.3
264	RAGUSA(RA)	208818	79339	37.9	37.9	36.3
265	SIRACUSA(SI)	223501	84294	37.7	37.1	36.3
266	LENTINI(SI)	59883	20934	34.9	37.1	36.3
267	CALTAGIRONE(CT)	109530	36961	33.7	37.6	36.3
268	CATANIA(CT)	435339	165119	37.9	37.6	36.3
269	ADRANO(CT)	73573	27077	36.8	37.6	36.3
270	GIARRE(CT)	131105	52980	40.4	37.6	36.3
271	TAORMINA(ME)	33043	13989	42.3	38.5	36.3
272	MESSINA(ME)	228030	80927	35.4	38.5	36.3
273	MILAZZO(ME)	121839	49562	40.6	38.5	36.3
274	PATTI(ME)	75634	31611	41.8	38.5	36.3
275	CARONIA(ME)	59793	22137	37.0	38.5	36.3
276	OLBIA(SS)**SARDEGNA**	42722	19544	45.7	41.6	40.4
277	CASTELSARDO(SS)	40384	16181	40.1	41.6	40.4
278	SASSARI(SS)	134414	57414	42.7	41.6	40.4
279	OZIERI(SS)	42116	16815	39.9	41.6	40.4
280	ALGHERO(SS)	59915	23214	38.7	41.6	40.4
281	BITTI(NU)	37899	15671	41.3	39.9	40.4
282	MACOMER(NU)	34613	13294	38.4	39.9	40.4
283	NUORO(NU)	50200	21930	43.7	39.9	40.4
284	SORGONO(NU)	37930	13969	36.8	39.9	40.4
285	LANUSEI(NU)	44708	17272	38.6	39.9	40.4
286	ORISTANO(OR)	117648	44951	38.2	38.2	40.4
287	VILLAMAR(CA)	30969	11786	38.0	40.2	40.4
288	VILLACIDRO(CA)	81153	31911	39.3	40.2	40.4
289	IGLESIAS(CA)	41293	15325	37.1	40.2	40.4
290	CARBONIA(CA)	69957	25404	36.3	40.2	40.4
291	CAGLIARI(CA)	310764	130615	42.0	40.2	40.4
	ITALY	44337100	20203600	45.6		

Table A.1.1: Population over 15 years, number of employed and activity rates in 291 Italian local labour markets. Source: ISTAT (1982).

APPENDIX A.2: Electricity consumption of medium sized manufacturing industries in the provincia of Arezzo, Italy in 1985

The following Table A.2.1 displays some variables connected with the consumption of electrical power by medium sized (that is with a power between 30 and 500 kw/h) manufacturing firms in the Italian provincia of Arezzo (Tuscany) in the first semester of 1985. These data have been kindly offered for our research purposes by the Italian Electric Energy National Company ENEL. The data are recorded at a communal level. There are 39 comuni in the provincia of Arezzo whose boundaries are displayed in Figure A.2.1.

The first column of Table A.2.1 contains the area code number. Column two contains the total number of users, i.e. the number of customers that receive electric energy through the network and that hold a contract for supplying. The contractual employed power (shortly power) measured in kilowatts per hour (kw/h) is the power, established in the contract at the beginning of each period that the user can exceed only under some restrictive conditions and paying different rates established in the contract. It is an indicator of the "electric dimension " of the firm and it can be used, under some conditions as a proxy of the capital stock of the firm. The consumption of electric energy is the quantity of electric energy, measured in kilowatts, consumed by the users, recorded at the power-meter by the suppliers.

The unitary consumption (column three in the table) is the ratio between the total consumption in the area and the number of users. Similarly the unitary power is the ratio between the total power in the area and the number of users, and it is displayed in column four. Finally column five of the table contains the number of worked hours given by the ratio between the consumption (kw) and the power (kw/h) and under some conditions can be viewed as a proxy of the plant utilization degree.

Comune	Code number	Users	Unitary consumption	Unitary power	Worked hours
Anghiari	01	134	2360	40.42	58.37
Arezzo	02	1667	3540	49.58	71.04
Badia Tebalda	03	25	1634	50.72	32.21
Bibbiena	04	435	5411	52.54	102.97
Bucine	05	171	2801	49.90	56.12
Capolona	06	118	3628	48.52	74.77
Caprese Michelangelo	07	25	4576	44.40	103.07
Castel Focognano	08	77	2017	44.87	44.97
Castelfranco di sopra	09	50	5125	50.80	100.88
Castel San Nicolo'	10	62	5625	48.59	115.75
Castiglion Fibocchi	11	24	5836	56.29	103.67
Castiglion Fiorentino	12	189	2339	45.80	51.07
Cavriglia	13	91	3585	48.03	74.64
Chitignano	14	10	4780	53.70	89.02
Chiusi della Verna	15	56	5024	76.96	65.27
Civitella Val Chiana	16	202	6126	68.80	89.04
Cortona	17	383	1867	40.59	46.01
Foiano della Chiana	18	187	3621	57.28	63.20
Laterina	19	55	7508	64.45	116.49
Loro Ciuffena	20	59	1824	41.22	44.25
Lucignano	21	63	2345	46.87	50.03
Marciano della Chiana	22	48	3057	63.41	48.21
Montemignaio	23	5	2310	30.60	75.49
Monterchi	24	43	2515	45.76	54.95
Monte San Savino	25	231	2661	42.91	62.01
Montevarchi	26	434	3364	50.74	66.28
Ortignano Raggiolo	27	11	715	48.72	14.68
Pergine Valdarno	28	85	3891	55.53	70.07
Pian di Sco	29	128	3285	51.37	63.95
Pieve Santo Stefano	30	69	2173	39.98	54.35
Poppi	31	182	2800	49.30	56.79
Pratovecchio	32	100	3239	54.64	59.29
San Giovanni Valdarno	33	278	2597	40.17	64.67
Sansepolcro	34	306	2789	45.19	61.71
Sestino	35	28	1769	53.28	33.21
Stia	36	79	2874	44.22	65.00
Subbiano	37	131	4818	59.56	80.89
Talla	38	25	1325	43.88	30.19
Terranova Bracciolini	39	195	3986	52.00	76.66

Table A.2.1: Nuber of users, unitary consumption, unitary power and worked hours for the medium sized manufacturing industries in the provincia of Arezzo (Italy) in the first semester of 1985.

Figure A.2.1: Map of the 39 comuni of the provincia of Arezzo (Italy).

APPENDIX A.3: Quadrat counts of houses in Hukuno Town, Tonami plain, Japan. (Matui, 1932)

2221010012000012010122011201111211201202
0201201112201100010102201221210010102012
1011001011101011012020013012102112001022
0111020120002200010012000100010900011111
1200000000102022012101110301201111001031
1310101000002202001001000012111210213111
0100010101201311413101100000002220120301
0010100100130010010010220200121220011001
0110110113113010201000133200001010100010
0000011200152000020021010020001001000120
0200111011102142101220112100001220000000
0001101000012220001013120000021200020111
0100120000000110111121113010110141120102
0001111011000012011113021000020003020112
0110001120010010020001100011100002002100
3411031000200010121001410022000101110440
0010011111100102032022310011013001101110
1101010021002200215200000000100122002101
0301000200020000010200001100200000013001
0110201000001100101000112110000110100212
1000110011100210000130221401001030011010
0211011000110031100101025211012001101200
0000020111200112101003214502111120200101
0011200010011000002001221003311010000010
1011001122110000010021100000110011002002
0011111000221200021000001103001207102002
0111122200203101010010001113101021210001
0210002120000010301100010010002211010110
0000100200000001100110100110111201021011
2001200000100112132000000000100011110210

APPENDIX A.4: Weights of wheat plots of grain. (Mercer and Hall, 1911).

W

	3.61	3.85	4.38	4.23	5.18	3.46	4.46	4.52	4.43	3.39	3.40	3.97	3.42	3.18	3.16	3.63	3.90	4.51	4.07	3.63	
	4.22	4.28	4.12	3.87	3.89	4.42	4.09	3.79	3.70	3.64	3.71	3.61	3.35	3.50	3.55	4.27	4.64	4.29	4.21	4.15	
	4.42	4.69	4.39	4.23	4.26	4.29	4.39	4.41	3.82	3.84	4.27	4.67	4.07	4.28	4.08	4.92	4.05	4.40	4.15	4.06	
	5.09	5.16	3.92	4.58	4.32	4.08	4.31	4.57	4.45	4.51	4.42	4.49	4.66	4.89	4.78	4.64	4.04	4.69	4.64	5.13	
	3.66	4.46	4.84	3.19	3.78	3.96	4.26	3.94	3.59	4.01	4.13	3.75	3.72	3.28	3.61	3.76	3.49	3.77	4.08	3.04	
	4.22	4.41	3.94	3.49	3.54	3.96	4.47	4.47	4.37	4.21	4.20	4.11	3.84	3.56	3.66	4.10	3.91	4.46	3.74	4.48	
	4.06	4.68	4.88	3.91	4.27	3.89	4.37	4.42	4.45	4.77	4.66	4.64	4.44	4.94	4.39	4.40	4.52	4.76	4.56	4.75	
	3.97	4.37	4.24	4.41	4.12	4.11	3.44	3.92	4.06	3.95	3.61	2.99	3.40	4.06	3.84	4.17	4.52	3.76	4.27	4.04	
	3.89	4.15	3.96	4.21	4.13	3.73	3.82	3.86	3.72	4.17	3.90	4.37	4.07	4.32	4.26	3.67	3.05	3.30	4.03	4.14	
	4.46	4.91	4.29	4.61	4.47	4.08	4.63	4.77	4.56	4.39	4.44	5.02	4.93	4.86	4.86	5.07	4.59	3.67	4.50	4.00	
	4.44	4.68	4.52	4.27	3.41	4.09	4.36	4.99	4.10	4.17	3.86	3.56	3.93	3.96	3.76	3.83	4.01	3.94	3.97	4.37	
	4.52	4.18	4.19	4.06	3.55	3.82	3.79	3.91	3.07	4.17	3.99	3.59	3.04	3.74	4.09	3.63	3.34	4.07	4.19	4.02	
S	3.70	4.19	4.49	3.75	3.16	3.57	3.56	4.09	3.99	4.09	3.37	4.05	3.72	4.88	3.72	3.74	4.06	3.78	4.05	4.58	**N**
	4.28	4.41	3.82	3.91	3.47	3.48	3.29	3.05	3.14	3.29	3.47	3.96	3.93	3.77	3.76	4.14	3.19	4.58	3.97	3.92	
	3.24	3.54	3.60	3.51	3.30	3.73	3.64	3.39	4.86	3.37	3.09	3.75	3.71	3.71	3.37	3.70	3.75	3.64	3.61	3.61	
	3.29	3.01	3.14	3.45	3.30	3.89	3.60	3.60	4.36	3.74	4.20	4.73	4.76	4.59	4.01	3.92	4.54	4.07	3.82	3.06	
	3.48	2.85	2.73	3.05	2.92	3.03	3.19	4.18	3.51	3.41	4.09	4.24	3.83	3.97	3.87	3.79	3.97	3.44	3.44	3.57	
	3.49	3.36	3.09	3.68	3.23	3.48	3.80	3.89	3.47	3.86	4.07	4.21	3.71	4.88	4.35	4.29	3.77	3.58	3.92	3.31	
	3.68	3.85	3.66	3.52	3.25	3.05	3.72	3.67	3.94	4.36	4.09	3.85	3.54	3.81	4.24	4.22	4.30	4.20	4.26	4.27	
	3.36	4.15	3.77	3.91	3.86	3.65	3.91	4.54	4.47	4.54	3.95	4.41	3.66	4.06	3.58	3.74	4.10	4.31	4.36	3.72	
	3.71	3.93	3.48	3.87	3.22	3.71	3.35	4.11	4.11	4.24	4.08	4.21	3.95	3.42	4.20	3.55	3.81	4.33	3.69	3.36	
	3.54	3.91	3.76	3.87	3.69	3.25	4.11	4.58	3.97	4.08	4.03	3.63	3.84	3.05	3.94	3.67	3.89	3.66	3.53	3.17	
	3.59	4.33	3.69	4.21	3.80	3.69	4.39	4.02	4.07	3.89	3.97	4.17	3.76	3.44	4.24	3.57	3.32	3.59	3.14	2.97	
	3.76	4.21	3.84	3.68	3.76	3.43	3.47	3.98	3.56	3.47	2.84	3.44	3.47	2.78	3.75	3.96	3.46	3.97	4.09	4.23	
	3.36	4.19	3.67	4.06	3.65	3.38	3.95	4.33	2.83	3.29	3.91	4.55	4.24	3.44	4.29	4.31	3.64	4.38	3.94	4.53	

E

APPENDIX A.5: Simulation methods in two dimensions

In this appendix we wish to review briefly some of the methods available in the literature to simulate series of data drawn from two-dimensional stochastic processes. A larger review can be found in Chambers (1977); Haining, Griffith and Bennett (1983), Johnson (1987) and Kleijnen (1987). A comparison between different procedures can be found in Arbia (1986b). Following Haining, Griffith and Bennett (1983) we will distinguish between a set of *distribution-based* methods and a set of *model-based* approaches.

DISTRIBUTION-BASED APPROACHES

A first set of methods is available when we can specify exactly the distribution of the process under study. As we are usually interested in Gaussian processes, all we need is to be able to specify the variance-covariance matrix of the process.
Let $\mathbf{V}$ be a symmetric positive definite matrix. A first method of obtaining random observations from a process having $\mathbf{V}$ as a variance-covariance matrix is to consider the matrix of the eigenvalues $\mathbf{\Delta}$ and the corresponding eigenvectors $\mathbf{H}$. We have that

$$\mathbf{V}\,\mathbf{H} = \mathbf{H}\,\mathbf{\Delta} \qquad \text{(A.5.1)}$$

Let us now set (see Cliff and Ord, 1981; p.152)

$$\mathbf{T} = \mathbf{H}\,\mathbf{\Delta}^{1/2}\,\mathbf{H}^{T} \qquad \text{(A.5.2)}$$

The random vector sample can be simulated by evaluating

$$\mathbf{X} = \mathbf{T}\,\mathbf{e} \qquad \text{(A.5.3)}$$

where $\mathbf{e}$ is a vector of independent identically distributed normal variates.
An alternative way of obtaining the same result is the following.
Let us assume that $\mathbf{e}$ is a vector of i.i.d. N(0,1) random variables. The variance-covariance matrix of the transform $\mathbf{Le}$ is $\mathbf{LL}^{T}$. As a consequence if we wish to generate random observations from a Gaussian process with a variance-covariance matrix $\mathbf{V}$ we take a matrix $\mathbf{L}$ such that

$$\mathbf{LL}^{T} = \mathbf{V} \qquad \text{(A.5.4)}$$

A way of doing this, is to exploit the Cholesky decomposition of **V**. In this case we have that the matrix **L** assumes the particular form of a lower triangular matrix (Chambers, 1977). This approach is the one we follow in Chapter 7.
Another way of decomposing the **V** matrix is suggested by Streitberg (1978). The author makes use of the spectral decomposition theorem (Bartlett, 1966) to give

$$\mathbf{V} = a_1 \mathbf{K}_1 + a_2 \mathbf{K}_2 + \dots\dots + a_m \mathbf{K}_m \tag{A.5.5}$$

where the a_i's represent the non-zero eigenvalues of **V**, and the sequence of matrices **K** are the associated products of row and column eigenvectors. Some problems with this approaches are discussed in Haining, Griffith and Bennett (1983).

MODEL-BASED APPROACHES

If it is not possible to specify exactly the variance-covariance matrix of the process we can base our simulation on a model of it. Let us assume that the autocorrelation structure of the process can be captured by a <u>simultaneous</u> autoregressive model (SAR) (Whittle 1954). For a first-order scheme we have

$$\mathbf{X} = \rho\, \mathbf{WX} + \mathbf{e} \tag{A.5.6}$$

with again i.i.d. $e_i \sim N(0,\sigma^2_e)$, ρ an autoregressive parameter, **W** the connectivity matrix of the spatial system, and **X** a vector sample drawn from the autocorrelated process. It follows that

$$\mathbf{X} = (\mathbf{I} - \rho \mathbf{W})^{-1} \mathbf{e} \tag{A.5.7}$$

Provided $(\mathbf{I}-\rho\mathbf{W})$ is not singular and, given a normal random number generator, Formula (A.5.7) simulates a process $\{X_i\}$ with (See Cliff & Ord 1981)

$$E(X_i)=0 \;;\; E(X_i^2)=\sigma^2_e;\; E(X_i X_j) = \sigma^2_e(\mathbf{I}-\rho\mathbf{W})^{-1}(\mathbf{I}-\rho\mathbf{W}^T)^{-1} \tag{A.5.8}$$

The problem with this approach is in the inversion of the matrix $(\mathbf{I}-\rho\,\mathbf{W})$. In most empirical situations this is large and sparse, with the determinant very close to zero. It therefore requires a high level of precision to be evaluated.
A possible alternative is to force the $(\mathbf{I}-\rho\,\mathbf{W})$ matrix into a block-diagonal structure and to perform the inversion separately in each block. A further solution is to consider the asymptotic duality between an autoregressive and a moving-average process (Haining, 1977) and re-express (A.5.7) as

$$\mathbf{X}=(\mathbf{I}+\rho\mathbf{W}+\rho^2\mathbf{W}^2+\rho^3\mathbf{W}^3 \dots\dots\dots)\mathbf{e} \tag{A.5.9}$$

where a good approximation can be reached often considering a finite number of terms (Arbia, 1986b).
Finally another possible solution is to use the fast Fourier transform as described by Larimore (1977).

References

Alker H.R. Jr. (1974) A typology of ecological fallacies, Social ecology, Dogan M. and Rokkan S. Editors. MIT Press. Reprint of the previous 1969 edition under the title: Qualitative ecological analysis in the social sciences.

Amemiya T. and Wu R.Y. (1972) The effect of aggregation on prediction in the autoregressive model, Journal of the American Statistical Association, **67**, 628-32.

Anderson T.W. (1957) An introduction to multivariate statistical analysis, John Wiley & Sons, New York.

Apostol T.M. (1974) Mathematical analysis, second edition, Reading, Addison Wesley.

Arbia G. (1985) Problems in the estimation of the spatial autocorrelation function arising from the form of the weights' matrix, Transformations through space and time, Haining R. and Griffith D. Editors, Martinus Nijhoff Publisher.

Arbia G. (1986a) The modifiable areal unit problem and the spatial autocorrelation problem: towards a joint approach, METRON, Vol.XLIV, **1-4**, 391 - 407, Roma.

Arbia G. (1986b) On the simulation of two dimensional stationary stochastic processes: a comparison of different procedures, COMPSTAT 86, Vol.II, Short communications and posters, De Antoni, Lauro and Rizzi Editors, Physica-Verlag, 17-18, Roma.

Arbia G. (1987) A stochastic approach to the modifiable areal unit problem in regional economics, Proceedings of the Fifth European Young Statisticians Meeting, Jensen J.L. and Sørensen M. Editors, Department of Theoretical Statistics, Århus University.

Arbia G. (1988a) On a lower bound to the negative correlation of stationary processes on a two dimensional lattice, Stochastic Processes and Their Application, Special issue for the 17th Conference.

Arbia G. (1988b) On second order non stationarity in two dimensional lattice processes, Computational Statistics and Data Analysis, Special issue for the First International Conference-Workshop on Optimal Design and Analysis of Experiments.

Arrow K.J. (1972) Exposition of the theory of choice under uncertainty, in Decisions and organizations, McGuire C.B. and Radner R. Editors, Amsterdam:North-Holland.

Bachi R. (1957) Statistical analysis of geographical series, Bulletin de l'Institut Internationale de Statistique, **36**, 229-40.

Bartels C.P.A. (1977) Economic aspects of regional welfare, income distribution and unemployment, Studies in applied regional science, Nijhoff.

Bartlett M.S. (1966) Stochastic processes: methods and applications, Cambridge University Press.

Bartlett M.S. (1975) The statistical analysis of spatial pattern, Chapman and Hall, Andower, Hants.

Bennett R.J. (1975) Dynamic system modelling of the north-west region. 1. Spatio-temporal representation and identification; 2. Estimation of spatio-temporal policy models; 3. Adaptive-parameter policy models; 4. Adaptive spatio-temporal forecast; Environment and Planning, **7**, 525-38, 539-66, 617-36, 887-98 .

Bennett R.J. (1979) Spatial time series analysis, forecasting and control, Pion, London.

Bennett R.L. and Bergman B.R. (1986) A microsimulated transaction model of U.S. economy, The John Hopkins University Press, Baltimore.

Besag J.(1972) On the correlation structure of two dimensional stochastic processes, Biometrika, **59**, 43-48.

Besag J. (1974) Spatial interaction and the statistical analysis of lattice systems (with discussion), Journal of the Royal Statistical Society, **36**, 192-235.

Blalock H.M. Jr.(1964) Causal inferences in nonexperimental research, The university of North Carolina Press, Chapel Hill.

Blinder A.S. (1974) Towards an economic theory of income distribution, Cambridge MIT Press.

Boots B. (1982) Comments on using eigenfunctions to measure properties of networks structure, Environment and Planning A, **14**, 1063-72.

Boots B. (1984) Evaluating principal eigenvalues as measures of network structure, Geographical Analysis, **9**, 351-65.

Boots B. (1985) Size effects in the spatial pattering of nonprincipal eigenvectors of planar networks, Geographical Analysis, **17**, 74-81.

Box G.E.P. and Jenkins G.M. (1970) Time series analysis, forecasting and control, Wiley.

Buchanan J.M. (1965) An economic theory of clubs, Economica, **32**, 1-14.

Caldwell S. et al.(1979) Forecasting regional energy demand with linked micro-macro models, Working paper in planning n.1, Department of City and regional planning, Cornell University, Ithaca,NY.

Chambers J.M. (1977) Computational methods for data analysis, John Wiley & Sons, New York.

Clark W.A.V. and Avery K. (1976) The effects of data aggregation in statistical analysis, Geographical analysis, **8**, 428-38.

Clarke M., Keys P. and Williams H.C.W.L.(1979) Household dynamics and socio-economic forecasting: a microsimulation approach, Paper presented at the European Congress of the Regional Science Association, Working Paper 257, School of Geography, University of Leeds,

Clarke M. Keys P. and Williams H.C.W.L. (1981) Micro-simulation, in Quantitative geography: a British view, Wrigley N. and Bennett R.J. Editors, Routledge & Keagan Paul, London, 248-56.

Clarkson G.P.E. and Simon H.A.S.(1960) Simulation of individuals and group behaviour, American Economic Review, **50**, 920-32.

Cliff A.D. and Ord J.K. (1973) Spatial autocorrelation, Pion, London.

Cliff A.D. and Ord J.K. (1975) Model building and the analysis of spatial patterns in human geography, Journal of the Royal Statistical Society, Series B, **37**, 297-348.

Cliff A.D. & Ord J.K. (1981) Spatial processes:models and applications, Pion, London.

Cliff A.D., Haggett P., Ord J.K., Bassett K.A. and Davies R.B. (1975) Elements of spatial structure, Cambridge University press.

Cochrane W.C. (1963) Sampling Techniques, John Wiley & Sons.

Cramer J.S. (1964) Efficient grouping, regression and correlation in Engel curve analysis, Journal of the American Statistical Association, **59**, 233-50.

Curry L. (1970) Univariate spatial forecasting, Economic Geography, **46**, Suppl, 241-58.
Curry L. (1972a) A bivariate spatial regression operator, Canadian Geography, **16**, 1-14.
Curry L. (1972b) A spatial analysis of gravity flows, Regional Studies, **6**, 131-47.
Curry L.(1978) Demand in the spatial economy: homo stochasticus, Geographical analysis, **10**,309-44.
De Jong P., Sprenger C. and Van Veen F. (1984) On extreme values of Moran's I and Geary's c, Geographical Analysis, **16**, 17-24.
Dixon R. and Spackman E.A. (1970) The three dimensional analysis of meteorological data, Scientific Paper, **31**, London, :H.M.S.O.
Doob J.L.(1978) Stochastic processes, John Wiley & Sons, New York.
Duncan O.D. and Davies B. (1953) An alternative to ecological correlation, American Sociological Review, **18**, 665-6.
Duncan O.D. , Cuzzort R.P. and Duncan B. (1961) Statistical geography: Problems in analysing areal data, The free press of Glancoe, Illinois.
Eliansson G.(1976) A micro-macro interactive simulation model of the Swedish economy, Stockholm. Industrial Institute for Economic and Social Research.
Feller W. (1943) On a general class of contagious distributions, Annals of Mathematical Statistics, **14**, 389-400.
Fisher R.A. (1941) The negative binomial distribution, Annals of Eugenetics, **11**, 182-7.
Gaile G.(1985) Measures of spatial equity, in Spatial statistics and models, Gaile G. and Willnott C.J. Editors, Reidel, 223-33.
Gehlke C.E. and Bihel K. (1934) Certain effects of grouping upon the size of the correlation coefficient in census tract material, Journal of the American Statistical Association, Suppl., **29**, 169-70.
Getis A. (1983) Spatial autocorrelation and the second-order analysis of spatial pattern, Paper presented at the North American meeting of Regional Science Association, November 13.
Getis A. (1985) A second-order approach to spatial autocorrelation, Ontario Geography, **25**, 67-73.
Ginsberg N.S. (1952) The pattern of Asia, Prenctice-Hall, Englewood Cliffs, NJ.
Goodchild M.F. (1980) Algorithm 9: Simulation of autocorrelation for aggregate data, Environment and Planning, A, **12**, 1073-81.
Goodman L.A. (1959) Some alternative to ecological correlation, American Journal of Sociology, **64**, 610-25.
Granger C.W.J. (1969) Spatial data and time series analysis, in Studies in regional science , Scott A. Editor, Pion, London.
Granger C.W.J. (1974) Aspects of the analysis and interpretation of temporal and spatial data, The statistician, **24**, 197-210.
Granger C.W.J. and Morris M.J. (1976) Time series modelling and interpretation, Journal of the Royal Statistical Society, Series A, **139**, 246-57.
Green H.A.J. (1964) Aggregation and disaggregation in economic analysis. Princeton University Press.
Grenader U. (1950) Stochastic processes and statistical inference, Arkiv. Mat.,**1**,195.
Greig-Smith P. (1952) The use of random and contiguous quadrats in the study of the structure of plant communities, Annals of Botany, **16**,293-316.
Griffith D.A. (1984) Measuring the arrangement property of a system of areal units generated by partitioning a planar surface, Recent developments in spatial

analysis: Methodology, measurements, models, G. Bahrenberg, M. Fisher and P. Nijkamp Editors,Aldershot, UK, Gower.

Griffith D. (1985) An evaluation of correction techniques for boundary effects in spatial statistical analysis: contemporary methods, Geographical Analysis, **17**, 81-88.

Griffith D.A. (1987) Toward a theory of spatial statistics: another step forward, Geographical Analysis, **19**, 69-82.

Griffith D. and Amrhein C.G. (1983) An evaluation of correction techniques for boundary effects in spatial statistical analysis: traditional methods, Geographical Analysis, **4**, 352-60.

Guyon X. (1982) Parameter estimation for a stationary process on a d-dimensional lattice, Biometrika , **69**, 85-105.

Haggett P. (1965) Locational analysis in human geography. First edition.

Haggett P., Cliff A.D. and Frey A. (1977) Locational analysis in human geography, Edward Arnold, London.

Haining R.(1977) Model specification in stationary random fields, Geographical Analysis, **9**, 107-29.

Haining R. (1978a) The moving average models for spatial interaction, Transactions of the Institute of the British Geographers, New Series, **3**, 202-25.

Haining R. (1978b) Interaction modelling on central place lattices, Journal of Regional Science,**18**, 217-28.

Haining (1978c) Specification and estimation problems in models of spatial dependence; Northwestern University Studies in Geography, n.24.

Haining R. (1979) Statistical tests and process generators for random field models, Geographical Analysis, **11**, 45-64.

Haining R. (1981) Analysing univariate maps, Progress in Human Geography, 58-78.

Haining R. (1983a) Modelling intra-urban price competition: an example of gasoline pricing, Journal of Regional science,**23**, 517-28.

Haining R. (1983b) Anatomy of a price war, Nature, **304**, 679-80.

Haining R. and Bennett R.J. (1985) Spatial structure and spatial interaction: modelling approaches to the statistical analysis of geographical data (with discussion), Journal of the Royal Statistical Society, B, **148**, 1-36.

Haining R., Griffith D. and Bennett R.J. (1983) Simulating two-dimensional autocorrelated surfaces, Geographical Analysis, **15**, 247-55.

Haining R., Griffith D. and Bennett R.J. (1984) A statistical approach to the problem of the missing spatial data using a first-order Markow model, Professional Geographer, **36**, 338-45.

Haitowsky J. (1973) Regression estimation from grouped observations, Griffin Statistical courses and monographs, **33**, Griffin.

Hannan E.J. (1970) Multiple time series, John Wiley & Sons, New York.

Hannan H.T. (1971) Aggregation and disaggregation in sociology, Lexington books, Lexington, Mass.

Harvey A.C. (1981) Time series models, Deddington, Philips.

Hägerstrand T.(1955) Statistika primäruppgifter flykartering och data processing maskmer, Meddelanden Frans Lunds Geografiska Institut, **344**, 223-55.

Heine V. (1955) Models for two dimensional stationary processes, Biometrika, **42**, 170-178.

Hildebrand W. (1971) Random preferences and equilibrium analysis, Journal of Economic theory, **3**,414-29.

Hooper P.M. and Hewings G.J.D. (1981) Some properties of the space-time processes, Geographical Analysis, **13**, 203-223.

Hopkins B.(1963) Observation of savanna burning in the Olokemeji forest reserve, Nigeria, Journal of applied ecology, **2**, 367-381.

Isserlis L. (1918) On a formula for the product-moment coefficient of any order of a Normal frequency distribution in any number of variables, Biometrika, **12** 134-9.

ISTAT (1982) Censimento Italiano della popolazione, Istituto Centrale di Statistica, Rome, Italy.

Johnston J. (1972) Econometric methods, McGraw Hill, New York.

Johnston R.J.(1976) Areal studies, ecological studies and social patterns in cities, Transaction of the Institute of the British Geographers, New Series, **1**, 118 22.

Jones E. and Sinclair D.J. (1968) Editors, Atlas of London and the London region, Pergamon Press, Oxford.

Kain J.F., Apgar W.C. and Ginn J.R. (1976) Simulation of market effects of housing allowance, Vol.1: Description of the NBER urban simulation model, Researc report Department of City and Regional planning, Harward University Cambridge, Mass.

Kendall M.G. and Stuart A. (1969) The advanced theory of statistics, second edition, Griffin, London.

Kendall M.G. and Stuart A. (1976) The advanced theory of statistics, third edition, Griffin, London.

Kershaw K.A. (1964) Quantitative and dynamic ecology, London, Edward Arnold.

Kirby A.M. and Taylor P.J. (1976) A geographical analysis of voting patterns in the EEC referendum, Regional Studies, **10**, 183-91.

Kleijnen J.P.C. (Statistical tools for simulation pratictioners, Dekker, New York.

Klein L.R. (1946) Remarks on the theory of aggregation, Econometrica, **14**, 303-12.

Klopotowsky A. (1977) Limits theorems for sum of dependent random vectors in R^d, Dissertationes Mathematicae., **151**, 1-62.

Kolmogorov A.N. (1941) Local structure of turbolence in a non-compressive fluid with very large Reynold numbers, Doklady Akademii Nank, SSSR, **30**, 259-303.

Kolmogorov A.N. (1950) Foundations of the theory of probability, New York, Chelsea publ.Co.

Koopmans T.C. (1950) Editor, Statistical inference in dynamic economic models, New York.

Larimore W. (1977) Statistical inference on stationary random fields, Proceedings of the IEEE, Special issue on multidimensional systems, **65**, 961-70.

Lebart L. (1966) Les variables socio-economiques departmentales ou regionales. I methodes statistique d'etude. Paris: Institut d'etude du Developpemen Economique et Social, Universite de Paris, **18**, 81-112.

Lebart L. (1969) Analyse statistique de la contiguite', Publication de l'Institut de Statistique de l'Universite de Paris, (mimeo).

Mardia K.V. (1988) Multi-dimensional Multivariate Gaussian Markow fields with application to image processing, Journal of Multivariate Analysis, **24**, 265-84.

Marsaglia G. (1954) Iterated limits and central limit theorem for dependent variables, Proceedings of American Mathematical Society, **5**, 987-91.

Martin R.J. (1979) A subclass of lattice processes applied to a problem in plane sampling, Biometrika, **66**, 209-17.

Martin R.L. and Oeppen J.E. (1975) The identification of regional forecasting models using space-time correlation functions, Transaction of the Institute of the British Geographers, **66**, 95-118.

Matern B.(1960) Spatial variations, Meddelanden fråns Statens Skogsforskninstitut,**49**,1-144.
Matui I. (1932) Statistical study of the distribution of scattered villages in two regions of the Tonami Plain, Toyama Prefecture, Japanese Journal of Geology and Geography, **9**, 251-66.
Mercer W.B. and Hall A.D. (1911) The experimental error of field trials, Journal of Agricultural Science , **4**, 107-32.
Modigliani F. and Brunberg R.(1959) Utility analysis and the consumption function, an interpretation of cross-section data, Post-Keynesian economics.
Moellering H. and Tobler W.R. (1972) Geographical variances, Geographical Analysis, **4**,34-50.
Moran P.A.P. (1954) Notes on continuous stochastic phenomena, Biometrika, **37**, 17-23.
Nephrash J.A. (1934) Some problems in the correlation of spatially distributed variables, Journal of the American Statistical Association, suppl., **29**, 167-8.
Neyman J. (1939) On a class of contagious distributions applicable in entomology and bacteriology, Annals of Mathematical Statistics, **10**,35-57.
Openshaw S. (1977a) A geographical solution to scale and aggregation problems in region-building, partitioning and spatial modelling, Transactions of the Institute of British Geographers, New Series, **2**, 459-75.
Openshaw S. (1977b) Algorithm 3: a procedure to generate pseudo-random aggregation of N zones in M zones where M is less than N, Environment and Planning, **9**,1423-8.
Openshaw S. (1977c) Optimal zoning systems for spatial interaction models, Environment and Planning, **9**,169-84.
Openshaw S. (1978a) An empirical study of some zone design criteria, Environment and Planning, **10**, 781-94.
Openshaw S.(1978b) An optimal zoning approach to the study of spatially aggregated data, Spatial representation and spatial interaction. Masser I. and Brown P.J.B. Editors, Martinus Nijhoff, London.
Openshaw S.(1981) The modifiable areal unit problem , Catmog n.38.
Openshaw S. (1984) Ecological fallacies and the analysis of areal census data, Environment and Planning, **16**,17-31.
Openshaw S. and Taylor P.J. (1979) A million or so of correlated coefficients: three experiment on the modifiable areal unit problem, in Statistical applications in the spatial sciences, Wrigley N. and Bennett R.J. Editors, Pion, London, 127-44.
Openshaw S. & Taylor P.J. (1981) The modifiable areal unit problem, Quantitative geography: a British view, Wrigley M. and Bennett R.J. Editors, Routledge and Keagan Publishers, London, 60-9.
Orcutt G. (1957) A new type of socio-economic system, Review of Economic and Statistics, **58**, 773-97.
Orcutt G. (1960) Simulation of economic systems, American Economic Review, **50**, 893-907.
Orcutt G., Caldwell S. and Wartheimer R. (1976) Policy explorations through microanalytic simulation, Washington D.C. Urban Institute.
Orcutt G. , Greenberger M. & Rivlin A. (1961) Microanalysis of socio economic systems: a simulation study, Harper and Raw , N.Y.
Orcutt G.H. , Watts H.W. and Edwards J.B. (1968) Data aggregation and information loss, American economic review, 773-787.
Ord J.K. (1972) Families of frequency distributions, Griffin, London.

Ord J.K. (1975) Estimation methods for models of spatial interaction, Journal of the American Statistical Association, **40**, 120-26.

Paelinck J.H. and Nijkamp P.(1975) Operational theory and method in regional analysis, Saxon house, Lexington Books.

Partzen E.(1957) A central limit theorem for multilinear stochastic processes American Mathematical Society, **28**, 252-6.

Passoneau J.R. and Wurman R.S. (1966) Urban atlas: 20 American cities, Cambridge Mass.

Patankar V.N. (1954) The goodness of fit of the frequency distribution obtained from stochastic processes, Biometrika, **41**, 450-62.

Pechman J.A. and Okner B.A. (1974) Who bears the tax burden?, Washington D.C., Brookins.

Pesaran M.H., Pierse R.G. and Kumar M.S. (1986) On the problem of aggregation in econometrics, Discussion paper on structural analysis of economic system Department of Applied Economics, Cambridge.

Pfeiffer P.E. and Deutsch J.E. (1980) A STARMA model building procedure with application to description and regional forecasting, Transaction of the Institu of the British Geographers, **5**, 330-349.

Pfeiffer P.E. and Deutsch J.E. (1981) Variance of the sample space-time autocorrelation function, Journal of the Royal Statistic Society, Series B, **43** 28-33.

Prais S. and Aitchinson J. (1954) The grouping of observations in regression analysis Review of the International Statistic Institute, **1**,1-22.

Priestley M.B. (1981) Spectral analysis and time series, Academic press, London.

Pryor F.L.(1973) Simulation of the impact of social and economic institutions on the size of the distribution of income and wealth, American Economic, Review **63**,50-72.

Quandt R.E. (1972) A probabilistic theory of consumer behaviour, in Evolution of Modern Demand Theory, Ekelund R.B. Jr. et al. Editors,Lexington Mass Lexington

Rayner J.N. (1971) An introduction to spectral analysis, Pion, London.

Rayner J.N. and Golledge R.C. (1972) Spectral analysis of settlement patterns in diverse physical and economic environments, Environment and Planning, **4**, 347-71.

Ripley B.D. (1977) Modelling spatial patterns (with discussion) Journal of the Royal Statistic Society, Series B, **39**, 172-212.

Ripley B.D. (1981) Spatial statistics, John Wiley & Sons, New York.

Robinson A.H.(1956) The necessity of weighting values in correlation of areal data, Annals of the Association of American Geographers,**46**,233-6.

Robinson A.H. Lindberger J.B. and Brinkman L.W. (1961) A correlation and regression analysis applied to rural farm population densities, Annals of the Association of American Geographers, **51**, 211-21.

Robinson W.S. (1950) Ecological correlations and the behaviour of individuals, American Sociological Review, **15**,351-57.

Rogers A. (1974) Statistical analysis of spatial dispersion: The quadrat method. Pion. London.

Rosenblatt D. (1956) On some stochastic processes formulation of individual preference and consumers behaviour, Econometrica, 347-8.

Scheffe' H. (1959) The analysis of variance, Wiley, New York.

Searle S.R. (1971) Linear models, John Wiley & Sons, New York.

Smith T.E. (1975) A choice theory of spatial interaction, Regional Science and Urban Economics,**5**, 137-76

Smith T.E. (1980) A central limit theorem for spatial samples, Geographical Analysis, **12**, 299-324.

Sokal R.R. and Oden N.L.(1978) Spatial autocorrelation in biology, 1. Methodology. Biological Journal of the Linnean Society, **10**, 199-228.

Spanos A. (1986) Statistical foundation of econometric modelling, Cambridge University Press.

Springer M.D. (1980) The algebra of random variables, John Wiley & Sons, New York.

Stocker T.M. (1982) The use of cross-section data to characterize macro functions, Journal of the American Statistical Association, **77**, 369-80.

Streitberg B. (1978) Multivariate models of dependent spatial data, Exploratory and explanatory statistical analysis of spatial data, Bartels C.P.A. and Ketellapper R.H. Editors, Martinus Nijhoff Publishing.

Taylor P.J. (1973) Some implications of the spatial organization of elections, Transactions of the Institute of British Geographers, **60**,121-36.

Taylor P.J. (1977) Quantitative methods in geography, Houghton Mifflin. Boston.

Taylor P.J. and Johnson R.J.(1979) Geography of elections, Penguin, Harmondsworth.

Telser L.G. (1967) Discrete samples and moving sums in stationary stochastic processes, Journal of the American Statistical Association, **62**, 484-99.

Theil H. (1954) Linear aggregation in economic relations, Amsterdam: North Holland Publ. Company.

Thomas E.N. and Anderson D.W. (1965) Additional comments on weighting values in correlation analysis of areal data, Annals of the Association of American Geographers, **55**, 492-505.

Thompson W .R. (1957) The coefficient of localization: an appraisal, Southern Economic Journal, **23**, 320-25.

Tiebout C.M. (1956) A pure theory of local expenditure, Journal of Political Economy, **64**, 416-24.

Tinkler K.J. (1977) An introduction to graph theoretical methods in geography, Norwich, Geo Abstract, Catmog n.14.

Tobler W.(1970) A computer movie simulating urban growth in the Detroit Region, Economic Geography supplement, **46**, 234-40.

Tooze M.J. (1976) Regional elasticities of substitution of the United Kingdom in 1968, Urban Studies, **13**, 35-44.

Unwin D. (1981) Introductory spatial analysis, Methuen , London.

Unwin D. and Hepple L.H. (1974) The statistical analysis of spatial series, The statistician, Vol.23, **3/4**, 211-27.

Upton G.J.G. and Fingleton B. (1985) Spatial data analysis by example, John Wiley and sons.

Wartenberg D. (1985) Multivariate spatial autocorrelation: a method for exploratory geographical analysis, Geographical Analysis, **17**, 263-83.

Watanada T. and Ben-Akiva M. (1978) Spatial aggregation of disaggregate choice models: an area-wide urban travel demand, sketch, planning model. Presented at the transportation research board annual meeting.

Whittle P.(1954) On stationary processes in the plane, Biometrika, **41**,434-49.

Whittle P.(1962) On the variation of yield variance with plot size, Biometrika, **43**, 337-43.

Whittle P.(1963) Stochastic processes in several dimensions, Bulletin of the International Statistical Institute, **49**, 974-93.

Wilkinson J.H. and Reinsh C. (1981) Handbook of automatic computation, Springer-Verlag, Vol.I.

Williamson (1965) Regional inequality and the process of national development: a description of patterns, in Economic development and cultural change **XIII**,**4**,3-84.

Wilson A.G. and Bennett R.J. (1985) Mathematical methods in human geography and planning, John Wiley.

Wilson A.G. and Pownell G.(1976) A new representation of urban system for modelling and for the study of micro-level interdependence, Area, **8**,246-54.9

Wold H. (1953) Demand analysis, New York.

Yaglom A.M. (1962) An introduction to the theory of stationary random functions (English translation of the 1952 Russian edition) Prenctice-Hall, Englewood Cliff, NJ.

Yule U. and Kendall M.S. (1950) An introduction to the theory of statistics, Charles Griffin, London.

Index

ADVANCED STUDIES IN THEORETICAL AND APPLIED ECONOMETRICS

---

1. Paelinck J.H.P. (ed.): Qualitative and Quantitative Mathematical Economics, 1982.
   ISBN 90 247 2623 9.
2. Ancot J.P. (ed.): Analysing the Structure of Econometric Models, 1984.
   ISBN 90 247 2894 0.
3. Hughes Hallet A.J. (ed.): Applied Decision Analysis and Economic Behaviour, 1984.
   ISBN 90 247 2968 8.
4. Sengupta J.K.: Information and Efficiency in Economic Decision, 1985.
   ISBN 90 247 3072 4.
5. Artus P. and Guvenen O. (eds.), in collaboration with Gagey F.: International Macroeconomic Modelling for Policy Decisions, 1986.
   ISBN 90 247 3201 8.
6. Vilares M.J.: Structural Change in Macroeconomic Models, Theory and Estimation, 1986.
   ISBN 90 247 3277 8.
7. Carraro C. and Sartore D. (eds.): Development of Control Theory for Economic Analysis, 1987.
   ISBN 90 247 3345 6.
8. Broer D.P. (ed.): Neoclassical Theory and Empirical Models of Aggregate Firm Behaviour, 1987.
   ISBN 90 247 3412 6.
9. Italianer A.: Theory and Practice of International Trade Linkage Models, 1986.
   ISBN 90 247 3407 X.
10. Kendrick D.A.: Feedback, A New Framework for Macroeconomic Policy, 1988.
    ISBN 90 247 3593 9 (HB). ISBN 90 247 3650 1 (PB).
11. Sengupta J.K. and Kadekodi G.K. (eds.): Econometrics of Planning and Efficiency, 1988.
    ISBN 90 247 3602 1.
12. Griffith D.A.: Advanced Spatial Statistics. Special Topics in the Exploration of Quantitative Spatial Data Series, 1988.
    ISBN 90 247 3627 7.
13. Guvenen O.: International Commodity Market Models and Policy Analysis, 1988.
    ISBN 90 247 3768 0.
14. Arbia G.: Spatial Data Configuration in Statistical Analysis of Regional Economic and Related Problems, 1989.
    ISBN 0 7923 0284 2